Linguistics: The Cambridge Survey

Volume III
Language: Psychological and
Biological Aspects

Linguistics: The Cambridge Survey

Linguistics: The Cambridge Survey

Edited by Frederick J. Newmeyer
University of Washington

Volume III
Language: Psychological and Biological Aspects

CAMBRIDGE
UNIVERSITY PRESS

Published by the Press Syndicate of the University of Cambridge
The Pitt Building, Trumpington Street, Cambridge CB2 1RP
40 West 20th Street, New York 10011-4211, USA
10 Stamford Road, Oakleigh, Melbourne 3166, Australia

© Cambridge University Press 1988

First published 1988
First paperback edition 1989
Reprinted 1990, 1994

Printed in Great Britain at the
Athenæum Press Ltd, Newcastle upon Tyne

British Library cataloguing in publication data

Linguistics: the Cambridge survey.
Vol. 3: language: psychological and biological aspects.
1. Linguistics
I. Newmeyer, Frederick J.
410   P121

Library of Congress cataloguing in publication data

Language: psychological and biological aspects.
(Linguistics, the Cambridge survey; v.3)
Includes indexes.
1. Psycholinguistics. 2. Biolinguistics.
I. Newmeyer, Frederick J.   II. Series.
P121. L567 vol. 3 [P37] 401'.9   87–25671

ISBN 0 521 30835 6   hard covers
ISBN 0 521 37582 7   paperback

Contents

Contributors to Volume III

Sheila E. Blumstein Department of Cognitive and Linguistic Sciences, Brown University

Ellen Broselow Department of Linguistics, State University of New York, Stony Brook

David Caplan Neuropsychology Unit, Massachusetts General Hospital

Robyn Carston Department of Phonetics and Linguistics, University College London

Richard A. Demers Department of Linguistics, University of Arizona

William Orr Dingwall Department of Hearing and Speech Sciences, University of Maryland

Karen D. Emmorey The Salk Institute for Biological Studies

Giovanni B. Flores d'Arcais Max Planck Institut für Psycholinguistik and University of Leiden

Victoria A. Fromkin Department of Linguistics, University of California, Los Angeles

Merrill F. Garrett Department of Psychology, University of Arizona

Henry Gleitman Department of Psychology, University of Pennsylvania

Lila R. Gleitman Department of Psychology, University of Pennsylvania

Catherine A. Jackson Department of Linguistics, University of California, Los Angeles

Barbara Landau Department of Psychology, University of Pennsylvania

MichaelK. Tanenhaus Department of Psychology, University of Rochester

Eric Wanner Russell Sage Foundation, New York

Preface

Language: psychological and biological aspects is the third volume of the four-volume series, *Linguistics: the Cambridge survey*. The first two volumes, *Linguistic theory: foundations* and *Linguistic theory: extensions and implications*, review the state of research on grammatical competence *per se*, both from the point of view of its structural properties and from the evidence from diverse areas of investigation that support the idea that the principles of generative grammer provide an adequate characterization of the human linguistic faculty. The focus of this volume is not the theory of grammar *per se*, but rather the broader psychological and biological aspects of language, including such topics as the role of language in cognition, its processing by speakers and hearers, its acquisition by first and second language learners, its representation in the brain, and its phylogenetic evolution. Roughly speaking, then, it covers the subfields of 'psycholinguistics' and 'neurolinguistics'. The fourth volume, *Language: the socio-cultural context*, treats sociolinguistics and allied subfields, such as ethnography of speaking, and conversation and discourse analysis.

In the first chapter of this volume, Michael K. Tanenhaus presents an overview of the field of psycholinguistics, giving a deft historical account not only of its achievements, but also of the tensions that have existed over the past generation between behavioral, cognition-based, and competence-based models of language. Tanenhaus reviews the effect on the field that the surge of interest in artificial intelligence has had (and will continue to have), and explains why psycholinguists are, on the whole, more receptive now to the rules and representations proposed by grammatical theorists than they were a decade ago.

Chapter 2, 'Language and cognition' by Robyn Carston, defends the idea that grammar is an 'input system' like vision: it is encapsulated (i.e. impenetrable to extralinguistic beliefs), domain-specific, processed rapidly and mandatorily, and innately specified. Unlike some psycholinguists, Carston takes an optimistic view about the possibility of understanding the principles governing the 'central systems' in which language is utilized in beliefs, inferences, and so on, and develops a theory of 'relevance' designed to explain its role in such processes.

The third chapter, Merrill F. Garrett's 'Processes in language production', investigates the systems that account for real-time lexical, phonological, and phrasal organization in the production of sentences. Garrett considers such interrelated questions as the extent of feedback among levels of language in information flow and the degree to which the known facts of production support a modular conception of language. Especially interesting are the speech error data that Garrett adduces in great detail as evidence for the nature of language production.

'Language perception' (Chapter 4), by Giovanni B. Flores d'Arcais, addresses the fundamental question of language perception, namely how hearers impose discrete structure on a continuous signal. The chapter deals with such topics as the nature and number of units of perception, parsing strategies, and the degree of cross-linguistic differences in perception. Like the authors of the first three chapters, Flores d'Arcais takes up the question of whether the facts from the domain under investigation support a modular or an interactive view of language.

Chapter 5, 'The mental lexicon', by Karen D. Emmorey and Victoria A. Fromkin, focusses on psycholinguistic models of lexical structure and relates the topic to online processes, such as word recognition and parsing. The authors show that lexical items have distinct orthographic representations, that affixes and base forms are represented and processed in distinct ways, and that the psycholinguistic evidence supports the distinction made in the model of lexical phonology between 'Level I' and 'Level II' morphological processes.

Chapter 6, written jointly by Lila R. Gleitman, Henry Gleitman, Barbara Landau, and Eric Wanner, 'Where learning begins: initial representations for language learning' focusses on the very first task facing infant language learners: picking out and relating significant pieces of sound and meaning from the welter of utterances with which their ears are bombarded. The authors discuss those cues that facilitate the analysis of language in terms of words, phrases, clauses, and so on, and pay particular attention to the role of 'Motherese' (the register typically used by adults when speaking to small children) in speeding acquisition.

In Chapter 7, Ellen Broselow's 'Second language acquisition', much attention is devoted to the similarities and differences between an adult's acquisition of a second language and a child's acquisition of a first. Broselow presents evidence in support of the idea that universal grammar plays a role in the former as well as the latter, and discusses such issues as language transfer, markedness, and the role of parameterized principles in second language acquisition.

Sheila E. Blumstein's 'Neurolinguistics: an overview of language–brain relations in aphasia' (Chapter 8), focusses primarily on language breakdown in adult aphasias. Much of the chapter is devoted to the still unresolved question of whether aphasias typically represent the breakdown of the underlying linguistic system or of those systems that are involved in its processing in speech. Blumstein concludes that the study of aphasia shows that language is independent (within limits) of cognition and that it is organized into sub-systems similar in kind to components of the grammar proposed in linguistic theory.

The ninth chapter, David Caplan's 'The biological basis for language', considers the localization and lateralization of the brain for language. Caplan shows that the core functions of language are localized in the neocortex surrounding the Sylvian fissure; nevertheless, particular aspects of language appear not to be narrowly localizable and might differ from individual to individual.

Chapter 10, Catherine A. Jackson's 'Linguistics and speech–language pathology', reflects the increasing interest by linguists and speech–language pathologists in each other's work. However, the two fields are still far apart in many ways: even many speech–language pathologists who see themselves as having a 'linguistic' orientation take a behaviorist approach in practice, while few theoretical linguists are aware of the potential significance of linguistic data from language disordered populations.

William Orr Dingwall's Chapter 11, 'The evolution of human communicative behavior,' stresses the continuities between the communicative behavior of the great apes and those of humans, in an attempt to unravel the evolutionary mystery of the latter. However, there are still fundamental discontinuities that remain to be explained: the great apes evidence no syntax or phonotactics, and their communication in the wild is homologous with human paralanguage rather than with structured speech.

The last chapter, 'Linguistics and animal communication' by Richard A. Demers, reviews the systems that have been proposed for the comparison of human language with the various types of animal communication. While Demers concludes that many forms of animal communication are more elaborate and structured than earlier researchers have assumed, the gulf between them and human language, as measured by a variety of parameters, is still great.

Frederick J. Newmeyer

1 Psycholinguistics: an overview[1]

Michael K. Tanenhaus

1.0. Introduction

Trying to write a coherent overview of psycholinguistics is a bit like trying to assemble a face out of a police identikit. You can't use all of the pieces and no matter which ones you choose it doesn't look quite right. Part of the difficulty is that psycholinguistics is concerned with three somewhat distinct questions: (1) how language is acquired during development; (2) how people comprehend language; and (3) how people produce language. The study of language comprehension and production forms one field, 'experimental psycholinguistics', and the study of language acquisition forms a separate field, 'developmental psycholinguistics'. In theory, many of the issues in experimental and developmental psycholinguistics are inter-related, but in practice there is little overlap between the two areas. As a result it is difficult to do justice to both within the same brief review.

A second problem is that contrary to what the name might suggest, psychology and linguistics have never been successfully integrated within psycholinguistics for more than short periods. Until recently, most psycholinguists were psychologists who were influenced in varying degrees by linguistics. In the last few years, an increasing number of linguists have begun to explore psycholinguistic issues. There is a fundamental disagreement about the relationship between language and cognition that more or less divides psycholinguists along disciplinary boundaries.

Linguists tend to follow Chomsky in assuming that the core of language is a specialized linguistic system or grammar which represents a sentence at a number of different levels and contains rules for relating these representations. While the linguistic system makes contact with other cognitive systems at the level of input and output, its rules and representations are

[1] I would like to thank a number of people who have shared their knowledge and insights about psycholinguistics as I was writing this chapter. Discussions with my colleagues at Rochester, Tom Bever and Gary Dell, were extremely helpful. Ginny Valian and Melissa Bowerman helped me sort through the issues in language acquisition, and Pim Levelt helped me frame the discussion of production. If I had taped these conversations, the chapter would have been improved. Thanks also to Alan Garnham for valuable comments on a draft of the manuscript and to Jane Oakhill for comments on the acquisition section.

1

distinct from those of other cognitive systems. According to the 'linguistic autonomy' or 'modularity' position, a theory of language performance must include among its explanatory primitives the rules and representations of the grammar. The modularity hypothesis as put forth by Chomsky (e.g. Chomsky 1980) is a theory of language competence, but it naturally translates into a perspective about language processing and language acquisition in which linguistic rules and representations form a distinct cognitive sub-system.

Psycholinguists working within the linguistic autonomy framework are guided by several assumptions. One assumption is that the structure of language can be studied independently from how that structure is used for communication. A second assumption is that sentence-level syntactic structure forms the core of the linguistic system. As a consequence these psycholinguists tend to focus on a narrow range of primarily syntactic phenomena, which are explained in terms of specialized principles of grammar. They argue that it is just these phenomena which form the core of language and the principles that explain them will thus form the basis for successful models of language processing and language acquisition.

The contrasting view, which most psychologists endorse, assigns a much less central role to the grammar. Language processing and language acquisition can best be understood within the same framework as other cognitive processes. The most radical form of this 'cognitivist' or 'linguistic minimalist' position is that the rules and representations proposed by linguistic grammars are epiphenomena of more general and basic cognitive processes (e.g. Bates & MacWhinney 1982). Linguistic minimalists generally reject the assumption that sentence-level processes, especially syntax, form the core of psycholinguistics, and they do not draw a sharp boundary between explanations of language use and language structure. As a consequence, they are often concerned with a broader range of phenomena than researchers working within the autonomy framework.

The history of psycholinguistics spans thirty years during which there have been radical changes in how the study of cognition is approached. When psycholinguistics was born during the 1950s, it was firmly rooted within the behaviorist tradition. There was widespread agreement that an association-based learning theory would ultimately explain the structure of language as well as how language is used and acquired. During the next decade, psycholinguistics was dominated by Chomsky's theoretical claims about the nature of linguistic knowledge, which provided a framework for the field. Psycholinguistics was at the frontier of a rapidly developing mentalist approach to cognition in which rules and representations formed the explanatory vocabulary.

During the 1970s psycholinguistics largely abandoned its ties with linguistic theory, as transformational grammar was widely seen as having failed to provide a useful explanatory framework for either experimental or developmental psycholinguistics. Psycholinguistics became absorbed into mainstream cognitive psychology and ideas drawn from artificial intelligence began to provide psycholinguistics with much of its theory. Within experimental psycholinguistics, questions about the role of language structure in language processing were largely abandoned, and within developmental psycholinguistics most research began to focus on the cognitive basis of language acquisition. More recently, the debate between proponents of linguistic minimalism and linguistic autonomy has emerged again with renewed vigor as linguistics has started to become reintegrated into psycholinguistics. Finally, the recent emergence of a new subsymbolic paradigm within cognitive science is beginning to challenge many of the fundamental assumptions of psycholinguistics.

The content of psycholinguistics can be defined independently of its history and without reference to broad disagreements such as the conflict between linguistic autonomy and linguistic minimalism. However, much of the excitement in the field comes from the role that psycholinguistics plays in debates about the nature of language and its relationship to cognition. In the remainder of this chapter I will use the continuing tension between the linguistic autonomy and linguistic minimalism positions to help structure a brief overview of psycholinguistics emphasizing its historical development. Comprehension, acquisition, and production will be discussed in separate sections. Many of the influences and trends that are common to the three areas will be introduced in the comprehension section, which will be more detailed than the acquisition and production sections.

1.1. The birth of psycholinguistics

Modern psycholinguistics began as a cooperative venture between linguists and psychologists during the early 1950s. Linguistics and psychology had each been strongly influenced by the logical positivist tradition in philosophy. According to this doctrine, the only meaningful statements were those that derived from logic or those that could be directly tested through empirical observation. Linguistic theories of this period classified language into units of different sizes, which were arranged in a strict hierarchy or 'taxonomy.' In theory, each unit was to be derived from lower level units. Substantial progress had been made in identifying low level units such as phones, phonemes, and morphemes, and linguists were beginning to extend the taxonomic approach to syntax. The goal of American linguistics was to develop a 'discovery' procedure that could be mechanically applied to a corpus of utterances to extract the units.

Within psychology, there was a general consensus that behavior could be explained by learned associations between stimuli and responses, with reinforcement providing the glue to cement associations. 'Radical behaviorists' such as B. F. Skinner argued that psychological explanation should be couched only in terms of observable stimuli and responses, whereas 'neobehaviorists' such as Clark Hull argued for the usefulness of mediating variables that were derived from observable stimuli and responses. Most research within the learning theory tradition examined animal behavior, on the assumption that the basic laws of learning would provide the building blocks for explanations of more complex behaviors. However, during the 1950s several prominent learning theorists turned their attention to more complex behaviors, with language, or 'verbal behavior' as it was more commonly called, being one of the primary targets for explanation. In 1957, Skinner published *Verbal behavior*, which provided an in-depth analysis of language within a radical behaviorist framework. Neobehaviorist treatments of meaning were developed by Osgood, Suci & Tannenbaun (1957) and Mowrer (1960).

In 1951 the Social Science Research Council sponsored a conference that brought together several leading psychologists and linguists. One of the participants, Roger Brown, credits this conference with directly leading to the birth of psycholinguistics (Brown 1970). The proceedings of the conference outlined a psycholinguistic research agenda that reflected a consensus among the participants that the methodological and theoretical tools being developed by psychologists could be used to explore and explain the linguistic structures that were being uncovered by linguists.[2]

At the same time as behaviorist psychologists were beginning to concentrate on language, two important developments were underway that would quickly undermine a psycholinguistics based upon behaviorist principles. The first development was Chomsky's work in generative grammar. The second was the development of the information processing approach to cognition pioneered by cognitive psychologists such as Miller and Broadbent and computer scientists such as Newell and Simon. Chomsky's ideas had the more immediate impact, so we will consider them first.

1.2. **The Chomskyan revolution**

There are at least three distinct ways in which Chomsky's ideas have shaped psycholinguistics: (1) Chomsky's criticisms of behaviorist treatments of

[2] The proceedings were edited by Osgood & Sebeok (1954) and published as a supplement to *The International Journal of American Linguistics* and reprinted in 1969 by Indiana University Press.

language and his view of the appropriate goals for linguistic theory played a major role in the development of cognitive science; (2) Chomsky's formulation of the logical problem of language acquisition has provided a framework for developmental psycholinguistics; and (3) Chomsky's theory of transformational grammar guided much of the first decade of research in experimental psycholinguistics.

1.2.1. Chomsky's methodological contribution

Chomsky rejected the discovery procedure as an unrealistic and scientifically inappropriate methodological goal for linguistics. He argued instead that linguistics should evaluate theories according to their explanatory power. These theories should account for the native speaker's tacit knowledge of sentences, or 'linguistic competence,' rather than the regularities observed in a recorded corpus of utterances. Linguistics was thus properly viewed as a branch of 'theoretical cognitive psychology' (Chomsky 1968). Chomsky argued that in order to model competence, linguists would have to abstract away from linguistic performance, which was affected by nonlinguistic factors such as attention and memory limitations.

Chomsky mounted a multifaceted attack on behaviorist explanations of language. He argued persuasively, if not conclusively, that natural language has properties that cannot be described by the class of formal languages (finite-state languages) that are, in principle, compatible with behaviorist assumptions. He also argued that behaviorist accounts of linguistic meaning and linguistic structure were plausible only in so far as they used scientific notions such as stimulus and response in a non-scientific metaphorical way. When these terms were defined operationally, the explanations were clearly incorrect (Chomsky 1959). Chomsky also argued that behaviorist learning theories did not provide adequate explanations of language acquisition by the child. Chomsky's critiques of behaviorist models focussed on Skinner's radical behaviorist analysis. However, Chomsky's arguments were quickly extended to neobehaviorist models by his students and colleagues. For instance, Fodor (1965) presented a detailed critique of Mowrer and Osgood's accounts of meaning. And, Bever, Fodor & Garrett (1968) challenged the adequacy of neobehaviorist accounts of language and cognition.

Bever *et al.*'s argument illustrates the flavor of these attacks on behaviorism. They pointed out that all behaviorist models accept the methodological constraint that all explanatory elements in a psychological theory must be derivable from potentially observable stimuli and responses. They dubbed this constraint the 'terminal meta-postulate' (TMP). However, no model that adheres to the TMP can generate all and only the strings produced by a mirror-image language, i.e. the language produced by the rules in (1):

(1)   a. X→aXa
       b. X→bXb
       c. X→O

The problem is that producing strings of a mirror-image language (e.g. abba, aa, bb, aabbaa) – which people can quickly learn after exposure to a few instances of grammatical and ungrammatical strings – requires a device that can keep track of what sequence of symbols was used early in the string, so that the sequence can be reproduced to complete the mirror image. The symbol X in (1) serves this function. There are numerous devices that will do the job (e.g. a push-down stack), but postulating such devices which clearly have no counterparts in stimuli or responses violates the TMP (Anderson & Bower 1973).

1.2.2. Language acquisition

Although Chomsky never put forward a serious model for language acquisition, his logical analysis of the problem has provided a framework for the field (see Gleitman & Wanner 1982). Chomsky argued that the linguistic input to which the child was exposed was too impoverished for him to induce the mapping between meanings and linguistic forms. Thus the child must begin the acquisition process with some innate linguistic knowledge that constrains the set of candidate grammars. Chomsky proposed that certain 'linguistic universals' constrained the 'hypotheses' that the child needed to consider and he restricted the notion of 'explanatory adequacy' to linguistic theories that provided an account of these universals. Chomsky's emphasis on the theoretical importance of language acquisition, his presentation of the simple fact that children acquire language as an intellectual puzzle, and his strong nativist claims all helped to create an atmosphere of intellectual excitement which led to an explosion of interest in how children learn language.

1.2.3. Experimental psycholinguistics

Chomsky's transformational theory of grammar shaped the first decade of research in experimental psycholinguistics. The theory of grammar presented in Chomsky 1957, in particular the notion of a transformationally related family of sentences built around a kernel sentence, generated a number of hypotheses that were experimentally tested in early studies of sentence perception and memory (e.g. Miller 1962; Clifton, Kurcz & Odom 1965). His 'standard theory' (Chomsky 1965) formed the basis for much of the psycholinguistic research done in the 1960s and early 1970s. The standard theory grammar contained three components: a phonological component, a syntactic component, and an interpretive semantic component. It also emphasized the distinction between surface structure and deep structure. Chomsky's ideas had the impact that they did in large part because of the influence of George Miller, one of the founders of modern cognitive psychology and cognitive science. We now turn to a brief history of language comprehension, beginning with Miller's early work.

1.3. Language comprehension

1.3.1. Psychological studies of grammar

In the early 1960s Miller began to explore the hypothesis that the language comprehension system directly incorporates a transformational grammar. One line of investigation was based on earlier studies by Miller and colleagues (e.g. Miller, Heise & Lichten 1951) that examined the recall of different linguistic units (e.g. phonemes, words, strings of words) presented in a noise background in order to determine the unit(s) of language processing. The central finding was that higher level (larger) units were better recalled than lower level units when presented against the same intensity noise background. Miller and Isard (1963) used the same technique with three types of stimuli: (1) random strings of words; (2) well-formed sentences; and (3) syntactically well-formed but semantically anomalous sentences. The best recall obtained in the normal sentence condition, but words from the syntactically well-formed but anomalous sentences were recalled better than words from the random strings, demonstrating that syntactic structure was being used during language comprehension.

Miller and his students also explored a specific proposal about how language structure was used in language processing that was later dubbed the 'derivational theory of complexity' (DTC) because it assumed that sentences with a more complex derivational history should be more difficult to process. The basic idea was that listeners first compute the surface structure of a sentence and then use transformations to map the surface structure on to the deep structure. The representation in memory was the kernel sentence plus its transformational tags. Although the DTC was supported by an initial series of experiments, it was quickly abandoned. Many of the results that supported the theory became difficult to interpret as transformational grammar changed. More importantly, the empirical predictions generated by the DTC were clearly disconfirmed by pairs of sentences in which the transforma-

7

tionally more complex member of the pair was easier to process (Fodor & Garrett 1966; Bever 1970).[3]

Other lines of research seemed to find evidence that listeners were recovering linguistic structure during comprehension. Fodor, Bever, and Garrett (in various combinations) conducted a well-known series of studies that demonstrated that brief clicks or tones embedded in sentences were perceived as occurring at linguistically defined boundary points. Other studies converged on the clause as a major boundary point in sentence processing. Syntactic variables became the focus of a growing number of studies using a variety of experimental paradigms. (Experimental paradigms such as phoneme monitoring, sentence–picture verification, lexical decision, and probe verification were all introduced during the middle 1960s.)

The studies of sentence memory conducted by Miller and his students had examined memory for syntactic structure (e.g. Mehler 1963). An important study by Sachs (1967) demonstrated that listeners rapidly forget the syntactic form but not the meaning of a sentence. This result was interpreted within the framework of Chomsky's (1965) theory as evidence that people remember the deep structure of a sentence. Studies by Blumenthal (1967) and Wanner (1974) provided the strongest experimental evidence that the deep structure of a sentence was stored in memory. For instance, Wanner had subjects memorize a set of complex sentences. Subjects were then presented with a probe word taken from the sentence as a cue to be used for recall. The effectiveness of the probe word as a recall cue was a function of the number of times that the word appeared in the deep-structure tree of the sentence.

The combination of evidence that listeners recover the deep structures of sentences and evidence that they do not use transformations posed a puzzle for theories of language comprehension, namely how do listeners map linguistic input on to deep structures without using transformations? Fodor & Garrett (1966) and Bever (1970) suggested that listeners use heuristic parsing strategies that Bever termed 'perceptual strategies.' Among the most compelling evidence for these strategies were examples of grammatical sentences that were difficult, if not impossible, to parse, because the strategies assigned the wrong structure to the sentence. The most famous example is Bever's sentence *The horse raced past the barn fell*, a grammatical sentence with a reduced relative clause (*The horse (which was) raced past the barn*) that is misparsed because the past participle is misanalyzed as a simple past tense of a main verb. Fodor, Bever & Garrett (1974) integrated perceptual strategies into a clausal model of sentence processing that incorporated three principles: (1) the clause is the primary unit of analysis; (2) within the clause

---

[3] The contrasts that provide evidence against the DTC are between sentences that are no longer transformationally related in current grammars. Thus it can be argued that rejection of the DTC needs to be reconsidered (e.g. Berwick & Weinberg 1983). See Garnham 1983 and note 6 for a discussion of some of the reasons why psycholinguistics are currently not interested in reviving the DTC.

perceptual strategies relate the elements of the clause; and (3) after the clause ends, it is recoded, freeing memory for further processing.

1.3.2. The end of the transformational era

The most detailed presentation of the strategies approach is in Fodor, Bever & Garrett (1974). Fodor *et al.* concluded that the structures assigned by transformational grammar are psychologically real (used during processing) but the rules (transformations) used to generate those structures are not, a position that Wanner (1977) has characterized as the 'weak theory of the psychological reality of transformational grammar.' This theory provided an integrated framework for psycholinguistics around a position that briefly represented a consensus and that has served as a reference point for sub-sequent work. By the time that the book was published, however, the consensus had already broken down. The next sections detail some of the reasons why.

.3.2.1. The constructive nature of sentence memory

The hypothesis that the memory representation for a sentence includes its deep structure did not survive the early 1970s. Bransford and Franks and colleagues conducted an influential series of studies that demonstrated that (1) stored representations do not respect sentence boundaries and (2) memory representations of a sentence combine information provided by the propositional content of the sentence with information drawn from inferences based on real-world knowledge. For example, after hearing a sentence such as (2):

(2) Three turtles rested on a log and a fish swam beneath them

subjects believed that they had heard (3) as often as (4),

(3) The fish swam beneath the log
(4) The fish swam beneath the turtles

even though the meaning of (3) is not in any sense represented in the deep structure of (2). Rather, it is inferred from the meaning of (2) by the use of knowledge of spatial relations in the real world. This study and others of the same period highlighted the ways in which context conditioned the interpret-ation of words, sentences, and larger texts. Although all of the experimental studies examined memory representations, the results were interpreted as providing evidence about the nature of the comprehension process as well. Studies of sentence-level mechanisms and representations were considered sterile and unexciting, given the constructive nature of comprehension.

1.3.2.2. Online processing

In the early 1970s, Marslen-Wilson conducted a series of influential experiments that highlighted the rapid real-time nature of language comprehension. For instance, Marslen-Wilson (1973) and Marslen-Wilson & Welsh (1978) demonstrated that lexical, syntactic, and nonlinguistic contextual information all determine the likelihood that people who are listening and repeating back a message at a lag of about one syllable (close shadowers) will fluently restore a distorted word in shadowing a running text. A series of studies with Tyler demonstrated that listeners rapidly use pragmatic information in resolving structural ambiguities and in interpreting both explicit and implicit anaphors (e.g. Tyler & Marslen-Wilson 1977). Thus listeners have rapid access to syntactic, semantic, and pragmatic knowledge, which they use to develop an integrated representation of an incoming sentence as each word is heard. Marslen-Wilson (1975b) argued that the weak theory of psychological reality was impeding progress in understanding language comprehension. Transformational grammar assumes simultaneous access to all aspects of a derivation. As a result, psycholinguists were led to explore processing models in which the input was more or less passively accumulated until it could be mapped on to a complete linguistic sequence. Marslen-Wilson and Tyler's work focussed attention on the temporal characteristics of language comprehension and on the interaction of different sources of information during online comprehension. They also identified the lexicon as the source of many of these processing interactions.

1.3.2.3. The linguistic wars

One of the factors that had contributed to the influence of transformational grammar within psycholinguistics was that Chomsky's theories represented a consensus among linguists. As this consensus broke down, the debates between proponents of Chomsky's variations of standard theory and proponents of generative semantics made it difficult for psycholinguists to incorporate linguistic theory into their experimental work. At the same time that psycholinguistic studies were finding that syntactic structures played a minimal role in sentence memory, generative semanticists such as Ross, Lakoff, and McCawley were arguing that the underlying structures were semantic rather than syntactic in nature and that there was at best a fuzzy boundary between syntax and semantics. The generative semanticists' work highlighted aspects of language, such as indirect speech acts, that were not easily integrated into generative grammars. It also emphasized the fuzziness of grammatical categories and the ways in which conceptual structure influenced judgements about linguistic well-formedness. The boundary between linguistic representations and conceptual representations seemed to be rapidly eroding, with some linguists beginning to appeal to cognitive psychologists for explanations for the cognitive foundations upon which language seemed to depend (see e.g. Ross 1974).

Despite its appeal to psychologists, generative semantics never had much of an influence within psycholinguistics.[4] Many of the phenomena that the generative semanticists explored were never plausibly incorporated into the transformational framework (e.g. speech acts). There was also a growing irritation on the part of psychologists with the prevailing attitude among linguists that performance data were irrelevant to the formulation of competence theories, especially after Chomsky had endorsed Miller's initial studies. But the primary reason was that psycholinguists no longer considered transformational grammars to be viable candidates for processing models.

1.3.3. Psycholinguistics without linguistics

By the middle 1970s there remained no unequivocal evidence that transformational grammar provided a model of either the rules or representations that listeners and speakers use during comprehension (Johnson-Laird 1974).[5] As a result, psycholinguistics largely severed its ties with linguistics and became absorbed into mainstream cognitive psychology. The field changed in a number of ways. During the 1960s psycholinguists had concentrated primarily on syntactic variables in sentence processing. During the 1970s, they focussed on higher level processes such as the comprehension and memory of discourse or text, and on lower level processes such as the recognition of lexical and sub-lexical units. The study of syntax was largely abandoned in favor of the study of meaning. In addition to studies of literal meaning, psycholinguists began to examine various aspects of nonliteral meaning such as indirect requests (e.g. Clark & Lucy 1975) and

---

[4] Among the few exceptions were studies by Kintsch (1974) and Fodor, Fodor & Garrett (1975) that tested the hypothesis that complex verbs such as causatives are more difficult to process than simple verbs. Generative semanticists decomposed causative verbs into underlying semantic primitives. For instance *kill* was analyzed as being derived from (CAUSE TO (BECOME (NOT ALIVE))). No differences were found in these experiments.

[5] The reader might wonder about the Wanner (1974) study discussed earlier that seemed to provide evidence for deep-structure representations in sentence memory. As Wanner (1977) later pointed out, the results can be explained without recourse to deep structure because the number of times that a word is mentioned in the deep-structure tree of a sentence is correlated with the number of propositions in which it participates. With a few exceptions, the studies that examined the psychological reality of grammar did not investigate properties of linguistic structure that were uniquely attributable to transformational grammar. One study (Bever, Lackner & Kirk 1969) found that listeners mislocate clicks towards clause boundaries only when the surface clause is also a deep-structure sentence. However, linguistic analysis of the materials used and the interpretation of results obtained with the click location methodology have been extremely controversial. Bever and his students have continued to develop the clausal model, but one of the first moves was to abandon the assumption that the major processing unit could be defined linguistically (e.g. Tanenhaus & Carroll 1975; Carroll, Tanenhaus & Bever 1978; Townsend & Bever 1978).

11

idioms and metaphor (e.g. Ortony 1979). These studies were influenced by Grice's (1967) theory of conversational logic and by Searle's (1969) analysis of sentences as speech acts.

Studies of word recognition were framed by two competing views about the nature of lexical access. On one view lexical access proceeds by parallel activation of a set of candidate 'logogens' (Morton 1969) and on the other by rapid serial search through a file (Forster 1976). At the sub-lexical level, researchers began to ask what codes and units of representation are computed during recognition, as well as how these units interact during processing. The role of morphological structure in word recognition emerged as an empirical issue (Taft & Forster 1975), as did the role of phonological representations in reading. The dual-route model of reading (Coltheart 1978), in which access to the lexicon can proceed either through a visually based whole word recognition process or through the application of spelling-to-sound rules, helped provide a framework for understanding normal visual word recognition (and later certain characteristics of acquired dyslexia: Coltheart, Patterson & Marshall 1980). Studies of auditory word recognition concentrated on the role of phonemes and syllables in lexical access and on the processing of ambiguous words (see Cutler & Norris 1979 for review). The structure of 'semantic memory' and the representation of concepts became the focus of extensive research. Seminal studies by Rosch and colleagues (e.g. Rosch 1975) challenged the classical view that concepts are represented in terms of defining and necessary features, arguing instead for prototype or instance-based representations.

The comprehension of stories and texts emerged as an important research topic in the middle 1970s. A number of propositional models for the representation of sentences and texts were developed (e.g. Norman & Rumelhart 1972; Anderson & Bower 1973; Kintsch 1974; Fredricksen 1975). The most influential of these models were the Anderson and Bower model, the subsequent model proposed by Anderson (1976), and the Kintsch and van Dijk (1977) model of text processing, which built upon the earlier Kintsch model. As cognitive psychologists became more interested in discourse and text, the interpretation of anaphora and inferential processing emerged as central research topics.

Studies of anaphora focussed primarily on how anaphoric expressions are associated with their antecedents. A number of factors were found to influence how easily an anaphor could be interpreted, including the number of potential antecedents for the anaphor, the distance of the antecedent from the anaphor, whether or not the antecedent was in focus and the 'implicit causality of verbs' (see Garnham in press for a review). Many of these studies were influenced by the work of Halliday & Hassan (1976) and other functionalist linguists.

More recent studies of anaphora have been influenced by the 'mental models' framework developed by Johnson-Laird and colleagues (e.g. Johnson-Laird 1983) in which the mental representation of a text is described in terms of discourse entities and their relationships rather than a set of propositions derived from the text. The mental models approach is closely related to recent work on discourse representation in linguistics (e.g. Kamp 1981; Heim 1982) and artificial intelligence (Webber 1981).

Studies of inferencing have focussed on when comprehenders draw various types of plausible or invited inferences. Haviland & Clark (1974) demonstrated that readers make 'bridging inferences' when they do not have a mental antecedent for a definite noun phrase. Other studies demonstrated that readers generally don't make forward (predictive) inferences. One question that received particular attention was whether or not comprehenders infer the plausible instrument for a verb such as *pound* (e.g. *hammer*) when an instrument is not mentioned. Experiments incorporating appropriate controls have concluded that instrument inferences are generally not made during comprehension (e.g. Corbett & Dosher 1978; McKoon & Ratcliff 1981). Work on inference was also influenced by proposals from artificial intelligence, especially Schank & Abelson's (1977) notion of a 'script' (a temporally organized memory structure that lists the sequence for stereotypical activities such as going to a restaurant). A number of studies (e.g. Bower, Black & Turner 1978) found that in recalling a story, readers tend to fill in from scripts information that was not explicitly mentioned in the text.

1.3.4. The influence of artificial intelligence

At the same time that Chomsky was beginning his work on syntactic theory within the framework of automata theory, Newell, Simon and Shaw were developing their thesis that symbol manipulation lies at the heart of intelligent behavior (e.g. Simon 1962). Digital computers, they argued, manipulate symbols and therefore provide both a theoretical and a methodological model for understanding intelligent behavior. The symbol manipulation idea merged with the view that the cognitive system is an information-processing system to form a new information-processing approach that quickly became synonymous with cognitive psychology. The earliest influence was seen in 'stage' models of memory in which information flow through the cognitive system was described in terms of transformations as it passed through different storage systems or buffers. The development of the additive factors logic for reaction time by Sternberg (1966) provided experimental psychologists with a powerful methodology for evaluating these models.

In an influential application of this approach in psycholinguistics, Clark & Chase (1972) used a task in which subjects were timed as they decided whether or not a sentence matched a schematic picture (see also Glucksberg, Trabasso & Wald 1974; Carpenter & Just 1975). The sentence and picture were assumed to be represented in a common propositional format and a stage model was developed to describe the mental operations of the subjects as they encoded the picture and the sentence and then compared them. The elegance of these models played an important role in integrating psycholinguistics within mainstream cognitive psychology and focussed attention on the proposition as an important theoretical construct.

The most important influence of artificial intelligence on psycholinguistics has come from work on language understanding and knowledge representation. The first work to have a major impact was Quillian's research in semantic memeory and natural-language processing. Quillian argued that successful natural-language processing required an explicit representation of conceptual knowledge. The format that he chose for representing knowledge was a propositional network in which conceptual relationships were computed by activation spreading between nodes connected by conceptual links. Collins and Quillian (1969) introduced the psychological community to some of Quillian's ideas in a report of some experiments in which subjects' reaction times were measured as they decided whether or not a proposition about a concept and a property was true (e.g. *Do birds have wings?*). This work initiated an extensive line of experimental research into the structure of conceptual representations. Perhaps more importantly, Quillian's ideas provided psychologists with both a representational format (the proposition) and a processing framework (spreading activation) for thinking about the representation of sentences and texts in memory and the retrieval processes that operated on these representations. Quillian's work, along with other early influential language understanding models such as Schank's (1972) conceptual dependency approach, and to a lesser extent, Winograd's (1972) SHRDLU system, emphasized the role of world knowledge in language understanding and downgraded the importance of syntax.

As the computational approach within artificial intelligence has developed, it has continued to influence psycholinguistics in a number of ways. One of these influences is methodological. Computer simulations are providing psycholinguists with a powerful tool for making their theories explicit. This in turn has led to an increased emphasis on mechanism within experimental psycholinguistics and more recently within developmental psycholinguistics. The computational approach has also helped to clarify the possible relationships between competence and performance theories. An influential example of this is Marr's (1982) distinction between a 'computational theory' and a program that implements the theory as an algorithm. Finally, psycholinguistics continue to be influenced by theoretical ideas from artificial intelligence in areas such as knowledge representation, discourse structure, and parsing.

1.3.5. Parsing with grammatical rules

The distancing of experimental psycholinguistics from linguistic theory began when psycholinguists rejected the hypothesis that grammatical rules are used in comprehension. During the last decade, the strategies approach of Fodor, Bever and Garrett, in which grammatical rules are not directly used in building a representation or 'parse' of a sentence, has been largely supplanted by alternative parsing proposals which explicitly use grammatical rules.

Kimball (1973) proposed a set of surface structure parsing principles that combined phrase structure rules with some decision principles for coping with indeterminacy. Kimball's principles provided an account for important aspects of sentence processing such as the relative difficulty of different types of constructions and peoples' preferences in interpreting ambiguous and locally ambiguous phrases. For instance, Kimball's principle of right association explains why *yesterday* is attached with *hit* and not with *said* in the sentence *Bill said his wife was hit by a car yesterday*. These principles were simplified in an influential paper by Frazier and Fodor (1978) into the minimal attachment principle. According to minimal attachment, each word is attached into the phrase marker that the parser is building using the phrase structure rule that requires the simplest attachment (e.g. building the fewest nodes). The Frazier and Fodor parser also assumes a limited viewing window so that minimal attachment only holds for local attachments. Fodor & Frazier (1980) later revised their model to readmit right association.

Work on parsing using grammatical rules with a more computational flavor also began to appear. Computational linguists had quickly rejected transformational grammars as computationally intractable; this led to a split between theoretical and computational linguistics that has only recently begun to close. In contrast to transformational grammars, phrase structure grammars can be naturally translated into a set of parsing instructions that can operate on input strings in a word by word (left to right) manner. The problematic cases that led Chomsky to adopt a transformational approach involve discontinuous constituents and unbounded dependencies. An alternative, explored extensively by Woods (1970), was to augment a phrase structure parser to allow it to keep track of long-distance dependencies. In the ATN approach, grammatical rules are directly used to recover the thematic structure of a sentence. Kaplan (1972) demonstrated how such an augmented transition network (ATN) could be used to provide an explicit computational model for Bever's strategies. In collaboration with Wanner, Kaplan developed an ATN parsing model that made explicit predictions about how people process relative clauses. Some of these predictions were experimentally confirmed by Wanner and Maratsos (1978).

The failure of transformational grammars as processing models influenced some linguists to reduce or eliminate transformations from generative grammar in order to make them more plausible candidates for performance models. Bresnan (1978) argued that competence grammars should be easily mapped onto processing models and that transformations presented a major obstacle to any simple mapping. In collaboration with Kaplan, she developed a syntactic theory, lexical functional grammar (LFG), that replaces transformational rules with lexical rules. Kaplan has developed a parser that uses the LFG grammar and Ford, Bresnan and Kaplan (1982) show that the parser, when it is combined with a number of decision rules, can provide an account of reader's preferences in interpreting sentences with attachment ambiguities. Ford *et al.* emphasize the importance of individual lexical items, especially verbs, in controlling decisions about how local syntactic attachments are resolved.

A more radical step was taken by Gazdar and colleagues (e.g. Gazdar, Klein, Pullum & Sag 1984). They have developed a generalized phrase structure grammar (GPSG) that completely eliminates underlying structure. The GPSG approach has been championed as a framework for language parsing and language acquisition by Crain & Fodor (1985).

Parsers handle local indeterminacy (ambiguity) in one of several ways. One is by computing parallel structures and holding on to the alternatives for some specified period. A second solution is to guess and then backtrack when necessary. Marcus (1980) developed a 'deterministic' parser with a three-constituent look-ahead buffer that never backtracks. Marcus claims that his parser can parse just those sentences that people can parse without special purpose recovery strategies. In addition his parser provides a computational explanation for some of the constraints on 'movement rules' that have featured prominently in Chomsky's recent syntactic theories. Marcus's approach has been extended in recent work by Berwick & Weinberg (1983) who argue that Chomsky's government and binding framework (Chomsky 1981) can be used to provide the competence framework for a computationally tractable parsing model. Finally, several researchers have proposed parsers that directly recover semantic representations without building syntactic representations (e.g. Ades & Steedman 1982; Johnson-Laird 1983).

After a decade in which the role of syntactic structure in processing was virtually ignored, the theoretical work on parsing has begun to stimulate experimental studies of syntactic processing. These studies are focussing on questions such as the relative contribution of rules and lexical structure, the degree to which grammatical knowledge is compartmentalized into different modules (as suggested by GB theory) or unified (as suggested by GPSG), and the autonomy of syntactic processing.[6] The experimental studies of Frazier and colleagues (e.g. Frazier & Rayner 1982; Frazier, Clifton & Randall 1983) have played a major role in rekindling interest in these issues. Many of these studies have been framed by the debate between interactive and modular models of language processing. We conclude our review of comprehension with a brief discussion of this issue.

1.3.6. Modular versus interactive models

During the last decade, there has been increased interest in how the different components of the comprehension and production system communicate during processing. For instance, there have been extensive studies on the interaction between phoneme recognition and lexical context (mostly using the phoneme monitoring task introduced by Foss 1969), the interaction of letter recognition and lexical context, and interaction of word recognition and syntactic and semantic context, and the interaction of parsing decisions and semantic and pragmatic context. These studies have been guided by a debate between two proposals about how different levels communicate. One extreme position is to have autonomous processing 'modules' in which each module computes a level or aspect of representation. Ambiguity at one level is passed on to the next. Higher level units exert their influence by filtering the outputs of lower level units. When a lower level unit does not receive sufficient input, then the processor may resort to special purpose strategies. The alternative position is to have a highly interactive system in which parallel processing takes place at a number of different levels with information from different levels communicating freely throughout the system.

One of the reasons that the modularity issue has attracted so much attention is that psycholinguists who believe in a rich linguistic system have

---

[6] Attempts to decide among competing grammatical theories on the basis of psycholinguistic data have been unconvincing at best. There are a number of reasons why one might expect this to be the case. First, the mapping between a grammatical theory and a parser is not straightforward. Thus predictions depend upon many assumptions that are not intrinsic to the grammatical theory. Also, there is no straightforward mapping or linking hypothesis between parsing operations and their behavioral reflexes. Simple mappings between processing complexity and number of operations by the parser or the richness of structure built by the parser are unlikely to be correct because many aspects of parsing require little or no measurable effort. Neither do we have a direct measure that the parser has proposed a node, for instance, or posited a gap. One approach has been to see whether there are processing differences between structures that are treated uniformly by one type of grammar but not by another (e.g. Freedman & Forster 1985; Frazier, Clifton & Randall 1983). This approach is complicated by the above considerations and by the fact that distinctions that are represented in one component in one grammar may be represented in a different component (e.g. the semantics) of another grammar.

generally proposed autonomous models (e.g. Forster 1979; Fodor 1983; Cairns 1984; Frazier 1985) whereas linguistic minimalists have generally endorsed interactive models. The attraction of modular systems for linguistic autonomists is primarily methodological: demonstrating that a putative process operates autonomously provides strong evidence for the existence of that process. The question of what units, or levels of representation, are used in processing, and the question of whether or not they interact during processing are logically orthogonal, however, as are the questions of formal autonomy and processing autonomy (see Tanenhaus & Lucas 1986 and Garnham 1985 for discussion). Fodor's (1983) provocative argument for the modular nature of input systems has also played a major role in focussing attention on the modularity issue (see Marshall 1984).

In the 1970s, the general consensus was that interactive models best characterized language perception. There were numerous empirical demonstrations that higher level structure facilitates lower level processing (e.g. Miller's demonstration that words are heard more clearly against a noise background when they are embedded in a syntactically well-formed sentence). In artificial intelligence, pattern recognition models that were based on stimulus-driven or contextually driven expectations were generally unsuccessful. However, including 'top-down' or contextually driven expectations markedly improved recognition. Interactive models seemed better able to capture the flexibility that is characteristic of perceptual and cognitive systems (Rumelhart 1977).

Non-interactive or autonomous models began to emerge as serious competitors in the late 1970s. As computational models became more sophisticated in vision and in speech, it became clear that there was more information in the bottom-up signal than earlier models had assumed. Moreover, some of the radical claims made by interactive models were not confirmed empirically. For example, readers do not skip words that are highly predictable and they rarely make forward inferences.

In an influential paper in which he proposed an autonomous model of sentence processing, Forster (1979) called into question the interpretation of many 'context' effects in the experimental literature. Forster argued that subjects may make use of higher level information in an experimental task that is intended to tap lower level processing, even when the initial processing is autonomous because higher level information generally becomes consciously available before lower level information. A number of experiments demonstrated the relative autonomy of lexical processing. For instance, contextually inappropriate senses of homographs (e.g. *rose*) are typically accessed even when they are incompatible with a biasing syntactic or semantic context (Swinney 1979; Tanenhaus Leiman & Seidenberg 1979) and the context has only weak effects on the speed with which familiar words can be read (Stanovich & West 1983). Consistently with Forster's suggestions, tasks that tap lower level processing without requiring an explicit decision tend to show minimal context effects, compared with tasks that involve an explicit decision (Seidenberg 1985). Recently, it has been proposed that parsing may proceed in a modular manner, with context failing to override structurally based attachment preferences (e.g. Rayner, Frazier & Carlson 1983; Ferreira & Clifton 1986; but cf. Crain & Steedman 1985).

In addition, there was a growing consensus that cognitive processes could be divided into two classes: 'strategic' or 'controlled' processes that were flexible but slow and demanding of limited capacity cognitive resources, and 'automatic' processes that were mandatory and rapid and that did not demand attentional resources (see Posner & Snyder 1975; Shiffrin & Schneider 1977). Interactive models that were couched in hypothesis-testing terms, bringing to mind strategic processes such as 'sophisticated guessing', began to seem less plausible given the rapidity of comprehension (Foder 1983). The flavor of these interactive models is illustrated by Goodman's famous description (1969) of fluent reading as 'a psycholinguistic guessing game.'

More recently, however, a new class of parallel interactive or 'connectionist' models has been developed in which large numbers of neuron-like units compute in parallel by sending activation to units to which they are connected. The nodes are connected in a network with each node sending simple numeric messages to the units to which its connects. The connections can be seen as coding micro-hypotheses that are evaluated rapidly and automatically. There are two groups of connectionist models: localist and distributed. In localist models structure is encoded fairly directly by nodes that 'stand' for concepts such as words and phonemes (McClelland & Rumelhart 1981; Feldman & Ballard 1982; Dell 1986). In the distributed approach, however, nodes don't represent anything, rather a concept is represented by a pattern of activity (McClelland & Rumelhart 1986; Rumelhart & McClelland 1986). Connectionist models provide natural computational mechanisms for a number of language phenomena such as the flexibility of word meanings and the fuzzy boundary between literal and nonliteral meanings. They also provide a plausible mechanism for communication among different components of the processing system and for the rapid convergence of information from different sub-systems. These models exhibit either modular or interactive properties depending on the strength and type of the connections between units. For example, the multiple activation of contextually inappropriate senses of ambiguous words, which has been presented as among the strongest empirical evidence for the autonomy view (e.g. Fodor 1983), is easily accommodated within the

19

connectionist framework (Cottrell 1984; Kawamoto in press). In general, recent interactive models, including connectionist models and Marslen-Wilson's influential 'cohort' model of auditory word recognition emphasize multiple activation of bottom-up candidates in much the same way as autonomous models.

1.4. Language acquisition

There are broad parallels between the historical trends in language acquisition and in experimental psycholinguistics. During the 1960s, Chomsky's proposals about language acquisition were contrasted with behaviorist accounts in which language was learned through mechanisms such as imitation and reinforcement. The results of these studies were broadly consistent with Chomsky's claims and extremely damaging to the behaviorist position. For instance, children clearly produce utterances that are not simple variations of sentences that they hear (e.g. 'Why Daddy no go?'). Also, the stages that children pass through in acquiring language suggest that they are learning rules. For instance, when children first learn the regular ending for the past tense, they begin to apply the ending to all verbs, including irregular verbs for which they had earlier used the correct ending.

An important series of studies by Brown and colleagues provided the strongest evidence against behaviorist accounts of language. One study demonstrated that children's production and imitation lags behind their comprehension. Thus, it is unlikely that language is learned directly through parents reinforcing successively closer approximations to adult grammar. When Brown and Hanlon (1970) actually examined the conditions under which parents reinforce their children's speech, they found that reinforcement is almost always based on the truth value of the child's utterance and not on its grammatical correctness. For example a child would be reinforced for saying 'He a girl' in describing a picture of a girl, but would be corrected for saying 'He a boy.' This result has taken on added significance as it has become clear that the absence of 'negative evidence' places constraints on what types of grammars can be learned in principle (Gold 1967; Wexler & Cullicover 1980).

As in experimental psycholinguistics, transformational grammar guided much of the early language acquisition research, which focussed primarily on how children learned syntax. Some studies documented the order in which different transformational rules were learned (e.g. Menyuk 1973) and there were attempts to correlate the derivational complexity of linguistic structures with their order of acquisition (Brown & Hanlon 1970). Several researchers tried to characterize the form of the child's earliest grammar in terms of underlying syntactic categories (e.g. Bloom 1970; McNeill 1970) and a number of attempts were made to write grammars for children at various stages of linguistic development. The most detailed empirical study was summarized in Brown 1973. Brown divided language development into five stages based on the mean length of a child's utterances in morphemes (MLU): Stage I (MLU 1.0–2.0) during which the child begins to use word order to code semantic relationships; Stage II (MLU 2.0–2.5) during which the child begins to use grammatical morphemes to modulate meaning; Stage III (MLU 2.5–3.0) during which sentence modalities begin to appear; Stage IV (MLU 3.0–3.5) during which the child begins to use embedded sentences; and Stage V (MLU 3.5–4.0) during which the child begins to use coordinate sentences.

In the early 1970s, there was a shift towards more cognitively based explanations of language acquisition (e.g. Bever 1970). To a large degree, this represented a cognitive counterattack on the strong nativist claims espoused by Chomsky and his proponents (e.g. McNeill 1970). A number of researchers proposed that the child's early utterances were better characterized by basic semantic–relational categories or case roles than by syntactic categories (Schlessinger 1970; Braine 1971; Bowerman 1973). Bruner (1975) argued that the child maps language on to existing cognitive categories that grow out of sensori-motor integration that is complete before language learning begins. Virtually all researchers now assume that the child's initial linguistic categories are semantic or that the child enters into the linguistic system assuming that there is a straightforward mapping between syntactic categories and semantic categories. The question of whether or not the child begins with innate hypotheses about syntactic categories remains one of the ongoing controversies in language acquisition. Linguistic minimalists assume that there is a relatively transparent mapping between semantic or conceptual notions and grammatical structure and thus little, if any, innate linguistic structure is required. For linguistic autonomists, the mapping is too complex for the child to accomplish without some innate linguistic knowledge or specialized skills for extracting syntactic regularities (Maratsos & Chalkley 1980). Gleitman (1981), using a tadpole–frog analogy, proposes that the child begins with a semantically based grammar and then switches at some point to syntactic categories.

.4.1. Motherese

Chomsky's argument for the innateness of linguistic knowledge depends heavily upon the assumption that the child's input is impoverished relative to the structure that he or she must extract from it. As more attention was paid to the caretaker's (usually the mother's) speech to the child, it became clear that the propositional content and the syntactic form of 'motherese' is simplified in systematic ways which seem tuned to the child's cognitive and linguistic capacities (Bowerman 1973; Snow 1973; Snow & Ferguson 1977). On the surface this would seem to make language learning easier for the child. If the input is simple and orderly, the child needs less innate apparatus to extract its structure. However, subsequent analyses of the motherese literature have cast doubts on whether the child's input really is linguistically simple (Newport, Gleitman & Gleitman 1977) and on whether the child attends to – and benefits from – the methods that caretakers used to make the structure of their language more transparent to the child (Shatz 1982).

The middle 1970s also saw the scope of developmental psycholinguistics widen to include studies of the child's acquisition of pragmatic or communicative competence (e.g. Bates 1976; Nelson 1976). As in language comprehension, much of this research was influenced by functionalist ideas in linguistics.

1.4.2. Learning word meanings

As the emphasis shifted away from syntax, the question of how the child acquires word meanings began to emerge as an important topic of research. Clark (1973) proposed that the child's initial word meanings have unspecified features (incomplete lexical entries) and that the components are learned in a fixed order (thus unmarked words are learned before marked words). A number of studies seemed to provide support for the theory. Children learn the unmarked form of adjectives before the marked form and they frequently overgeneralize word meanings. Moreover, children seem to interpret more complex forms as if they were synonomous with simpler forms, for example using *large* as if it meant *big*. More recently, the componential model has been seriously challenged on both theoretical and methodological grounds (e.g. Carey 1982). For instance, the unmarked form of an adjective, which is learned before the marked form is also far more frequent. Children also seem to undergeneralize as frequently as they overgeneralize (e.g. Saltz 1972; Anglin 1977). Carey (1982) also points out that while children do sometimes use *large* as if it meant *big*, they do not do so across a range of tasks and contexts, as would be expected on the incomplete entries hypothesis. Finally, the componential theory of concepts which underlies the feature model has been seriously challenged during the last decade (Smith & Medin 1981).

One alternative approach has been suggested by Keil (1981), who proposes an 'ontological' theory of concepts, in which words are classified in terms of the types of predicates that they can be used with (e.g. animate things can die but not be broken). Keil's theory provides a principled account of how the child's hypotheses about word meanings might be constrained. More recently, Keil and Batterman (1984) have suggested that children's initial lexical concepts are defined in terms of prototypical features (e.g. the concept of *dog* is an animal that has certain physical characteristics), and then they subsequently switch to a more definitional or 'theory-based' meaning. These changes do not appear to be linked to a general developmental stage but rather to the amount of knowledge that the child has about the domain of the concept. Carey (1982) and Pinker (1984) suggest that the child might exploit correlations between word meanings and syntactic structure in learning lexical concepts (e.g. verbs of transfer typically occur with three arguments and undergo dative shift). Clark (1986) has recently proposed that children use the principle that all forms contrast in meaning to constrain their hypotheses about word meanings.

1.4.3. Cross-linguistic studies

In contrast to experimental psycholinguistics, cross-linguistic studies have featured prominently in developmental psycholinguistics. The most extensive cross-linguistic project has been directed by Slobin. Slobin has developed a number of proposals to account for the order of acquisition for various aspects of languages that differ in structure (e.g. word-order versus inflectional languages). For example, Slobin suggests that the child assumes that words (wordlike concepts) are mapped on to acoustically salient units. He also argues that local grammatical cues such as inflection are easier to learn than global cues such as word order.

Comparisons of spoken language with sign language, usually American Sign Language (ASL), have also figured in the developmental psycholinguistic literature. Gardner and Gardner (1969) made the startling claim that they had succeeded in teaching ASL to a young chimpanzee. Their conclusions have since been challenged both by psycholinguists and by behaviorist psychologists (e.g. Seidenberg & Petitto 1979; Terrace 1979). Pioneering work by Bellugi and colleagues (e.g. Bellugi & Klima 1979) has mapped out the linguistic structure of ASL and established that it has the characteristics of a natural language. Thus if there is a special language facility or module, it is not specialized for vocal language (Newport 1982). Pettito (1984) has examined the transition from gesture to sign in ASL. On the basis of certain discontinuities, she argues that language does not emerge out of gesture as has often been suggested.[7]

---

[7] Recent work by Pettito (e.g. Pettito 1984) demonstrates that children learning ASL as their first language exhibit discontinuities when they shift from the gesture system to the ASL system. For example, children who point correctly to indicate *you* and *me* later make confusions when they use the same gestures as part of the pronominal system.

1.4.4. **Learnability**

During the middle 1970s, Wexler and colleagues (see Wexler & Cullicover 1980) introduced the mathematical study of learnability into developmental psycholinguistics. In contrast to mainstream developmental psycholinguistic research, which focussed on empirical studies of what children say, this work began with some basic assumptions, namely that children learn a transformational grammar based only on positive evidence, and sought to determine under what conditions, if any, a transformational grammar could be learned. Their work demonstrated that a transformational grammar could be learned only if certain 'locality' or 'boundedness' constraints were placed on transformational rules. The formal study of learnability now forms an important sub-area within developmental psycholinguistics.

1.4.5. **Mechanisms for acquisition**

Perhaps the major trend in development psycholinguistics within the last several years is an increased emphasis on the mechanisms by which children construct and modify their language. The concern with mechanism reflects, in part, a feeling that language acquisition research had become too descriptive in the 1970s. In this context, Pinker (1984) has noted that during the 1970s people began to talk and write about 'child language' instead of 'language acquisition'. It also reflects a growing computational influence. Pinker (1984) has provided the most ambitious attempt to develop an integrated theory of acquisition. He proposes a series of procedures that describe how the child learns an LFG grammar. Pinker adopts the proposal made by Grimshaw (1981) and Macnamara (1982) that children begin with innate knowledge of linguistic categories and then assumes that they have a straightforward semantic mapping in order to bootstrap themselves into the system.

Bowerman (1987) identifies two issues that researchers in language acquisition are converging on. One is the problem of how the child avoids ending up with an overly general grammar. More specifically, how, in the absence of evidence about which utterances cannot be grammatical sentences, does the child ever revise a hypothesis that is initially too general (Braine 1971; Baker 1979)? This problem has motivated Chomskyans to shift their view of language acquisition from hypothesis testing to 'parameter setting.' According to the parameters setting hypothesis, all of the differences in the world's languages can be described in terms of how the parameters are set for a small number of rule schemata. The child's task is to learn how to set the parameters. Berwick (1985) proposed that children initially hypothesize the narrowest possible rule, a view that has been challenged on both theoretical and empirical grounds (e.g. children make errors of overgeneralization). Pinker proposes that children can recover from an overly general hypothesis by noticing generalizations among a subset of examplars that share a linguistic property (cutting back to a subset). Other possibilities are that the child preempts existing rules based on positive instances and that the child is equipped with strong innate constraints about the form of rules or specified principles of grammar (e.g. Roeper 1982).

The second issue is whether change occurs 'online,' as a function of the child failing to correctly parse a sentence, or offline as a result of a more reflective reorganization. Rumelhart and McClelland (1986) have recently developed a connectionist model for learning the past tenses of verbs that exhibits the three-stage sequence (irregular forms used correctly, followed by overgeneralizations, followed by the correct adult pattern) without explicitly representing the past tense rule. Their model provides a mechanism for offline reorganization without conscious reflection and it also raises the radical possibility that other apparently rule-governed phenomena might have similar explanations. An important issue is whether this approach can be extended to handle other types of lexical and syntactic reorganization such as those identified by Bowerman (1982). For instance children who use certain verb–event combinations correctly later make overgeneralizations (e.g. 'He pulled it untied') as they apparently discover commonalities among different verbs.

1.5. Language production

Production has been the least studied and perhaps the least understood of the three major areas within psycholinguistics. It is only recently that production has achieved an equal status with comprehension within experimental psycholinguistics. One of the reasons is that language production is difficult to study experimentally because the processes by which speakers translate a conceptual message into a linguistic form are largely inaccessible and not easily subject to experimental manipulation. Many of the issues that have shaped research in comprehension and acquisition (for example, the role of a competence grammar), have played only a minor role in production.

1.5.1. Planning units in production

In the late 1950s and early 1960s, a number of researchers used hesitations and pauses in natural and experimentally elicited speech to draw inferences about the planning units of production. Goldman-Eisler (1958) found that speakers pause at points of high uncertainty (where uncertainty was defined

25

in statistical terms) and concluded that speech is planned left-to-right. Maclay and Osgood (1959) and Goldman-Eiser both found that speakers hesitate and pause more before content words than before function words. While some word choices might be made in a left-to-right manner, Lashley (1951) provided strong arguments that some sort of hierarchical structure was planned in advance, using examples such as the agreement of the verb and the subject in sentences such as *Are all of the boys planning to come.* Boomer (1965) proposed that speech is planned in a several-word unit that he termed the 'phonemic clause.' Foder, Bever & Garrett (1974) suggested that the major unit in production was the surface clause. Ford & Holmes (1978) later examined processing load during ongoing speech and suggested that the deep structure clauses are the more important planning unit. However, they argued against a transformational explanation for their data.

Unlike comprehension and acquisition, transformational grammar has had only a limited influence on theory and research in production. Valian & Wales (1976) observed how people modified sentences when a listener occasionally responded 'What.' Transformationally complex sentences tended to be replaced by simpler forms, leading the authors to claim that speakers have access to deep structures. Foss & Fay (1975) argued that speakers use transformation during production. They suggested that speech errors such as *Put on some rouge on* were due to speakers failing to complete the deleting portion of a transformation that had a copying (moving the particle) and deletion component. Stemberger (1982) argues that these errors come about when two activated phrase structures are blended together, as occasionally happens with word blends.

1.5.2. Slips of the tongue

The primary source of data in language production has come from speech errors or 'slips of the tongue.' Merringer & Meyer (1895) first suggested that speech errors revealed the properties of the linguistic system, and influential analyses were also conducted by Lashley (1951) and Wells (1951). Fromkin (1971) argued that the linguistic forms that participate in slips correspond to the units of language that are posited by theoretical linguists (see also MacKay 1970). In the middle 1970s, Shattuck-Hufnagel and Garrett provided the outline of a processing model of sentence production using speech errors as their primary data. Shattuck-Hufnagel (1979) introduced the notion of a frame-and-slot model in which linguistic segments are selected to fill independently computed slots. For example, the production system might generate a slot for a consonant and a vowel which would then be filled by the appropriate phonemes.

Garrett (1975) used an analysis of a large corpus of speech errors to outline a framework for a theory of sentence production that has been extremely influential. Garrett proposed that sentence production, which he defined as the translation of an intended message into a linguistic form, was accomplished in a number of serially ordered independent stages. In Garrett's model syntactic processing takes place in two stages, a 'functional' level stage during which lexical representations and their underlying grammatical relations are constructed, and a 'positional' stage during which a representation consisting of phonologically specified morphemes in the order in which they are to be spoken is constructed. The two-stage assumption explains a number of regularities in speech errors, including the fact that word exchanges and sound exchanges have different characteristics. Word exchanges typically occur with words of the same syntactic class, they can occur across a span of several words, and the participating words need not be phonologically similar. In contrast, sound exchanges can involve sounds from words that differ in syntactic class, the participating sounds are usually close to one another, and they are usually phonologically similar. Garrett accounts for these differences by assuming that word exchanges take place at the functional level and sound exchanges at the positional level. The assumption that phonetic forms are not inserted until the positional level also explains why inflectional forms typically 'accommodate' to the phonetic environment created by the error. For example, the plural *s* is voiced or voiceless depending on the preceding sound. When the plural shifts during a speech error, it takes on the voicing characteristics of the new environment. Garrett also suggested that function words tend not to participate in sound exchanges because they are inserted at the functional level.[8] Lapointe (1985) has recently extended Garrett's approach by providing a detailed model for how inflectional and derivational affixes are accessed in order to account for the pattern of inflectional errors produced by agrammatics.

The interactive–autonomy issue has also recently emerged within language production. The issues are the same as in comprehension, although production researchers tend to agree on the levels of representation that are needed to characterize production. Dell and Reich (1981) challenged Garrett's claims about the autonomy of the functional and positional stages. They demonstrated that a number of speech error phenomena involve interactions between the functional and positional levels. For instance, sound errors tend to create words more than nonwords, words that

---

[8] Dell (1986) has recently shown that function words and phonologically matched content words (e.g. *by* and *buy*) participate equally often in experimentally elicited slips of the tongue. The claim that function words and context words are accessed differently has also been made in the comprehension literature. Bradley (1978) argued that function words have a privileged access route on the basis of experimental evidence that function words do not show a frequency effect in recognition. However, this result has not been replicated in subsequent studies by Gordon and Carammazza (1982) and Garnsey (1985).

participate together in sound errors tend to be phonologically related, and the semantic and phonological similarity jointly predict the likelihood that a given word will substitute for an intended word. Dell (1986) accounts for these and other phenomena in a parallel-interactive model of sentence production. The model is formalized as a computer simulation that makes predictions about speech errors that have been confirmed in both the natural speech error corpora and in experimental studies that induce slips.[9] Dell's is one of several recent models that share a spreading activation framework (e.g. MacKay 1982; Stemberger 1985).

One domain where the two models propose different mechanisms is in editing. In interactive models, feedback through spreading activation can act as an automatic and unconscious editor to help prevent errors. It also increases the likelihood that the errors that do occur will be well-formed units. In autonomous models, these effects are explained as the result of editing that occurs as speakers monitor their intended output. Editing that is clearly conscious occurs when speakers correct or 'repair' their utterances, as in 'I want the croissant . . . I mean the breadroll.' Levelt (1983) provides the most detailed analysis of repairs to date, including a well-formedness constraint which restricts the form of possible repairs.

1.5.3. Lexical retrieval

The mechanism underlying lexical retrieval, especially the processes by which conceptual representations are used to access lexical meanings, has received relatively little attention. Levelt and Schriefers (1986) argue that lexical access must begin with a 'preverbal message,' which encodes conceptual information that is relevant to grammatical encoding. The preverbal message is used to access a 'lemma,' a stored lexical item that is specified for syntactic, semantic, and productive morphological structure. Schriefers (discussed in Levelt & Schriefers) has shown that longer latencies in retrieving marked forms as compared with unmarked forms (e.g. 'small' versus 'large') are most likely due to greater complexity at the lemma access stage.

1.5.4. Determinants of structure

One of the central problems in production is how intended speakers choose the syntactic form of their utterance. Osgood (1963; 1971) conducted some pioneering studies on this issue in which he asked speakers to describe

---

[9] The technique that Dell used to induce slips was developed by Baars, Motley & MacKay (1975). Subjects are presented with pairs of words and occasionally asked to repeat the last word pair. Slips are elicited by creating a phonological set, which is broken by the target stimuli (the sequence for which the experimenter is trying to induce a slip).

simple situations. For example, Osgood would roll one of several balls of different colors across a table at various speeds and ask subjects to describe what they saw. He demonstrated that speakers tend to use an indefinite article the first time an object is used and then they shift to define articles. Subsequent studies have used a picture description task in which the experimenter manipulates various aspects of the picture and observes the effects on the syntactic form chosen by the speaker (see Bock 1982). Another domain where the issue of autonomy has emerged is in the relationship between lexical retrieval and syntactic planning. Levelt and Maassen (1981) and Levelt and Schriefers (1986) argue for the relative autonomy of word-order formulation and lexical accessibility. Bock (1982) proposed that word order is determined by an interaction of the availability of lexical items and of syntactic structures, both of which can be influenced by functional, as well as other, factors. She has recently demonstrated that speakers choose syntactically primed structures more frequently than other possible structures in picture description tasks. She has also found that the accessibility of a word (manipulated experimentally) affects whether the word is used early or late in a sentence. Kempen and Hoenkamp (in press) present a computational theory of the syntactic formulation process.

Clark has conducted an extensive line of research, beginning with his work in the 'given–new' contrast, that examines the ways in which speakers' utterances are determined by the conversational context, including the speaker's knowledge of the listener (e.g. Clark 1979; Clark & Marshall 1981; Clark & Carlson 1982). Clark argues that the notion of shared knowledge between the speaker and listener, or 'common ground,' is essential for understanding phenomena such as which nominal and referential forms are chosen by speakers.

1.6. **Psycholinguistics in the 1980s: summary and conclusion**

Where does psycholinguistics stand in the middle 1980s? In many respects the field is more vibrant than it has been since the middle 1960s, when it briefly played a leadership role in the overthrow of behaviorism and in the development of a cognitive psychology based on mentalist constructs. However, as the initial attempts to incorporate linguistic theory into processing models failed, linguists rapidly distanced themselves from psycholinguistic research, and psychologists began to distance themselves from linguistic theory. Moreover, the two major branches of psycholinguistics, experimental and developmental psycholinguistics, began to drift apart, as they often appeared to have little more than their name in common. By the middle 1970s experimental psycholinguistics had almost become completely absorbed into cognitive psychology.

29

In the 1980s there has been a reemergence of interest in the role of linguistic structure in language behavior. This trend can be seen in a number of areas. The study of syntactic processing, which was largely abandoned in the 1970s, is rapidly becoming a productive area again. The study of word recognition has been broadened to include higher level syntactic and semantic structure (e.g. argument structure), and lower level morphological and phonological structure. The latter trend is particularly apparent in the study of auditory word recognition, where psycholinguists are beginning seriously to explore the possibility that listeners use phonological and prosodic representations to help parse incoming words (Frauenfelder & Taylor 1987). Until recently, linguistic semantics has had only a limited influence within psycholinguistics, in part because many of its practitioners explicitly deny that semantics is psychological. However, work in computational linguistics is beginning to integrate recent ideas about semantics into psychologically plausible models of discourse representation. Within the next few years these models are likely to become influential in psycholinguistics.

One of the reasons for the renewed interest in linguistic structure is that the rules and representations posited by current linguistic theories are easier to embed in plausible processing models than were those used by earlier theories. In phonology, for example, linear rules based on segments or features have been replaced by hierarchical representations. In syntax, transformations have been reduced or eliminated and the lexicon has been enriched. Linguists have also become more interested in processing and psycholinguistics is emerging as a respectable sub-area within linguistics.

Psycholinguistics has also benefited from the development of cognitive science. Beginning in the middle 1970s, with considerable encouragement in the United States from the Sloan Foundation, researchers in cognitive psychology, artificial intelligence, philosophy of mind, and linguistics began to interact with one another at workshops and conferences. The result of this interaction was increased interdisciplinary awareness and, occasionally, collaboration as researchers learned of new developments in related disciplines. The cognitive science approach is reflected in a small but growing number of computationally explicit models that incorporate insights about representation from linguistic theory and that attempt to model psycholinguistic data.

And what of the debate betwen linguistic minimalists and linguistic autonomists? On the one hand, the debate has taken on a renewed vigor as linguists have begun to contribute more to the theoretical and empirical literature in both experimental and developmental psycholinguistics. On the other hand, as psycholinguistics has become more computational, and therefore more explicit, researchers with different perspectives are increasingly able to translate their metatheoretical disagreements into empirical questions.

However, at the same time that the development of cognitive science is beginning to lead to a more integrated approach to the study of language, the connectionist approach is beginning to challenge many of the basic assumptions of the information processing paradigm. Most work within psycholinguistics, as well as other branches of the cognitive sciences, has assumed that explanatory theories of cognitive processes will be couched in terms of rules and representations, with computations operating on symbols. However, all connectionist models downplay the importance of rules, and distributed models explicitly reject the assumption that cognition is symbolic. Language, with its apparently logical, rule-governed properties, represents one of the most difficult challenges for the connectionist approach. Thus psycholinguistics is likely to become actively involved again in a debate about the basic nature of cognition.

REFERENCES

Ades, A. E. & Steedman, M. J. 1982. On the order of words. *Linguistics and Philosophy* 4: 517–58.
Anderson J. R. 1976. *Language, memory and thought*. Hillsdale: Erlbaum.
Anderson, J. R. & Bower, G. H. 1973. *Human associative memory*. Washington: Winston.
Anglin, J. M. 1977. *Word, object, and conceptual development*. New York: Norton.
Baars, B., Motley, M. & McKay, D. 1975. Output editing for lexical structure from artificially elicited slips of the tongue. *Journal of Verbal Learning and Verbal Behavior* 14: 382–91.
Baker, C. L. 1979. Syntactic theory and the projection problem. *Linguistic Inquiry* 10: 533–81.
Bates, E. 1976. *Language and context: studies in the acquisition of pragmatics*. New York: Academic Press.
Bates, E. & McWhinney, B. Functionalist approaches to grammar. In Wanner & Gleitman 1982.
Bellugi, U. & Klima, E. 1979. *The signs of language*. Cambridge, MA: Harvard University Press.
Berwick, R. 1985. *The acquisition of syntactic knowledge*. Cambridge, MA: MIT Press.
Berwick, R. & Weinberg, A. 1983. The role of grammars as components of models of language use. *Cognition* 13: 1–61.
Bever, T. G. 1970. The cognitive basis for linguistic structures. In Hayes 1970.
Bever, T. G., Fodor, J. A. & Garrett, M. F. 1968. A formal limitation of associationism. In T. R. Dixon & D. C. Horton (eds.) *Verbal behavior and general behavior theory*. Englewood Cliffs: Prentice-Hall.
Bever, T. G., Lackner, J. R. & Kirk, R. 1969. The underlying structures of sentences are the primary units of immediate speech perception. *Perception and Psychophysics* 5: 225–31.
Blumenthal, A. L. 1967. Prompted recall of sentences. *Journal of Verbal Learning and Verbal Behavior* 6: 203–6.
Bock, J. K. 1982. Towards a cognitive psychology of syntax: information processing contributions to sentence formulation. *Psychological Review* 89: 1–47.
Boomer, D. S. 1965. Hesitation and sentence encoding. *Language and Speech* 8: 145–58.
Bower, G., Black, J. & Turner, T. J. 1978. Scripts in memory for text. *Cognitive Psychology* 11: 177–220.

Michael K. Tanenhaus

Bowerman, M. 1973. *Early syntactic development: a cross-linguistic study with special reference to Finnish.* Cambridge: Cambridge University Press.

Bowerman, M. 1982. Reorganizational processes in lexical and syntactic development. In Wanner & Gleitman 1982.

Bowerman, M. 1987. Discussion: mechanisms of language acquisition. In MacWhinney 1987.

Bradley, D. S. 1978. Computational distinctions of vocabulary type. Doctoral dissertation, MIT.

Braine, M. D. S. 1971. On two models of the internalization of grammars. In D. I. Slobin (ed.) *The ontogenesis of grammar.* New York: Academic Press.

Bransford, J. D. 1979. *Human cognition: learning, understanding and remembering.* Belmont: Wadsworth.

Bresnan, J. 1978. A realistic transformational theory. In Halle, Bresnan & Miller 1978.

Bresnan, J. (ed.) 1982 *The mental representation of grammatical relations.* Cambridge, MA: MIT Press.

Brown, R. N. 1973. *A first language: the early stages.* Cambridge, Mass.: Harvard University Press.

Brown, R. N. & Hanlon, C. 1970. Derivational complexity and order of acquisition in child language. In Hayes 1970.

Brown, R. W. 1970. *Psycholinguistics.* New York: The Free Press.

Bruner, J. 1975. The ontogenesis of speech acts. *Journal of Child Language* 2: 1–19.

Cairns, H. S. 1984. Research in language comprehension. In R. C. Naremore (ed.) *Language science.* San Diego: College-Hill Press.

Carey, S. 1982. *Semantic development: the state of the art.* In Wanner & Gleitman 1982.

Carpenter, P. A. & Just, M. A. 1975. Sentence-comprehension: a psycholinguistic processing model of verification. *Psychological Review* 82: 45–73.

Carroll, J. M., Tanenhaus, M. K. & Bever, T. G. 1979. The perception of relations: the interaction of structural, functional, and contextual factors in the segmentation of speech. In W. J. M. Levelt & G. B. Flores d'Arcais (eds.) *Studies in the perception of language.* New York: Wiley.

Chomsky, N. 1957. *Syntactic structures.* The Hague: Mouton.

Chomsky, N. 1959. Review of Skinner's *Verbal behavior. Language* 35: 26–58.

Chomsky, N. 1965. *Aspects of the theory of syntax.* Cambridge, Mass.: MIT Press.

Chomsky, N. 1968. *Language and mind.* New York: Harcourt Brace Jovanovich.

Chomsky, N. 1980. *Rules and representations.* Oxford: Blackwell.

Chomsky, N. 1981. *Lectures in government and binding.* Dordrecht: Foris.

Clark, E. V. 1973. What's in a word? On the child's acquisition of semantics in his first language. In T. Moore (ed.) *Cognitive development and the acquisition of language.* New York: Academic Press.

Clark, E. V. 1987. The principle of contrast: a constraint of language acquisition. In MacWhinney 1987.

Clark, H. H. 1979. Responding to indirect speech acts. *Cognitive Psychology* 11: 430–77.

Clark, H. H. & Carlson, T. B. 1982. Context for comprehension. In J. Long & A. D. Baddeley (eds.) *Attention and performance*, Vol. 9. Hillsdale: Erlbaum.

Clark, H. H. & Chase, W. 1972. On the process of comparing sentences against pictures. *Cognitive Psychology* 3: 472–517.

Clark, H. H. & Lucy, P. 1975. Understanding what is meant from what is said: a study in understanding conveyed requests. *Journal of Verbal Learning and Verbal Behavior* 14: 56–72.

Clark, H. H. & Marshall, C. R. 1981. Reference relations and mutual knowledge. In Joshi, Webber, & Sag 1981.

Clifton, C., Kurcz, I. & Jenkins, J. 1965. Grammatical relations as determinants of sentence similarity. *Journal of Verbal Learning and Verbal Behavior* 4: 112–17.

Collins, A. M. & Loftus, E. F. 1975. A spreading activation theory of semantic processing. *Psychological Review* 82: 407–28.

Collins, A. M. & Quillian, M. R. 1969. Retrieval time from semantic memory. *Journal of Verbal Learning and Verbal Behavior* 8: 240–7.

Coltheart, M. 1978. Lexical access in simple reading tasks. In G. Underwood (ed.) *Strategies of information processing.* London: Academic Press.

Coltheart, M., Patterson, K. & Marshal, J. C. (eds.) 1980. *Deep dyslexia.* London: Routledge & Kegan Paul.

Cooper, W. E. & Walker E. C. T. (eds.) 1979. *Sentence processing: psycholinguistic studies presented to Merrill Garrett.* Hillsdale: Erlbaum.

Corbett, A. C. & Dosher, B. A. 1978. Instrument inferences in sentence encoding. *Journal of Verbal Learning and Verbal Behavior* 27: 479–71.

Cottrell, G. W. 1985. A connectionist approach to word sense disambiguation. Doctoral dissertation, University of Rochester.

Crain, S. & Fodor, J. D. 1985. How can grammars help parsers? In Dowty, Kartunnen & Zwicky 1985.

Crain, S. & Steedman, M. 1985. On not being led up the garden-path: the use of context by the psychological syntax processor. In Dowty, Kartunnen & Zwicky 1985.

Cutler, A. & Norris, D. G. 1979. Monitoring sentence comprehension. In Wales & Walker 1979.

Dell, G. S. 1986. A spreading activation theory of retrieval in sentence production. *Psychological Review* 93: 283–321.

Dell, G. S. & Reich, P. A. 1981. Stages in sentence production: an analysis of speech error data. *Journal of Verbal Learning and Verbal Behavior* 20: 611–29.

Dowty, D. R., Kartunnen, L. & Zwicky, A. (eds.) 1985. *Natural language parsing: psychological, computational, and theoretical perspectives.* Cambridge: Cambridge University Press.

Feldman, J. & Ballard, D. 1982. Connectionist models and their properties. *Cognitive Science* 6: 205–54.

Ferreira, F. & Clifton, C. 1986. The independence of syntactic processing. *Journal of Memory and Language* 25: 348–68.

Fodor, J. A. 1965. Could meaning be an r_m? *Journal of Verbal Learning and Verbal Behavior* 4: 73–81.

Fodor, J. A. 1983. *The modularity of mind: an essay of faculty psychology.* Cambridge, MA: Bradford.

Fodor, J. A., Bever, T. G. & Garrett, M. G. 1974. *The psychology of language: an introduction to psycholinguistics and generative grammar.* New York: McGraw-Hill.

Fodor, J. A. & Garrett, M. F. 1966. Some reflections on competence and performance. In J. Lyons & J. R. Wales (eds.) *Psycholinguistics papers.* Chicago: Aldine.

Fodor, J. D., Fodor, J. A. & Garrett, M. F. 1975. The psychological unreality of semantic representations. *Linguistic Inquiry* 4: 513–31.

Fodor, J. D. & Frazier, L. 1980. Is the human parsing system an ATN? *Cognition* 8: 417–59.

Ford, M., Bresnan, J. & Kaplan, R. 1982. A competence-based theory of syntactic closure. In Bresnan 1982.

Ford, M. & Holmes, V. 1978. Planning units and syntax in sentence production. *Cognition* 6: 35–53.

Forster, K. I. 1976. Accessing the mental lexicon. In Wales & Walker 1976.

Forster, K. I. 1979. Levels of processing and the structure of the language processor. In Cooper & Walker 1979.

Foss, D. J. 1969. Decision processes during sentence comprehension: effects of lexical item difficulty and position upon decision times. *Journal of Verbal Learning and Verbal Behavior* 8: 457–462.

Foss, D. J. & Fay, D. Linguistic theory and performance models. In D. Cohen & J. R. Wirth (eds.) *Testing linguistic hypotheses.* Washington: Hemisphere.

Frauenfelder, U. H. & Tyler, L. K. 1987. The processes of spoken word recognition: an introduction. *Cognition* 25: 1–20.

Frazier, L. 1985. Modularity and the representational hypothesis. *Proceedings of the Northeastern Linguistics Society.* Amherst: GLSA.

Frazier, L., Clifton, C. & Randall, J. 1983. Filling gaps. Decision principle and structure in sentence comprehension. *Cognition* 13: 187–222.

Frazier, L. & Fodor, J. D. 1978. The sausage machine: a new two-stage model of parsing. *Cognition* 6: 291–325.

Frazier, L. & Rayner, K. 1982. Making and correcting errors during sentence comprehension: eye movements in the analysis of structurally ambiguous sentences. *Cognitive Psychology* 14: 178–210.

Fredricksen, C. H. 1975. Representing logical and semantic structure of knowledge acquired from discourse. *Cognitive Psychology* 7: 371–457.

Freedman, S. & Forster, K. I. 1985. The psychological status of over-generated sentences. *Cognition* 19: 101–31.

Fromkin, V. A. 1971. The nonanomalous nature of anomalous utterances. *Language* 47: 27–52.

Gardner, R. A. & Gardner, B. T. 1969. Teaching language to a chimpanzee. *Science* 165: 664–72.

Garnham, A. 1983. Why psycholinguists don't care about DTC: a reply to Berwick and Weinberg. *Cognition* 15: 263–9.

Garnham, A. 1985. *Psycholinguistics: central topics.* London: Methuen.

Garnham, A. in press. Understanding anaphora. In A. W. Ellis (ed.) *Progress in the psychology of language,* Vol. 3. London: Erlbaum.

Garnsey, S. M. 1985. Function words and content words: reaction time and evoked potential measures of word recognition. University of Rochester Cognitive Science Technical Report URCS-29.

Garrett, M. F. 1975. The analysis of sentence production. In G. H. Bower (ed.) *The psychology of learning and motivation.* New York: Academic Press.

Gazdar, G., Klein, E., Pullum, G. & Sag, I. 1984. *Generalized phrase structure grammar.* Cambridge, MA: Harvard University Press.

Gleitman, L. R. 1981. Maturational determinants of language growth. *Cognition* 10: 103–14.

Gleitman, L. R. & Wanner, E. 1982. Language acquisition: the state of the state of the art. In Wanner & Gleitman 1982.

Glucksberg, S., Trabasso, T. & Wald, J. 1974. Language structure and mental operations. *Cognitive Psychology* 5: 338–70.

Gold, E. M. 1967. Language identification in the limit. *Information and Control* 10: 447–74.

Goldman-Eisler, 1958. Speech production and the predictability of words in context. *Quarterly Journal of Experimental Psychology* 10: 96–106.

Goodman, K. S. 1969. Reading: a psycholinguistic guessing game. *Journal of the Reading Specialist* 6: 126–35.

Gordon. B. & Caramazza, A. 1982. Lexical decision for open- and closed-class lexical items: failure to replicate differential frequency sensitivity. *Brain and Language* 15: 143–62.

Grice, H. P. 1967. *Logic and conversation: the William James Lectures.* Cambridge, MA: Harvard University Press.

Grimshaw, J. 1981. Form, function, and the language acquisition device. In C. L. Baker & J. J. McCarthy (eds.) *The logical problem of language acquisition.* Cambridge, MA: MIT Press.

Halle, M., Bresnan, J. & Miller, G. A. (eds.) 1978. *Linguistic theory and psychological reality.* Cambridge, MA: MIT Press.

Halliday, M. A. K. & Hassan, R. 1976. *Cohesion in English.* London: Longman.

Haviland, S. E. & Clark, H. H. 1974. What's new? Acquiring new information as a process in comprehension. *Journal of Verbal Learning and Verbal Behavior* 13: 512–21.

Hayes, J. R. (ed.) 1970. *Cognition and the development of language.* New York: Wiley.

Heim, I. 1982. *The semantics of definite and indefinite noun phrases.* Doctoral dissertation, University of Massachusetts.

Johnson-Laird, P. N. 1974. Experimental Psycholinguistics. *Annual Review of Psychology* 25: 135–60.

Johnson-Laird, P. N. 1983. *Mental models: towards a cognitive science of language, inference, and consciousness.* Cambridge: Cambridge University Press.

Joshi, A. K., Webber, B. L. & Sag, I. A. 1981. *Elements of discourse understanding.* Cambridge: Cambridge University Press.

Kamp, J. A. W. 1981. A theory of truth and semantic representation. In J. Gorenendijk, T. Janssen & M. Stokholf (eds.) *Formal methods in the study of language.* Amsterdam: Mathematical Centre Tracts.

Kaplan, R. 1972. Augmented transition networks as psychological models of sentence comprehension. *Artificial Intelligence* 3: 177–200.

Kawamoto, A. H. in press. Resolution of lexical ambiguity using a network that learns. In S. Small, G. W. Cottrell & M. K. Tanenhaus (eds.) *Lexical ambiguity resolution in the comprehension of natural language.* New York: Morgan-Kauffman.

Kempen, G. & Hoenkamp, H. in press. Incremental procedural grammar for sentence production. *Cognitive Science*.

Keil, F. 1981. Constraints on knowledge and cognitive development. *Psychological Review* 88: 197–227.

Keil, F. & Batterman, N. 1984. A characteristic-to-defining shift in the development of word meaning. *Journal of Verbal Learning and Verbal Behavior* 23: 221–36.

Kimball, J. 1973. Seven principles of surface structure parsing in natural language. *Cognition* 2: 15–47.

Kintsch, W. 1974. *The representation of meaning in memory*. New York: Wiley.

Kintsch, W. & van Dijk, T. A. 1977. Toward a model of text comprehension and production. *Psychological Review* 85: 63–94.

Lapointe, S. 1985. A theory of verb form use in the speech of agrammatic aphasics. *Brain and Language* 24: 100–55.

Lashley, K. S. 1951. The problem of serial order in behavior. In L. A. Jeffries (ed.) *Cerebral mechanisms in behavior*. New York: Wiley.

Levelt, W. J. M. 1983. Monitoring and self-repair in speech. *Cognition* 14: 41–104.

Levelt, W. J. M. & Maassen, B. 1981. Lexical search and order of mention in sentence production. In W. Klein & W. J. M. Levelt (eds.) *Crossing the boundaries in linguistics: studies presented to Manfred Bierwisch*. Dordrecht: Reidel.

Levelt, W. I. & Shriefers, H. 1986. Issues of lexical access in language production. Unpublished paper. Nijmegen: Max Planck Institute for Psycholinguistics.

Maclay, H. & Osgood, C. E. 1959. Hesitation phenomena in spontaneous English speech. *Word* 15: 19–44.

McClelland, J. L. & Rumelhart, D. E. 1981. An interactive activation model of context effects in letter perception: Part 1. An account of basic findings. *Psychological Review* 88: 375–405.

McClelland, J. L. & Rumelhart, D. E. (and the PDP research group). 1986. *Explorations in the microstructure of cognition: Part 2, psychological and biological models*. Cambridge, MA: Bradford.

MacKay, D. W. 1970. Spoonerisms: the structure of errors in the serial order of speech. *Neuropsychologia* 8: 323–50.

MacKay, D. W. 1982. The problems of flexibility, fluency, and speed accuracy trade-off in skilled behavior. *Psychological Review* 89: 483–506.

McKoon, G. & Ratcliff, R. 1981. The comprehension processes and memory structures involved in instrumental inference. *Journal of Verbal Learning and Verbal Behavior* 20: 671–82.

MacNamara, J. 1982. *Names for things*. Cambridge, MA: MIT Press.

McNeill, D. 1970. *The acquisition of language*. New York: Wiley.

MacWhinney, B. 1987. *Mechanisms of language acquisition*. Hillsdale: Erlbaum.

Maratsos, M. & Chalkley, M. A. 1980. The internal language of children's syntax. The ontogenesis and representation of children's categories. In K. Nelson (ed.) *Children's language*, Vol. 2. New York: Gardner.

Marcus, M. 1980. *A theory of syntactic recognition for natural language*. Cambridge, MA: MIT Press.

Marr, D. 1982. *Vision*. San Francisco: Freeman.

Marshall, J. M. 1984. Multiple perspectives on modularity. *Cognition* 17: 209–42.

Marslen-Wilson, W. 1973. Linguistic structure and speech shadowing at very short latencies. *Nature* 244: 522–3.

Marslen-Wilson, W. 1975a. Sentence perception as an interactive parallel process. *Science* 189: 266–8.

Marslen-Wilson, W. 1975b. The limited compatibility of linguistic and perceptual explanations. In R. Grossan, J. San & T. Vance (eds.) *Papers from the parasession on functionalism*. Chicago: Chicago Linguistic Society.

Marslen-Wilson, W. & Welsh, A. 1978. Processing interactions and lexical access during spoken word recogntion. *Cognition* 10: 29–63.

Mehler, J. 1963. Some effects of grammatical transformations on the recall of English sentences. *Journal of Verbal Learning and Verbal Behavior* 2: 346–51.

Merringer, R. & Meyer, K. 1895. *Versprechen und verselen*. Stuttgart: Goschensche.

35

Miller, G. A. 1962. Some psychological studies of grammar. *American Psychologist* 17: 748–62.

Miller, G. A., Heise, G. & Lichten, W. 1951. The intelligibility of speech as a function of the context of the test materials. *Journal of Experimental Psychology* 41: 329–35.

Miller, G. A. & Isard, S. 1963. Some perceptual consequences of linguistic rules. *Journal of Verbal Learning and Verbal Behavior* 2: 217–28.

Morton, J. 1969. The interaction of information in word recognition. *Psychological Review* 76: 165–78.

Mowrer, O. H. 1960. *Learning theory and the symbolic processes.* New York: Wiley.

Nelson, K. E. 1976. Facilitating children's syntax. *Developmental Psychology* 13: 101–70.

Newport, E., Gleitman, H. & Gleitman, L. 1977. Mother, I'd rather do it myself: some effects and non-effects of maternal speech style. In Snow & Ferguson 1977.

Norman, D. & Rumelhart, D. E. (and the LNR research group). 1982. *Explorations in cognition.* San Francisco: Freeman.

Ortony, A. (ed.) 1979. *Metaphor and thought.* Cambridge: Cambridge University Press.

Osgood, C. E. 1963. On understanding and creating sentences. *American Psychologist* 18: 735–51.

Osgood, C. E. 1971. 'Where do sentences come from?' In Steinberg, D. D. & Jakobowitz, L. A. *Semantics: an interdisciplinary reader in philosophy, linguistics and psychology.* Cambridge: Cambridge University Press.

Osgood, C. E. & Sebeok, T. A. (eds.) 1954. Psycholinguistics: a survey of theory and research problems. *Supplement to the International Journal of American Linguistics* 20. Reprinted by Indiana University Press, 1969.

Osgood, C. E., Suci, G. J. & Tannenbaum, P. H. 1957. *The measurement of meaning.* Urbana: University of Illinois Press.

Petitto, L. A. 1984. From gesture to symbol: the relationship between form and meaning in the acquisition of personal pronouns in American Sign Language. Doctoral dissertation, Harvard University.

Pinker, S. 1984. *Language learnability and language development.* Cambridge, MA: Harvard University Press.

Posner, M. & Snyder, C. R. 1975. Attention and cognitive control. In R. L. Solso (ed.) *Information processing and cognition.* Hillsdale: Erlbaum.

Rayner, K. E., Carlson, M. & Frazier, L. 1983. The interaction of syntax and semantics during sentence processing: eye movements in the analysis of semantically biased sentences. *Journal of Verbal Learning and Verbal Behavior* 22: 358–74.

Roeper, T. 1982. The role of universals in the acquisition of gerunds. In Wanner & Gleitman 1982.

Rosch, E. H. 1975. Cognitive representation of semantic categories. *Journal of Experimental Psychology* 104: 192–223.

Ross, J. R. 1974. Three batons for cognitive psychology. In W. B. Weimer & D. S. Palermo (eds.) *Cognition and the symbolic processes.* Hillsdale: Erlbaum.

Rumelhart, D. E. 1977. Toward an interactive model of reading. In S. Dornic (ed.) *Attention and performance*, Vol. 6. Hillsdale: Erlbaum.

Rumelhart, D. E. & McClelland, J. 1986. *Explorations in the study of microcognition: Part 1: fundamentals.* Cambridge, MA: Bradford Books.

Sachs, J. S. 1967. Recognition memory for syntactic and semantic aspects of connected discourse. *Perception and Psychophysics* 2: 437–42.

Saltz, E. 1971. *The cognitive basis of human learning.* Homewood: Dorsey Press.

Schank, R. C. 1972. Conceptual dependency: a theory of natural language understanding. *Cognitive Psychology* 3: 552–631.

Schank, R. C. & Abelson, R. P. 1977. *Scripts, plans, goals, and understanding.* Hillsdale: Erlbaum.

Schlessinger, I. M. 1971. Production of utterances and language acquisition. In D. I. Slobin (ed.) *The ontogenesis of language.* New York: Academic Press.

Searle, J. R. 1969. *Speech acts: an essay in the philosophy of language.* Cambridge: Cambridge University Press.

Seidenberg, M. S. 1985. Constraining models of word recognition. *Cognition* 14: 169–90.

Seidenberg, M. S. & Petitto, L. A. 1979. Signing behavior in apes: a critical review. *Cognition* 7: 177–215.

Shattuck-Hufnagel, S. 1979. Speech errors as evidence for a serial ordering mechanism in sentence production. In Cooper & Walker 1979.

Shatz, M. 1982. On mechanisms of language acquisition: can features of the communicative environment account for development? In Wanner & Gleitman 1982.

Shiffrin, R. & Schneider, W. 1977. Controlled and automatic human information processing: II, perceptual learning, categorization, automatic attending, and a general theory. *Psychological Review* 84: 127–90.

Simon, H. S. 1962. *The science of the artificial.* Cambridge, MA: MIT Press.

Skinner, B. F. 1957. *Verbal behavior.* New York: Appleton-Century Crofts.

Smith, E. E. & Medin, D. L. 1981. *Categories and concepts.* Cambridge, MA: Harvard University Press.

Snow, C. E. 1972. Mothers' speech to children learning language. *Child Development* 43: 549–65.

Snow, C. E. & Ferguson, C. A. 1977. *Talking to children.* Cambridge: Cambridge University Press.

Stemberger, J. P. 1982. Syntactic errors in speech. *Journal of Psycholinguistic Research* 11: 313–45.

Stemberger, J. P. 1985. An interactive activation theory of language production. In A. Ellis (ed.) *Progress in the psychology of language*, Vol. 1. London: Erlbaum.

Stanovich, K. E. & West, R. F. 1983. On priming by a sentence context. *Journal of Experimental Psychology: General* 112: 1–36.

Sternberg, S. 1966. High-speed scanning in human memory. *Science* 153: 652–54.

Swinney, D. A. 1979. Lexical access during sentence comprehension: (re)consideration of context effects. *Journal of Verbal Learning and Verbal Behavior* 18: 645–60.

Taft, M. & Forster, K. I. 1975. Lexical storage and the retrieval of prefixed words. *Journal of Verbal Learning and Verbal Behavior* 14: 638–47.

Tanenhaus, M. K. & Carroll, J. M. 1975. The clausal processing hierarchy . . . and nouniness. In R. Grossman, L. J. San & T. J. Vance (eds.) *Papers from the Parasession on Functionalism.* Chicago: Chicago Linguistic Society.

Tanenhaus, M. K., Leiman, J. L. & Seidenberg, M. S. 1979. Evidence for multiple stages in the processing of ambiguous words in syntactic contexts. *Journal of Verbal Learning and Verbal Behavior* 18: 427–41.

Tanenhaus, M. K. & Lucas, M. M. 1986. Context and lexical processing. *Cognition* 25: 213–34.

Terrace, H. S. 1979. *Nim.* New York: Knopf.

Townsend, D. J. & Bever, T. G. 1978. Inter-clausal relations and clausal processing. *Journal of Verbal Learning and Verbal Behavior* 17: 509–21.

Tyler, L. K. & Marslen-Wilson, W. 1977. The on-line effects of semantic context on syntactic processing. *Journal of Verbal Learning and Verbal Behavior* 16: 683–92.

Valian, V. & Wales, R. 1976. What's what: talkers help listeners hear and understand by clarifying sentential relations. *Cognition* 4: 155–76.

Wales, R. J. & Walker, E. C. T. (eds.) 1979. *New approaches to language mechanisms.* Amsterdam: North–Holland.

Wanner, E. 1974. *On remembering, forgetting, and understanding sentences.* The Hague: Mouton.

Wanner, E. 1977. Review of J. A. Fodor, T. G. Bever & M. F. Garrett, *The psychology of language. Journal of Psycholinguistic Research* 6: 261–70.

Wanner, E. & Gleitman, L. R. 1982. *Language acquisition: the state of the art.* Cambridge: Cambridge University Press.

Wanner, E. & Maratsos, M. 1978. An ATN approach to comprehension. In Halle, Bresnan & Miller 1978.

Webber, B. N. 1981. Discourse model synthesis: preliminaries to reference. In Joshi, Webber & Sag 1981.

Wells, R. 1951. Predicting slips of the tongue. *Yale Scientific Magazine* 3: 9–30.

Wexler, K. & Cullicover, P. 1980. *Formal principles of language acquisition.* Cambridge, MA: MIT Press.

Winograd, T. 1972. Understanding natural language. *Cognitive Psychology* 3: 1–191.

Woods, W. A. 1970. Transition network grammars for natural language analysis. *Communication of the ACM* 13: 591–606.

2 Language and cognition
Robyn Carston

2.0. Chomskyan linguistics

Before Chomsky, linguistics tended to be a taxonomic enterprise, involving collecting a body of data (utterances) from the external world and classifying it without reference to its source, the human mind; it was a kind of verbal botany, as Searle has put it. Since Chomsky, linguists have thought of themselves as investigating mental representations and rules, and thus as engaged in a branch of theoretical cognitive psychology.[1] Chomsky himself recently characterized the study of generative grammar as having effected a shift of focus in language study from E-language (=externalized language) to I-language (=internalized language), that is, 'from behaviour or the products of behaviour to states of the mind/brain that enter into behaviour' (Chomsky 1986: 3).[2] The mentalist picture of language is now a familiar one and I shall do no more here than sketch those of its basic contours which have implications for work on cognitive systems in general:

1. The interesting questions in studying language concern the nature of our knowledge of language, how we come to have this knowledge, and how we put this knowledge to use.

2. These questions are to be approached within a general view of the mind as a system of computational principles forming and transforming representations; linguistic knowledge is a set of such principles and putting that knowledge to use involves the interaction of these principles with other systems of mental representation and computation. The characterization of these systems is to be given formally and explicitly in such a way that it involves no appeal to unanalyzed intelligence or intuitions of the subject.

3. While exposure to linguistic input from the environment is essential to

[1] Jesperson (1924) held a very similar view of language as mental structure earlier this century, before structuralism and the anomalous conception of the 'behavioral sciences' took hold. And he was, of course, not the first; Chomsky (1972) outlines the evolution of views on language over the centuries, and places himself in the tradition of the seventeenth-century rationalists.

[2] See Chomsky 1986, especially Chapter 2, for an account of this shift and a much more detailed discussion of the E-language view, which encompasses a broad range of non-psychological views of language from Bloomfield's 'totality of utterances' to David Lewis's 'pairing of sentences and meanings (the latter taken to be set-theoretic constructions in terms of possible worlds).'

our coming to reach this state of knowledge, its role is to trigger and minimally shape a given (innate) richly delineated complex structure, rather than (somehow or other) to create or induce this structure. Such input is too unsystematic and degenerate to give any *learning* account of how we reach linguistic maturity.

4. The notion of knowledge here is clearly distinct from any of the philosophical analyses of the concept of knowledge. These usually involve some variation on the definition of knowledge as 'true, justified, belief,' and assume there is an external reality that the beliefs can be said to be true of.[3] In the case of the principles of I-language, there is no such external reality; a grammar grows in a largely predetermined way and is no more an evidenced belief system than are the principles that account for our visual perception. Knowledge of grammar does give rise to propositional knowledge or beliefs, such as knowing *that* a certain string is syntactically ill-formed. But this is not knowledge justified by evidence or grounded in experience either; as mentioned in (3) above, the appropriate evidence is neither necessary nor available for the development of the system. Knowledge here is a mental structure which grows along with all the other standard characteristics of the human species in the normal course of maturation of the individual.[4]

5. I-language is, or is a part of, a specific mental sub-system with its own idiosyncratic structure and design (the language faculty); it is one of a system of interacting modules which make up the mind, each of which has its own particular properties, and each of which may itself comprise distinct though interacting components. This point connects closely with (3) above regarding the richly specified innate structure. While it is quite possible to believe in innateness without modularity, it seems to be verging on the incoherent to go for modularity without innateness. If mature systems of the mind are organized according to sets of principles which are specific to each system it seems impossible to account for their development unless the mind is innately programmed for these separate faculties, each destined to grow in its own way under the triggering influence of appropriate environmental conditions.[5]

6. The data of linguistic performance are a product of our knowledge of language (competence), but not of that mental system alone. Behavioral data are the result of an interaction of intentional systems of beliefs and goals with the language system and of the stresses and strains on these various systems, which share limited resources of memory and attention

---

[3] As Chomsky (1980: 27) says of the *principles* of grammar, 'the question of truth, conformity to an external reality, does not enter in the way it does in connection with our knowledge of the properties of objects.' The grammar is what enables the formation of linguistic representations (phonological, syntactic), given the input to the system of an appropriate acoustic stimulus.

[4] See Chomsky 1980 (especially pp. 89–100) for extensive discussion of this view of knowing, or 'cognizing' as he renames it.

[5] See Chomsky 1980: 40 for further discussion of this point.

focus, as well as whatever systems of motor coordination underlie speech. Anyone confining his or her study to performance is dealing in linguistic–nonlinguistic hybrids whose ingredients do not conveniently separate out at the touch of his or her classificatory tools. These data may provide some of the evidential material for testing proposed principles of underlying competence, but such principles cannot be derived from them without a theory of what to look for.[6]

The relevance of each of these six points to cognitive systems in general should emerge from, or at least be lurking in the background of, the ensuing discussion, though I will concentrate directly on (2) and (5) only.

Conceived of as a cognitive sub-system, I-language (henceforth 'language') has a theoretical vocabulary and principles which are defined independently of other cognitive systems. In this conception of linguistics, the theoretical constructs of linguistic theory are to be taken as denoting *real* mental entities. An alternative view is that the structure of language is to be explained by the principles of general intelligence and that linguists' grammars are just convenient organizational frameworks rather than theories of something real and distinct. On such an *instrumentalist* view, linguistic constructs may be useful descriptive tools, but they are not mental primitives, as they are derived from elements and principles of the perceptual and conceptual information processing systems. As Tanenhaus, Carlson and Seidenberg put it (1985: 360), on such a view 'the structure of the language would fall out as a consequence of the structure of the cognitive system itself.' It is notable how little by way of theory is ever offered with this 'language fallout' view. It is often nonlinguists who find it plausible, for instance philosophers such as Quine and Putnam and developmental psychologists following Piaget,[7] who maintain that the mind develops as a whole rather than as a modular structure with specific capacities developing in their own ways.[8] One would like some inkling of a theory which shows how a common set of principles underlie (say) visual perception, logical inferencing and linguistic competence.

[6] See Fodor 1981 for a dismissal of the view that there is any specifiable database for linguistics, be it utterances, grammaticality intuitions, or the results of experiments on language processing.

[7] However, there are linguists who are sympathetic with this view; for instance, Hudson (1984), who sees linguistic knowledge as a part of general knowledge and belief systems. Another slant, but from the same general perspective, is taken by Lakoff, who has a notion of 'cognitive grammar' which is a collection of (performance) strategies for understanding and producing sentences and therefore denies a competence/performance distinction. See Lakoff & Thompson 1975 for an early account along these lines, and Smith 1979 for an assessment. More recently Lakoff has developed a view of cognition as 'experientialist' (very much in the Piagetian spirit) with language as one of its manifestations: all syntactic categories and constructions are semantically, pragmatically, or otherwise functionally motivated. See Lakoff 1986a, case study 3, and Lakoff 1986b.

[8] See Piatelli-Palmarini 1980, where Chomsky and Fodor specifically address Piaget's idea that a child's cognitive development, including language, is 'constructed' out of its sensori-motor capacities.

The fallout view faces strong disconfirming evidence in the detailed and very complex knowledge of language which investigations by Chomsky and his colleagues have shown very young children to have.[9] To take just one of a vast range of distinct cases, a child may well not yet have grasped the property of conservation of volume nor be able to perform any but the most rudimentary arithmetic calculations, yet will have the knowledge linguists formulate as the binding principles, none of which has been explicitly taught; for instance, the child will know that the pronoun *she* may be referentially dependent on *Susan* or refer to someone else in *Susan believes she is clever*, but that *she* cannot be referentially dependent on *Susan* in *She believes Susan is clever*. Linguistic knowledge seems to develop at its own rate rather than in tandem with other systems of knowledge, and moreover, to involve principles that don't seem to have any analogue in other systems – two properties which are surely indicative of an autonomous system. Actually there is not just a single issue here concerning the relation of the grammar and the 'general cognitive system,' but several, involving relations between the three distinct notions of grammar, language processing system, and general cognitive system (also called the central systems: where 'thinking' is located). An attempt at separating out these often entwined concerns will be made later, but let us first consider what is meant by autonomous mental systems and what it means for linguistic knowledge to be one of them.

2.1. **Mental modularity**

The champions of mental modularity are Chomsky and J. A. Fodor. Chomsky (1975 and 1980) goes so far as to propose that there are distinct faculties for such capacities as deductive reasoning, arithmetic, problem solving and scientific theory formation, as well as for language. Fodor (1983) is more modest in his claims, arguing for the modularity of the various input systems such as vision and audition and, more controversially, for language as an input system, and thus as modular.

'Input' system is a functional notion: such a system takes as its input the output of a sensory transducer, a device that maps in a one to one fashion from a noncomputational pattern of physical energy into a symbolic

---

[9] Anderson (1983) remains a fallout advocate. He claims that his cognitive theory, ACT, provides a basic framework for a unified theory of the human mind. He says (p. 3) 'it seems more plausible that the language-specific adaptations are few and minor, that the language faculty is really the whole cognitive system. In our evolution we may have developed or enhanced certain features to facilitate language, but once developed, these features were not confined to language and are now used in nonlinguistic activities. Thus the mind is a general pool of basic structures and processes.'

format;[10] this input is a 'representation'[11] of a proximal stimulus (say, a pattern of light waves impinging on the retina); it is transformed by the input system into a representation of the distal layout (say, a friend's face) and then into a format that makes it accessible to the central thought processes, say a conceptual representation of *Here's Susan*. The particular input system here is, obviously, the visual perception system, but the same sort of story could be told for the others: the auditory, the tactile, the olfactory, the gustatory, and, so it is claimed, the linguistic. All of these deliver up information about the outside world to thought, making it possible to integrate information whose initial contact with the organism is in radically different formats according to the receptor sensitive to it. Fodor claims that all of these input systems share a cluster of properties which are characteristic of modular structures. Firstly, they are special-purpose (or domain-specific). I take it that there are several aspects to this (only the first of which he explicitly mentions): (a) they are sensitive to representations of only some subset of the full set of environmental stimuli which the organism is capable of processing; (b) the vocabulary and format of the representations they manipulate are specific to the particular system, not shared with other input systems nor with the central systems; and (c) similarly, they each have a proprietary database and set of computational principles directing their processes. Other properties are the fastness and automaticity of their operations, their limited access to data (informational encapsulation, as he puts it; cognitive impenetrability, as Pylyshyn 1984 puts it), and their being largely genetically specified and thus maturing at their own preprogrammed rate. Fodor (1985) talks of natural language parsing and visual processing as *reflex-like*; they are reflex-like in their automaticity and encapsulation. However, this analogy breaks down with regard to the other main property of reflexes, that is their direct unmediated response to the appropriate stimulus. Input systems are not 'straight-through' but computational; in this respect they are not to be distinguished from the 'thinking' capacities of the mind. He sums up the crucial properties of input systems in the statement:

[10] Transducers contrast with computational mechanisms such as the input systems in that they are assumed to preserve the informational content of their inputs, simply altering their format so that they become accessible to computational systems. See Pylyshyn 1984 (Chapter 6, 'The bridge from physical to symbolic') for a more extensive discussion of transduction.

[11] The property of being 'true or false of' is generally thought to apply only to conceptual representations, i.e. those amongst which the relation of entailment holds. It obviously doesn't hold amongst grammatical or visual representations. So what property do all representations have in common? The answer seems to be that it is 'aboutness,' i.e. some sort of systematic covariance with environmental states (Fodor 1983: 39). This would seem to encompass everything from proximal stimulations (retinal images and whatever effect acoustic stimuli have on the appropriate mechanism) through conceptual representations to external representations such as utterances, models (letting x 'stand for' y) and works of art. These latter are after all not true or false of an external reality, though they may bear greater or lesser degrees of resemblance to it. This very broad definition needs to be made relative to certain conditions of normal functioning, lest wild patternings of a mind breaking down are taken to qualify as representations of some external thing.

'Although perception is smart like cognition in that it is typically inferential, it is nevertheless dumb like reflexes in that it is typically encapsulated' (1985: 2).

The central systems (or general cognitive system) are functionally distinguished from the input systems: Fodor characterizes them as the set of systems employed in the fixation of belief (i.e. in deciding what is true or false about the world). A range of activities may be involved in this, including reasoning, problem solving, and speculating; also located here, presumably, are other *thinking* pastimes of a more playful, less utilitarian nature such as fantasizing, daydreaming and mental rehearsals of forthcoming interactions – activities we normally identify with 'persons' rather than with sub-personal 'systems.' These seem to have the hallmarks of *non*modular systems. They are nonspecialized, at least in the sense of (a) above since they deal in representations whose original sources (whether environmental or internal) are all those that the organism is capable of responding to. However, they too must deal in representations of a particular format type, that is, conceptual, since the whole point of the input systems is to get information which enters the organism in a range of distinct forms into this format so that it can be centrally compared, integrated, and sometimes stored. Another way of putting this is to say that the central systems are modality and domain neutral and independent. They have unrestricted access to data from memory and from the various input systems and so may be slower and less automatic (one may be aware of conscious effort in exercising them). There is no fixed neural architecture for these specific activities or for the subject areas they may work on. Here, then, we have the basis for a principled distinction between perception (including language) and cognition.

Central systems are of course computational, i.e. they perform operations on representations and they have access to information about the world solely from the *form* (syntax) of these representations. The computations of the central systems are inferential, both demonstrative (deductive) and nondemonstrative (reasoning to the best explanation on the basis of nonproving evidence). As mentioned above, input systems must also be computational given the standard poverty of the stimulus arguments; as Fodor (1985: 2) puts it, perception must involve 'the *contribution* of information by the processing organism' since there is typically more information in the perceptual output than there is in the proximal stimulus input. In this respect input systems are not reflex-like. He mentions the perceptual constancies as exemplifying this: despite fluctuations in the size and shape of the retinal image produced by a single object, the perception is usually of a stable object whose size and shape does not change. Since there is no direct correspondence between fluctuating two-dimensional retinal images and our stable percepts, it seems that computational processes of some sort or other must transform the one into the other.

Just as the format of representations within the input systems is of a different order from that of the central systems, let us say perceptual as opposed to conceptual, so the kinds of computation performed in bringing about the transformation from proximal stimulus to representation of the world seem of a different order from the reasoning processes characteristic of the rational fixation of belief, decision-making and formation of desires and goals. As we will see shortly, the series of transformations of representations from light images through to three-dimensional object description cannot be construed as inferential in any useful sense. And the same goes for the operations that mediate different levels of syntactic representation in natural-language processing: say there are operations which move elements around in structures so as to fill in gaps, which is one possibility which has been entertained, such a computation bears no resemblance to standard inferential processes. It is even harder to conceive of inference as what relates representations at different linguistic levels, say the phonetic, the phonological, and the syntactic. It seems that we do well to confine our use of the term 'inference' to central systems operations, and, for want of any other term, call the operation of input systems 'perceptual computations.'

Let's briefly consider the case of the visual perception system, which is perhaps fairly immediately recognizable as having the properties given as characteristic of a modular system. It does seem to be fast and automatic and, given the evidence from optical illusion studies, that *knowing* the truth of the matter makes little difference to our perception of an illusion, it does seem to be sealed off from contexual information in just the way Fodor takes to be standard for a module: even after measuring the Müller–Lyer lines and finding them identical in length, people still see one as longer than the other.

As an input system, the business of vision is to construct and present to the central system information about some part of the external world (the distal layout), taking as its input data the (transduced) retinal image(s) caused by that bit of the world. The retinal image is a two-dimensional array of measurements of levels of light intensity (registered by some 160 million light receptors making up the retina). From this 'gray-level' image all the visual information about shapes, surface contours, colors, etc., is derived.

The input system makes explicit information that is only implicit in the gray-level pattern (just as the language system makes explicit information which is only implicit in the acoustic properties of an utterance). According to the computational view of Marr 1982 (summarized in Rosenfield 1984 and Roth & Frisby 1986), this 'making explicit' involves a sequence of mental representations formed on the basis of the gray image together with strong assumptions about image–world correlations which are internal to the system. The first major representational level is 'the primal sketch'; the crucial assumption at work here is that changes in illumination level (i.e. changes in the level of grayness from one set of dots to another) are the edges and shifts in surface contours of objects. In accordance with this principle, a two-dimensional representation marking in object boundaries and object regions is set up.

In the next major representation, called the 2½-D sketch, three-dimensionality is made explicit, but only from the viewer's perspective; relative distance of each patch of surface from the viewer, orientation with respect to line of sight, and the presence of edges are shown here but information about the object as an entity in space is not yet available. If the object is in motion, computation over changes in successive images also enters into formation of this representation; Ullman (1979) gives experimental evidence that the structure of an object can be derived from the dot patterns caused by its movement, and hypothesizes an assumption of object rigidity built into the visual system. The existence of this principle can be demonstrated by tricking it into inappropriate operation: if a square is projected on to a screen and its sides are expanded and contracted in a regular fashion, what a viewer *should* see is a small square, then a large square, then a small square, etc. But what *is* seen is a single square that does not change in size, but that alternately recedes and approaches. That is, the visual systems misinterprets the cues as if a rigid object were being observed. The final stage is the computation of a generalized view of an object, the 3-D model, which can then be matched to one of a stored collection of 3 D object models in the process of object identification. The intermediate representations such as the primal and 2½-D sketches are generally inaccessible to the central system; they are simply the means to an end, and once that end has been achieved (object or scene recognition) the means is irrelevant to the organism. The various perceptual computations sketched here are peculiar to the visual system and the representations (sketches) are in a particular format which distinguishes them from conceptual representations and from other input system representations (such as linguistic ones), thus satisfying the full range of properties characteristic of modular systems.[12]

Language processing, it is argued, evinces the same general modular properties as vision, the crucial and controversial one being encapsulation from, or impenetrability to, extralinguistic beliefs; making the case for this will occupy the next section of the chapter. Language certainly seems to have the cluster of other characteristic properties. It is domain-specific in

[12] The skeletal sketch of the visual system given here is derived largely from Rosenfield 1984 and Roth & Frisby 1986, hence the concentration on Marr's theory. Pinker 1984 gives a comprehensive overview of issues and theories in visual cognition, placing Marr's approach in the context of others.

the sense of bringing to bear a set of specific principles on a deliminated stimulus domain; such principles as subjacency and binding do not seem to apply generally in information processing but just to language; the same is true for the formats the system handles (phonetic, phonological, syntactic). It is fast and mandatory: you have no choice but to hear an utterance of a sentence as an utterance of a sentence; you can't switch off the language processor as it were and simply perceive a voice making sounds; experiments in which subjects repeat continuous speech as they hear it show that the standard 'shadowing' time is a quarter of a second (Marslen-Wilson 1973). Given the amount of input and output processing involved in this behavior, it would seem to qualify as a fast psychological process if anything does. The various interlevels of processing are generally inaccessible to the central systems; subjects cannot report on the phonetic or syntactic structure of an utterance (the linguist's task would be much diminished if this were possible); what they retain is the gist of the meaning conveyed. Language is innately specified as already argued. More tentatively, Fodor suggests as further characteristics that language has a fixed neural architecture, a relatively fixed pattern of growth across individuals, and that it breaks down in a patterned way as in the case of the various aphasias.[13]

So language, like vision, is special rather than typical of the mind's workings; it is not a case of thought in microcosm. Study of a perceptual capacity such as parsing isn't going to tell us how, say, nondemonstrative inference in problem solving works; nor for that matter is it likely to generalize to other areas of perception.

Many challenging questions are raised by Fodor's modularity thesis. Questions concerning his views on the central systems are discussed in the final section; the immediate and pressing question of the rightness or not of the modularity thesis for language occupies the next section. Among the interesting issues that cannot be pursued here are the following:[14]

1. Assuming modularity is right in the general case, how modular are the modules themselves? For instance, are there separate modules for color perception, the analysis of shape, face recognition, etc., within the visual module, and for phonological analysis and syntactic analysis within the language input system?

2. Does the cluster of properties associated with modular systems rule out cross-modular connections? For instance, it has been suggested (McGurk & MacDonald 1976) that speech perception is influenced by the visual input of observed vocal movements, i.e. mechanisms of phonetic analysis are

[13] See Fodor 1983: 98–101.
[14] Fodor's monograph has aroused much response, positive and negative; many of the questions raised here are discussed along with others in *Cognition* 17.2, which is devoted to the modularity issue, and in the peer commentary following Fodor's precis in *The Behavioral and Brain Sciences* 8.1.

activated by this particular visual stimulus. Another case is mentioned by Mattingly & Liberman (1985), who see nonlinguistic acoustic phenomena accompanying speech, such as voice quality, loudness, and pitch, being passed on from the language processor to some other auditory input system when they prove not to be susceptible to phonetic analysis.

3. Unlike the other systems discussed, language is an output system as well as an input system, that is, it is both perceptual and motor, so we might ask what the relation is between its input function and its output function. Are there two language modules, or just one with corresponding input and output operations (parsing and sentence planning; speech perception and speech production) relying on the same grammar?

4. Do certain *learned* activities, such as the capacity to read fluently, qualify as modular? Reading is domain-specific, fast, automatic, and encapsulated, in much the same way as spoken language processing. Obviously, however, it is not innately specified as the latter is. This is an interesting and problematic case, since it is surely highly parasitic on the language module, and the question looks to be how, through learning, the language processor comes to be receptive to a particular visual stimulus type.

5. What is the relation between the grammar (competence) and the language input system (a performance system)? Since the perception process performed by the language module must involve the assigning of linguistic types to the received linguistic tokens (uttered sentences and phrases) the system must encompass a theory of linguistic types, i.e. a grammar (or an I-language). Linguistic knowledge, then, is module-internal and its use in sentence perception is no threat to encapsulation. Exactly how it is employed, what its relation is to the parsing procedures involved in language perception and whether either has any bearing on the development, ontogenetic or phylogenetic, of the other, are open questions.[15]

6. Assuming modularity is right, what are the outputs of the modules like and how is the interface with the central systems effected? It's reasonably easy to discern clearly low level modular processes (such as forming a primal sketch or phonological analysis) and clearly high level central processes (such as interpreting someone's utterance as ironic or deciding to pursue some course of action after weighing up the pros and cons), but where the one ends and the other starts is a far more difficult problem. If we suppose that at the language/cognition interface there is a process of mapping from lexical items on to concepts stored centrally, the question of the structural information carried over into the conceptual representation remains; some notion of logical form setting up an incomplete central system represen-

---

[15] See Valian 1979 for different views of the relation between competence and performance. See Bever 1970 and 1975, Frazier 1978 and 1985, and Frazier & Fodor 1978, on parsing strategies and their relation to the grammar, and Crain & Steedman 1985 for an alternative view. J. D. Fodor 1981 explores ways in which the grammar has been shaped over time by performance pressures.

tation has to come in here, whether it is Chomskyan logical form (LF), the Sperber & Wilson 1986 idea of logical form as an incomplete conceptual representation, or some other. LF seems in some respects too low level a notion, not only because of its lexical vocabulary but also because of the language specificity of its syntactic structure. Sperber & Wilson assume that logical form employs the vocabulary of the central system (concepts) and they envisage a syntax for that system which generalizes across natural languages.[16] The output of the visual processor is just as wide open to conjecture; it would be very nice if it could be shown that what is involved here is a mapping from 3-D models on to concepts, providing the central system with such hypotheses as *There is a dog* and *It is raining*, in the conceptual format which the system deals in, so permitting their inferential interaction with evidence derived from nonvisual sources.

2.2. The cognitive impenetrability of language perception

Fodor's modularity thesis is directly at odds with a mainstream view in twentieth-century psychology, that of the New Look Cognitivists who considered perception to draw on all manner of beliefs, memories and expectations in the process of constructing percepts.[17] They were impressed by the 'intelligent' (=computational) nature of perceptual processes and inferred from it to the continuity of perception with cognition; Fodor is impressed by the 'dumb' (=encapsulated) nature of perceptual processes and infers from it to the *dis*continuity of perception from cognition. Fodor's logic is tighter than the NLCs', since computationality is consistent with modularity while encapsulation is inconsistent with perception–cognition continuity. So the crucial question is whether he is right or not about the encapsulation (cognitive impenetrability) of particular mental faculties, and that can be ascertained only empirically. In particular we are interested in whether he is right with regard to the encapsulation of *language* processing.

The basic assumption of work in AI on programming machines to understand texts takes it as more or less obvious that human language processing is cognitively penetrated, and aims at computer simulations with this feature. The following statements from Schank and Hunter are typical: 'No utterance can make sense to an understander unless the understander knows something about the topic of the utterance; a thoroughly unencapsulated process' (1985a: 30); 'the program must have some idea of what will happen next, based on what has happened previously and what it already knows about these kinds of situations . . . a conceptual parser uses informa-

---

[16] Kempson (forthcoming) gives an interesting discussion of the vocabulary and structural properties of logical form within a relevance-theoretic framework.
[17] For the views of one of the best-known exponents of this school, see Bruner 1957.

tion from many sources, grammatical and otherwise . . . syntax is only one of many sources of information used simultaneously to understand text' (1985b: 144).

On the face of it, there appears to be a fair amount of evidence to support this assumption. Recall the well-known cloze effects: words are far more predictable in some sentential contexts than in others. In sentence (1) for example, there is a narrow range of high probability completions, which is not the case for sentence (2):

(1)   The doctor handed the blood sample to the —
(2)   On Tuesday we went to the —

General knowledge in western cultures includes a stereotypic script about doctors, nurses, and blood samples, but no such script about what people do on Tuesday. Sentence (1) is said to have a high cloze value and (2) a low one, and it has been shown that people's ability to understand sentences in noisy conditions is directly related to the average cloze value of the sentence (averaging across all positions in the sentence), that is, the more predictable the more easily and accurately understood. Similarly, a lexical decision task, in which, for example, sentence (1) was presented visually followed by a string of letters which the subject had to judge as a word or not, showed significantly longer latencies (i.e. time taken to decide correctly) for a coherent but unlikely competition such as 'janitor' than for the highly likely 'nurse.' This looks like the direct involvement of background/contextual knowledge in sentence perception.

Further evidence comes from the psychologists Marslen-Wilson and Tyler, who continue the New Look tradition in the area of language. They advocate 'an on-line interactive language processing theory, in which lexical, structural (syntactic), and *interpretive knowledge* sources communicate and interact during processing in an optimally efficient and accurate manner' (Marslen-Wilson & Tyler 1980: 1; my emphasis). They present an impressive range of experimental evidence to support this view, some of which I look at here but which is comprehensively surveyed in Marslen-Wilson & Tyler 1981 and Tyler & Marslen-Wilson 1982.

Tyler & Marslen-Wilson (1977) presented listeners with structurally ambiguous fragments such as 'landing planes' preceded by a clause that was biased towards one reading (e.g. 'If you walk too near a runway' or 'Even if you are a trained pilot'). Each fragment was followed by a target word, either *is* or *are*, which was presented visually. The context clause determined whether *is* or *are* was the grammatical continuation of the phrase 'landing planes.' Reaction times to read the target word were faster when the word was a contextually appropriate continuation, suggesting that listeners were evaluating the ambiguous fragments relative not only to the meanings of the words involved, but also to the pragmatic plausibility of each reading in the given context.

In another experiment referred to in Marslen-Wilson & Tyler 1981, the on-line availability of information from different levels of representation in resolving anaphoric reference was demonstrated. Context sentences as in (3) were followed by one of three possible fragment strings as in (4):

(3)   As Philip was walking back from the ship, he saw an old woman trip and fall flat on her face. She seemed unable to get up.
(4)   a. Philip ran toward . . .
      b. He ran toward . . .
      c. Running toward . . .

Following each of the fragments, listeners were presented with a visual target word, which was either a pragmatically plausible or an implausible continuation, assuming the subject had linked the anaphor ('he' in (b), zero in (c)) to the appropriate antecedent *Philip*. The plausible target was *her*, the implausible one *him*. Plausible continuations were named faster than implausible ones in all three cases, showing that listeners had assigned a referent to the anaphor by the end of the fragment, and the size of the difference did not vary significantly across the three cases. In (c), the only way the runner can be identified is by some inferential process relating the verb phrase 'Running toward . . .' to the properties of the potential antecedents in the context, i.e. one must infer who is most likely to be running toward whom. This is taken to indicate that pragmatic inferences are drawn online and in parallel with the grammatical analysis of a sentence.

This does look rather compelling and calls for some sort of response from the believer in language encapsulation. Fodor's response is to point out several conditions that any *apparent* counterevidence to encapsulation must meet if it is to achieve the status of *real* counterevidence:

1. The information bearing on a computation that the system performs must be shown to be extramodular and not part of the stock of premises which are particular to that module.

2. The computation must be shown to be linguistic (perceptual in the general case) and not postperceptual since obviously perception and cognition interact *somewhere*, the point on the modular view being that it's not just anywhere.

3. The system putatively penetrated must be the system standardly employed in language processing and not some backup system brought in when conditions are not standard.

This third point is relevant to the cloze effects since it seems that the disparity mentioned above disappears when sentences are presented in undistorted conditions and at a rapid rate (as in a set of experiments by Fischler &

Bloom 1980) – thus it looks as if what goes on in noisy conditions is a guessing strategy, which certainly would employ real-world knowledge but which is not the way sentence perception is *standardly* achieved. In the clear quick case where guessing is neither necessary nor possible (guessing takes time), speed and accuracy of sentence perception bear no relation to cloze value.

Now let us consider Marslen-Wilson & Tyler's results. I don't think that anyone now would want to dispute the *online* nature of processing: a speech signal is extended in time over periods ranging from a few hundred milli-seconds to several seconds, and, as speech shadowing has shown, a hearer is able to perceive and reproduce a signal with only a 250-msec delay (between onset of the word heard and onset of the word uttered). Every word has phonetic, syntactic, and semantic properties and the experiments cited indi-cate unequivocally that hearers begin their analysis at each of these levels as soon as they can. The old idea that all syntactic work on a clause was executed before any semantic processing began (a radically *non*interactionist account) was a relic of a misplaced attachment to the idea of directly incorporating linguistic competence levels of representation into a performance model, ignoring the facts of real-time processing; Marslen-Wilson & Tyler's work has certainly demonstrated the error in this. Clearly phonetic analysis begins as soon as a few phones have been uttered, lexical accessing part way through the utterance of the first word, and syntactic and semantic processing as soon as the first word has been identified.

But what matters to us here is the *interactive* bit of the theory. Fodor's position on interaction *within* the language module is less restrictive than that of other modularity theorists such as Forster (1979), who maintains that there are hierarchically arranged autonomous sub-systems for phonological, lexi-cal, syntactic, and semantic processing within the language module and information flow amongst these is strictly bottom-up, i.e. restricted to passing the output of lower levels of processing to the next higher level. There seems to be some evidence against this strong position. For instance Ganong (1980) shows that knowledge that *gift* is a word, while *kift* is not, may directly affect whether [g] or [k] is perceived at the beginning of a phonologically ambiguous utterance. Ryder & Walker (1982: 138) cite evidence that suggests that a syntactic analysis may be available to guide lexical access when the ambiguity is purely syntactic; so, for example, the presence of a determiner or the infinitive indicator *to* may lead to the accessing of only one or the other of the two lexical items *call* (the two differing only in verb/noun categorization). This is of no consequence to Fodor, who explicitly allows for top-down interaction *within* the language module and cites some further evidence in its favor (Fodor 1983: 65).

But what does have a crucial bearing on Fodor's encapsulation hypothesis is the interaction of *non*linguistic knowledge (such as that pilots land airplanes) with linguistic information (such as the two structural analyses of 'landing planes'). Again, Marslen-Wilson and Tyler's results can leave us in no doubt that there is a pretty minute interaction of processes, both linguistic and contextual, at the level of the word or morpheme. The important question that their work raises for the advocate of encapsulation is whether, in the terms of Crain & Steedman (1985), the interaction is *weak* or *strong*. On the weak view syntactic processing independently sets up the alternatives which semantics and context choose amongst; on the strong view semantics and context are predictive, that is, they influence which linguistic entities are accessed in the first place. Marslen-Wilson & Tyler (1980) seem to equivocate between the two versions. Clearly the strong version is incompatible with encapsulation. The question is whether the experimental results cited above entail the strong view.

It could be reasonably maintained that the response biases in the ambiguity experiment referred to above are the product of *post*perceptual processes and thus don't meet Fodor's second requirement on counterevidence, thereby supporting a weak but not a strong interactive theory. One possibility is that the structures are accessed *serially* by the processor; one of them is presented to the central processes for integration with the message so far received (e.g. 'If you walk too near a runway . . .'), and either accepted or rejected; if rejected, the other analysis is accessed and proffered. Alternatively, the two might be accessed simultaneously and *parallel* attempts at integration made with some measure of 'best fit' (see the discussion of the theory of relevance in section 2.3) deciding between them. A few milliseconds later the next word, whether 'are' or 'is' is processed; in the inappropriate case the hearer is going to be confused, since here is a word which is lexically and structurally unambiguous and which simply won't integrate with the message so far; hence the longer response latency.[18]

A similar story can be told for the anaphor case: by the time 'her' or 'him' leaves the processor, the identity of the agent as Philip has been established by postperceptual processes and the occurrence of another masculine pronoun leaves the hearer without any plausible antecedent to assign to it; processing thus falters. One might wonder about the absence of time differences among the three cases: if the anaphoric link is made *post*perceptually, that is *after* linguistic processing in the third case, shouldn't it take longer? We're dealing in such tiny time spans here that it's difficult to know what's going on, but since in the first two cases the perceptual processor has 'Philip' or 'he' to deal with, its work is fractionally greater than in the third case, which may be taken to offset the time taken to make the pragmatic inference in the third case. The point of interest here is that an

[18] See Forster 1979 for a discussion of Marslen-Wilson & Tyler's results.

online *weakly* interactive theory of language processing is the strongest theory needed to explain the results of these experiments, and this is entirely compatible with a modular view of the language processor.[19]

The weakly interactive theory seems to have been established beyond all reasonable doubt with regard to one particular language process, that of lexical *access*, in experiments by Swinney (1979), Tanenhaus, Leiman & Seidenberg (1979), Onifer and Swinney (1981), and Seidenberg, Tanenhaus, Leiman and Bienkowski (1982). The sort of finding that led New Look theorists to believe that context directs lexical access came from the facilitation of lexical decisions by biasing contexts, so, for example, lexical decision on the italicized word in 'All of the animals escaped when the gate of the *pen* was left open' was faster than when it appeared in a neutral context where the word was acceptable but had a low cloze value. In the first Swinney experiment subjects listened to sentences containing an ambiguous word (such as the one above) and simultaneously made lexical decisions about letter strings presented visually *immediately following* the ambiguity. As expected, the response time to the word *pig* was faster than to the contextually unrelated word *king*. However the important result was that response time to the word *ink* was also comparably faster; it is just as contextually irrelevant as *king* but is of course related to the other meaning of *pen*. The effect was shown to hold for sentence contexts favoring the other reading of the ambiguous word, too, such as 'I wanted to write a letter to my mother but I couldn't find my *pen*' (i.e. *pig* was facilitated by this). That is, both lexical items *pen* are accessed in all contexts, whether neutral or biased towards one of the meanings.

This is an interesting result for the first of the conditions given by Fodor for cognitive penetration of perception: what at first looked like evidence for extramodular information influencing a perceptual process now no longer does. In Fodor's words: '[it] looks a lot less like the intelligent use of contextual/background information to guide lexical access. What it looks like instead is some sort of associative relation among lexical forms . . . a relation pitched at a level of representation sufficiently superficial to be *in*sensitive to the semantic content of the items involved' (1983: 79). That is, if facilitation is due to associative links among lexical items the influence is *intra*modular and purely linguistic, not conceptual. There are two forms

---

[19] Obviously I am presupposing the automaticity of semantic processing and reference assignment – there seems to be ample evidence that even in very fast shadowing hearers can't help but carry out these processes though they are not required by the task (see Marslen-Wilson 1973). Note that this implies that manditoriness is not peculiar to input systems but that it is a feature of at least some central processes as well. Marslen-Wilson & Tyler (1981) make it clear that they are opposed to modularity, and I gather they still hold this position from the title of a recent talk, 'Against modularity,' presented at Amherst in 1985, which I have not yet seen. I do not see why they should take this line, given the compatibility of their experimental results with modularity and their insistence that perceptual processing is *data-driven* and *obligatory* (1981: 327).

pen, each with its particular constellation of node connections in a network of connections: the one to a set of forms which encode the subject's animal and farm concepts, the other to a set of forms encoding concepts to do with writing. This network idea is a familiar one: accessing an item in the network activates its node with a spread of activation to connected nodes; relative levels of excitation are directly proportional to distance from the original activated node (other things being equal). The existence of such module-internal connections cuts processing costs as it will presumably often facilitate lexical access and obviate the need for a rendezvous with context. For example, accessing *hot* in understanding 'I'm always either too cold or too hot' should be quicker than in 'This room is too hot' given a pretty direct connection between *cold* and *hot*. (Note that in the process the other lexical item, *hot* meaning 'spicy' will be assessed as well, i.e. *cold* and *spicy* will indirectly activate each other via *hot* as will *pig* and *ink* via *pen*, but, Fodor maintains, such a system will produce processing savings overall.)

The second Swinney experiment was identical except that the visual words were presented *three syllables after* the ambiguity; in this case the effect was lost, that is, only words related to the contextually relevant meaning of the ambiguity (e.g. *pig*) were facilitated. Onifer & Swinney (1981) ran a set of experiments using the same paradigm but with a different set of ambiguous words: they used highly polarized lexical ambiguities – words having one very frequent meaning (75%–89% frequency of use) and one very infrequent meaning (11%–25% frequency of use) – and tested them in strongly biasing contexts. The results here were identical in form to Swinney's original results; that is, all meanings for the ambiguity were activated immediately after the ambiguity was heard, including the very infrequent meaning in a context biased towards the frequent meaning. And, as in the Swinney experiments, by 900 msec later only the contextually appropriate meaning of the ambiguity – whether the most or the least frequent meaning – was still active. Swinney (1982: 161) mentions an experiment he carried out to see whether ambiguous words, differing in the grammatical category of each sense, such as *watch* or *cross*, which are both nouns and verbs, would also be exhaustively accessed even when preceded by a disambiguating cue word, say *the* or *to*. Again the evidence was that in *all* contexts *both* meanings of the ambiguity were momentarily accessed even when the grammatical class of one of the meanings was inappropriate.[20] All the evidence points one way: to exhaustive access of homophonic lexical items followed by rapid post-access disambiguation.

---

[20] However, Ryder & Walker (1982) present evidence that when a word is merely syntactically ambivalent (i.e. not also semantically ambiguous), such as *defeat*, *offer*, *cart*, only the more frequent usage is immediately accessed, i.e. the verb *offer*, the noun *cart*.

Given the lexical network idea, the way is open for a module-internal account of disambiguation. Taking the original example 'All of the animals escaped when the gate of the pen was left open,' *animal* and maybe *gate* have some reasonably close connection to *pen*, so that *pen* is already activated to some extent when the processor comes to the utterance of *pen*. At this point both lexical items *pen* become highly activated, though one more highly so than the other, given the push from *animal* etc., so this is the one chosen. Either the other gets 'turned off' once the choice is made or its relatively lower level of activation has faded out a few milliseconds later (i.e. after four syllables). One prediction from this is that though items related to both senses of an ambiguous word are activated, as the experiments show, the ones related to the chosen sense should be more highly activated, hence more quickly responded to, than those connected to the rejected sense. This does seem to be the case in the reaction-time statistics Swinney gives: lexical decisions to words related to the inappropriate sense of the ambiguity are consistently fractionally slower than those to words related to the appropriate sense.

However the lexical network story is not the only one compatible with the results: it could be that lexical forms map directly to a conceptual address in the central system where encyclopedic information about the denotation of the concept is stored and it is this 'knowledge' which is responsible for the disambiguation rather than 'dumb' network connections. A central system of multiply cross-referenced encyclopedic entries has to exist anyway – it's a crucial part of memory, providing us with a store of propositional information, varying in accessibility, and used all the time in inferential thought (see section 2.3). On this story there would be exhaustive module-internal lexical access followed by parallel mappings and attempts at contextual integration which lead to a rapid choice between the options. Both conceptual addresses are accessed briefly, which accounts for the Swinney effects, and all disambiguation is postperceptual – which is still of course quite compatible with the encapsulation of the language processor.

It is rather difficult to see how to decide between these alternatives. However, it does seem reasonable to suppose that language processing precedes central processing (for the appropriate unit), so one might compare the cases we've looked at so far with one that undoubtedly requires central processing: such a case would be one in which a *non*linguistic context clearly biases the interpretation of an ambiguity, that is, because the crucial disambiguating information reaches the central system via a different input system, its effect on the linguistically conveyed information can only be postperceptual. For example, the subject sees a picture on a screen of two people watching animals running around wrecking a garden, and hears one of them utter: 'We need a *pen*.' Assuming activation of both senses of *pen*, only contextual interaction (i.e. postperceptual processes) could perform the disambiguation. If the Swinney type cases, where preceding sentential context dictated one sense, were found to be significantly quicker, this would seem to support the interlexical network idea. Another possibility would be to set up cases contrasting in plausibility but not involving associative links such as the following:

(5)   On the train he looked at his paper/plan
(6)   Walking in, he took off his coat/clothes
(7)   In the distance she heard the sound of a train/trumpet

It doesn't seem likely that there should be a lexical link between *sound* or *distance* and *train*, in fact it's rather more likely that there is such a link between *sound* and *trumpet*, but the first is a more common experience than the second. If reaction times in a lexical decision task or a naming task proved to be facilitated in the more plausible case, this would have to be due to postperceptual processes of context integration. If this facilitation is on a par with the effect in the assumed lexically associated cases mentioned above it would begin to look as if positing a lexical network is redundant. If postperceptual processes account for the plausibility effect in the one case, why shouldn't they do so in the other?[21]

There seems already to be some *prima facie* evidence telling against the network: Swinney (1982) mentions a study carried out by Onifer which replicated the cross-modal lexical priming experiments they had already done but with a different population of subjects, chronic schizophrenics, who have 'a well documented symptom that involves their interpreting ambiguous words (almost solely) in terms of the inherently most frequent meaning of those words. Further, they often appear to completely ignore the context in choosing this interpretation' (1982: 159). The results were that both the high and the low frequency meanings of ambiguities were activated immediately upon occurrence of the ambiguity in all context conditions (biased and neutral), as for normal subjects. But on the three-syllable delay test only the *most* frequent meaning for the ambiguity was still active, whether contextually relevant or not. Now if there is a lexical network in operation it is responsible for the first set of results, i.e. momentary activation of both the homophonic lexical items (*pen*, say) and thus of words related to the two senses (*pig*, *ink*, etc.). But then it seems to play no role in subsequent processing since subjects choose the most frequent item with apparently no regard for levels of activation in the network. It is difficult to see how this

---

[21] Some of the examples here are taken from Morton & Long (1976), whose study is concerned with the relative difference in processing of high and low transitional probability words. Naturally, the high group includes the lexically associated cases as well as those I picked out, so that their results would need careful categorization and analysis to see how they bear on the current issue.

could be possible, since there are not two distinct mechanisms at work here. The alternative view, an automatic parallel mapping on to conceptual addresses and attempts at contextual integration, is both compatible with all the results so far and can more reasonably be seen as involving two distinct processes, with the schizophrenic subjects unable to perform the latter one, that is, assessment of contextual relevance. On such a view the damage lies with a central process; the language module remains still intact.

No matter which ultimately proves correct, the overall picture is consistent with the weakly interactive theory, that is, lexical access is exhaustive and autonomous, uninfluenced by context, and choice amongst the alternatives is made rapidly online, either via an internal network or post-perceptually, in accordance with contextual fit;[22] encapsulation of the language processor is not threatened.

2.3. Relevance: a theory of the central systems

A major theme of Fodor 1983 and 1985 is that the central cognitive processes are not amenable to investigation: while the input systems have problem status, the central systems have mystery status; we can tackle problems but mysteries are beyond us. There are two major difficulties arising from the nonmodular nature of central systems:

1. The function of the central systems is to fix beliefs. Yet this is a process involving nondemonstrative inference (or inference to the best explanation), about which almost nothing is known.

2. Central processes are unencapsulated, that is, there is no way to limit the range of facts or beliefs that may play a role in fixing further beliefs.

Fodor sees the higher cognitive processes as similar to those at work in scientific discovery; the hypothesis confirmation process, involved in fixing beliefs and in scientific theory formation, requires bringing to bear the structure of an entire belief system and inference of a nondemonstrative sort that we don't understand 'in either its macrocosmic or its microcosmic incarnation' (Fodor 1985: 4).

Undeterred by these gloomy observations, Sperber & Wilson (1986) have developed a theory of the central systems which offers solutions to both of the difficulties mentioned above. The particular central thought process they investigate, the interpretation of utterances, is one they consider more typical of central cognitive processes than is the forming and confirming of scientific hypotheses, which is special in a number of ways, not least of which is the vast

---

[22] There is now a vast literature on lexical processing (in particular on lexical ambiguity), all of which bears on the modularity issue even when it is not directly addressed; as well as the references cited in the text the following are relevant: Cairns & Hsu 1980, Cairns, Cowart & Jablon 1981, Tanenhaus & Seidenberg 1981, Seidenberg *et al.* 1984, Seidenberg 1985, Norris 1986, Seidenberg & Tanenhaus forthcoming. See also Chapters 1, 3, and 4 in this volume and also Volume II, Chapter 2.

amount of time and effort it involves. Very little of either is spent on the hundreds of hypotheses we make, and confirm to our satisfaction every day, such as that the phone is ringing, that it's time for dinner, that it's going to rain or that Mary has just said that she's tired, thus implying that she doesn't want to go out.

The idea that a principle of least effort governs much of human behavior, mental and physical, is well established. Clearly, however, the species would be extinct if this were not offset by other instincts and goals; living involves solving problems and that requires effort. In the realm of language, least effort has been invoked as one of the two crucial factors in causing languages to change over time (Zipf 1949, Martinet 1962); the other, opposing, force being the requirements of communication: *speakers* expend the minimum energy compatible with achieving their goal of conveying messages.

A different trade-off with the principle of least effort operates for human beings in their role as *hearers*. Hearing and interpreting utterances is simply one means by which we receive information about the world. As information processors (and so as utterance interpreters) we have another goal, that of improving our representation of the world. This means increasing our stock of information, improving its accuracy, integrating it into a connected picture and organizing it so it is accessible when it can be useful, etc. But individuals are constantly exposed to hundreds of *potential* stimuli in their environment, of which only a small subset act on them as *actual* stimuli. What determines which phenomena actually impinge on them? The answer Sperber & Wilson (1986)[23] give is that it is those phenomena which are likely to provide individuals with *relevant* information, where relevant information is information which interacts in certain ways with their representation of the world. There are three kinds of impact (or cognitive effect) which a phenomenon might have so as to qualify as relevant: it might strengthen a tentative assumption that one has; it might weaken or even contradict an assumption; or it might combine with existing assumptions to yield new ones via deductive inference.[24] Clearly, then, relevance is a matter of degree: the more cognitive effects a phenomenon has, the more relevant it is. But that can't be the whole

[23] Summary accounts of relevance theory are given in Wilson & Sperber 1986b, Sperber & Wilson forthcoming, and also Volume II, Chapter 8, and Volume IV, Chapter 13, of this series.
[24] The system of deductive rules used by humans in processing information is importantly different from standard formal logical systems set up to meet certain requirements of a non-psychological sort. Such systems typically consist of inference rules for the set of so-called 'logical particles': – *and, or, if . . . then, not, some, all*, so there are no rules for other connectives like *before, after, although, since* or to account for the great range of inferences hinging on predicate words such as *mother, bachelor, dog, yellow, murder, chase*, etc. On the other hand, they include a range of rules which don't seem to have a counterpart in spontaneous human inferencing, that is, the *introduction* rules, such as the rule that says that, given as input any proposition P, it follows deductively that P or Q, where Q is any proposition at all. Such rules can apply recursively to their own output *ad infinitum*. It is obvious that in processing information we don't link it arbitrarily to other possible bits of information, nor do the rules we use apply indefinitely. Sperber & Wilson (1986: Chapter 2) claim that all the deductive rules used in information processing are elimination rules and thus yield only what they call *nontrivial* conclusions.

story, since it would predict that in our bid to realize our goal of the greatest possible cognitive effects we would go on endlessly processing a conceptual representation delivered up by the input system, bringing to bear on it more and more of our stock of beliefs to see whether they interact to alter our representation of the world. This is where the principle of least effort comes in and is incorporated into a comparative definition of relevance:

> *Relevance*
>
> (a) Other things being equal, the greater the cognitive effects, the greater the relevance.
>
> (b) Other things being equal, the smaller the processing effort, the greater the relevance.   (Sperber & Wilson forthcoming a)

The key to cognition is the goal of *maximizing relevance*: that is, of getting the greatest possible cognitive effects for the least expenditure of effort.

But how do individuals 'know' which phenomena are likely to give them good returns for their efforts? Clearly they don't process each possibility, assess its relevance and then take it on or discard it. They don't have the processing resources to do this (for every phenomenon in their environment) apart from which such a practice would involve enormous and wasteful expenditure of energy, as if they were operating in accordance with some principle of *maximal* effort, and thus be directly at odds with the very aim of relevance maximization. While perceptual systems are designed to handle a particular phenomenal domain, they have the additional feature of picking and choosing within that domain, passing on only a subset of the information they monitor to the central systems. Certain phenomena seem automatically to preempt attention, such as the smell of appetizing food, bright colors, the sight of a raging fire, loud noises, the cry of a baby; responses to these are frequently of survival value and reflect a relevance-directed adaptation of the perceptual systems.

Among the phenomena that automatically preempt attention are utterances. Utterances are a rather different sort of stimulus from those so far considered, which are the offerings of an indifferent world; utterances are *ostensive* stimuli, where an ostensive stimulus is one which has its source in an intentional organism whose intention is to inform by having its audience recognize its intention to inform (i.e. whose intention is communicative). Other ostensive stimuli are a pointing at something, a waving hand, a ringing doorbell or telephone: all of these are means by which an intentional organism focusses the attention of an information processor on his or her communicative intention. There is a crucial difference between ostensive stimuli and other phenomena that one attends to: while one might hope for relevance (that is, cognitive effects for a small amount of processing effort) in one's self-directed observations of the world, one can have definite *expectations* of relevance from ostensive stimuli, since they come with a *presumption* of relevance. By demanding attention from an audience the communicator indicates that he or she is offering something which is of sufficient relevance to be worthy of attention, that is, an expenditure of mental effort by the audience will be repaid by cognitive gains.

The presumption of relevance is not a presumption of maximal relevance (maximum cognitive effects for least processing effort) but of *optimal* relevance (*adequate* cognitive effects for least processing effort). Optimal relevance takes into account the interests of both speaker and hearer. Speakers are as much ruled by a principle of least effort as hearers are so a speaker can't be expected to have cast about for an utterance which will have maximum cognitive effect on a hearer's belief system. However, speakers also have the goal of conveying a message and since they know that a hearer will expend only as much effort as is necessary to identify the message, it is in their interest to frame their utterance so that the first plausible interpretation the hearer arrives at is the one they wanted to convey; this will be the first interpretation consistent with the *principle of relevance*:

> Every act of ostensive communication communicates the presumption of its own optimal relevance. (Sperber & Wilson 1986: 158)[25]

In this 'cooperation' between information source and information processor (speaker and hearer) we have one major difference from scientific theory construction, during which theorizers receive no help from their source of evidence – the nonintentional natural world.

It's important here to distinguish the role of the language input system, which goes into automatic action when the appropriate acoustic (or visual) phenomenon is present, and the role of the principle of relevance, which directs the processing of utterances by the central systems. For instance, we might see two people in conversation and overhear one of them say 'She was far too young,' and though we have no particular interest in these people or their conversation, our language processor, highly sensitized to this kind of stimulus, processes it quickly and automatically up to the output representation, a logical form (incomplete conceptual representation). Since the utterance was not directed at us we have no guarantee of its relevance to us and the utterance is just another *possibly* relevant phenomenon thrown up by the world; the fact that it gets as far as our central systems is simply a by-product of the design of the language module. On the other hand, if the

[25] Note that the principle of relevance does not say that communicators necessarily succeed in producing optimally relevant stimuli or even that they always try to do so. Many utterances are boring and irrelevant, and some are diversionary. What the principle of relevance says is that communicators can't help but communicate to their addressees that in producing the stimulus they did they are being optimally relevant. As with anything one communicates it may not be true and/or it may not be honest.

utterance is directed at us and thus guaranteed relevant to us we will set about finding a referent for 'she,' narrowing the pastness given by 'was' to some determinate time and supplying the ellipsed material telling what she was too young for, all of which are guaranteed immediately accessible (requiring minimal effort) by the presumption of relevance which the fact of the utterance communicates. This complete conceptual representation is then processed in a highly accessible context of assumptions which the new piece of information modifies in one or more of the three ways mentioned above. It might strengthen a suspicion one already had that Susan was too young to marry, contradict an assumption one had that the speaker thought Susan's marrying was a good idea, or interact deductively with an assumption one had that people who marry young usually regret it, to give the implication that Susan probably regrets her marriage.

It should be clear from the discussion so far that utterance interpretation differs from scientific theory formation again in that only a small subset of one's belief system (representation of the world) is brought to bear on the new information in arriving at an interpretation of it (a confirmed hypothesis about it); this subset is the *context* for the interpretation of the new item of information. There are various sources of the assumptions that make up the context: long-term or encyclopedic memory, short-term memory (which would include the interpretation of the immediately preceding utterance) and concurrent outputs of other perceptual systems such as vision. The total set of assumptions comprising the individual's representation of the world are by no means all equivalently available for use in the interpretation process at any given time. Encyclopedic information is organized into blocks filed at conceptual addresses so that, for instance, processing incoming information which involves as a subpart a mapping on to one's *dog* concept makes available whatever information one has filed there about dogs. That block of information is internally organized so that it too varies in degree of accessibility. Information lodged at one conceptual address is multiply cross-referenced with entries at other conceptual addresses; so, for instance, new information which involves a mapping on to one's *pet* concept might lead to one accessing *dog* information too, though this will involve more steps than in the previous case, i.e. it will be slightly less accessible; if the point of origin were *farm*, *dog* information might be less accessible again, and if *city* even more so, etc. Other factors, interacting with each other, enter into the accessibility of information; the more recently information has been processed the more accessible it is, the more stereotypical (i.e. the more frequently used) the more accessible, and, assuming we hold our beliefs with varying degrees of strength, the more strongly held the more accessible (other things being equal, in each case). A detailed theory of accessibility is wanting but that there is some such organization seems clear.

The whole of long-term (encyclopedic) memory is connected up in this way; from a single concept one could ultimately access every assumption one has (given lots of time and suspension of the principle of least effort). The selection of a particular context on a particular occasion is, however, always determined by the bid for relevance; in processing any new item of information we try to obtain as great a cognitive (we can now say *contextual*) effect as possible for the least possible processing effort, i.e. we select a context which will maximize relevance. In communicating, a speaker tries to produce an utterance that has a range of effects in a context that is as small and easily accessible as possible. In interpreting an utterance, a hearer has not determined a context in advance; the context is not a given but a variable, fixed by an interaction of what *is* given, which is the presumption of its own optimal relevance that every utterance communicates and the output of the language module (an incomplete conceptual representation). This will be illustrated directly.

So in choosing the case of utterance interpretation, Sperber and Wilson show that, while unencapsulated in principle, at least some central processes are highly constrained in practice: given the criterion of consistency with the principle of relevance, an information processor puts only as much work into accessing contextual assumptions as is necessary to yield an adequate range of contextual effects. Now what of the other, related, difficulty Foder finds with the central systems: the problem of non-demonstrative inference? There are two worries here: (a) the system of rules used, (b) the degree of confirmation of one's assumptions and how this is arrived at.

Consider the kind of inference process involved in interpreting B's utterance in (8):

(8) A: Let's go to a movie this afternoon
     B: I've got a lecture

Given a complete conceptual representation of the proposition expressed by B (which involves some considerable enrichment of the representation output by the language module) as in (a), and an appropriate set of contextual assumptions as in (b), the implication of a negative response, (c), to A's proposal can be *deduced*:

(8) a. B has a lecture to attend this afternoon
     b. If someone has a lecture to attend this afternoon he/she cannot go
        to a movie this afternoon
     c. B cannot go to a movie this afternoon

The rules involved here are straightforward deductive rules: universal instantiation and modus ponens. Wilson & Sperber (1986a and Sperber & Wilson 1986: Chapter 2) show the essential role of deductive rules in arriving at implicated conclusions of this sort; there isn't some other non-demonstrative or inductive rule type called upon here. So in what does the nondemonstrative (unproved) nature of such inferential processes in comprehension consist? The conclusion (c) is not the only one A could have drawn from B's utterance; it is crucially dependent on A recovering the assumption (b) from encyclopedic memory. If, for example, A knew B hated lectures and always looked for something else to do while they were on, he might instead have accessed assumption (d):

d.   If B has a lecture to attend this afternoon she'll be happy to go to a movie this afternoon

and thus have derived as conclusion a positive response to the suggestion. The recovery of these assumptions, which interact with the proposition expressed, is part of the worry Fodor has about the central processes: even given that B must be understood as implying an answer to A there are hundreds of *logically* possible ways of deriving either an acceptance or rejection of A's proposal from B's utterance, for instance:

a.   B has a lecture to attend this afternoon
e.   New Zealand isn't in the northern hemisphere
f.   If B has a lecture to attend this afternoon or New Zealand is in the northern hemisphere then B cannot go to a movie this afternoon
d.   B cannot go to a movie this afternoon

Relevance theory, and an associated account of the accessibility of encyclopedic information, provides a direct answer to this problem. A will simply not access (e) or (f) since, although they may both be his beliefs, they will both be far less accessible than (b) (or (d)), which is derived from sets of information filed at conceptual addresses made directly accessible by the conversational reference to 'a movie' and 'a lecture' and the fact that it is B talking. A will access (b) or (d) (or some other related assumption), whichever is the more accessible, in accordance with his search for maximal relevance and on the presumption of the optimal relevance of B's utterance. If the processing in this context of the proposition expressed has an adequate range of contextual effects, the interpretation is consistent with the principle of relevance and must be the one the speaker intended.

So one difference between the inferences of comprehension and those of standard mathematical or formal logical proofs is that, in the case of proofs, all the premises are explicitly given, whereas in interpretive inferring (and in nondemonstrative inference in general) some are implicit and must be supplied by the hearer/interpreter. There is an element of risk in this; the utterance itself and the presumption of relevance it carries provide the hearer with guidelines as to interpretation, not with a fail-safe algorithm ensuring perfect communication. For instance, given his knowledge of B, (d) might be A's most accessible assumption, but if B has recently reformed her ways and become serious about lecture-going, A will arrive at a conclusion which differs from the one B intended; miscommunication of this sort may be the fault of neither party, both acting in good faith, but simply reflect a mismatch in assumptions. What an utterance offers the interpreter is evidence, a set of clues, and there are always alternative ways of interpreting a piece of evidence; the criterion of consistency with the principle of relevance may yield a best hypothesis, but sometimes this won't be the correct one, i.e. the one intended by the speaker.

Another difference between interpretive inference and logical proofs is that in proofs all premises are assumed true and thus the conclusion is true, while in utterance interpretation we may have varying degrees of confidence in the conclusions we draw, dependent on our degree of confidence in the premises used in the deductive inference. So, for instance, A might hold (b) to be highly likely but less than absolutely certain (since after all it might be possible to fit both a movie and a lecture into the one afternoon); hence his conclusion, (c) will be held with a high but less than total degree of conviction. All factual assumptions are held with varying degrees of conviction: those derived from direct observation tend to be very strong (on the whole we trust our own senses); the strength of those derived from utterances will depend on our faith in the speaker; those we entertain in our private musings about, say, the future may be fairly weak. The strength of an assumption arrived at deductively depends on the strength of the premises used in the deduction; it will be only as strong as the weakest premise used. An assumption one already holds may acquire extra confirmation from a new piece of information (whether directly observed or inferred from an utterance) and thus be independently strengthened, or it may be retroactively strengthened by functioning effectively in one's mental life, for example, by causing some modification of contexts in which it is placed.[26]

Summing up, what is envisaged here is a set of psychologically real deductive rules, an organization of memory in terms of degrees of accessibility, and an assignment of degree of strength to assumptions dependent on their source and subsequent processing history. Given these reasonable assumptions about the central cognitive systems, the nature of nondemonstrative inference, at least in utterance understanding, begins to look much less of a mystery.

Finally, let's look briefly at the account relevance theory gives of how a

---

[26] Sperber & Wilson (1986: 75–83) explain why they do not envisage the logical notion of *subjective probability value* as being appropriately carried over into the psychology of belief; they prefer a comparative concept of relative *strength* of assumptions, a functional property of representations determined by their processing history.

choice is made among hypotheses delivered by the language input system in the case of an utterance containing an ambiguous linguistic expression. According to the picture that was beginning to emerge in section 2.2, access of homophonous items is exhaustive, and choice among them seems to be a postperceptual (i.e. central) process. The items are mapped in parallel on to conceptual representations and attempts at their contextual integration are made, some criterion of best fit leading to choice of one of the options. We now have the criterion in question: there is always at most one interpretation which is consistent with the principle of relevance.

Consider an utterance of 'We need a pen,' which gives rise to the following possible interpretations of (hypotheses about) its explicit content, which are simultaneously tested for consistency with the principle of relevance:

a.   We need a writing instrument
b.   We need an enclosure

Suppose that the hearer has easy access to a context in which (b) has an adequate range of contextual effects (speaker and hearer are gazing disconsolately at a yard of animals running wild), while a context for (a) is much less accessible or not accessible at all. A rational speaker must have foreseen this, so hypothesis (b) is consistent with the principle of relevance, and is the only interpretation consistent with the principle of relevance: the assumption that the speaker intended (b) is retroactively strengthened (confirmed) because it has a function in that easily accessible context and makes an impact on it. Consider now the same scenario, but add to it a speaker who is worrying about all the letters that need to be written this weekend and thus wants to convey (a), and say the utterance of 'We need a pen' is shortly followed by 'I loathe letter-writing.' The speaker could easily have saved the hearer processing effort by rephrasing the utterance ('We need something to write with') to eliminate the unwanted interpretation. If the speaker doesn't do this, the hearer has to process both (a) and (b), first choosing (b) and then subsequently having to backtrack and go for (a). Given the readily accessible context provided by the output of the visual system, the speaker could not expect (a) to be optimally relevant (i.e. to have adequate contextual effects with minimum possible processing effort) to the hearer and thus the assumption that the speaker intended (a) receives no confirmation in *that* context, though it does in the context made accessible by the following utterance.

It holds quite generally that the first interpretation tested and found consistent with the principle of relevance is the only interpretation consistent with the principle of relevance; a speaker who does not intend this interpretation should rephrase the utterance to eliminate it. Sperber & Wilson (1986: Chapter 4) show this principle at work in all the other aspects of interpreting utterances too: assigning referents to referring expressions, supplying ellipsed material, deriving implicit assumptions (implicatures), interpreting metaphors, irony and the other rhetorical figures, and identifying illocutionary force or propositional attitude.[27] While much current work on utterance interpretation (pragmatics) proliferates arbitrary maxims and principles in an effort to account for the ease and general accuracy with which we interpret each other's utterances, relevance theory offers a complete pragmatic theory turning on a single principle. This principle is in no way arbitrary since it emerges from general facts about human cognition together with certain basic assumptions about the ostensive nature of communication.[28]

[27] For work on various aspects of utterance interpretation within a relevance-theoretic framework see Blass 1985, in preparation; Blakemore 1986; Carston forthcoming; Kempson 1984a, 1984b, 1986; Maclaren 1982.

[28] Many thanks to Deirdre Wilson for very enjoyable talks about the content of this chapter and for excellent advice which I've tried to heed.

REFERENCES

Anderson, J. R. 1983. *The architecture of cognition*. Cambridge, MA: Harvard University Press.
Bever, T. G. 1970. The cognitive basis for linguistic structures. In J. R. Hayes (ed.) *Cognition and the development of language*. New York: Wiley.
Bever, T. G. 1975. Functional explanations require independently motivated functional theories. In R. Grossman, L. J. San & T. Vance (eds.) *Papers from the parassession on functionalism*. Chicago: Chicago Linguistics Society.
Blakemore, D. L. 1986. Semantic constraints on relevance. Doctoral dissertation, University of London.
Blass, R. 1985. Cohesion, coherence and relevance. University College London. MS.
Blass, R. in preparation. Discourse and syntax in Sissala. Doctoral dissertation, University of London.
Bruner, J. 1957. On perceptual readiness. *Psychological Review* 64: 123–52.
Cairns, H. S., Cowart, W. & Jablon, A. D. 1981. Effect of prior context on the integration of lexical information during sentence processing. *Journal of Verbal Learning and Verbal Behavior* 20: 445–53.
Cairns, H. S. & Hsu, J. R. 1980. Effects of prior context on lexical access during sentence comprehension: a replication and reinterpretation. *Journal of Psycholinguistic Research* 9.4: 319–26.
Carston, R. forthcoming. Saying and implicating. University College London. MS.
Chomsky, N. 1972. *Language and mind*. New York: Harcourt Brace Jovanovich.
Chomsky, N. 1975. *Reflections on language*. New York: Pantheon.
Chomsky, N. 1980. *Rules and representations*. Oxford: Blackwell.
Chomsky, N. 1986. *Knowledge of language: its nature, origin, and use*. New York: Praeger.
Cooper, W. E. & Walker, E. C. T. (eds.) 1979. *Sentence processing: psycholinguistic studies presented to Merrill Garrett*. Hillsdale: Erlbaum.
Crain, S. & Steedman, M. 1985. On not being led up the garden path: the use of context by the psychological syntax processor. In Dowty, Karttunen & Zwicky 1985.
Dowty, D. R., Karttunen, L. & Zwicky, A. M. (eds.) 1985. *Natural language parsing*. Cambridge: Cambridge University Press.
Fischler, I. & Bloom, P. A. 1980. Rapid processing of the meaning of sentences. *Memory and Cognition* 8.3: 216–25.
Fodor, J. A. 1981. Some notes on what linguistics is about. In N. Block (ed.) *Readings in philosophy of psychology* Vol. 2. London: Methuen.

Fodor, J. A. 1983. *The modularity of mind.* Cambridge, MA: MIT Press.
Fodor, J. A. 1985. Precis of *The modularity of mind. The Behavioral and Brain Sciences* 8: 1–42.
Fodor, J. D. 1981. Does performance shape competence? *Philological Transactions of the Royal Society London*, B 295: 285–95.
Forster, K. I. 1979. Levels of processing and the structure of the language processor. In Cooper & Walker 1979.
Frazier, L. 1978. On comprehending sentences: syntactic parsing strategies. Doctoral dissertation, University of Connecticut.
Frazier, L. 1985. Syntactic complexity. In Dowty, Karttunen & Zwicky 1985.
Frazier, L. & Fodor, J. D. 1978. The sausage machine: a new two-stage parsing model. *Cognition* 6: 291–325.
Ganong, W. F. 1980. Phonetic categorization in auditory word perception. *Journal of Experimental Psychology: Human Perception and Performance* 6.1: 110–25.
Hudson, R. A. 1984. *Word grammar.* Oxford: Blackwell.
Jesperson, O. 1924. *The philosophy of grammar.* London: Allen & Unwin.
Kempson, R. M. 1984a. Anaphora, the compositionality requirement, and the semantics–pragmatics distinction. *North-Eastern Linguistics Society Proceedings* 14: 183–206.
Kempson, R. M. 1984b. Pragmatics, anaphora, and logical form. In D. Schiffrin (ed.) *Georgetown University Round Table on Languages and Linguistics.* Washington: Georgetown University Press.
Kempson, R. M. 1986. Ambiguity and the semantics–pragmatics distinction. In Travis 1986.
Kempson, R. M. forthcoming. Logical form: the grammar cognition interface. School of Oriental and African Studies, London.
Lakoff, G. 1986a. *Women, fire, and dangerous things: what categories reveal about the mind.* Chicago: University of Chicago Press.
Lakoff, G. 1986b. Cognitive semantics. *Berkeley Cognitive Science Report* No. 36.
Lakoff, G. & Thompson, H. 1975. Introducing cognitive grammar. *Proceedings of the 1st Annual Meeting of the Berkeley Linguistics Society:* 295–313.
Maclaran, R. 1982. The semantics and pragmatics of English demonstratives. Doctoral dissertation, Cornell University.
McGurk, H. & Macdonald, J. 1976. Hearing lips and seeing voices. *Nature* 264: 746–8.
Marr, D. 1982. *Vision.* San Francisco: Freeman.
Marslen-Wilson, W. D. 1973. Linguistic structure and speech shadowing at very short latencies. *Nature* 244: 522–3.
Marslen-Wilson, W. D. & Tyler, L. K. 1980. The temporal structure of spoken language understanding. *Cognition* 8: 1–71.
Marslen-Wilson, W. D. & Taylor, L. K. 1981. Central processes in speech understanding. *Philosophical Transactions of the Royal Society London* B 295: 317–32.
Martinet, A. 1962. *A functional view of language.* Oxford: Clarendon Press.
Mattingly, I. G. & Liberman, A. M. 1985. Verticality unparalleled, commentary on Fodor: *Modularity of mind. The Behavioral and Brain Sciences* 8.1: 24–6.
Mehler, J., Walker, E. C. T. & Garrett, M. (eds) 1982. *Perspectives on mental representation: experimental and theoretical studies of cognitive processes and capacities.* Hillsdale: Erlbaum.
Morton, J. & Long, J. 1976. Effect of word transitional probability on phoneme identification. *Journal of Verbal Learning and Verbal Behavior* 15: 43–51.
Norris, D. 1986. Word recognition: context effects without priming. *Cognition* 22: 92–136.
Onifer, W. & Swinney, D. A. 1981. Accessing lexical ambiguities during sentence comprehension: effects of frequency of meaning and contextual bias. *Memory and Cognition* 9.3: 225–36.
Piatelli-Palmarini, M. (ed.) 1980. *Language and learning: the debate between Jean Piaget and Noam Chomsky.* Cambridge, MA: Harvard University Press.
Pinker, S. 1984. Visual cognition: an introduction. *Cognition* 18: 1–63.
Pylyshyn, Z. W. 1984. *Computation and cognition.* Cambridge, MA: MIT Press.
Rosenfield, I. 1984. Seeing through the brain. A review of *Vision* by David Marr. *The New York Review of Books:* 11 October 1984.
Roth, I. & Frisby, J. P. 1986. *Perception and representation.* Milton Keynes: Open University.
Ryder, J. & Walker, E. 1982. Two mechanisms of lexical ambiguity. In Mehler, Walker & Garrett 1982.

67

Robyn Carston

Schank, R. & Hunter, L. 1985a. Encapsulation and expectation, commentary on Fodor's *Modularity of mind. The Behavioral and Brain Sciences* 8.1: 29–30.
Schank, R. & Hunter, L. 1985b. The quest to understand thinking. *Byte* April 1985: 143–55.
Seidenberg, M. S. 1985. Lexicon as module. *The Behavioral and Brain Sciences* 8: 31–2.
Seidenberg, M. S. & Tanenhaus, M. K. forthcoming. Modularity and lexical access. In I. Gopnik (ed.) *Proceedings of McGill Cognitive Sciences Workshops*. Norwood: Ablex.
Seidenberg, M. S., Tanenhaus, M. K., Leiman, J. M. & Bienkowski, M. 1982. Automatic access of the meanings of ambiguous words in context: some limitations of knowledge-based processing. *Cognitive Psychology* 14: 489–537.
Seidenberg, M. S., Waters, G. S., Sanders, M. & Langer, P. 1984. Pre- and postlexical loci of contextual effects on word recognition. *Memory and Cognition* 12.4: 315–28.
Smith, N. V. 1979. Syntax for psychologists. In J. Morton & J. C. Marshall (eds.) *Structures and processes*. London: Elek.
Sperber, D. & Wilson, D. 1985. *Relevance: communication and cognition*. Oxford: Blackwell.
Sperber, D. & Wilson, D. forthcoming. A précis of relevance theory. To appear in *The Behavioral and Brain Science*.
Swinney, D. A. 1979. Lexical access during sentence comprehension: (re)consideration of context effects. *Journal of Verbal Learning and Verbal Behavior* 18: 645–59.
Swinney, D. A. 1982. The structure and time-course of information interaction during speech comprehension: lexical segmentation, access, and interpretation. In Mehler, Walker & Garrett 1982.
Tanenhaus, M. K., Carlson, G. N. & Seidenberg, M. S. 1985. Do listeners compute linguistic representations? In Dowty, Karttunen & Zwicky 1985.
Tanenhaus, M. K., Leiman, J. M. & Seidenberg, M. S. 1979. Evidence for multiple stages in the processing of ambiguous words in syntactic contexts. *Journal of Verbal Learning and Verbal Behavior* 18: 427–40.
Tanenhaus, M. K. & Seidenberg, M. S. 1981. Discourse context and sentence perception. *Discourse Processes* 26: 197–220.
Travis, C. (ed.) 1986. *Meaning and interpretation*. Oxford: Blackwell.
Tyler, L. K. & Marslen-Wilson, W. D. 1977. The on-line effect of semantic context on syntactic processing. *The Journal of Verbal Learning and Verbal Behavior* 16: 683–92.
Tyler, L. K. & Marslen-Wilson, W. D. 1982. Speech comprehension processes. In Mehler, Walker & Garrett 1982.
Ullman, S. 1979. *The interpretation of visual motion*. Cambridge, MA: MIT Press.
Valian, V. 1979. The wherefores and therefores of the competence–performance distinction. In Cooper & Walker 1979.
Wilson, D. & Sperber, D. 1986a. Inference and implicature. In Travis 1986.
Wilson, D. & Sperber, D. 1986b. Pragmatics and modularity. In *Parasession on pragmatics and grammatical theory*. Chicago: Chicago Linguistic Society.
Zipf, G. K. 1949. *Human behavior and the principle of least effort*. Cambridge: Addison Wesley. Wesley.

3 Processes in language production
Merrill F. Garrett

3.0. Introduction

A number of years ago, the distinguished psychologist Charles Osgood became interested in the problem of language production (1971). He held the view that the study of production processes was the natural arena for exploring fundamental relations between cognitive structure and language forms. From his perspective, the focus of interest was the intention of speakers to achieve particular semantic and pragmatic consequence; those intentions drove, more or less directly, syntactic and lexical selection, and hence were the proper domain of study for the analysis of real-time sentence planning activities.

He began his inquiry by asking what variation in language form was associated with changes of perspective and presupposition in a simple descriptive task. So, for example, he asked what perceptual and cognitive conditions would demonstrably trigger a shift from active to passive voice, what would trigger the use of a definite article, or the contrastive use of a modifier. And he was able to effect such changes by systematic alteration of the conditions in his scene description task.

In this case, as in many others, Osgood was ahead of his time. Description of language-particular processes was not then well developed, nor were there accessible characterizations of the conceptual-level semantic structures that interact with language structures to yield connected discourse. The experimental results he attained were, thus, not readily connected to formal linguistic and logical systems, and the theory of language-particular processes was only nascent.

These problems are not solved at present, but the outlines of solutions have begun to emerge, and there are prospects for the serious pursuit of the goals Osgood avowed. We have, moreover, a clearer understanding of the theoretical options that relate conceptual and linguistic structures (see e.g. Fodor 1984). The next sections outline major features of basic language production processes, summarize their empirical support, and consider some relations between language processes and more general cognitive factors.

3.1. **Sentence production: principal processes**

3.1.1. **Message level formulation**

The major focus of research in language production has been the systems that account for real-time lexical, phonological, and phrasal organization, with less attention given to mechanisms of message construction that will insure that the linguistic constructions produced will reflect the semantic intentions of the speaker. This is hardly surprising, for the latter is a problem that implicates the whole of human cognition.

Broadly speaking, three things determine the form of a message's expression: (1) The content the speaker wishes to convey, (2) the effect the speaker wishes to produce in his or her auditors, and (3) the forms permitted by the structure of the language being spoken. The joint effect of (1) and (2) is deemed to give rise to a specific message and that in turn interacts with (3) to yield a series of specific sentences.

Let me make the terminology to be used here more explicit. I will use the term 'message' (M) to refer to the proximal cause of sentence production: it is the real-time representation that controls the integration of sentence form. Diverse inferential processes underlie the construction of a message representation, but not without limit; M expresses what the speaker is, in fact, committed to at the time of utterance of the sentence forms that encode M.

These matters are, of course, not determined by the empirical facts about sentence production to be considered here; they are stipulated for convenience of discussion (for relevant commentary, see e.g. Bach & Harnish 1979; Block in press, Fodor in press). The postulation of M places useful boundary conditions on the discussion of possible interactions between sentence formulation and conceptual factors. The limiting idealization treats the elements of M as contemporaneous with respect to sentence formulation. But the elaboration of both message-level structures and sentence-level structures is deployed in time, even though not to the same scale. Thus, while discussion below initially treats the relation of M to sentence processes as feed-forward only (i.e. no decision about a feature of M is contingent on a feature developed by sentence-level processes), that position is amended to include editorial processes that can alter, albeit indirectly, the course of message construction.

With these preliminaries, we turn to specific problem areas. These address the study of language production in terms of *sentence* production. The presumption is that embedding a sentence in a discourse will not fundamentally alter the character of the computations that generate its form. What then are the processing systems that underly the real-time generation of sentence form? We will discuss three classes of such systems: lexical selection, phrasal construction, and phonological coding.

3.1.2. Lexical selection in sentences

The three principal sources of constraint on the computations that determine the lexical content of sentences are conceptual, syntactic and phonological: lexical selection processes are governed by conceptual and syntactic factors, and retrieval is from an inventory of forms sufficient to determine the surface phonetic form of phrases. Further, note that the productivity of syntax requires some separation of lexical selection from phrasal construction. The performance data reviewed below indicates the way these constraints are expressed in processing.

Two phenomena with straightforward face validity for this problem have been widely remarked. Both of these are species of abortive efforts to retrieve a known word. In the one case, often called in normal speakers a 'tip-of-the-tongue' (TOT) state, and in certain language-disordered speakers anomia, the word in question, though known, cannot be recalled on the occasion of its use, and the speaker is aware of this failure. The regularities in the consequent attempts at retrieval are the data to which we appeal. In the second case, the failure manifests itself as the substitution of another word for the intended word, usually, though not invariably, with the immediate apprehension of error by the speaker. The relations between target and intrusion are the data to which we appeal.

.1.2.1. TOT states

Tip-of-the-tongue states have been studied through both natural observation and experiment. Brown & McNeill (1966) reviewed the history of psychological interest in TOT states and provided the initial experimental study of them. Their findings, since several times replicated and extended, match in essential respects those from studies of spontaneously occurring TOT states (see e.g. Browman 1978). Brown and McNeill presented a list of definitions of infrequently used words to a large group of students, tabulated the incidence of subjective TOT states, and made measures of available information about aspects of word form. They found, as earlier observational studies indicated, greater than chance ability to guess the initial sounds of words, and significant, though weaker, knowledge of word length. For the same experimental conditions, Rubin (1975) subsequently reported evidence for knowledge of morphemic structure: if the target word had an initial or final morpheme (not the stem), that morpheme tended to be available as a whole, otherwise only one or two sounds were available.

Merrill F. Garrett

These findings also connect to studies of word finding difficulty in aphasia and related disorders (see Buckingham 1979 and Pate *et al.* in press for review and discussion). For example, when aphasics fail in a picture-naming task, those not primarily anomic ('conduction aphasics') have been found able to provide the information normally available in TOT states, while those aphasics classified as anomic appear to lack such information (Goodglass *et al.* 1976). Moreover, anomic aphasics benefit more than other clinical groups when provided with initial word sounds as cues for eliciting picture names (Myers & Goodglass 1978).

Such findings suggest a special status for these parameters of word form, namely that initial sounds and length are the basis for organization of the inventory of lexical forms, and hence are the normally effective descriptions for retrieval. That, as we will see, is also the implication of regularities in word substitution errors.

3.1.2.2. Word substitutions

Word substitutions are diverse in their superficial properties and apparent causes (see e.g. Garrett 1980a; Harley 1984). Where theoretical interest is specifically in lexical selection and retrieval, one selects for analysis those errors that seem to indicate retrieval failures. The substitution type with a *prima facie* case for such interpretation is that for which there is no topical relevance and of which there has been no mention in prior discourse, either topic relevant or topic irrelevant. When one so restricts the data set, the remaining substitutions are, by and large, those that have a relation of syntax and of form, e.g. (1), or meaning, e.g. (2), to the intended target word:

(1)   'mushroom' for 'mustache'; 'cabinet' for 'catalog'; 'considered' for 'consisted'
(2)   'sword' for 'arrow'; 'mother' for 'wife'; 'listen' for 'speak'

The most influential discussion of such word substitutions is Fay and Cutler's (1977). They evaluated relations between target and intrusion for form-related substitution pairs and found a significant correspondence for length and stress placement, and a marked similarity of initial segments, with decreasing likelihood of overlap progressing left to right through the word. Later work (Hurford 1981; Cutler & Fay 1982) indicated that although greatest similarity is for word-initial segments, there is also strong overall similarity of form. Morphological structure, particularly prefixation, is also implicated (Fay 1983). The intersection of these findings with those for TOT states is striking. Moreover, these regularities are robust, appearing in

72

several independent corpora, including some evidence that they hold for children as well as adults (Aitcheson & Straf 1983).

Fay and Cutler interpreted the patterns in word substitutions as indicating two things: first, that word selection was based on a direct mapping from meaning representations to words, and when defective, such a selection process would yield semantically related word substitutions; second, that word *forms* were stored in an inventory organized on the basis of phonological resemblance. An error in retrieval of a word form would thus yield a nearby item in this space, similar in respect of the parameters that determine distance in the space. They argued that the motivation for such an organization is primarily perceptual, and hence that the form inventory was the same as that used by the word recognition system. This hypothesis comports not only with the observed phonological similarities, but also with indications that prefix structure affects word recognition (Taft & Forster 1975; Lima 1986).

3.1.2.3. A two-step lexical retrieval process

Two further features of word substitutions are striking. First is a virtually absolute constraint of grammatical category – target and intrusion correspond; second is a dissociation between meaning and form relations – target and intrusion words related in form rarely show a meaning relation, and conversely. This latter is unsurprising, in the sense that the relation between word form and word meaning is conventional. Nevertheless, it is a fact that has import for the way in which the stored representations of words are organized for retrieval during sentence construction.

The basic properties of the system being attested are that meaning and form based retrieval are separate operations, and that both such processes are syntactically constrained, hence part of language-specific processes, not of those that determine M. This has been expressed as a two-step retrieval process (Fromkin 1971; Butterworth 1980; Garrett 1976, 1978) in the context of systems for phrasal integration in sentence production (see section 3.1.3). Directly put, the claim is that information about word form is not available at the stage of initial lexical selection, and that a separate retrieval operation is required at the point when segmental structure is specified.

Several other observations bear on this issue. Butterworth & Beatty (1978) have argued that patterns of hesitation and gaze control in conversational speech reflect a two-stage retrieval process, and Butterworth (1979) has linked this to hesitation and neologistic speech in jargon aphasia. (See Buckingham 1979 and Garrett 1982 for related discussions.) Bock (in press) notes the correspondence of the two-step retrieval hypothesis in sentence production to stages offered in accounts of experimental studies of object naming. Levelt & Maassan (1981) report distinct effects of the perceptual/semantic determinants of word order and those that depend on efficiency of access to phonological form. Similarly, Kempen & Huijbers (1983) report experimental effects that suggest a lexically *specific* but phonologically uninterpreted stage of processing in picture description. They argue for parallel selection of abstract lexical elements, and subsequent retrieval of form after the syntactic consequences of that selection have been assessed.

The difference between meaning and form based errors that fuels the two-step retrieval theory is indisputable in its superficial form, but it has been argued to be less absolute than it seems (i.e. suitably assessed, form and meaning similarities for target and intrusion words may exceed base probabilities of random convergence: Dell & Reich 1981). This is an important issue to which we will return (section 3.2.1).

3.1.3. **Phrasal processing**

Processing accounts of phrasal construction have been approached in two general and complementary ways. One is to accept the levels of organization required for a formal description of grammatical structure, and to incorporate those levels in a performance model (see e.g. Fry 1969; Bierwisch 1971; Fromkin 1971). The complementary approach is initially agnostic about the realization of the rule systems of formal grammars in the organization of the real-time language processor. It accepts the basic phrasal, lexical, and segmental linguistic categories as candidates for processing vocabulary and seeks a basis for the postulation of levels in the features of production processes (see e.g. Garrett 1975, 1980a; Bock 1982).

There is encouraging convergence between the outcomes of these approaches. In particular, we can say that more than one level of processing that implicates phrasal structure is required to account for the patterns in hesitation distributions, speech errors, sentence recall, and experimentally constrained descriptive speech. But, though multiple levels of process are generally agreed upon, the character of those processes and their associated representations is not settled. We will consider some of the alternatives after sketching some basic findings.

3.1.3.1. A working model from speech error data

A departure point for much of the inquiry about language production has been the patterns of error in spontaneous speech. Those errors that involve two identifiable error loci are of particular relevance to phrasal level processes (e.g. shifts and exchanges), for they display characteristic patterns from which the organization of processing structure may be inferred.

Sound errors and morphophonemic accommodations

One of the clearest indications that multiple levels of processing intervene between M and articulatory control derives from the phenomenon of accommodation in speech errors (Fromkin 1971; Bierwisch 1971). Regular morphological and phonological rules must apply after the processing stage(s) that give(s) rise to errors that mislocate sound elements, e.g. (3) and (4):

(3) an eating marathon, uttered as:
   'a meating arathon' (a/an alternation. Fromkin 1971)
(4) even the best teams lost, uttered as: 'even the best team losts' (/z/ changes to /s/)

Such evidence dictates a separation of the processing level(s) that fix(es) detailed phonetic representation from that representing abstract segmental and lexical structure.

What is the nature of the higher level(s)? Other aspects of sound errors suggest important features. The majority of such errors occur within phrases, the source syllables are metrically similar, and the word with primary phrasal stress is involved more often than chance would predict; moreover, there are strong phonological similarities among the interacting elements and their environments (Merringer 1908; Boomer & Laver 1968; Fromkin 1971; MacKay 1969; Nooteboom 1969). From these facts, we know that the level at which these processing errors occur is constrained by phrasal boundaries, and that sufficient phrasal detail is present to represent major phrasal stress features. Both syntactic and prosodic characterization of the relevant phrasal structure has been suggested (see section 3.1.4.3 below).

Word exchanges

The preceding observations distinguish two processing levels. These, however, are not sufficient to cover the full range of error data. In particular, properties of word exchanges (e.g. Bierwisch 1971; Fromkin 1971; Garrett 1975) dictate a processing level distinct from that at which sound movement errors occur. Word exchanges and sound movement errors, particularly sound exchanges, contrast sharply. Word exchanges are predominantly between phrases, and in a significant number of cases, between clauses; they occur almost exclusively for words of corresponding grammatical category, and frequently span several intervening words. Sound exchanges rarely cross clause boundaries, and are predominantly phrase internal; they do not show a category constraint, and usually span only a word or two. These constraints

Merrill F. Garrett

have been argued to be independently defensible even though there is covariance in the conditions (Garrett 1975, 1980b). Finally, there is a marked difference in the degree of phonological involvement: word exchanges show little evidence of such influence (see section 3.2 for counterarguments). These differences, and some others to be discussed in a moment provide a basis for hypothesizing a level of processing for which the syntactic relations among words, but not their surface phonological representation, is calculated. It is a multiphrasal level (as compared with the single phrasal processes implicated in sound errors), probably with a two-clause limit – word exchanges rarely implicate elements of non-adjacent clauses.

Stranding exchanges

The discussion so far has compared the properties of sound exchanges and word exchanges. A third class of errors, those exchanges that implicate morphemes, provides a revealing contrast with these. Such errors appear to move only stem morphemes; affixal morphemes, primarily inflectional, are 'stranded', e.g. (5)–(8):

(5)   That's why they sell the cheaps drink
(6)   They were turking talkish (talking Turkish)
(7)   Make it so the apple has more trees
(8)   How many pies does it take to make an apple?

These exchanges appear to arise in two ways – either at the stage that gives rise to the word exchanges, or that which gives rise to sound exchanges (Garrett 1980a). The key fact is that when morpheme stranding errors occur for elements of distinct phrases, the categorial constraint holds; otherwise not. But for sound errors, there is no change in categorial constraint for the (relatively few) errors that cross phrase boundaries.

These facts have been combined in a hypothesis about all exchange errors (Garrett 1975, 1980a), namely that they arise from misassignment of a lexical form, or segments of a lexical form, to a planning frame, and these latter may be those appropriate either to syntactic or to phonological phrasing (Garrett 1982). On this hypothesis, all non-lexical formatives are features of planning frames, and hence not subject to exchange processes. This provides a natural account of the stranding errors, and correctly predicts that stranded elements should not themselves be observed to exchange in other error cases. Note also that this construal fits a further observation about stress: phrasal stress is preserved in exchanges, i.e. moved elements do not take their stress with them, but are stressed according to their error-induced environment. If stress is a feature of the planning frames (or computed from it), stress should be so 'stranded' in word and morpheme exchanges.

76

These regularities may be summarized in the form of a proposal for the successive assignment of lexical content to phrasal structures outlined in Figure 1 (from Garrett 1984).

At this point, we take note of the natural fit between the independently motivated double retrieval hypothesis and the distinction between syntactic and phonological levels of phrasal integration (F and P in Figure 1). The meaning-based word substitutions may be associated with selection of lexical content for F structures, and form-based substitutions with the selection of lexical forms for P level structures.

Shift errors

There is one further category of movement errors to be compared with exchanges. These are 'shift errors,' e.g. (9)–(11):

(9) [mermaids move their legs together] uttered as 'mermaid moves their legs together'
(10) [what that adds up to] uttered as 'what that add ups to'
(11) [you do hafta come] uttered as 'you hafta do come'

The elements that predominate in these errors are just those notable by their absence from exchange errors – minor category words and inflectional affixes. A hypothesis that can account for this is that morpheme shifts arise posterior to all exchanges, and do so as a consequence of operations that interpret features of phrasal frames for insertion into the terminal string of phrase markers. Two other observations reinforce this view. First, there is evidence that word and morpheme exchanges yield lexically dependent accommodations of form, while shifts produce only those for regular phonological processes (Garrett 1980b). Second, and most tellingly, exchanges preserve stress, but shifts often distort it (Cutler 1980). Some further implications of these processes are considered in 3.1.4.

The evidence reviewed heretofore indicates three processing levels: the F level is a multiphrasal level of syntactic planning with a two-clause limit; the two other levels implicate segmental and prosodic structure. The P level provides for segmental interpretation of phrasal structures, and subsequent processes determine phonetic detail. The indicated levels are represented as independent, feed-forward only processes.

.1.3.2. The projection onto other data classes

Studies of nonfluency

The distribution of hesitation pauses, false starts, and retracings in spontaneous speech provides evidence regarding speech planning. Goldman-

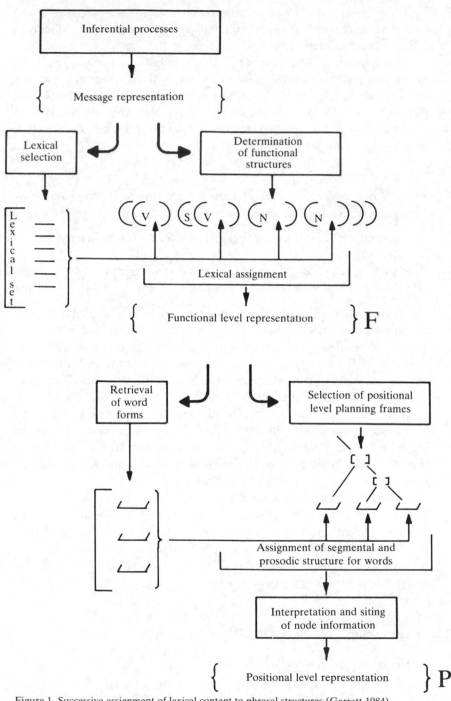

Figure 1. Successive assignment of lexical content to phrasal structures (Garrett 1984)

Eisler's (1968) pioneering work in this area emphasized the role of lexical processes, and supported the idea that general cognitive load and lexical selection influence hesitation patterns. More to the current issue, several other studies indicate phrase structure effects as well.

Levelt (1983) reviews past work on immediate self-corrections in speech and reports a controlled descriptive study of such repairs. His analysis elegantly supports surface phrase structure conditions on repair processes. Boomer (1965) attributed a significant role in the patterning of hesitations to phrasal structure, specifically 'phonemic clauses' (major stress and juncture groups). Subsequent work by Ford (1978) argued for an influence of underlying phrasal structure. That conclusion was supported in experimental work by Ford and Holmes (1978) using a reaction-time measure of processing load during sentence construction. Though the question is not settled, it is likely that both of these levels dictate hesitation. (See Garrett 1982 for related discussion.)

Experimental analysis of production

Recent experimental findings connect in significant ways to speech error arguments. These provide convergent support for some features of the working model, and indications for certain modifications.

Levelt & Maassan (1981) used a task in which speakers had to describe moving parts of simple visual arrays. Time to initiate utterance was measured. By independent test, they determined response latencies for naming the figures used in the arrays, and related these to utterance order for nouns in array descriptions. Strong effects were found for conceptual constraints on lexical ordering and choice of sentence type, but relative availability of lexical forms did not affect ordering, thus indicating a separation of conceptual/syntactic sequencing and retrieval of word forms. (But see section 3.2 for a caveat.)

Bock has addressed these issues in a series of systematic experiments. In one experiment (Bock 1986a), she compared the influence of conceptual and phonological variables on sentence form. She used a picture description task and preceded the target by a prime word that was either phonologically or semantically related to one of the nouns needed to label objects or participants in the pictured activities. The two classes of primes produced different patterns of description: semantically primed nouns were more likely to be sentence subjects than unprimed nouns, with concomitant shifts between active and passive voice; phonological primes (equated for effectiveness as primes for the target words) did not produce a similar effect.

Bock relates this outcome to the way in which words are integrated into phrasal schemata. She postulates two levels of integration, with the proviso that conceptual availability of words affects their assignment to surface

79

grammatical roles (e.g. surface subject, direct object). Items in a lexical net are first selected (primed) by conceptual factors and tagged with thematic roles (e.g. agent, patient). 'Functional integration' links primed items together as verb structure specifies. The conceptual accessibility effect determines which (appropriate) argument is assigned to the subject role – the more highly activated an item, the quicker it is linked to a surface role in the structure.

This view is supported in Bock & Warren's report (1985) of the patterns of change in grammatical role assignments for NPs differing in conceptual accessibility (as indexed by their imagery value). In a recall task, more accessible nouns shifted to subject roles. This is not just a serial order effect, they argue, since order for conjoined nouns showed no influence of this variable. On this point, note that phonological variables can affect order of conjuncts (as in cases of frozen word order: Cooper & Ross 1975; Pinker & Birdsong 1979), and Bock and Warren did find such effects for conjuncts in their experiment. Other findings by Kelly, Bock & Keil (1986) also implicate conceptual accessibility. They found systematic effects of prototypicality in sentence recall: terms designating a prototype were mentioned earlier than non-prototype terms, with sentence form adjusted accordingly. See Bock (in press) for further discussion.

In this, and related proposals (e.g. Stemberger in press; Dell 1986), the activation level in a conceptual or lexical net accounts for the ordering (or misordering) of elements in a structural framework. Bock's proposal stresses that, because of lexical dependency of structure at F level, the availability of a lexical item affects the selection of a structural frame.

A final point needs emphasis. Bock's work with alternations of active and passive as a function of conceptual accessibility – as it may be reflected in prototypicality, imageability or concreteness – opens the door to experimental work on the problems that so intrigued Osgood. The identification of experimentally controlable lexical parameters effective at the conceptual level is essential to effective investigation of the discourse factors that people are responsive to when they opt for specific sentence structures in normal communicative situations.

3.1.4. Phonological processing

Word and morpheme exchanges indicate a separation of lexical content from phrasal frames, as sound exchanges indicate a separation of segmental content from lexical frames. Particularly compelling examples of this are the complementary errors sometimes seen in attempts at self-correction, e.g. (12) and (13):

(12) [pack rat] uttered as 'rack pat, . . . no, I mean, pat rack, . . . PACK RAT'
(13) Successive blends of [pack/batch] uttered as 'back, . . . no, I mean patch' (from Shattuck-Hufnagel 1986)

The separation of lexical content from phrasal frame is required by the productivity of syntax, hence the evidences of that separation in lexical and phrasal processes are not surprising. But the same kind of processing separation holds for the segmental content of lexical items, where, seemingly, it is not imperative: the lexical inventory is a finite set (but see Hankamer 1986). Thus, Shattuck-Hufnagel (1986) poses the question why a segment ordering operation should be required: given the order stored with the lexical record, a process that assigns segmental elements to serial positions in a lexical frame seems redundant.

An answer to this question is that surface phrasal groups are assembled without segmental content as initial baggage: they are built from F level structure, which lacks that information, and hence, the segmental composition of words must be added. Errors arise as token occurrences of stored lexical forms are called for during utterance construction and lexical records integrated into a phrasal package for pronunciation. Several specific proposals concerning those processes have been put forward on grounds of both experimental work and observation of speech errors.

3.1.4.1. Some general observations

The relevant evidence for phonological processing implicates subanalyses of words in terms of phonemes, syllables, and features. A variety of observations attests to the governing role of syllable structure in production processes.

Syllables
Experimental work by Treiman (1983, 1984) studied subjects' relative facility with phonological manipulations that preserved or violated aspects of syllable structure – as division into onset and rhyme and analysis of the rhyme into peak and coda. That work shows strong performance constraints for syllable structure, as do related studies by Cowan, Braine & Levitt (1985) of 'backward talkers' (speakers who have acquired an ability to fluently reverse the order of segments or segment groups in their speech). Similarly, Stemberger & Treiman (1986) report error dependencies that distinguish the slots in syllable-initial consonant clusters: the second position in a cluster is far more vulnerable to error than the initial position. This and a number of

related observations indicate that in processing, the cluster must be treated as analyzed rather than unitary.

More generally, speech errors involving segments are strongly affected by syllable structure (see Crompton 1982 for a recent review and interpretation). With respect to speech error patterns, syllables appear to constrain error rather than indulge in it the way that simple phrases, words and sound segments do (Shattuck-Hufnagel 1983). Movement errors do not generally involve syllable-sized chunks, except where the latter are ambiguous as to their classification (i.e. they coincide with morphemes, or the segmental make-up of the error unit is ambiguous). In short, the evidence indicates that syllabic structure provides a processing framework rather than units of retrieval in a processing vocabulary. On such a view, syllabic structure should, as it does, determine the potential interactions of segments in errors: initial segments interact with other initial segments, and similarly for medial and final segments. This result agrees with contemporary metrical theory in a straightforward way, and is all the more cogent given the evidence for an independent representation of stress as part of the processing framework that segments are attached to.

Features

The status of phonological features in the production process was put succinctly by Fromkin (1971). Though errors that involve complementary single-feature changes are not common (the modal sub-lexical error is a single segment slot), most segmental errors are readily construed as feature errors, since the norm is for similar segments to interact. As Fromkin points out, the issue is not really acute since features are properties of segments. The characterization of sound errors in terms of feature bundles associated with segmental slots in a syllabic framework covers the empirical ground and readily assimilates to formal theories of phonology.

Word onsets

Shattuck-Hufnagel (1986) argues that word-onset consonants must also be considered a processing class. Two observations are relevant: (1) In error corpora, those elements predominate in sound error processes. This bias resides primarily in complex errors (those with a source in the intended utterance). (2) Experimentally induced errors indicate that such a bias may depend on phrasal structure. In a memory/repetition task (with phonetically balanced 'tongue twisters'), Shattuck-Hufnagel found a word-initial bias, as is typical of natural error corpora. That bias was linked to phrasal structure in the test strings: word *lists* did not show a consistent word-initial error bias, but the same test words in phrasally organized strings showed a strong and consistent asymmetry.

Shattuck-Hufnagel suggests that an account of the word-position bias depends on transfering word-initial and non-initial segmental information at different times, and this, given her experimental findings, calls for a link between such an ordering and the process of associating lexical forms with phrasal environments. Such a link is provided by the assumption that the onsets of words are retrieval cues that govern this phase of the phrasal process. Recall that we have already argued in section 3.1.2 for such a retrieval feature. (See also section 3.2.2.1.)

1.4.2. Two processing proposals

Shattuck-Hufnagel (1979, 1986) postulates an utterance-specific framework that guides processing, and a segment to slot association process for serial ordering (a 'scan-copier'). Elements are sequentially copied from the lexical source set to marked sites in the framework and a monitor mechanism checks off elements as they are assigned to frame slots. She accounts for different types of interactive errors (exchanges, anticipations, perseverations) in terms of different patterns of monitor failure. Such failures are prompted by segmental similarity, parallel frame positions, and phonetic similarity of frame environments; all interactive errors are assumed to occur at a common processing level. One of the strong features of the model is its descriptive power – it succinctly characterizes a broad range of error types. Recently, Buckingham (1986) has described an adaptation of Shattuck-Hufnagel's model for the description of segmental errors in aphasic speech. That adaptation embeds the scan-copier at the P level of Figure 1.

Dell (1986) proposes a production model that uses spreading activation (see below) in a lexical network to account for natural and experimentally induced sound errors and for outcomes in a simulation of the lexical net. The network lexicon in Dell's system does not do computational work in respect of organizing sentence form. It feeds independently constructed sentence representations; these provide controlling activation that is distributed in the network in terms of connectivity among the postulated levels of lexical structure. The lexicon is thus a repository of promissory notes which it must deliver on when selection is made by each sentence processing level.

Different types of sound errors in this system, as in Shattuck-Hufnagel's, are all deemed to arise at the same level, and are driven by similarity relations among processing elements. To this, Dell adds the factor of a 'confusion of levels' – lexical activity at levels other than the phonological can interfere with sound planning processes. To illustrate briefly: for anticipations, the phonetic elements of the lexical node that is the focus of processing at, for example, the syntactic level will receive some activation because of that syntactic activity. Since higher levels are on average ahead of lower levels, that will boost activation for phones ordered later than those for current phonological processing. Such phones may thus occasionally exceed activation levels for correct phones and intrude in their stead. Note the importance of phonetic similarity: similarities permit intruding phones to share activation from phonological nodes, thereby increasing the likelihood of intrusion.

Perseverations are caused by 'rebound activation': the act of correctly assigning a word to its position in a structure sets its activation to zero. But because of its high activation prior to this selection, its neighbors get excited; their heightened activation sends a late boost to the already selected word, thus resuscitating what should be dead. This spurious activation can combine with functional activation from involvement of the node at lower levels, where it may be current.

Exchanges arise by a logical continuation of these processes. The phone displaced in an anticipation has a relatively high level of activation, not dissipated by the selection process, and hence may occur in the position intended for the intruding phone. Note that these accounts are compatible with Shattuck-Hufnagel's monitor mechanism. For example, the checkoff step is represented by the assumption in the activation scheme that levels drop to zero immediately upon assignment to a frame position. In general, the computations described in the scan-copier component of Shattuck-Hufnagel's model seems to be implementable in terms of such mechanisms, though there are areas in which the fit is not good. The word-onset bias, for example, is not represented, nor are deletion effects triggered by similar sounds. Modifications suggested by Dell for dealing with these and related problems would enhance the correspondence between the two models.

Dell's network simulation provides a number of interesting predictions for rate-dependent effects in sound errors not otherwise readily identified: e.g. increased featural similarity at slower rates, an interaction between sound error types (exchange, anticipation and perseveration) as a function of rate, and a greater effect of lexical bias on exchange errors than other sound errors. These provide a basis for futher analysis of error corpora and scope for useful experimental inquiry.

3.1.4.3. Some extensions of speech error arguments

Some further features of speech error patterns are relevant to phonological processing claims. These concern the exchange and shift errors discussed in section 3.1.3.1. Recall that exchange errors, both sounds and words, are restricted to major category words, whereas shifts involve minor category words and inflectional elements preferentially. Moreover, the word classes that appear in, or contribute sound elements to, exchanges are, by and large, the word classes that appear in the substitutions discussed in section 3.1.2. The contrasts between the error processes characteristic of major category words and those of inflections and minor category words have been expressed as a hypothesis about computational vocabularies in the production system: 'open class' (oc) elements (those that appear in exchanges) are recruited by the retrieval processes inferable from word substitution errors, while the 'closed class' (cc) elements (that rarely appear in exchanges, but commonly appear in shifts) are recruited by the processes that select phrasal frames (Garrett 1975, 1980a).

An exception to the regularities of sound and word exchanges just noted provides an argument for construing the structures of P in Figure 1 as phonological phrases: prepositions appear in word substitutions and in word exchanges, but do not contribute to sound exchanges. Prepositions are classed with major category items at the syntactic level (they introduce a phrase type), but are treated as minor category words at the phonological level. If the processes at P are deemed phonological, the contrasting behavior of prepositions in the two error classes would be accounted for: prepositions are oc at F, and cc at P.

A possible implication of this line of argument is that cc items are not segmentally specified at the point that oc items are. If access is ordered, and cc elements are specified late, they may be subject to interactive sound errors only at the stage of detailed phonetic specification, to which stage Garrett (1979, 1980a) has argued anticipations and perseverations should be assigned; such errors do violate the constraint against oc/cc interaction that is observable for sound exchange errors.

These observations run counter to the thesis of the models in section 3.1.4.2: that oc and cc words are segmentally interpreted by the same processes, and that anticipation/perseveration errors and exchanges occur at the same level. Either an alternative account for the vocabulary interaction with sound error types will be required, or modification of the those models is indicated.

3.2. Some considerations of mechanism

Section 3.1 outlined major features of production processing, and although distinct classes of processing constraints were identified, these might be represented in various ways. One might treat lexical processing as a two-stage system integrated with phrasal and phonological processes as outlined in section 3.1, or postulate instead a single network representation of the lexicon in which form and meaning descriptions interact to govern the insertion of lexical items into phrasal environments. Similarly, information flow might be characterized as one way from higher to lower levels, or as including feedback relations between adjacent and non-adjacent levels. These and related issues are considered in the following sections.

3.2.1. **Phonological influences on semantic and syntactic errors**

Two kinds of findings act as counterweight to the sharp contrasts outlined in section 3.1. Both indicate joint effects of variables that, by working hypothesis, operate at distinct levels, and phonological influences are at issue in each case.

3.2.1.1. Phonological effects on semantic word substitutions

Two kinds of effects are relevant. The general claim (Dell & Reich 1981; Harley 1984; Stemberger 1984) is for a phonological infiltration of semantic errors, indicated by an overlap of initial consonants in target and intrusion. A related claim (Stemberger 1983; Aitcheson & Straf 1982; Harley 1984) is that word substitutions showing both strong semantic and strong phonological similarity, while infrequent, are still more likely than chance (e.g. 'lobster' for oyster; 'amnesia' for anaesthesia). These observations have been interpreted as support for a version of production processes in which spreading activation determines lexical selection. Such a mechanism might, however, be used to implement either a two-step retrieval system, or one in which meaning and form descriptions are simultaneously functional. Available evidence favors the former alternative.

The reported level of phonological contamination does not compromise the basic processing contrast between meaning related and form related substitutions: similarities of phonologically mediated substitutions are qualitatively and quantitatively different. Compare, for example, the segmental overlap in serial positions 1–4 for form and meaning related substitutions shown in Table 1. Such a comparison actually underestimates the strength of the contrast, for the featural differences at mismatch points in form based errors are less than for semantic errors, and form related errors, unlike semantic errors, often show overall similarity.

Table 1.

Overlapping segments	0	1	2	3	4
Semantic substitutions (Dell & Reich; n=137)	0.58	0.28	0.12	0.02	0.00
Phonological substitutions (Fay & Cutler; n=156)	0.15	0.37	0.24	0.17	0.08

Other evidence also suggests that the phonological effects on semantic errors are not robust. Substitution errors internal to semantic fields should provide ideal conditions for interaction. But an experimental study by Levelt (1983) found no effect of sound similarity on the likelihood of color term substitutions. Similarly, for a spontaneous error corpus, Garrett (1987) found (for several semantic fields, e.g. body parts, clothing terms, motion verbs) very strong effects of semantic relations within fields, but no consistent effect of phonological similarity.

Cutler (1983) has suggested an account of the strong overlap cases (e.g. read/write; lobster/oyster) that accepts the notion of spreading activation in a lexical net, but as a factor in distinct processes. She argues that when a semantic specification is made, (semantic) neighbors are primed; if any of these are very similar in form, the probability of an incorrect phonological choice is increased. This proposal predicts a small, but stable, incidence of mixed cases (those with both malapropism and semantic substitution features). Such a view construes the interaction as an effect of conceptual facilitation on form selection, not of form similarity on conceptual interaction, and might be extended to accommodate the possibility of 'subtle semantic effects' in form based word substitutions – viz. indications (Kelly 1986, cited in Bock in press) that phonological intrusions are more concrete or imageable than the words they displace.

.2.1.2. Phonological influences on word exchanges

Dell and Reich also report phonological similarity for F level word exchanges (where, by working hypothesis, word form is not specified). The assessed similarity here, as in the meaning related word substitutions, is incidence of initial segment overlap. The reported effects of form are, though significant by the estimates of chance used, of lesser force than those for processes in which phonological form is functional. Moreover, while the finding of a phonological influence on such errors requires explanation, it does not obviate the original point of contrast between the word and sound exchange errors.

There is an important distinction that must be brought to the fore in interpreting these findings and those of section 3.2.1.1. That distinction is between performance effects that reflect the computational objectives of a system and those that reflect adventitious correlates of the mechanisms implementing those objectives. Dell's characterization of the phonological effects on meaning based and syntactic errors seems apt: they reflect possible connectivity in the lexical system that feeds the independent systems that determine sentence form.

3.2.2. **Relations between levels**

Several lines of evidence suggest processing relations between levels that differ from those of Figure 1. These are evidences of lexical biases in sound errors, of priming biases for particular surface syntactic forms, and of lexical accessibility effects on surface structure.

3.2.2.1. Lexical bias: sound errors create words

A basic observation about error corpora is that a *majority* of error products for sound errors are nonwords (55–60%, Fromkin 1971; Garrett 1976). Against this we must set reports that the incidence of created words in error corpora, even though a minority, exceeds chance estimates (Dell & Reich 1981) in experimentally induced errors (Baars, Motley & McKay 1975), and in a network simulation of sound errors (Dell 1986).

An implication of the lexical bias is that the processes that assign phonological form to words are in contact with the lexicon after the point at which retrieval has taken place. In terms of the working model, this means that after the point at which lexical forms are assigned to their surface phrasal environments, some communication with the lexicon is maintained.

These effects may indicate assembly of phonological forms in a network that links nodes for phonological structures (phonemes, syllables, features) to lexical nodes (Dell 1986), or as the reflection of an editorial bias effective at the phonological process level or at some interpretive monitoring level. There is some evidence in favor of editorial processes as a factor in the experimental effects of Baars *et al.*: subjects' appreciation of the lexical status of the stimuli affected the bias.

An interesting, but currently unevaluated, possibility is that the lexical bias is, as Dell's network simulation suggests, most characteristic of exchanges, and is linked to the word-onset bias discussed by Shattuck-Hufnagel via an error checking routine that uses word-onset information to determine the accuracy of assignment of segmental content to phrasal slots. Such an account would simultaneously render sensible the empirical intersection of word-form retrieval parameters, exchange error locus, and a late applied lexical constraint on phonological processing.

3.2.2.2. Surface form biases

Though each sentence in the context of a discourse must have the semantic content the speaker seeks to convey, the forms of the language permit expressive variation that preserves its semantic force. Such variation is at the disposal of the speaker for the furtherance of those communicative objectives that go beyond the mere presentation of the chosen discourse interpretation – viz. to persuade, enthral, outrage, entertain, or otherwise affect the response to communication apart from its literal content. These variations in form often involve the surface form of sentences, hence making higher order decisions contingent on lower level outcomes.

This general observation has its specific demonstrations in observational and experimental work showing structural bias for conversational exchanges. For example, Levelt & Kelter (1982) report that the syntactic form of an answer often corresponds to the surface form of its question. See Schenkein 1980 for related discussion. Bock (1986b) reports an experiment showing such syntactic pattern matching: the forms that subjects (unaware of the experimental contingencies) use in picture descriptions can be biased by the form of an immediately preceding, referentially unrelated, sentence. One might construe this as 'syntactic priming,' and as reinforcement for the view that surface forms influence higher order planning. We turn momentarily to the question of how this can be accommodated in a model like that of Figure 1.

.2.2.3. Lexical accessibility effects again

A basic problem of coordination inheres in the scheme represented in Figure 1. The separation of phrasal construction from lexical retrieval implies, among other things, that a planned phrase may not be utterable because the segmental content of one of its constituent words is not available at the right time. Hence, variations in efficiency of lexical form retrieval must be accommodated by the processing system. One obvious accommodation is to wait, and studies of nonfluency support such an idea (Goldman-Eisler 1968; Butterworth 1979). Another solution is to switch to a phrase that doesn't require the offending form, and a third is for higher order systems to index lexical availability and formulate accordingly.

There is experimental evidence suggesting some form of feedback between functional level processing and assignment of lexical forms to surface phrases. The work of Levelt and Maassan (see 3.1.3.2) shows that less accessible lexical forms may cause shifts from one surface form to another. Similarly, Bock (1986a) showed phonological priming effects on word order in a picture description task similar to that described in section 3.1.3.2 for the contrast of semantic and phonological primes. Here, all the primes are very similar in form to the target words; their effect in this experiment is inhibitory – the primed word tends to come later in the picture descriptions, with concomitant shifts in active/passive use. Bock also observed effects on fluency: more nonfluencies occurred when a primed target word was uttered in initial position. The Levelt and Maassan results showed a compatible effect: when less accessible forms occurred first, time to onset of utterance was increased.

These syntactic variations seem most naturally characterized as 'failure triggered' switches in form, rather than as evidence for preplanning at F level processing, for it makes sense of both the nonfluency effect and the form switches. When a first ordered form is unavailable, and integration of its constituent phrase accordingly delayed, there is a switch to an expression that uses an available lexical form (originally slated for incorporation in a later constituent). In this connection, note that Levelt and Maassan's results show an increase in utterance duration just prior to switches between alternate sentence forms.

The price one pays for this construal is some form of parallelism in the processing scheme. In the experimental cases, the competing surface forms were equally acceptable for the required descriptions, and were repeatedly called for. Therefore, it is possible that both forms were routinely readied and the one most suitable to the available lexical item was used. Is such parallelism representative of normal production processes? Other evidence that we now turn to strongly indicates that it is.

3.2.3. Serial and parallel processes in sentence construction

3.2.3.1. Parallel construction

True parallelism requires simultaneous, multiple representations at one or more of the processes intervening between conceptual activity and articulation. There is a sense in which a parallelism in normal production is intuitively quite plausible. If one countenances the reality of more than a single train of thought, one must be prepared for the possibility that two M level representations coexist, only one of which is meant for expression. Further, our ability to adjust our expression, in apparent real time, to accommodate stylistic variation suggests coexistence of more than one set of *sentence* level representations. Making message-formulation system directly privy to variations in surface form would entail a penetration of the sentence level processing by conceptual level decision making. A way to avoid this, without giving up the intuition of real-time stylistic control, is to postulate multiple encodings that are interpretively filtered at M. This sort of evidence might not be deemed strongly relevant to the issues we have been addressing. It could be a pseudo-parallelism, with alternatives computed serially. A particular error phenomenon, however, argues for a parallelism internal to the sentence construction system.

2.3.2. Blend errors

Blends come in both lexical, e.g. (13) and (14), and phrasal e.g. (15) and (16), varieties. Word blends differ from word substitutions in an essential feature. They hold between items that are equally acceptable as candidates for a given phrasal slot (i.e. they preserve intended truth value; word substitutions do not). Phrasal blends show the same meaning constraint as word blends: they reflect competition between two ways to say the same thing.

(14) Blends of: [evade/avoid]: 'evoid'; [athlete/player]: 'athler'; [spank/ paddle]: 'spaddle'; [terrible/horrible]: 'torrible'
(15) Successive blends of [I don't care] and [It doesn't matter]: 'It doesn't care . . . no . . . I don't matter'
(16) A blend of [the day of the week] and [the mood I'm in]: 'It depends on the day of the mood I'm in'

In discussing blend errors, Butterworth (1982) distinguishes 'plan internal' errors, 'alternative plan' errors (those with equivalent meanings), and 'competing plan' errors (those with different meanings). He argues that current theories of error processes focus on plan internal errors, and that the stages of processing so indicated do not lend themselves to an account of alternative plans errors; some form of parallelism is required. Canonical blends do indeed seem to be alternative plan errors – the result of interaction between distinct encodings of a given message rather than an interaction between the distinct elements of a single encoding of a message. To account for them, two or more higher order representations (from which the interacting error elements are derived) must be assumed. Note that these errors show simultaneous influence from what are usually argued to be distinct levels of processing activity (semantic, syntactic, and phonological). Both word (MacKay 1972) and phrasal (Fay 1982) blends show effects of syntactic and phonological structure. The simultaneous influence of the different types of constraint can readily be accommodated by assuming that meaning similarity is a condition on initiating parallel encodings and that form similarity is a condition on path blending (rather than pruning). These observations apply to alternative plan errors. What about the competing plans case – those that represent a train of thought not intended for utterance? The level of processing duplication necessary is different for alternative and competing plans since the former do not require distinct representations at M, nor it might be argued, even at F. There most certainly are instances in which error seems to be linked to thought trains outside the intended message – Freud's accounts of error (1901; see also Motley 1980) provide an obvious example of competing plan influences, though with extra theoretical baggage. Harley (1984)

91

discusses some relevant cases that he terms 'cognitive intrusions' (e.g. 17 below), and the error category of 'environmental contaminants' (e.g. 18 below) provides another illustration:

(17) [I've read all my library books] uttered as 'I've eaten all my library books,' when the speaker was hungry and thinking about preparing some food (from Harley 1984)

(18) [Please turn off the TV] uttered as 'Please turn off the flower,' while looking at a flower pot on top the TV

These latter are instances in which a description for an environmental object or event, quite outside the intended message, but coincidentally in the visual or auditory purview of the speaker, intrudes itself into the stream of speech. Such cases provide clear evidence for a capacity to generate multiple messages and to maintain them to the phonological level, as well as the capacity to entertain more than a single phrasal or lexical encoding for a given message.

Editorial functions of considerable power and flexibility will be required to adjudicate between competing lines of processing activity. Indeed, Baars (1980) has argued that sundry sorts of failure to control such competition account for most speech errors. However, it is worth noting that the devices we are contemplating are relevant to more than the phenomena of speech error. They also answer the independently demonstrable need for a capability to control the stylistic and functional conventions of the language in order to adjust our expression in real time to the demands of a multiply determined communication task.

3.3. **Summary comment**

It is presently fashionable to claim, though generally not in one breath, both that cognitive processes are in some interesting degree modular and that language processes are interactive. But if language doesn't constitute a modular system, the first thesis is in trouble, for there aren't many other good candidates around. Incompatibility between those views is more apparent than real, of course. We surely do have grounds, both from study internal to language processing and from study of cognition at large, to claim computationally significant contrasts of sentence comprehension/construction and general cognitive activity. But the exercise of language in aid of real communication goes greatly beyond sentence construction, and the latter is very much in the service of the former. It is in this respect that language processing is, indeed, highly interactive. As the issues considered in section 3.2 attest, the evidence for direct conceptual influence on sub-processes internal to sentence construction is not compelling, though the evidence for its rapid, automatic, ubiquitous, but *indirect* influence is very persuasive.

What about structure internal to the sentence construction part of the language system? Is modularity defensible there? The evidence is somewhat mixed, but fairly summarized by saying that in those cases where informational contact seems a bit promiscuous for a modular system, it also seems describable in terms of purely lexical processes. The evidence for separation of effect in the systems that determine sentence form is better than that for insulation of the corresponding classes of information associated with lexical items.

Withal, it is encouraging to contemplate the rapid development in the past decade of experimental means for the examination of real-time processing questions in the production domain. The evolution of theory in the area is greatly facilitated by such convergent approaches to an inquiry long dominated by observational methods of speech error collection and analysis of hesitation distributions. These latter will not be dispensed with by any means, but they will be put to a welcome acuteness of test because of the evolution of the tools of experiment and simulation.

REFERENCES

Aitcheson, J., & Straf, M. 1982. Lexical storage and retrieval: a developing skill? In Cutler 1982.
Baars, B. J. 1980. The competing plans hypothesis: a heuristic viewpoint on the causes of errors in speech. In H. Dechert & M. Raupach (eds.), *Temporal variables in speech: studies in honor of Frieda Goldman-Eisler*. The Hague: Mouton.
Baars, B. J., Motley, M. & McKay, D. G. 1975. Output editing for lexical status in artificially elicited slips of the tongue. *Journal of Verbal Learning and Verbal Behavior* 14: 382–91.
Bach, K. & Harnish, R. 1979. *Linguistic communication and speech acts*. Cambridge, MA: MIT Press.
Bierwisch, M. 1971. Linguistics and language error. Reprinted in Cutler 1982.
Block, N. in press. Advertisement for a semantics for psychology. In X. P. A. French, T. E. Uehling & H. K. Wettstein (eds.) *Midwest Studies in Philosophy*.
Bock, J. K. 1982. Toward a cognitive psychology of syntax: information processing contributions to sentence formulation. *Psychological Review* 89: 1–47.
Bock, J. K. 1986a. Meaning, sound and syntax: lexical priming in sentence production. *Journal of Experimental Psychology, Learning, Memory and Cognition* 12: 575–86.
Bock, J. K. 1986b. Syntactic persistence in language production. *Cognitive Psychology* 18: 355–87.
Bock, J. K. 1987. An effect of the accessibility of word forms on sentence structures. *Journal of Memory and Language* 26: 119–37.
Bock, J. K. in press. Coordinating words and syntax in speech plans. In A. Ellis (ed.) *Progress in the Psychology of Language*, Vol. 3. London: Erlbaum.
Bock, J. K. & Warren, R. K. 1985. Conceptual accessibility and syntactic structure in sentence formulation. *Cognition* 21: 47–67.
Boomer, D. 1965. Hesitation and grammatical encoding. *Language and Speech* 8: 145–58.
Boomer, D. & Laver J. 1968. Slips of the tongue. *British Journal of Disorders of Communication* 3: 2–12.
Browman, C. 1978. Tip of the tongue and slip of the ear: implications for language processing. *UCLA Working Papers in Phonetics* No. 42.
Brown, R. & McNeill, D. 1966. The tip of the tongue phenomenon. *Journal of Verbal Learning and Verbal Behavior* 5: 325–37.

Merrill F. Garrett

Buckingham, H. 1979. Linguistic aspects of lexical retrieval disturbances in the posterior fluent aphasias. In H. Whitaker & H. A. Whitaker (eds.) *Studies in Neurolinguistics*, Vol. 4. New York: Academic Press.

Buckingham, H. 1986. The scan-copier mechanism and the positional level of language production: evidence from phonemic paraphasia. *Cognitive Science* 10: 195–217.

Butterworth, B. 1979. Hesitation and the production of verbal paraphasias and neologisms in jargon aphasia. *Brain and Language* 8: 133–61.

Butterworth, B. 1980. Some constraints on models of language production. In B. Butterworth (ed.) *Language production*: Vol. I, *Speech and talk*. London: Academic Press.

Butterworth, B. 1982. Speech errors: old data in search of new theories. In Cutler 1982.

Butterworth B. & Beatty, G. 1978. Gesture and silence as indicators of planning in speech. In R. Campbell & G. T. Smith (eds.) *Recent advances in the psychology of language; formal and experimental approaches*. New York: Plenum.

Cooper, W. E. & Ross, J. R. 1975. World order. In R. E. Grossman, L. J. San & T. J. Vance (eds.) *Papers from the parasession on functionalism*. Chicago: Chicago Linguistic Society.

Cowan, N., Braine, M. D. S. & Levitt, L. 1985. The phonological and metaphonological representation of speech: evidence from fluent backward talkers. *Journal of Memory and Language* 24: 679–98.

Crompton, A. 1982. Syllables and segments in speech production. In Cutler 1982.

Cutler, A. 1980. Errors of stress and intonation. In V. Fromkin (ed.) *Errors in linguistic performance*. New York: Academic press.

Cutler, A. 1982. The reliability of speech error data. In Cutler 1982.

Cutler, A. (ed.) 1982. Slips of the tongue. Amsterdam: Mouton.

Cutler, A. 1983. Perfect speech errors. In L. M. Hyman & C. S. Li (eds.) 1988. *Language, speech and mind*. New York: Cumm & Helm.

Cutler, A. & Fay, D. 1982. One mental lexicon, phonologically arranged: comments on Hurford's comments. *Linguistic Inquiry* 13: 107–13.

Dell, G. 1986. A spreading activation theory of retrieval in sentence production. *Psychological Review* 93: 283–321.

Dell, G. & Reich, P. 1981. Stages in sentence production: an analysis of speech error data. *Journal of Verbal Learning and Verbal Behavior* 20: 611–29.

Fay, D. 1982. Substitutions and splices: a study of sentence blends. In Cutler 1982.

Fay, D. 1983. The mental representation of prefixed words: evidence from prefix errors in spontaneous speech. *Journal of Verbal Learning and Verbal Behavior*.

Fay, D. & Cutler, A. 1977. Malapropisms and the structure of the mental lexicon. *Linguistic Inquiry* 8: 505–20.

Fodor, J. A. 1984. *The modularity of mind*. Cambridge, MA: MIT Press.

Fodor, J. A. in press. *Psychosemantics: the problem of meaning in the philosophy of mind*.

Ford, M. 1978. Planning units and syntax in sentence production. Doctoral dissertation, University of Melbourne.

Ford, M. & Holmes, M. Planning units and syntax in sentence production. *Cognition* 6: 35–53.

Freud, S. 1901. (first German edition). *Psychopathology of everyday life*, trans. by A. A. Brill (1958). New York: Mentor.

Fromkin, V. 1971. The non-anomalous nature of anomalous utterances. *Language* 47: 27–52.

Fry, D. B. 1969. The linguistic evidence of speech errors. *Brno Studies in English* 8: 69–74.

Garrett, M. F. 1975. The analysis of sentence production. In G. Bower (ed.) *The Psychology of learning and motivation: advances in research and theory*, Vol. 9. New York: Academic Press.

Garrett, M. F. 1976. Syntactic processes in sentence production. In R. Wales & E. Walker (eds.) *New approaches to language mechanisms*. Amsterdam: North Holland Press.

Garrett, M. F. 1978. Word and sentence perception. In R. Held, H-L. Teuber and H. Leibowicz (eds.) *Handbook of sensory physiology*, Vol. 8: *Perception*. New York and Heidelberg: Springer-Verlag.

Garrett, M. F. 1980a. Levels of processing in sentence production. In B. Butterworth, (ed.) *Language production*, Vol I, *Speech and talk*. London: Academic Press.

Garrett, M. F. 1980b. The limits of accommodation: arguments for independent processing levels in sentence production. In V. Fromkin (ed.) *Errors in linguistic performance*. London: Academic press.

94

Garrett, M. F. 1982. Production of speech: observations from normal and pathological language use. In A. Ellis (ed.) *Normality and pathology in cognitive functions*. London: Academic Press.

Garrett, M. F. 1984. The organization of processing structure for language production: applications to aphasic speech. In D. Caplan (ed.) *Biological perspectives on language*. Cambridge, MA: MIT Press.

Garrett, M. F. 1987. Meaning and form in word retrieval: substitution errors within semantic fields. MIT Center for Cognitive Science Occasional paper No. 41.

Goldman-Eisler, F. 1968. *Psycholinguistics*. London: Academic Press.

Goodglass, H., Kaplan, E., Weintraub, S. & Ackerman, N. 1976. The 'tip-of-the-tongue' phenomenon in aphasia. *Cortex* 12: 145–53.

Hankamer, J. 1986. Morphological parsing. Paper presented at the Conference on Lexical Representation and Process. The Max Planck Institute for Psycholinguistics and the Interfacultaire Werkgroep Tall- en Sprachgedrag, Nijmegen, 1986.

Harley, T. 1984. A critique of top-down independent models of speech production: evidence from non-plan-internal errors. *Cognitive Science* 8: 191–219.

Hurford, J. R. 1981. Malapropisms, left-to-right listing, and lexicalism. *Linguistic Inquiry* 12: 419–23.

Kelly, M. H., Bock, J. K. & Keil, F. C. 1986. Prototypicality in a linguistic context: effects on sentence structure. *Journal of Memory and Language* 25: 59–74.

Kempen, G. & Huijbers, P. 1983. The lexicalization process in sentence production and naming: indirect election of words. *Cognition* 14: 185–209.

Levelt, W. J. M. 1983. Monitoring and self-repair in speech. *Cognition* 14: 41–104.

Levelt, W. J. M. & Kelter, S. 1982. Surface form and memory in question answering. *Cognitive Psychology* 14: 78–106.

Levelt, W. J. M. & Maassan, B. 1981. Lexical search and order of mention in sentence production. In W. Klein & W. Levelt (eds.) *Crossing the boundaries in linguistics*. Dordrecht: Reidel.

Lima, S. D. 1986. Morphological analysis in sentence reading. *Journal of Memory and Language* 26: 84–99.

MacKay, D. G. 1969. Forward and backward masking in motor systems. *Kybernetik* 6: 57–64.

MacKay, D. G. 1972. The structure of words and syllables: evidence from errors in speech. *Cognitive Psychology*. 3: 210–27.

Merringer, R. 1908. *Aus dem Leben der Sprache*. Berlin: Behr.

Meyers, D. & Goodglass, H. 1978. The effects of cueing on picture naming in aphasia. *Cortex* 14: 178–89.

Motley, M. 1980. Verification of 'Freudian slips' and semantic prearticulatory editing via laboratory-induced spoonerisms. In V. Fromkin (ed.) *Errors in linguistic performance*. London: Academic Press.

Nooteboom, S. G. 1969. The tongue slips into patterns. In A. G. Sciarone, A. J. van Essen & A. A. Van Raad (eds.) *Leyden studies in linguistics and phonetics*. The Hague: Mouton.

Osgood, C. E. 1971. Where do sentences come from? In D. Steinberg & L. Jakobivits (eds.) *Semantics*. Cambridge: Cambridge University Press.

Pate, D. S., Saffran, E. M. & Martin, M. in press. Specifying the nature of the production impairment in a conduction aphasic. *Language and Cognitive Processes*.

Pinker, S. & Birdsong, D. 1979. Speakers' sensitivity to rules of frozen word order. *Journal of Verbal Learning and Verbal Behavior* 18: 497–508.

Rubin, D. 1975. Within word structure in the Tip-of-the-Tongue phenomenon. *Journal of Verbal Learning and Verbal Behavior* 14: 392–7.

Schenkein, J. 1980. A taxonomy for repeating action sequences. In B. Butterworth (ed.) *Language production*, Vol. 1: *Speech and talk*. London: Academic Press.

Shattuck-Hufnagel, S. (1979) Speech errors as evidence for a serial ordering mechanism in speech production. In W. E. Cooper & E. C. T. Walker (eds.) *Sentence processing*. Hillsdale: Erlbaum.

Shattuck-Hufnagel, S. 1983. Sublexical units and supralexical structure in speech production planning. In P. F. MacNeilage (ed.) *The production of speech*. New York: Springer-Verlag.

Shattuck-Hufnagel, S. 1986. The role of word-onset consonants: speech production priming. In E. Keller & M. Goprik (eds.) *Motorsensory processes*. Hillsdale: Erlbaum.

Stemberger, J. P. 1983. Inflectional malapropisms: form based errors in English morphology. *Linguistics* 21: 573–602.

Stemberger, J. P. 1984. Structural errors in normal and agrammatic speech. *Cognitive Neuropsychology* 1: 281–313.

Stemberger, J. P. in press. An interactive activation model of language production. In A. Ellis (ed.) *Progress in the psychology of language*, Vol. I. London: Erlbaum.

Stemberger, J. P. & Treiman, R. 1986. The internal structure of word-initial consonant clusters. *Journal of Memory and Language* 25: 163–80.

Taft, M. & Forster, K. I. 1975. Lexical storage and retrieval of prefixed words. *Journal of Verbal Learning and Verbal Behavior* 14: 638–47.

Treiman, R. 1983. The structure of spoken syllables: evidence from novel word games. *Cognition* 15: 49–74.

Treiman, R. 1984. On the status of final consonant clusters in English syllables. *Journal of Verbal Learning and Verbal Behavior* 23: 343–56.

4 Language perception

Giovanni B. Flores d'Arcais

4.0. Introduction

The present chapter is a selected overview of the issues concerning language perception that have been most heavily debated during the last ten years and are still very much current at the time of writing.[1]

It is not easy to design the structure and scope of a chapter on language perception. Depending on the area of research and on the interest of the researcher, the term 'perception' has been synonymous with *identification, recognition, discrimination, understanding,* and *comprehension*. In speech perception research, the term covers almost every sensory and perceptual operation, in psycholinguistics the term has been used to designate such diverse processes as word recognition, the segmentation of the speech signal, judgements of similarity between two linguistic structures, and even the comprehension of connected discourse.

It is also impossible to define a sharp boundary between language perception and language comprehension. As Fodor asks, 'Where does sentence recognition stop and more central activities take over?' (1983:61). In vision, we recognize a world of objects, people, faces; we do not 'perceive' corners, shadows, and edges. When dealing with speech, we perceive words and sentences, not just sequences of sounds. Perceiving language means carrying out various psychological operations such as isolating and segmenting words, phrases, and longer units, and attributing meaning to them. Listening to an unknown language and to a familiar one involves perception in both cases. However, the experience of being exposed to an unknown foreign language is completely different from that of listening to our native language, or to one which bears structural similarities to languages we know. Even with an unknown language we might occasionally be able to infer something about the structure of a sentence or about word boundaries; to a minor extent we might be able to carry out some segmentation solely on

[1] For a more systematic treatment and a broader presentation of the area, the reader is referred to Garrett 1978; Levelt 1978; Cole & Jakimik 1978, 1980; Danks & Glucksberg 1980; Flores d'Arcais & Schroeder 1983.

the basis of pauses, intonation, and accent. But in order to organize the incoming speech signal perceptually, we have to be able to assign to it an appropriate linguistic structure. In order to isolate words, we have to know what the words of the language we hear are. If by perceiving a word we mean 'recognizing' it, we must not only segment a sequence of sounds, but also access a representation in the mental lexicon. In this chapter, consequently, I will not try to hold to a sharp distinction between perception and comprehension. We will consider the study of language perception as the domain of psycholinguistics, which tries to explain the processes through which a sequence of spoken language or a piece of written text is segmented, interpreted and given a mental representation.

Traditionally, speech perception and language perception have been two distinct fields of study. Research in the two areas has proceeded on separate routes, with separate journals and congresses, and in different scientific 'circuits,' the first looking at the perception of units such as the, phoneme or the syllable, the second dealing with phrases and sentences. During the last decade or so, however (see e.g. Cohen & Nooteboom 1975), the picture has begun to change. Speech perception research is no longer limited to the syllable or to typical CVC sequences, but is now studying connected speech; psycholinguistic models include the contribution of acoustic phonetic patterns and intonation. Several contemporary attempts to construct automatic language recognition systems have been successful only to the extent to which they have been able to take into account the contribution of different sources and levels of information in the perceptual process.

The main issues debated within the area of language perception in the mid 1980s are much the same as earlier, and many of the questions asked earlier are still open. The basic question of psycholinguistics in the 1960s was, and to some extent still is, 'How do we understand a sentence?' Word perception, which had initially been studied within cognitive psychology at large, has for a long time been one of the focal topics of psycholinguistics: in this area there has recently been a convergence of interest from fields such as psychology of reading, neuropsychology, and neurolinguistics. However, the researchers' attention has also shifted to newer problems. For example, while early psycholinguistic research almost ignored the role of suprasegmental information in sentence perception, there has recently been much interest in the effects of intonation cues on language perception (see e.g. Cutler & Clifton 1984).

While in the 1960s most models of sentence perception tended to be serial, and generally autonomous, in the 1970s interactive models were predominant. Now autonomous models have been revived, albeit of a less radical type. Many of the assumptions taken for granted in the 1970s are now being challenged. For example, the then current assumption that the speech signal contains so little phonetic information that speech perception is possible only with a large contribution of top-down processing, utilizing considerable syntactic and semantic knowledge, has recently been questioned. As another example, while the goal of earlier artificial intelligence systems was primarily to function successfully with respect to a minimum standard, recent systems have attempted to approach human performance more closely, including even such human properties as making errors and operating in real time.

Space constraints allow this chapter to deal with only a selection of the theoretically interesting areas. It will, in fact, deal at length with only two classes of problems. The first concerns the basic units of segmentation in language perception. The second concerns the nature of the processes underlying linguistic perception, in particular whether perception at various linguistic levels results from independent mechanisms and processes or from interrelated processes with mutual influences. Thus, I will first discuss the possible ways in which the speech signal can be segmented at different levels, and will look closely at two levels which have attracted much attention in psycholinguistic research throughout the years: the word and the clause. The chapter will also discuss perceptual strategies in language perception, and consider a few models of parsing which are of direct interest for language perception theories. Finally, the important issue of autonomy and interaction in language perception processes will be addressed and related to the notion of modularity. As a side issue, attention will be given to the possible impacts of certain cross-linguistic studies on theories of language perception.[2]

4.1. Perceptual segmentation of speech

The listener is faced with two basic perceptual problems. In the first place he or she has to locate *boundaries*, and in the second place identify words or other units despite *variations* in the signal. The acoustic signal consists of an almost continuous stream of sounds, and boundaries are rarely available. Word boundaries are not given in the speech wave, but are the result of perceptual processes. At some point, therefore, the (almost) continuous signal has to be segmented and made discrete.

When dealing with words in isolation, the problem of segmentation might not be very important. Words spoken in isolation tend to display a great amount of stability at the acoustic and phonetic level (Cole & Jakimik 1978). This means that the perception of words spoken in isolation could

---

[2] For discussion of the application of the results of work in language perception to the design of speech recognition systems, see Volume II, Chapter 11 of this series.

successfully be modeled by pattern-matching techniques. In fact, computer systems can be programmed to perform rather well in recognizing words spoken in isolation by a known speaker, by comparing the parameters of the incoming signal with stored representation of the sound patterns of the words (Reddy 1976). However, the same procedures fail when applied to fluent speech.

Most utterances can in principle be segmented in a variety of ways. Allophonic variations give rise to different perceptual events. The following examples of allophonic contrasts are clear cases of alternative segmentation of the same acoustic event: *night rate/nitrate; a tease/at ease; big gate/big eight.* Many such cases are the result of *geminate reduction*, according to which two identical consonants across word or syllable boundaries reduce to one, such as in *that train* versus *that rain* or *that drain; more ice* versus *more rice*, etc. Alternative parsing of the same sequence of sounds can produce rather distinct syntactic structures: *he gave the example* and *he gave the eggs ample* (Cole & Jakimik 1978).

Beside alternative segmentations, the same acoustic signal can produce different perceptual results because of the phonological, or more general linguistic and contextual, knowledge listeners normally use, as can be demonstrated by a variety of 'slips of the ear,' spontaneous perceptual errors such as those collected by Garnes & Bond (1977) and Bond & Garnes (1980) in spontaneous conversations: hearing 'tenure' for 'ten years,' 'chocolate' for 'chalk dust,' 'inter tube' for 'inner tube,' etc.

Although recent work suggests that there might be more markings for word boundaries than so far estimated (see e.g. Nakatami & Dukes 1977), it is certain that segmentation cues in the signal are not extremely numerous and not unequivocal.

A basic problem for the perception of spoken language is thus the problem of *segmentation*, and an immediately related question is that of the *units* in speech perception. Since the acoustic signal has to be perceptually organized to yield a linguistic structure having a meaningful representation, the question is: what are the basic units of segmentation of the signal? On the way from an unanalyzed acoustic signal to a meaningful representation, various discrete levels of organization are involved. Which of these intermediate organization levels are perceptually real?

The basic mechanism organizing the speech segment perceptually is a *parser*. Traditionally, parsers have been devices constructed to operate at the level of the word, phrase or clause units. However, a device capable of parsing the speech segment into syllabic structure and of matching the resulting constituents against the lexicon has been proposed and implemented by Church (1983).

Evidence for the existence of units in production and perception is apparent from a variety of sources, including experimental data. Psychologically real perceptual units have been proposed at different levels, from the phoneme to the syllable, to words, to immediate constituents, and to complete clauses.

Perhaps the most radical proposal claims that speech perception takes place directly from an analysis of the spectral information, without any intermediate levels (Klatt 1976, 1980). In this model, the basic unit is taken to be the *diphone*, defined in terms of the transition between a speech segment and the one which follows.

Several models of perception rely on phonetic feature analyzers (see e.g. Pisoni & Sawusch 1975; Oden & Massaro 1978): the signal is analyzed by detectors capable of reacting selectively to various aspects of the speech signal, such as changes in the frequency of the formants. It is still an open question whether these detectors are sensitive to auditory or to phonetic properties.

Among the most popular candidates for the basic units of speech perception are, of course, the phoneme and the syllable. Evidence for segmentation at the level of the syllable is abundant (see among others Warren 1971; Massaro 1975; Studdert-Kennedy 1976; Mehler, Dommergues, Frauenfelder & Segui 1981; Segui 1984). On the other hand, some recent work (Cutler, Mehler, Norris & Segui 1983) provides evidence that the syllable might not always function as the appropriate processing unit in English.

Words are *prima facie* the most likely candidates as structural and functional units in speech perception. Several psycholinguistic models have taken this for granted, and the main questions concern not so much the nature of the unit, as the processes and mechanisms through which words are perceived, recognized, and accessed in the mental lexicon. We will briefly return to this problem in the section on word perception (4.2).

Units larger than the word, such as the constituent or the clause, have also been proposed as units of perception. Of course, they are a different kind of perceptual unit than, say, the syllable or the word: they represent not strict segmentation units, but rather units of processing within working memory.

Evidence for the perceptual reality of a unit at a given level does not necessarily mean that 'higher' or 'lower' perceptual units are not possible. The existence of a phonological unit as perceptually real, for example, does not preclude the word being a distinct perceptual event.

4.2. **Word perception**

An essential phase of language perception consists of the process of isolating and identifying a single word. Whatever the status of the word is in linguistic theory, psychologists have always taken it to be an important unit of language, and it is certainly the one whose existence has been most widely taken for granted. Contemporary cognitive psychology (including much work in psycholinguistics) has provided numerous models of the process of perceiving words in isolation and in sentences, and much experimental data to support them. Since the process of perceiving a word goes together with the identification of its meaning, most of these models also represent models of both the organization of, and access to, the mental lexicon.

The different types of word recognition models can be reduced to two basic classes, namely *search models* and *activation models*.

The prototype of the search model is Forster's (1976) *autonomous search model*, characterized by a lexicon and by access files which select appropriate subsets of lexical entries on the basis of perceptual attributes. The word entries in the access files contain pointers to appropriate entries in the mental lexicon. The model is autonomous and bottom-up. Top-down information is used only at a *post-access* stage of word recognition.

The most influential activation model is undoubtedly Morton's (1969, 1970) *logogen*, which is a standard reference and a starting point for all activation models available. Each word entry in Morton's model corresponds to a unit in the mental lexicon, the logogen. A logogen is characterized by a threshold which specifies the amount of activation necessary for the unit to give a response. When enough evidence has been collected from the stimulus input and/or from the semantic system to exceed the threshold value, the logogen fires and a response is made available to the system. Logogens are sensitive both to sensory and conceptual information, and in this sense the model is non-autonomous.

Among the activation models of word perception, two interactive ones are particularly interesting, namely the cohort model in its original form and the model by McClelland & Rumelhart (1981) which has been modified by Elman & McClelland (1984). Both models, as well as most contemporary interactive models of word recognition (see e.g. Cole & Jakimik 1980), share the following assumptions: listeners recognize words sequentially, often before having heard them entirely, and by using much contextual information (particularly syntactic and semantic knowledge).

Let us briefly consider the *cohort* of Marslen-Wilson and his associates (Marslen-Wilson & Welsh 1982; Marslen-Wilson & Tyler 1980). In this model, each entry in the mental lexicon corresponds to a single recognition unit, which represents a coordination of acoustic phonetic and of syntactic and semantic specifications. The process is initiated by sensory information provided by the speech signal. The result of an acoustic phonetic analysis of the input is matched against the acoustic phonetic pattern specified for a given unit. Very early, the recognition devices corresponding in the mental lexicon to all the word units which begin with the initial sequence will be activated. These elements constitute the word-initial cohort, which monitors the continuing sensory input and the compatibility of the words with the available syntactic and semantic constraints. Whenever a mismatch occurs with either source of constraints, that is, whenever the new sensory information does not match with members of the activated cohort, or these are not compatible with the contextual information, the word candidates which do not match are dropped, until a single word candidate remains. Thus, the final selection of a word candidate from the cohort is based on the ability both to satisfy contextual criteria and to match the acoustic phonetic input. The outcome and the timing of the perceptual process reflects not only the positive evidence available over a stimulus item, but also the negative evidence.

Evidence in favor of the model comes from a variety of ingenious experiments with shadowing techniques, gating, etc. (Marslen-Wilson & Tyler 1980; Tyler & Wessels 1983; Marslen-Wilson 1987). The cohort model is characterized by a series of properties: the model emphasizes the continuous, left-to-right character of language perception; the initial phase of the process is purely stimulus driven, and interaction between stimulus information and knowledge sources does not start until some evidence has been accumulated. In the most recent version of the cohort theory (Marslen-Wilson 1987), lexical entries failing to match the input are not dropped, but, in absence of further bottom-up support, their level of activation starts decaying.

An important issue in word recognition concerns the earliness of the process. If the process starts, as the cohort model claims, before enough acoustic phonetic information has become available to ensure correct identification of the intended word, then either word perception is in part the result of guessing, or context influences the perceptual process. In this case, then, the process of perceiving a word can hardly be taken to be autonomous. There is in fact evidence from a variety of experiments with shadowing, gating,[3] and other techniques that listeners are capable of iden-

[3] The 'gating' technique (Grosjean 1980), makes it possible to test hypotheses about the nature of the 'left-to-right' processing of linguistic material. The technique consists of presenting a subject with segments of speech, starting with the initial part of a word and increasing the length of the segment by very small portions of speech each time, until the subject can correctly identify the word. This procedure has allowed researchers to obtain evidence pertaining to an essential question, namely the time involved in the perceptual identification of a word.

tifying a word before it is uniquely specified in the signal against possible alternatives (see e.g. Tyler & Wessels 1983; Marslen-Wilson 1985).

4.3. **Word recognition and lexical decomposition**

A major question in word recognition concerns the comprehension of lexically complex words. In several languages, most words are longer than the single morpheme: they carry prefixes and suffixes, verbs are inflected for tense and person, nouns are inflected for number and often for gender. It is obviously very unlikely that all this information is represented in the mental lexicon in the same surface form as it has in a passage of spoken or written language. Especially in languages with a rich morphology, this would require a very large mental lexicon. For each 'regular' verb in Italian, for example, there are no less than 38 different inflected forms. To assume a separate entry for each of these forms would put severe demands on the mental lexicon. To be sure, no serious theory has ever made this extreme assumption. On the other hand, the existence of derivational suffixes, of prefixes capable of encoding semantic distinctions, and of compound nouns, poses a number of constraints on any theory of word recognition.

Within a psycholinguistic attempt to account adequately for the process of recognizing and comprehending a word, several questions can be formulated. What are the units represented in the mental lexicon? Does morphological analysis take place during the process of language comprehension? Are words decomposed into morphemic constituents during this process? Is morphological decomposition an obligatory stage in word recognition? At which moment in the process of word recognition does this decomposition take place?

A variety of experimental findings, most of which emerged from recent research motivated by a new interest in morphology, give some support to the notion of morphological decomposition during word recognition. The idea that the morpheme, and not the word, is a basic unit in the mental lexicon has been proposed by several authors such as Murrell & Morton (1974) and Snodgrass & Jarvella (1972). More recently, a number of studies on morphological analysis during word recognition have become available, which begin to offer an interesting picture on the questions outlined above.

Perhaps the largest amount of the literature available concerns prefixes. Some experimental evidence suggests that prefixes are stripped off the stem before search is made. For example, according to Taft & Forster (1975), when the reader or a listener encounters a prefixed word, he/she strips off the prefix. Unprefixed words which look like a prefix ('pseudoprefixed' words, such as *relish*) take longer to process, because the reader first attempts to strip off the prefix and then would be left with a nonword. Only after search in the mental lexicon has failed (*lish* is not found), would the recognition system search again for the complete word. Similarly, in lexical decision tasks, prefixed nonwords such as *devive* take longer to classify as nonwords than nonprefixed nonwords such as *lomalk* (Taft 1979a; Taft & Forster 1975). Again, the recognition system first attempts prefix stripping, and this abortive attempt takes some time. A nonword combining a prefix and a stem (*dejuvenate*) takes longer to reject than a word containing a prefix and a nonstem (*depertoire*).

Prefixed forms facilitate recognition of their free stems as much as identical repetition of the stem: for example, the priming effect of *unaware* on *aware* is not statistically different from the priming effect of *aware* on the same word *aware* (Stanners, Neiser & Painton 1979). Frequency effect for prefixed words turn out to be based on stem frequency, not on the frequency of the prefixed words themselves (Taft 1979b; Bradley 1980).

Are suffixes stripped off the same way prefixes are taken to be? The evidence available here is less univocal and does not allow us to take this conclusion. For example, Manelis & Tharp (1977) failed to obtain any difference in lexical decision latencies between truly suffixed words (such as *hissing*) and pseudosuffixed words (such as *pudding*). Similarly, Henderson, Wallis & Knight (1984) could not obtain any substantial decomposition effect for suffixes. This asymmetry between prefixes and suffixes effects has allowed the conclusion (Lima 1987) that words might tentatively be prelexically stripped of any initial letter pattern regardless of whether that could be a prefix or not.

Some evidence for morphological decomposition of suffixes, however, comes from letter search tasks. When a reader is requested to search for a given target letter in a text he/she is more likely to miss a target that is part of an inflectional suffix (Smith & Sterling 1982). The letter *e* is missed more frequently in the *-ed* inflection than in a corresponding stem position. An intermediate missing rate emerged in this study for derivational suffixes.

Are compound words decomposed in their constituent words or morphemes during the process of word recognition? Do both constituents constitute separate access codes, or only the first or the second, or is the whole compound accessed as a unit? Is *fireman* accessed as a unit, or does the recognition system first look for an entry under *fire*? Evidence on this area is scarce and not univocal. On the basis of Osgood & Hoosain's (1974) results it can be concluded that compound words are identified and perceived as units. On the other hand, from a series of interesting experiments, Taft & Forster (1975, 1976) conclude that the access code is not the whole word, but a representation of the first constituent of the word: lexical access would be mediated by the first constituent or syllable of the compound noun. This conclusion is also supported by results of another experiment by the same authors, which compared pairs of compounds having equal surface frequency, but with first constituents having high frequency against pairs characterized by low-frequency first constituents. High-frequency first constituents yielded faster recognition times of the compounds than low-frequency first constituents (Taft & Forster 1976).

It is also doubtful whether Taft and Forster's hypothesis that the first component is the access code really holds against further experimental evidence. For example, compound words which are reverse of existing compound words (e.g. *berryblack*) (Taft 1985) are more difficult to classify as nonwords than compound 'nonwords' made of constituents which were not part of any compound nor possible productive combinations, such as *brandlink*. This result seems to indicate that not just the first, but both constituents might be accessed. In fact, Lima & Pollatsek (1983) also found that nonwords in which both constituents formed real words such as *turntribe* take longer to reject than nonwords in which only the first constituent formed a word.

The degree of semantic opacity or transparency of the components also seems to have something to do with lexical access, as demonstrated by a study of Wilson (1984, quoted in Henderson 1985). Transparent compounds primed their first constituents and not their second, but opaque compounds did not. Notice that priming effects are related to constituent position and not to semantic relation (*doormat* primes *door* and not *mat*, while the word is probably to be taken as more closely related semantically to *mat* than to *door*), a fact speaking for prelexical decomposition.

The available data allow the following conclusion. There is some evidence for prefix stripping during word comprehension, but little evidence for suffix stripping. As for compounds, while morphological decomposition has been shown in some cases, it is by no means a general process.

That some form of morphological decomposition can take place during word recognition seems a reasonable conclusion on the basis of the available evidence. A different question, of course, is whether morphological decomposition is an obligatory, prelexical stage during word recognition. According to such a strong theory of morphological analysis, decomposition would take place obligatorily during word recognition, and the process would be prelexical. Thus a few well-known orthographical or phonological units would be stripped off prelexically before searching for an appropriate stem in the mental lexicon. According to a weaker form of this hypothesis, morphological decomposition would not be an obligatory stage of decomposition, but would depend on the type of words presented, and the process of decomposition would not necessarily have to be prelexical.

The most prominent position centered on the notion of obligatory decomposition at a prelexical stage is Taft and Forster's theory (1975). In their model of lexical decomposition, essentially derived from Forster's search model of word recognition (Forster 1976), a distinction is made between an access file and the mental lexicon proper. The access file contains the representation of the stem morphemes of the language, listed in order of decreasing frequency. Thus, the access code for lexical access would be the stem morpheme, that is, a word with the prefix stripped off. In a modified form of this basic model, Taft (1979a) proposed that the appropriate access code for lexical access is the Basic Orthographic Syllabic Structure (the BOSS) which is the orthographically defined first syllable of a word, and which includes the consonant following the first syllable.

Although, as we have seen, there is some evidence consistent with Taft and Forster's idea, especially concerning prefix stripping, this evidence does not seem enough to support a strong theory, but is not inconsistent with a weaker theory of morphological decomposition (see Henderson 1985).

The fact that the picture is not clear, and that the experimental results are much related to the items used and to the composition of the stimulus set, is to be put in relation to the fact that complex nouns, be they affixed or compounds, have various derivational histories, obey different principles and not seldom display little systematicity. For several compounds and derivations, the possibility of a morphological distinction is a purely etymological fact. While in some cases the components are rather transparent, in many cases they have no more than the status of fossil. Several phonological changes take place as a result of compounding, thus obscuring the nature of the components. Stripping off the prefix from *illiterate* or *irregular* requires a different operation from that necessary to separate the surface form *in* from *incongruent*. And does the processor attempt to strip away the suffix *-in* both in *caffein* and in *cousin*? In order to decompose the word *infant* one has to have a substantial knowledge about the etymology of the word, which includes the derivation of *-fans* from *fari*. And even when the listener has appropriately the feeling of prefixation about the word *include*, some effort is still required to relate the element *-clude* (Latin *claudere*) to surface lexical forms such as *closure*.

There are several other problems with a strong theory of morphological decomposition. For example, does the decomposition process of the word *interminable* attempt at stripping away *inter-* from *-minable*, or, more appropriately, *in-* from *terminable*, or does it attempt both, and in which order? What about multiple *pre-* suffixing, and multiple morpheme words? Does a model assume the same type and amount of decomposition for *insert* and for *intertransformability*, a compound of no less than 5 morphemes?

A further problem for any model assuming decomposition of compounds during recognition, of course, is that compounds do not display a consistent relation between constituent position and a given semantic function. Rules that govern the formation of the compounds are very numerous. A *fireman* extinguishes *fire*, but a *snowman* is a kind of statue made of *snow*, and a *milkman* delivers *milk*.

Still other questions are open and have remained so far almost unexplored within psycholinguistics. For example, what about *blends* such as *smog*? Does the recognition system look for *smoke* and for *fog*? Or does it, as is more likely, search directly for the entry for *smog*?

The work reviewed here is an indication of an increasing interest in morphological processing with psycholinguistics, which has paralleled new developments in morphology within linguistics. Given the number and the interest of the questions still open it is not difficult to predict an intensive development of theories and research effort in this area in the years to come.

4.4. Sentence perception: the clausal hypothesis

In this section we will review some evidence regarding the status of the clause as a perceptual unit, and point out certain theoretically interesting changes in opinion on this point during the last decade.

The clausal hypothesis (see e.g. Jarvella 1971; Carroll & Tanenhaus 1978; Flores d'Arcais 1978) is characterized by two main features. First, the clause is taken to be a primary unit of language perception: the speech segment is organized in the receiver's immediate memory clause by clause, and the signal is accumulated until the end of the clause. Second, at the end of the clause, working memory is cleared of surface grammatical information and the content of the clause is sent to a long-term store where it is represented in a more abstract form.

In its early form, the clausal hypothesis was formulated in strictly structural terms, and processing units were defined in terms of grammatical categories. This notion has been challenged by Carroll & Bever (1976) and by Carroll & Tanenhaus (1978). According to these authors, the listener, rather than constructing well-formed syntactic units of the size of the clause, isolates complete and coherent sets of grammatical relations. In a sequence of speech, the receiver might tend to isolate a complete subject-verb-object relation as a perceptual unit. The units in terms of which the listener segments speech are not structural units, but functional ones. The basic unit of sentence segmentation would then be not a structural clause, but a *functional* one. This often corresponds to a structural clause, but also to some shorter segments. Segmentation is affected by a variety of factors, such as grammatical completeness, surface marking, length, and complexity. Tanenhaus & Carroll (1975) proposed a hierarchy of functional clauses, ranging from simple sentences to nominalizations, and argued that more complete clauses serve as better functional segmentation units. Main clauses make better functional clauses than adverbial subordinate ones, which are in turn better than relative clauses, etc. Some experimental support for this view is available: for example, Carroll & Tanenhaus (1978) found that if brief tones are superimposed on sentences, listeners tend to mislocate them towards clause boundaries more often with functionally complete clauses than with functionally incomplete ones.

A second feature of the clausal hypothesis in its 'classic' form is that upon completion of a clausal unit, working memory is cleared of its contents, which are stored in some abstract form in long-term memory. Data from Jarvella (1971) and Caplan (1972), among many others, offer evidence in favor of this feature. Some more recent evidence, however (e.g. Flores d'Arcais 1978), suggests some modification of this view, in the sense that the operation of 'clearing' working memory at the end of the clause does not consist of an all-or-none operation, but a gradual process, and that linguistic material is kept in working memory more or less in its surface form, depending on the degree of cohesion with the material which follows and on the extent to which it might be necessary for processing that material. This might be the case, for example, when the full interpretation of a later clause is strongly dependent on the previous one, as in the following example: *Although he was very tired, John continued his work.*

Evidence from other experiments (e.g. Flores d'Arcais 1978; Marslen-Wilson, Tyler & Seidenberg 1978) also seems to point toward a modification of the clausal hypothesis, according to which some information is still retained in its literal form even after a clause structure is completed, as long as it is necessary for further processing. On this view, interpretation of the initial clause should provide the processor with the information necessary for deciding to what extent the memory store can be cleared of surface information.

A third characteristic of the clausal hypothesis, even in its weakest form, is that the process of sentence segmentation presents discontinuities. This notion is not easy to maintain in the light of the evidence from online studies of sentence processing. For example, in rhyme and category monitoring experiments,[4] the speed of judgements near clause boundaries does not vary significantly before or after the boundary between two linguistic clauses (Marslen-Wilson, Tyler & Seidenberg 1978). These data are com-

[4] Monitoring tasks (phoneme monitoring, rhyme monitoring, etc.) are typical procedures used in psycholinguistic studies of language perception, and are based on the assumption of limited capacity of the perceptual system. These methods assume that if the system is busy processing information within a task *A*, it won't have much energy left over for another task *B*. The more attention, energy, or processing capacity *A* takes, therefore, the less remains available for *B*. Under this assumption, performance on *B*, which is the dependent variable, can be taken as an indicator of the processing load required for *A*, which is what the psycholinguist is primarily interested in.

patible with only a weaker form of the clausal hypothesis, according to which the end of the clause would be marked perceptually and by concomitant freeing of the working memory. However, there is still a need for theoretical integration of two sorts of data, namely the evidence for processing clause by clause and the results favoring the notion of continuous processing in constructing an interpretation of the incoming signal.

4.5. **Perceptual strategies in language segmentation**

In principle, perceptual segmentation of the incoming speech signal could be accomplished by a parser using two different types of procedures. On the one hand, the human parser could proceed by applying well-defined algorithms, such as the rules of a grammar. At the other extreme, the perceptual structure could be the output of heuristics consisting of isolating and relating to each other major grammatical classes, constructing constituents, etc. According to this point of view, the human parser would operate not on the basis of a grammar, but by using various strategies and operating principles.

Since Bever (1970), several authors have proposed perceptual strategies of language segmentation, consisting of heuristics based on gestalt-like principles, some syntactic and some semantic. The perceptual operation of segmenting and organizing the incoming signal by using syntactic strategies consists of identifying various levels of constituents, by using linguistic cues to impose on the signal a syntactic structure on which a semantic representation can be attached. An example of such a strategy is the following: 'Whenever you find a determiner, begin a noun phrase' (Clark & Clark 1977). The use of this kind of strategy typically appeals to function words, prefixes, suffixes and other items that are capable of marking important linguistic boundaries. More strictly semantic strategies consist of picking up content words and constructing as early as possible putative propositions which make sense semantically and pragmatically. The string of words is then parsed accordingly: the syntactic information available in the signal is mainly disregarded and the parser operates on the basis of the proposition constructed.

To give an example of other parsing principles, according to Frazier & Rayner (1982) many decisions taken during the processing of ambiguous sentences can be reduced to two general parsing strategies, namely the principle of *late closure* and the principle of *minimal attachment*. According to the first principle, incoming lexical items tend to be attached to the phrase or the clause which is currently being processed (namely to the lowest possible non-terminal node dominating the last item being analyzed). According to the principle of minimal attachment, incoming material is placed in the phrase marker being constructed by using the fewest nodes consistent with the well-formedness rules of language. Notice that by using these two strategies, the processor often constructs an incorrect analysis of some portions of the sentence: he is led into a 'garden-path' with a perceptual result which does not match the linguistic structure intended by the speaker.

Much research on parsing strategies during the last years has focussed on processing dependencies between elements which may be rather distant in the incoming signal. Various models of sentence perception and comprehension both with natural language and within AI have been based on consideration of both local and non-local dependencies.

The notion of perceptual strategies in language perception has produced many interesting models of parsing, a few of which will be mentioned in the next section. The principal problem with this approach, however, is that the choice of strategies often tends to be *ad hoc*, and the strategies proposed generally remain at an intuitive and descriptive level. It is only in the most recent models, mainly those dating from the introduction of augmented transition network (ATN) models, that an attempt has been made to formalize the proposed strategies, and much formalization remains to be done.

4.6. Parsing models

Of particular interest for psycholinguistic theories of language perception are the attempts to produce sentence parsers which operate like human listeners and readers, with their capacities and defects (including limited working memory) and which have the same kind of difficulties humans have in processing multiple embeddings and garden-path sentences. Among the natural language parsers proposed, those most important to a psychological theory of language perception are Kimball's (1973) model, Frazier and Fodor's (1978) 'sausage machine', and Bresnan's parser (1978).

In Kimball's model, a first-stage parser operates from left to right to connect each lexical unit to a phrase marker. When a phrase unit is completed, it is sent to a second-stage parser which reassembles the elements and performs further syntactic processing by dividing the utterance into constituents which are assigned appropriate syntactic categories. The parser operates by using seven principles which are made like perceptual heuristics of the type discussed above, and are capable of joining units into a phrase. As an example, consider Kimball's 'closure' principle: 'A phrase is closed as soon as possible, unless the next node parsed is an immediate constituent of that phrase.'

Frazier and Fodor's sausage machine (1978) is another interesting attempt to produce a psychologically plausible sentence parser. The device operates in two steps. The first is performed by the *preliminary phrase packager* (the sausage machine) which assigns lexical and phrasal nodes to groups of a few words. The second step is performed by the *sentences structure supervisor*, a device which joins the phrases produced by the first component into complete phrase markers, thus producing the definitive structure of the sentence analyzed. The first level works as a heuristic device which moves through the input sentence by accommodating a few (say, half a dozen) words at a time into a kind of 'window.' The component works by searching for local structure, using syntactic cues such as determiners, conjunction, and the like, and principles such as minimal attachment. The units which are linked in this stage may constitute clauses, combinations of clauses, or simply phrases. These units are not necessarily structural units. The integration of this preliminary analysis and higher level monitoring is then performed by the sentence structure supervisor. The size of the processing unit seems rather flexible and can accommodate different levels of material. The units computed by Frazier and Fodor's sausage machine show some correspondence with the functional units of Carroll & Bever (1976), to which we alluded in Section 4.4.

The nature of these parsers seems to point to a model of sentence perception which operates essentially on two levels. The first one is constrained by local principles, namely perceptual operating principles and applications of local syntactic relations. The second, higher, level of processing assembles and organizes these units.

Within AI, several parsers have been proposed which bear directly on psychological theories, and which have sometimes been sources of inspiration for psycholinguistic studies. One of the best known is Wood's ATN parser (see Levelt 1978 for a brief presentation of ATN models within a psycholinguistic framework), and a whole series of parsers derived from it. Another such parser is *Parsifal* (Marcus 1980). Whether such parsers have been successful in simulating the human system is another question. For example, Parsifal is deterministic, that is, it does not back up, as does any human parser sent on a garden-path. Moreover, Parsifal is able to parse only grammatical sentences: ungrammatical sentences will simply not be handled, and the parser will not be able to tell where the trouble is. Some recent programs have attempted to deal with this problem. For example, *Paragram* (Charniak 1983) is capable of identifying some of the trouble spots in ungrammatical sentences. Developments within AI are so rapid that it is difficult to predict what kind of models will remain viable, though it is easy to predict that these developments will have more impact on psychological theories of language perception.

4.7. Is language perception an interactive or an autonomous process?

A long-debated issue in psycholinguistics is whether language processing is an autonomous or an interactive process, that is whether it is the output of a series of processes performed by single components, or of a process taking place through the simultaneous cooperation of different sources of knowledge. Originally more specifically focussed on the domain of syntactic comprehension, it is an issue which concerns all levels of linguistic processing, from the perception of phonemes to the perception of words and sentences. The issue represents one of the most important theoretical problems in language perception – and, of course, in all domains of cognitive psychology at large.

According to a radical autonomous position, processing at each level is independent of influences from processing at other levels. Lexical access would be unaided by other levels and syntactic processing would be performed without assistance from, or relation to, any semantic processing. According to an extreme interactionist position, processing at one level is affected by, and affects processing at, all other levels. Perceiving a word is the output of simultaneous activations of phonological, semantic, and lexical mechnisms. Perceiving sentences is the result of interactive processes between syntax, semantics, and pragmatics. Intermediate positions have also been proposed, including the possibility that interaction takes place only at the level of output, once the perceptual process has been exhausted, and is limited to the process of selecting from information already processed.

For perceptual theory, the consequences of choosing one or the other position are obvious. A radical or a moderate autonomous position entails that the contribution of various sources of knowledge to perception is essentially postperceptual. On the other hand, truly interactive positions require perceptual mechanisms capable of accommodating the contributions of different components or levels *during* the perceptual process.

In the following, I will briefly discuss the autonomous and the interactive position to highlight the effects of context, and introduce the notion of modularity and the position of automaticity in language perception.

While evidence for an autonomous stage of syntactic processing in sentence comprehension is found in early 1970s work by Forster and his associates (e.g. Forster & Ryder 1971; Forster & Olbrei 1973), the advocacy of autonomous models has found a recent revival. Most recent autonomous models tend to be less radical than the early ones, however, in that they concede the presence of interaction at least at some output level. For example, according to Holmes (1979), some semantic processing takes place

113

before full syntactic computation has made the sentence's deep structure available.

As for the interactive position, all present interactive theories of language perception recognize a contribution of both top-down and bottom-up information to the processing of the linguistic signal. Interaction means on the one side the contribution of both stimulus information and conceptual information to processing, and on the other side the interaction among levels of processing, for example between semantic and syntactic information. Among the most important properties of interactive models, the following are worth mentioning: first, processing proceeds in parallel at all levels; second, the results from one processing level are available at all other levels; third, the processor is free at any moment to use evidence available from any level.

Evidence for top-down effects and for a simultaneous use of various sources of knowledge in word and sentence perception is so abundant in contemporary psycholinguistic literature that there is almost no need for any exemplification. However, if it is easy to find evidence for interaction, the problem is to decide *what* interacts with what, and *where*. Notice that the notion of interaction is not incompatible with the idea of specific processing at a given level. The question is whether interaction is restricted to the *output* of the processing level or is necessary for the processing at a given level.

Directly related to the autonomy and interaction issue is the question whether there are autonomous *modules* of language perception. According to the main proponent of the modular view (Fodor 1983), a module is a domain-specific piece of neural architecture designed to perform specific computations of input information to be transmitted to central cognitive processes. The computation performed by a module is 'informationally encapsulated' and as such is not accessible to real-world knowledge nor to any cognitive bias. Linguistic perception is probably one of the human functions for which the most convincing evidence for modularity can be adduced. Various levels of linguistic perception seem impenetrable to influences from knowledge sources or from strategic decisions. For example, phonetic analysis and word perception are fast, automatic, and unavoidable. An interesting question is whether it is possible to reconcile the modular view with the existence of interactive processes in perception. The issue is still very highly debated, (see e.g. the first issue of 1985 of *The Behavioral and Brain Sciences*), and will no doubt continue to be so for the next few years (see also the following sections).

4.8. Context effects in language perception

Context effects in language perception bear directly on the autonomy inter-action debate and the modularity issue. Such effects consist in the action of a given source of knowledge, linguistic or extralinguistic, on the processing of a given unit or level of linguistic material. The actions examined are typically facilitatory, but can also be inhibitory. There is ample evidence of contextual effects at all levels, such as on the identification of phonemes and of words and at the level of sentence processing. So, for example, detecting a letter in a string of letters is easier if the string spells a word than if it is a nonsense string. The reaction time to the letter *d* in the word *read* is shorter than the reaction time to the same letter embedded in the nonword *aerd*. This well known 'word superiority effect' has been repeatedly replicated (e.g. Reicher 1969; Wheeler 1970) and is one of the simplest and clearest cases of context effects in perception of linguistic material.

One of the most dramatic demonstrations of context effect in word perception is the phenomenon of *phoneme restoration* (Warren 1970): if a phoneme is erased from a word in context and replaced by a nonlinguistic sound of equal intensity, when the word is presented in context the perceiver does not note the substitution and perceives the word as it is normally heard. Some recent experiments, however, suggest that at least some bottom-up confirmation is necessary to obtain restoration (Samuel 1981).

Top-down effects in the perception of words or parts of sentences are particularly evident when stimulus information is incomplete or ambiguous. In the process of perceiving a word, there is probably some trade-off between stimulus information and context: when the input signal is undis-torted and unambiguous, contextual effects may be of limited importance, but when the signal is impoverished or indeterminate, the context exercises a much stronger influence (see e.g. Garner & Bond 1976). On the other hand, contextual information seems always to be used when available, not only when the stimulus input is degraded (Morton & Long 1976).

The question which is at issue in the autonomy–interaction debate is not whether context effects exist or not, for even the most radical autonomous position recognizes their existence. The problem concerns the locus and the nature of the effect. No available model of word perception has been able to make clear predictions about the specific contextual effects of the various sources of knowledge on the perceptual process. The main differences between models concern the locus of the effect, whether it is pre-access, during the access, or post-access. A central question is whether there are data specific enough to allow a precise answer to this question.

Many data showing context effects, such as the priming effect on word recognition and syntactic facilitation based on semantic knowledge, can be interpreted in two ways. Either they are truly interactive effects, in the sense that they operate in the perceptual process, or they are post perceptual. Modularity and autonomy are violated by the first condition, but remain unaffected by the second. A choice between these two alternatives can perhaps be made more easily once we know something more about the course of the processes of word perception, syntactic processing, and so on.

Consider the problem with regard to word recognition. According to radical autonomous models, context effects are completely post-access. In logogen-like models, on the other hand, context effects are prelexical, in the sense that context directly affects the recognition threshold. If we had more evidence as to the time course of the process, then we would be on firmer ground with respect to the context effect in word perception. It would be very important, for example, to know if context affects the selection of a word only after some stimulus information has been processed, but before the whole stimulus information which is necessary to determine the word uniquely has been presented. Studies designed to test the cohort model with the gating techniques have provided important evidence in this respect (see e.g. Tyler & Wessels 1983).

Context effects such as priming in word recognition are *prima facie* evidence against a modular view of word perception. However, if context effects are postlexical, as many authors have claimed, then word recognition can be the product of a blind, modularly organized system. Moreover it is possible to incorporate the priming effects within the module (Fodor 1983, 1985). In fact, Seidenberg (1985) advocates this modular view of word recognition, claiming the existence of a module for word recognition, and at the same time allowing for the presence of contextual effects. Similar arguments, of course, apply to context effects in syntactic processing.

4.9. **Language perception as an automatic process**

Another theoretically interesting question, taken up in recent years, and which is directly related to the issue of modularity and to the autonomy hypothesis, concerns the automaticity of language perception. The distinction between *automatic* and *controlled* processes constitutes a very important theoretical notion in contemporary cognitive psychology (see e.g. LaBerge & Samuels 1975; Posner & Snyder 1975; Schneider & Shiffrin 1977; Shiffrin & Schneider 1977; LaBerge 1981). Schneider and Shiffrin make the distinction clear:

Automatic processing is activation of a learned sequence of elements in long-term memory that is initiated by appropriate inputs and then proceeds automatically. . . . Controlled processing is a temporary activation of a sequence of elements that can be set up quickly and easily but requires attention, is capacity limited . . . and is controlled by the subject (1977: 1)

An automatic process is characterized by the following properties. It occurs (a) without intention (and is therefore unavoidable), (b) without giving rise to any conscious awareness, and (c) without producing interference with other ongoing mental activities. Another essential characteristic of an automatic process is that (d) it does not require special resources and, therefore, in principle (e) does not reduce the processing capacity of this system. Moreover, automatic processes (f) have a high efficiency and (g) are highly resistant to modification. Controlled processes, on the other hand, are taken to be (a) resource demanding and (b) of limited capacity. Further, they are in principle (c) conscious or accessible to awareness, and (d) under strategic control of the subject, and therefore also (e) highly flexible and modifiable.

That much of language processing in normal conditions takes place in an automatic and probably effortless way can be concluded both on the basis of our own intuitions and on a large amount of empirical evidence. Both our experience of suffering through a neighbor's television program and the listener's perceptual awareness of a spoken message on a given topic on the rejected channel of a dichotic listening experiment are evidence of the unavoidability of language perception. Furthermore, interference effects of several kinds explored in the literature on word recognition, such as Stroop effects and many other phenomena, are evidence of the automatic character of the access to the mental lexicon. Language perception is fast and mandatory, and therefore at least some levels of perceptual organization are likely to be the output of specialized modules.

Some evidence available from normal and from agrammatic subjects, however, suggests that although linguistic perception is likely to be to a large extent a highly automatic process, the results of the computation might be used only to a limited extent. For example, eye fixation data during reading of sentences containing syntactic or semantic violations showed that subjects fixate longer on the locus of the syntactic violations even when they are not consciously aware of them and fail to report the violations (Flores d'Arcais 1982). There is also some evidence suggesting that language perception and comprehension systems may still be intact in patients showing severe agrammatic disturbances. For example, it has been shown that agrammatic patients can be sensitive to grammatical structure (Linebarger, Schwartz & Saffran 1983) and seem to possess a substantially intact language perception system even when their performance in ordinary tests of sentence understanding is very poor. Thus, sentence comprehension disturbances do not necessarily reflect a loss of the capacity to perform the appropriate perceptual computation correctly. These results suggest that at least some of the difficulties in language comprehension in agrammatics may not be so much a problem at the perceptual or comprehension level, but rather one at the level of use and control of the results of automatic perceptual processing. This hypothesis is not without resonance in contemporary cognitive neuropsychology (see e.g. Milberg & Blumstein 1981; Linebarger *et al.* 1983). The claim, based on aphasia research, of a specialized neural architecture for language computation might thus require some attenuation or modification.

In conclusion, the results mentioned suggest a view of an automatic language perception process accompanied by selective use of the results of this processing. The hypothesis is related to the ongoing debate on modularity, and in this context may open interesting perspectives in language perception theories.

4.10. **Selective functional cues to language perception**

A tacit assumption underlying most theories of language perception is that within a range of individual differences, language users function more or less in the same way, independently of variations in the language spoken. Although no specific claims have been made about the identity of perceptual principles used in language segmentation by speakers of different languages, the general features of language perception models have been implicitly taken to have a validity across language boundaries. Thus, until recently, models of language perception have hardly considered the possibility that, in the process of mapping the acoustic signal onto a linguistic structure and constructing a meaningful interpretation, the listener might give differential weight to various elements of the speech signal, or use different cues in segmenting and organizing the incoming signal, depending on the efficiency of the cues in a given language.

While cross-cultural studies abound in psycholinguistic literature, it has not been until recently that specific attention has been given to the process whereby segmental and suprasegmental elements would be used with various 'weights' in different languages, to work through the input material until a representation is obtained. Thus, while in a given language *A* certain linguistic features would be critical in the process of constructing a perceptual organization, for a language *B* other features would convey more critical information and be functionally more relevant for the perceptual process. In language *A*, for example, specific syntactic features could be critically relevant for perception, while in a language *B* a more valid cue would be provided by prosodic information. Accordingly, speakers of different languages might have learned to use various such cues differentially. This would have consequences for any attempt to model language perception.

A series of interesting investigations in this direction has been carried out by Bates, MacWhinney and associates (Bates *et al*. 1982; MacWhinney, Bates & Kliegl 1984). The approach taken has been formulated in a model of sentence processing called the 'competition model,' which makes a series of claims about the control of sentence processing, some of which are of interest for the present discussion. Two such claims, tested in an experiment in MacWhinney *et al*. (1984), refer to the notion of *cue strength* and *cue validity*. According to the first claim, mappings between form and function in different languages would have different weights. The weight which a given cue would have in a given language would be a reflection of the relative 'cue validity' in that particular language.

In an attempt to test their model, MacWhinney *et al*. (1984) placed in competition the following four types of cues: word order, agreement marking, stress, and animacy, and examined the role of these four elements in English, German, and Italian. For each of the experimental sentences, the subjects were requested to assign the role of actor. The results indicate that in this assignment American speakers of English rely almost exclusively on word order, Germans tend to rely more on agreement and animacy, and Italians prefer using agreement marking.

Although these experimental results, as well as those of other studies by the same authors, have been based on judgements of the subjects rather than on direct indicators of linguistic performance, and although the theoretical relevance of this approach is not completely clear, in the sense that it opens a series of questions about sentence processing rather than solving them, still interesting perspectives emerge from this work. If the indications obtained about the differences in 'weight' for the various linguistic cues in the languages investigated can be shown to correspond to functional differences during the perceptual processes, then intriguing consequences might follow for psycholinguistic models of language perception.

4.11. Conclusions

During the last decade, theories about language perception have progressed substantially and interesting answers to old questions have been provided. Robust data are available from a variety of paradigms; these might have to be accommodated in alternative theoretical frameworks, but their value will survive theoretical changes. Consider word perception as an example: from a variety of studies, such as the one carried out within the framework of the cohort model (e.g. Tyler & Wessels 1983; Marslen-Wilson 1984), we have a greater understanding of the time course of word recognition. We also know that when we are presented with a polysemic word, it is likely that all of its meanings become available to the processing system, at least for a very short period, independently of context (Swinney 1979; Tanenhaus, Leiman & Seidenberg 1979). Or take sentence perception: from eye fixation data (e.g. Frazier & Rayner 1982), we know how people deal with certain kinds of structural ambiguities and what kind of perceptual interpretations are probably constructed during reading.

Many of the questions presently under debate in language perception are unlikely to fade from the spotlight in the near future. Among these, to name a few, the modularity issue, the time course of word and sentence perception, the specific contribution of the different sources of knowledge to the perceptual process, and the locus of the interaction effects in perception will provide rich fields of theoretical speculation and experimentation for years to come.

REFERENCES

Bates, E., McNew, S., MacWhinney, B., DeVescovi, A. & Smith, S. 1982. Functional constraints on sentence processing: a cross-linguistic study. *Cognition* 11: 245–99.
Bever, T. G. 1970. The cognitive basis for linguistic structures. In J. R. Hayes (ed.) *Cognition and the development of language*. New York: Wiley.
Bond, Z. S. & Garnes, S. 1980. Misperception of fluent speech. In Cole 1980.
Bradley, D. C. 1980. Lexical representation of derivational relation. In M. Aronoff & M. L. Kean (eds.) *Juncture*. Saratoga: Anima Libri.
Bresnan, J. 1978. A realistic transformational grammar. In M. Halle, J. Bresnan & G. A. Miller (eds.) *Linguistic theory and psychological reality*. Cambridge, MA: MIT Press.
Caplan, D. 1972. Clause boundaries and recognition latencies for words in sentences. *Perception and Psychophysics* 12: 73–6.
Carroll, J. M. & Bever, T. G. 1976. Sentence comprehension: a case study in the relation of knowledge to perception. In E. C. Carterette & M. P. Friedman (eds.), *The handbook of perception*, Vol. 8: *Language and speech*. New York: Academic Press.
Carroll, J. M. & Tanenhaus, M. K. 1978. Functional clauses and sentence segmentation. *Journal of Speech and Hearing Research* 21: 793–808.
Charniak, E. 1983. A parser with something for everyone. In M. King (ed.) *Parsing natural language*. London: Academic Press.
Church, K. W. 1983. *Phrase-structure parsing: a method for taking advantage of allophonic constraints*. Indiana University Linguistic Club.
Clark, H. H. & Clark, E. 1977. *Psychology and language: an introduction to psycholinguistics*. New York: Harcourt, Brace, Jovanovich.
Cohen, A. & Nooteboom, S. G. 1975. *Structure and process in speech perception*. New York: Springer-Verlag.
Cole, R. A. (ed.) 1980. *Perception and production of fluent speech*. Hillsdale: Erlbaum.
Cole, R. A. & Jakimik, J. 1978. Understanding speech: how words are heard. In G. Underwood (ed.) *Strategies of information processing*. New York: Academic Press.
Cole, R. A. & Jakimik, J. 1980. A model of speech perception. In Cole 1980.
Cutler, A. & Clifton, C. 1984. The use of prosodic information in word recognition. In H. Bouma & D. G. Bouwhuis (eds.) *Attention and performance*, Vol. 10: *Control of language processes*. Hillsdale: Erlbaum.

Cutler, A., Mehler, J., Norris, D. & Segui, J. 1983. A language specific comprehension strategy. *Nature* 304: 159–60.

Danks, J. H. & Glucksberg, S. 1980. Psycholinguistics. *Annual Review of Psychology* 31: 391–417.

Elman, J. L. & McClelland, J. L. 1984. Speech perception as a cognitive process: the interactive activation model. In N. J. Lass (ed.) *Speech and language: advances in basic research and practice*, Vol. 10. New York: Academic Press.

Flores d'Arcais, G. B. 1978. The perception of complex sentences. In W. J. M. Levelt & G. B. Flores d'Arcais (eds.) *Studies in the perception of language*. Chichester: Wiley.

Flores d'Arcais, G. B. 1982. Automatic syntactic computation and use of semantic information during sentence comprehension. *Psychological Research* 44: 231–42.

Flores d'Arcais, G. B. & Schreuder, R. 1983. The process of language understanding: a few issues in contemporary psycholinguistics. In G. B. Flores d'Arcais & R. J. Jarvella (eds.) *The process of language understanding*. Chichester; Wiley.

Fodor, J. A. 1983. *The modularity of mind. An essay on faculty psychology*. Cambridge, MA: MIT Press.

Fodor, J. A. 1985. Precis of the modularity of mind. *The Behavioral and Brain Sciences* 8: 1–5.

Forster, K. I. 1976. Accessing the mental lexicon. In R. J. Wales & E. Walker (eds.) *New approaches to language mechanisms*. Amsterdam: North Holland.

Forster, K. I. & Olbrei, I. 1973. Semantic heuristics and syntactic analysis. *Cognition* 2: 319–47.

Forster, K. I. & Ryder, L. A. 1971. Perceiving the structure and meaning of sentences. *Journal of Verbal Learning and Verbal Behavior* 9: 699–706.

Frazier, L. & Fodor, J. D. 1978. The sausage machine: a new two-stage parsing model. *Cognition* 6: 291–325.

Frazier, L. & Rayner, K. 1982. Making and correcting errors during sentence comprehension: eye movements in the analysis of structurally ambiguous sentences. *Cognitive Psychology* 14: 178–210.

Garnes, S. & Bond, Z. W. 1977. The relationship between semantic expectation and acoustic information. In W. V. Dressler & O. E. Pfeiffer (eds.) *Phonologica 1976: Akten der dritten Internationalen Phonologischen Tagung, Wien 1976*. Innsbruck: Phonologische Tagung.

Garrett, M. F. 1978. Word and sentence perception. In R. Held, H. W. Leibowitz & H. L. Teuber (eds.) *Handbook of sensory physiology*, Vol. 3: *Perception*. Berlin: Springer-Verlag.

Grosjean, F. 1980. Spoken word recognition and the gating paradigm. *Perception and Psychophysics* 28: 267–83.

Henderson, L. 1985. Towards a psychology of morphemes. In A. W. Ellis (ed.) *Progress in the psychology of language*. London: Erlbaum.

Henderson, L., Wallis, J. & Knight, D. 1984. Morphemic structure and lexical access. In H. Bouma & D. Bouwhuis (eds.) *Attention and performance*, Vol. 10. Hillsdale: Erlbaum.

Holmes, V. M. 1979. Some hypotheses about syntactic processing in sentence comprehension. In W. E. Cooper & E. C. T. Walker (eds.) *Sentence processing: psycholinguistic studies presented to Merrill Garrett*. Hillsdale: Erlbaum.

Jarvella, R. J. 1971. Syntactic processing of connected speech. *Journal of Verbal Learning and Verbal Behavior* 10: 409–16.

Kimball, J. 1973. Seven principles of surface structure parsing in natural language. *Cognition* 2: 15–47.

Klatt, D. H. 1976. Linguistic uses of segmental duration in English: acoustic and perceptual evidence. *Journal of the Acoustical Society of America* 62: 1345–66.

Klatt, D. H. 1980. Speech perception: a model of acoustic-phonetic analysis and lexical access. In Cole 1980.

LaBerge, D. 1981. Automatic information processing: a review. In J. Long & A. Baddeley (eds.) *Attention and performance*, Vol. 9. Hillsdale: Erlbaum.

LaBerge, D. & Samuels, S. J. 1975. Toward a theory of automatic information processing in reading. *Cognitive Psychology* 6: 293–323.

Levelt, W. J. M. 1978. A survey of studies in sentence perception: 1970–1976. In W. J. M. Levelt & G. B. Flores d'Arcais (eds.) *Studies in the perception of language*. Chichester: Wiley.

Liberman, A. M. & Mattingly, I. G. 1985. The motor theory of speech perception revisited. *Cognition* 21: 1–36.

Lima, S. D. 1987. Morphological analysis in sentence reading. *Journal of Memory and Language* 26: 84–99.

Lima, S. D. & Pollatsek, A. 1983. Lexical access via an orthographic code? The Basic Orthographic Syllable Structure (BOSS) reconsidered. *Journal of Verbal Learning and Verbal Behavior* 22: 310–92.

Linebarger, M. C., Schwartz, M. F. & Saffran, E. M. 1983. Sensitivity to grammatical structure in so-called agrammatic aphasics. *Cognition* 13: 361–92.

McClelland, J. L. & Rumelhart, D. E. 1981. An interactive activation model of context effects in letter perception: Part 1, an account of basic findings. *Psychological Review* 88: 375–407.

McWhinney, B., Bates, E. & Kliegl, R. 1984. Cue validity and sentence interpretation in English, German and Italian. *Journal of Verbal Learning and Verbal Behavior* 23: 127–50.

Marcus, M. P. 1980. *A theory of syntactic recognition for natural language*. Cambridge, MA: MIT Press.

Manelis, L. & Tharp, D. A. 1977. The processing of affixed words. *Memory and Cognition* 5: 650–95.

Marslen-Wilson, W. D. 1973. Linguistic structure and speech shadowing at very short latencies. *Nature* 244: 522–3.

Marslen-Wilson, W. D. 1975. Sentence perception as an interactive parallel process. *Science* 189: 226–8.

Marslen-Wilson, W. D. 1980. The temporal structure of spoken language understanding. *Cognition* 8: 1–71.

Marslen-Wilson, W. D. 1984. Function and process in spoken word recognition. In H. Bouma & D. G. Bouwhuis (eds.), *Attention and performance*, Vol. 10: *Control of language processes*. Hillsdale: Erlbaum.

Marslen-Wilson, W. D. 1987. Functional parallelism in spoken word recognition. *Cognition* 25: 71–102.

Marslen-Wilson, W. D. & Tyler, L. K. 1980. The temporal structure of spoken language understanding. *Cognition* 8: 1–71.

Marslen-Wilson, W. D., Tyler, L. K. & Seidenberg, M. 1978. Sentence processing and the clause boundary. In W. J. M. Levelt & G. B. Flores d'Arcais (eds.) *Studies in the perception of language*. Chichester: Wiley.

Marslen-Wilson, W. D. & Welsh, A. 1978. Processing interactions and lexical access during word recognition in continuous speech. *Cognitive Psychology* 10: 29–63.

Massaro, D. W. 1975. *Understanding language: an information processing analysis of speech perception, reading and psycholinguistics*. New York: Academic Press.

Mehler, J., Dommergues, J. Y., Segui, J. & Frauenfelder, U. 1981. The role of the syllable in language acquisition and perception. In T. Myers, J. Laver & J. Anderson (eds.) *The cognitive representation of speech*. Amsterdam: North–Holland.

Milberg, W. & Blumstein, S. E. 1981. Lexical decision and aphasia: evidence for semantic processing. *Brain and Language* 14: 371–85.

Morton, J. 1969. The interaction of information in word recognition. *Psychological Review* 76: 165–78.

Morton, J. 1970. A functional model of human memory. In D. A. Norman (ed.) *Models of human memory*. New York: Academic Press.

Morton, J. & Long, J. 1976. Effect of word transition probability on phoneme identification. *Journal of Verbal Learning and Verbal Behavior* 15: 43–51.

Murrell, G. & Morton, J. 1974. Word recognition and morphemic structure. *Journal of Experimental Psychology* 102: 963–8.

Nakatami, L. H. & Dukes, K. D. 1977. Locus of segmental cues for word juncture. *Journal of the Acoustical Society of America* 62: 714–19.

Oden, G. C. & Massaro, D. W. 1978. Integration of featural information in speech perception. *Psychological Review* 85: 172–91.

Osgood, C. E. & Hoosain, R. 1974. Salience of the word as a unit in the perception of language. *Perception and Psychophysics* 15: 168–82.

Pisoni, D. B. & Sawusch, J. R. 1975. Some stages of processing in speech perception. In Cohen & Nooteboom 1975.

Posner, M. I. & Snyder, C. R. R. 1975. Attention and cognitive control. In R. Solso (ed.) *Information processing and cognition: the Loyola symposium*. Hillsdale: Erlbaum.

Reddy, D. R. 1976. Speech recognition by machine: a review. *Proceedings of the IEEE* 64: 501–23.

Reicher, G. M. 1969. Perceptual recognition as a function of meaningfulness of stimulus material. *Journal of Experimental Psychology* 81: 276–80.

Samuel, A. G. 1981. The role of bottom-up confirmation in the phonemic restauration illusion. *Journal of Experimental Psychology: Human Perception and Performance* 7: 1124–31.

Schneider, W. & Shiffrin, R. M. 1977. Controlled and automatic human information processing: I. Detection, search and attention. *Psychological Review* 84: 1–66.

Segui, J. 1984. The syllable: a basic perceptual unit in speech processing? In H. Bouma & D. G. Bouwhuis (eds.) *Attention and performance*, Vol. 10: *Control of language processes*. Hillsdale: Erlbaum.

Seidenberg, M .S. 1985. Lexicon as module. Open peer commentary to Fodor's *Modularity of mind*. *The Behavioral and Brain Sciences* 8: 31–2.

Shiffrin, M. & Schneider, W. 1977. Controlled and automatic human information processing: II. Perceptual learning, automatic attending and a general theory. *Psychological Review* 84: 127–90.

Smith, P. T. & Sterling, C. M. 1982. Factors affecting the perceived morphemic structure of written words. *Journal of Verbal Learning and Verbal Behavior* 21: 704–21.

Snodgrass, J. G. & Jarvella, R. J. 1972. Some linguistic determinants of word classification times. *Psychonomic Science* 27: 220–2.

Stanners, R. F., Neiser, J. J. & Painton, S. 1979. Memory representation for prefixed words. *Journal of Verbal Learning and Verbal Behavior* 18: 399–412.

Studdert-Kennedy, M. 1976. Speech perception. In N. J. Lass (ed.) *Contemporary issues in experimental phonetics*. New York: Academic Press.

Swinney, D. A. 1979. Lexical access during sentence comprehension: (re)consideration of context effects. *Journal of Verbal Learning and Verbal Behavior* 18: 645–59.

Taft, M. 1979a. Lexical access via an orthographic code. The Basic Orthographic Syllabic Structure (BOSS). *Journal of Verbal Learning and Verbal Behavior* 18: 21–40.

Taft, M. 1979b. Recognition of affixed words and the word frequency effect. *Memory and Cognition* 7: 263–72.

Taft, M. 1981. Prefix stripping revisited. *Journal of Verbal Learning and Verbal Behavior* 20: 289–97.

Taft, M. 1985. The decoding of words in lexical access: a review of the monographic approach. In D. Besner, T. Gary Weller & G. E. MacKinnon (eds.) *Reading research advances in theory and practice*, Vol. 5. Orlando: Academic Press.

Taft, M. & Forster, K. I. 1975. Lexical storage and retrieval of prefixed words. *Journal of Verbal Learning and Verbal Behavior* 14: 638–47.

Taft, M. & Forster, K. I. 1976. Lexical storage and retrieval of polymorphemic and polysyllabic words. *Journal of Verbal Learning and Verbal Behavior* 15: 607–20.

Tanenhaus, M. K. & Carroll, J. M. 1975. The clausal processing hierarchy and nouniness. In R. Grossman, J. San & T. Vance (eds.) *Papers from the parasession on functionalism*. Chicago: Chicago Linguistic Society.

Tanenhaus, M. K., Leiman, J. M. & Seidenberg, M. S. 1979. Evidence for multiple stages in the processing of ambiguous words in syntactic contexts. *Journal of Verbal Learning and Verbal Behavior* 18: 427–40.

Tyler, L. K. & Wessels, J. 1983. Quantifying contextual contributions to word recognition processes. *Perception and Psychophysics* 34: 405–20.

Warren, R. M. 1970. Perceptual restoration of missing speech sounds. *Science* 167: 392–3.

Warren, R. M. 1971. Identification times for phonemic components of graded complexity and for spelling of speech. *Perception and Psychophysics* 9: 345–9.

Wheeler, D. D. 1970. Processes in word recognition. *Cognitive Psychology* 1: 59–85.

5 The mental lexicon

Karen D. Emmorey and Victoria A. Fromkin

5.0. Introduction

The mental lexicon is that component of the grammar that contains all the information – phonological, morphological, semantic, and syntactic – that speakers know about individual words and/or morphemes.

It is an open question whether there is an isomorphism between the units and components of the grammar and those implemented and accessed in the linguistic processing system(s), even though a linguistic performance model is ultimately dependent on the grammar. Lexical structure as part of grammatical theory is discussed in Volume I, Chapter 3, of this series; this chapter will therefore focus on psycholinguistic models of the lexicon. Both models are equally 'mental' but are directed toward answering different questions.

Psycholinguistic models have generally been concerned with how lexical information is accessed or processed and have been less explicit about the representation and structure of the information. The nature of the stored representations is important, however, because it may in part determine the nature of the access mechanisms. In addition, the proposed lexical access procedure has implications for internal lexical structure and representation within the mental lexicon. In this chapter we will examine a number of processing models of the lexicon, focussing on what they imply about the mental representation of words.

Many psycholinguistic models of the lexicon hypothesize separate sub-components containing phonological, orthographic, and semantic information about words (Forster 1976; Morton 1979; Allport & Funnell 1981; Fromkin 1985). There is much evidence in support of this modular lexical structure. For example, access to phonological, orthographic, syntactic, and semantic information about words can be independently affected by damage to the brain. Schwartz, Marin and Saffran (1979) discuss a demented patient who maintains preserved phonological and syntactic knowledge about words in the face of a severe breakdown in semantic knowledge. This patient was impaired in assigning semantic categories to words, overgeneralizing *dog* to *cat* while still able to utilize grammatical morphemes to interpret complex sentences (e.g. passives, comparatives). The patient was also able to make better use of subcategorization cues to differentiate homophones (the *sea*; to *see*) than semantic cues (*lake, sea*). Preserved access to the phonological representation of words through grapheme-to-phoneme pronunciation rules accompanied by a loss of access to orthographic representations is found in some forms of dyslexia (Marshall & Newcombe 1966, 1973; Shallice & Warrington 1975; Saffran & Marin 1977; Patterson 1982; Newcombe & Marshall 1985). Some of these patients can read regularly spelled words (e.g. *road*) which can be pronounced by use of these rules but cannot read irregularly spelled words (e.g. *broad*) which require access to the orthographic representation since these rules will not produce correct pronunciations. (See below for further discussion of this issue.)

Within a componential lexicon, a lexical entry consists of information (phonological, orthographic, semantic, etc.) stored in separate information-specific components. Lexical knowledge about a word is therefore not stored in one 'place,' but is represented in different sub-lexicons. Although these subcomponents are argued to be independent, they must interface and interrelate in a complex network. Such a lexicon appears to be formally equivalent to one in which phonological, orthographic, syntactic, and semantic representations are listed as part of a single entry, the model of the lexicon usually assumed in grammatical theory or in language-specific grammars. Our argument, here, for a modular structure of the lexicon (in addition to the overall modularity of the grammar) has no theoretical bearing for models of grammar or competence, but does bear on psycholinguistic models of word recognition and language parsing. We will discuss below the structure of the subcomponents in the performance model, their stored representations, and their interconnections with respect to different processing models of the lexicon.

5.1. **Phonological and/or phonetic representations**

Most models of lexical processing assume some phonemic (or morpho-phonological) representation for each entry, given the abundant evidence from speech errors (Fromkin 1973, 1980), language games (Sherzer 1970), and speech perception and production studies, which reveal phonological knowledge more abstract than systematic or physical phonetic representations (Chomsky & Halle 1968).

The question remains as to whether the lexicon also includes phonetic representations. The resolution of this question has particular relevance to the cohort model, which was developed by Marslen-Wilson and his colleagues (Marslen-Wilson & Welsh 1978; Marslen-Wilson 1980; Marslen-Wilson & Tyler 1980) to account for spoken word recognition. According to this model, word recognition is achieved in the following manner: the first one or two phonemes serve to 'activate' all words in the listener's lexicon which begin with that initial sequence, and these words form the 'word-initial cohort.' A word is recognized (in isolation) by matching the word candidates in this cohort with the incoming sensory information. When a mismatch occurs between the sensory input and a word candidate, that word drops out of the cohort. This matching process continues until only one candidate remains which is consistent with the sensory input. At this point the listener is claimed to have recognized the word. When the word is heard in the context of an utterance, semantic and syntactic constraints are assessed along with the sensory input. Word recognition occurs when a single word candidate matches both the sensory and the contextual information. Thus, according to this model, a word can be 'recognized' even before the end of the word is heard if it is uniquely defined by context and sensory information prior to the end of a word. For example, *dwindle* can be recognized with the [ɪ] is 'heard' since at this point it is uniquely distinguished from *dwell* and all other English words.

Whether the stored lexical representations contain phonetic information about words has important implications for this model. Because word recognition (in isolation) is said to occur when one word candidate remains which alone matches the sensory information, it is important to determine on what basis – phonetic or phonemic – the elimination of the other candidates is made. If the representation with which the stimulus is matched is phonetic, a larger number of candidates will be eliminated than if it is phonological. For example, if the stimulus word (presented in isolation) were *clone* the initial (phonologically based) cohort would be all the words in the listener's lexicon which begin with /klo/, e.g. *cloak, close* [klos], *close* [kloz], *clothe, clove, clover, cloture.* Note that compounds (e.g. *close-knit*) and derived or inflected words (e.g. *closely, closed*) are not included here; we will return to the question of how morphologically complex items are stored and accessed.

What is interesting to note is that if the incoming stimulus ([klōn]) is matched against phonetic representations (words beginning with ([klō]) recognition will occur as soon as the listener hears the nasalized vowel, since none of the words in the cohort above contains a nasalized vowel. On the other hand, if the stimulus is matched against more abstract phonological representations, the listener will recognize the word at /n/ where it is distinguished from the rest of the cohort. The size of the cohort will be larger if phonemic representations are stored. Marslen-Wilson & Tyler (1981) suggest that phonetic effects may play a role in the word recognition processes, but state that it is unclear if they do. We can see here how representations and processes interrelate. If phonetic representations are stored in the lexicon, and if the assumption of many psycholinguists that additional tasks require more processing time is correct, then words will be recognized earlier and the cohort size will be smaller than if phonemic representations alone are stored. If phonetic representations are not stored, the matching process must then compute the phonological representation from the acoustic signal – a long-standing problem in linguistic phonetics (Fromkin 1977; Ladefoged, 1980; Halle 1985). Experiments to determine whether phonetic information can be used to eliminate members of the cohort are yet to be conducted.

Furthermore, the hypothesis that words are accessed by their initial segments has implications for the organization and structure of the lexicon, i.e. it suggests that words are listed in the lexicon by their initial segments. In fact, a fair amount of evidence indicates some type of phonological organization by initial segment. Subjects in a 'tip-of-the-tongue' state are most often able to remember the initial sound or syllable of the target word (Brown & McNeill 1966). Anomic patients are often able to access a word if they are given the initial segment or syllable (Benson 1979). Baker (1974) found that in a timed test subjects were able to list many more words that began with the same segment than words that shared the same vowel, the same middle consonant, the same final consonant, or the same last syllable. These results suggest that a word is most easily accessed by its initial segment. This does not mean, however, that listings based on other characteristics do not also exist, and there is evidence for other phonological organizations within the lexicon, not accounted for by the cohort model.

According to the cohort model, final segments are not always necessary for recognition; one might infer that they should thus be the least important and the least salient part of a word. However, Cutler, Hawkins & Gilligan (1985) argue that the endings of words are more salient than the middle of words. Misperceptions occur less often on the ends of words than on medial segments (Browman 1978), and speech errors occur less often on the final segments than on medial ones (Cutler & Fay 1982). The final segments of a word are also remembered more often than the medial segments in a tip-of-the-tongue state (Brown & McNeill 1966), and Baker (1974) found that subjects could list rhymes (for monosyllabic words) as easily as listing words with the same initial consonants, but words that shared the same medial vowel were much harder to produce.

These findings do not necessarily support the notion that words are listed in a sort of backwards dictionary, but do suggest the importance of these phonological aspects in lexical processing. It may be the case that words are also listed by final rhyme structure or final (stressed) syllable, which accounts for the greater saliency and/or stability of word endings (in comparison to middle segments) in speech perception and production and the ease with which rhyming words can be located in the lexicon. But these facts can be accounted for by processing strategies separate from the order of listing, or by 'recency effects' found in many memory experiments, i.e. the end of a word is heard most recently and thus might be more easily remembered.

5.2. **Orthographic representation and grapheme-to-phoneme conversion rules**

In addition to phonological representations, each lexical entry must include its orthographic representation for literate speakers. These are in addition to the grapheme/phoneme conversion rules which permit the reading aloud and writing to dictation of nonsense words which have no lexical representation or of new words which we have not yet acquired. Such rules are insufficient to account for our ability to pronounce or spell the 'irregular' words in English. That is, the rules we use to pronounce *mile* as /mayl/ or *zile* (a nonsense string) as /zayl/ cannot explain our ability to read *lisle* as /layl/ or *aisle* as /ayl/. The regular rules may account for our reading *hymn* as /hɪm/ since English phonology requires the deletion of a final post-consonantal nasal, but they cannot account for our ability to read the noun *lead* as /lɛd/ and the verb as /lid/.

That both 'spelling–pronunciation' rules and orthographic representations are part of the lexicon is supported again by the fact that they can be differentially affected by brain damage. Furthermore, phoneme-to-grapheme rules may not be simply the reverse of grapheme-to-phoneme rules. Beauvois & Dérousné (1979), for example, report on a patient who could read nonwords but could not write nonwords to dictation.

The evidence from reading studies also suggests that words can be accessed either by grapheme-to-phoneme conversion processes or by a purely visual orthographic process, i.e. different strategies may be used (see McCusker, Hillinger & Bias 1981 for a review).

There is striking evidence from deep dyslexic patients that the grapheme-to-phoneme conversion rules are not the only path to understanding written words; these brain-damaged patients are able to read words but have difficulty with nonwords, showing an inability to utilize these rules (Coltheart, Patterson & Marshall 1980). Nor can they judge whether printed nonwords rhyme – a task which also requires translation from spelling to sound. It thus appears that deep dyslexic patients can read real words by matching the printed stimulus to their orthographic representations, i.e. by a purely visual process, which then permits them to access the phonological representations of these words; grapheme-to-phoneme conversion rules play no part in this process. The nature of the grapheme-to-phoneme conversion process is currently being debated (dual access or analogy? see Seidenberg 1985), but it is clear that some type of orthographic code must be listed separately from a phonological representation with each lexical entry.

Both the Fromkin model (1985) and the logogen model (Morton 1979, 1982) include a separate component in the lexicon containing orthographic representations. These models differ about whether there are connections between the phonological and orthographic representations of words. The logogen model contains separate systems for recognizing written and spoken words, and Jackson & Morton (1984) and Morton (1979) reject any direct connections between these two systems. The input systems of the logogen model are presented in Figure 1.

In Morton's model, a logogen is a word (or morpheme; see below) detection unit that receives stimulus information from the analysis systems and semantic and syntactic information from the cognitive system. When a certain threshold of information is attained the logogen corresponding to a particular word 'fires' or generates a word response as output to the cognitive system. The cognitive system is not well defined but contains a linguistic parser and processing system (Morton & Patterson 1980). Some phonological (or phonetic) representations must be contained in the auditory logogens, since each logogen responds most to the acoustic information for a particular word, and that information must somehow be coded in the logogen in order for it to respond. By the same argument, orthographic representations must be coded in the visual logogens.

The Fromkin model also contains separate phonological and orthographic 'sub-lexicons' and other components, e.g. semantic. Each entry in each sub-lexicon includes the addresses which connect the various representations, i.e. a word's phonological representation includes its orthographic, semantic, syntactic, etc., addresses. The coaddressing model is shown in Figure 2.

The numerical addresses in this model obviously have only metaphorical meaning. Entries are posited to have addresses that are close numerically or which occur 'on the same street' when they are similar in structure or in the same semantic class. This is to account, in a simplistic fashion, for normal or aphasic speech errors. For example, typical word substitutions in which an incorrect but semantically related word is used may be caused by the speaker going to the correct 'street' or 'page' in that sub-lexicon but (for reasons not relevant to this paper) selecting a wrong but 'close' entry. Suppose, for example, a speaker says 'cape' but had intended to say 'dress'. In the lexical selection process, instead of accessing *dress* with a possible

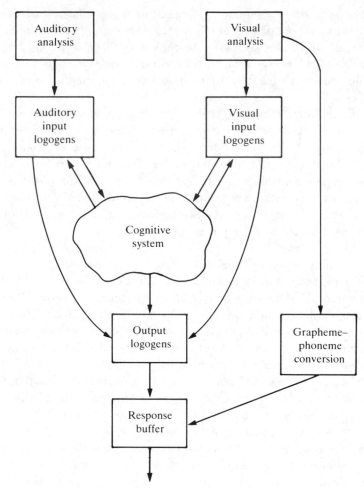

Figure 1. Logogen model (Morton & Patterson 1980)

semantic address of S123, S124 is accessed, the address for *cape*, which includes its phonological address P2007, which when selected for pronunciation produces /kep/. The point we wish to make is that the lexical model must account for all the data which pertain to lexical access or selection, normal and disturbed, and separate but interconnected modules appear to be required.

The problem the logogen model faces by disallowing connections between phonological and orthographic representations is that the model cannot explain the effects of phonology on visual word recognition or the effects of orthography on auditory word recognition. Anecdotal evidence

130

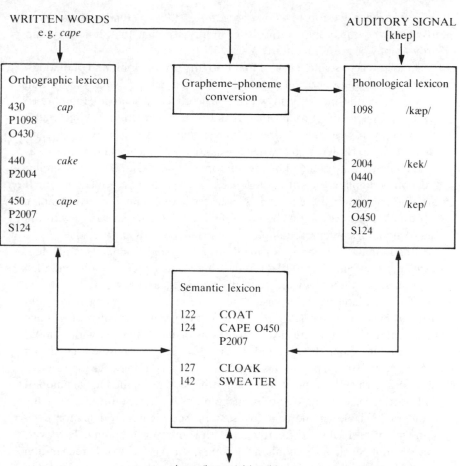

Figure 2. Modular coaddressing model for single words (Fromkin 1985)

from linguistics students learning the IPA (International Phonetic Alphabet) suggests strong connections between the orthographic and phonological representations of words. Students often find it extremely difficult to suppress their knowledge of the orthography of a word and to attend solely to the sounds. Early linguists were also lead astray in their study of languages by their inability to separate the sounds of a language from its orthography (see Bloomfield 1933). In addition, Baker (1974) found that subjects often made 'spelling errors' when they were asked to list words that contained similar sounds. For example, when asked to list words beginning with the same first consonant and vowel sounds as *bone*, /boʊ/, subjects produced errors like *boss*, *boot*, *box*, and *body*. One explanation as to why orthography is so difficult to suppress is that the phonology and orthography of words are interconnected.

In fact, recent studies suggest that both the orthographic and phonological representations are automatically accessed during word recognition regardless of the modality in which the word is presented. Humphreys, Evett & Taylor (1982) found that visual word recognition was facilitated when the word was preceded by a homophone prime. For example, subjects' ability to recognize *pale* when it was covered by a masking pattern was better when it was preceded by the homophone *pail*. Graphemically similar but non-homophonous words (e.g. *pack*) did not facilitate recognition. If the phonological representation is accessed along with the orthographic representation, recognition should be facilitated for target words with the same phonological representation as the priming words.

In addition, Seidenberg & Tanenhaus (1979) and Donnenworth-Nolan, Tanenhaus & Seidenberg (1981) found that when subjects monitored a list of spoken words for a word that rhymed with a cue word, the rhyme identification latencies were faster when the cue and rhyming word were orthographically similar (e.g. *glue, clue* versus *grew, clue*). If orthographic representations automatically become available, rhymes with similar orthographies should be detected faster. However, it could be argued that the effect of orthography in this experiment occurs in the decision stage of monitoring which takes place in the cognitive system (in the logogen model) and not in the lexicon. If the listener adopts a strategy of accessing the orthographic code via the cognitive system (see Figure 1), detection decisions might be facilitated for rhymes with similar orthography. However, this cannot explain homophone priming in visual word recognition (Humphreys *et al.* 1982) because recognition of the homophone prime was poor, indicating that it would be very difficult for subjects to adopt a recognition strategy based on accessing the phonological code in the auditory input logogen via the cognitive system, and that the phonological representation is automatically (unconsciously) activated. If there is no connection between the orthography of a word and its phonology, this result is difficult to explain, especially since Humphreys *et al.* (1982) show that the facilitation is not due to the grapheme-to-phoneme conversion process, because irregular words which cannot be read via these rules also facilitated recognition (e.g. *suite* primed *sweet*).

Support for separate orthographic and phonological representations, as well as active grapheme↔phoneme conversion rules is provided by cases of acquired dyslexia mentioned above, and exemplified by a surface dyslexic, Kram, discussed by Newcombe & Marshall (1985) and Fromkin (1985). This patient, following brain injury, appears to have lost all access routes to the orthography (as well as the standard orthography-to-phonology rules, substituting his own). If the orthographic representation is not listed separately from the phonological representation one would have to posit either impairment to the orthographic representation of each lexical item, or a complex impairment of the multitude of connections to these representations, leaving the pathways to the phonology intact. By positing separate sub-lexicons with interconnecting addresses (as in Figure 2) the impairment is more simply explained.

In reading aloud, Kram pronounces *cape* as /sæpi/ and writes KAP when hearing the word. He can tell you its meaning when he hears it but not when he sees the printed version; he can get to the meaning of a word only through its phonology, i.e. he can not say what the written word *cape* means, because /sæpi/ is not in the phonological lexicon. Returning to Figure 2, Kram either is unable to access the orthographic lexicon and the address for *cape*, O450, or after accessing it, cannot 'read' its phonological address, i.e. the connecting pathway between the two sub-lexicons is unavailable to him. He therefore uses his grapheme-to-phoneme rules in which, for example, all vowels are [+syllabic] and the letter 'c' is pronounced /s/ to produce /sæpi/, for which there is no phonological listing and therefore no semantic address. However, upon hearing /kep/, he knows its meaning, since the acoustic signal permits him to access the phonological address, P2007, which also lists the semantic address S124. But again, the pathways between the phonology and orthography are cut off, preventing him from accessing the orthographic address O450; again using his phoneme-to-grapheme rules he writes KAP. Further, asked to read his own written word, he says /kep/ and can then state what it means.

The model presented in Figure 2, therefore, can account for Kram's impairment by erasing the arrows connecting the orthography and phonology, and from the semantic component to the orthography.

Kram also illustrates that any model which includes only a phonetic representation is not viable. In his dialect of English, all words which in the standard dialect include an interdental fricative have instead an /f/ or /v/ for the /θ/ or /ð/, respectively. In writing to dictation, for example, Kram writes FING for thing; he matches the acoustic [θ] with his /f/ and can arrive at the semantic representation of /fing/ which means 'thing.'

Such data from normal and from brain-impaired subjects, from psycholinguistic experiments, and from reading, argue for a lexicon with abstract phonological representation of words in at least one listing according to initial phonemes with separate orthographic representations addressed or connected in some fashion.

5.3. **Morphology**

Up to this point we have been discussing the phonological and orthographic representations of words, but what may be stored in the lexicon are morphemes – roughly classified (in English) as affixes and base forms. There is considerable evidence that the linguistic processing system differentiates between affixes and base forms. Garrett (1980), for example, shows that affixes and word stems exhibit different patterns in speech errors. Word stems often participate in exchange (reversal or spoonerism) errors in speech, but affixes (as bound morphemes not as syllables), seldom if ever do. In addition, affixes often participate in shift or movement errors but word stems (of major grammatical categories: nouns, verbs, adjectives) rarely do.

(1) Word or stem exchanges:
   a. I left the cigar in my briefcase → I left the briefcase in my cigar
   b. This seat has a spring in it → This spring has a seat in it
   c. We have a lot of ministers in our church → . . . churches in our minister
   (a and b from Garrett 1980; c from Fromkin 1971)

Bound morpheme exchanges such as *The boying are goes* for *The boys are going* have not been reported, but affix shifts or movements are observed (examples from Garrett 1980).

(2) Affix shifts:
   a. That would be the same as adding ten → . . . as add tening
   b. I'd forgotten about that → I'd forgot abouten that

In contrast, word shifts such as *I left the in my cigar briefcase* (for the targeted utterance (1a) above) are not reported, although word shifts involving minor grammatical categories (e.g. adverbs, intensifiers, determiners) do occur.

(3) Minor category word shifts:
   a. I frankly admit to being subjective in my evaluation → I admit to being frankly subjective . . .
   b. I really hate to correct exams → I hate to really correct exams
   c. Did you stay up very late last night →Did you stay up late very last night?
   (a and b from Fromkin corpus; c from Garrett 1980)

Garrett (1980) proposes an explanation for these category distinctions based on levels of processing. These examples serve here to illustrate (1) that lexical category information must be stored in the lexicon and (2) that there appear to be different constraints regarding the processing of stems and affixes.

Aphasia data also show that affixes and base forms are apparently processed differently. Buckingham (1981) discusses patients who produce many neologistic jargon forms which are appropriately inflected or derived:

(4)   a. The leg [vɪltəd] from here down
      b. This is the [kreibəkæks] where the [frəjəz] get out after the [čuw]

In these examples, nominal suffixes attach to 'nouns' in noun phrases and verbal suffixes attach to 'verbs.' The jargon affects primarily the lexical or stem morpheme.

The reading errors of some acquired dyslexics also often involve morphologically complex derived words in which the stem is read correctly but either the affixes are stripped or other affixes are substituted (Patterson 1982). This may reflect the subject's ability to decompose the written form and access the stripped stem, but inability to access complex forms (if they are listed separately) or inability to access separate listings of bound morphemes. Such a morpheme list must be part of the normal lexicon because of speakers' ability to form new derived forms with nonsense stems and regular affixes.

Inflectional and derivational affixes may not form a single class; it is an open question whether a processing or representational distinction exists between these two morphological types. As we argued earlier, while process and representation may not in all cases be identical, the representation of morphemic structure will affect the nature of the access mechanism and the proposed access mechanism may argue for a particular morphemic representation. The cohort model provides a clear example of this interdependency. Whether base forms or complex affixed forms in addition to base forms are stored in the lexicon will affect the size of the word-initial cohort. Recall that according to this model words are recognized by accessing all words that begin with the initial segments of the word. Candidate words are eliminated when they fail to match the incoming stimulus, and a word is recognized when it is the only remaining candidate. For example, if the word *Robert* is heard in isolation, the candidate base morphemes compatible with the first syllable are *robin* and *rob* (estimated from Kenyon & Knott 1953); *Robert* will be recognized at [t] where it is the only remaining candidate compatible with the incoming stimulus. However, if affixed forms are also compared, the cohort will include *robber*, *robins*, *robs*, *robbing*, *robbed*, and *robbery*. In this case, *Robert* will be recognized at [t] where it is distinguished from *robber* and *robbery*. If only base forms are accessed recognition can occur earlier: thus how morphemes are stored influences the recognition process.

The nature of the cohort model can also constrain morphological representation. Tyler and Wessels (1983) present evidence that suggests that only base morphemes are contained in the cohort set used for recognition. They hypothesize that 'words are represented in the mental lexicon as base morphemes with inflectional and derivational markers attached to them' (1983: 418). However, if derived words are accessed via their base morpheme, words in which the affix changes the phonological shape of the base could not be accessed. For example, the suffix *-ity* changes the vowel in *sane* from [e] to [æ] in *sanity*. The word-initial cohort for *sanity* consists of all words beginning with the initial sequence [sæ] (e.g. *sand, salamander*, etc.) The base *sane* is not included and therefore could not be accessed. *Sanity* must have an entry distinct from *sane*. This same problem is present for prefixed forms as well, because the word-initial cohort does not contain the base form, but rather all words beginning with that prefix in addition to words which are monomorphemic but have the same phonological form as the prefix (e.g. *insane* and *interrupt*). The serial nature of the cohort access mechanism requires that prefixed words and words whose morphology changes the phonological form of the base must be stored and accessed independently of their root morpheme.

Taft & Forster (1975), on the other hand, propose a model of the lexicon in which prefixed words do not have separate entries but are accessed by their root. According to this model, prefixed words are recognized in the following manner:

(1) Recognize that a prefix is present and remove it for lexical search.
(2) Search the lexicon for the stem.
(3) When the root is found, recombine it with the prefix to form the word. At this point recognition occurs.

This procedure is based on evidence which indicates that nonwords derived from prefixed words (e.g. *vive* from *revive*) take longer to reject in a lexical decision task than nonwords derived from pseudoprefixed words (e.g. *lish* from *relish*). Taft & Forster (1975) suggest that the stem *vive* is initially found in the lexicon but rejected with post-access checking of the combination of stem and prefix. The nonword *lish* can be rejected immediately since there is no stem *lish* represented in the lexicon. In addition, Taft (1981) found that pseudoprefixed words take longer to recognize than prefixed words, suggesting that they are initially misanalyzed as prefix+stem (but see Henderson, Wallis & Knight 1984).

However, there are some problems with this hypothesis. First, no distinction is made between words whose morphological analysis results in syntactic or semantic information relevant to the interpretation of the word and words whose morphological structure is a historical relic and not psychologically 'real' in any nontrivial sense. For example, Taft (1981) considers *intrigue* and *replica* as prefixed bimorphemic words (*in+trigue* and *re+plica*) which he compares to *indigo* and *regime* which are considered pseudoprefixed monomorphemic words. In this experiment the morphological status of a prefix was determined on the basis of ratings of 'prefixedness' by 10 judges. In another experiment (Taft & Forster 1975) words were considered pseudoprefixed if either they were not listed as prefixed in the Shorter Oxford Dictionary or the prefix did not 'add meaning' to the word. But one may question these methods as a measure for determining the morphemic structure for the mental representation of words. How do children (or adults) learn the correct morphological analysis of these words? One would like to know whether those judges who consider *intrigue* to be bimorphemic have a different internal representation from those judges who considered *intrigue* to be monomorphemic. Different subjects in these experiments might have a different morphological analysis of the words from that assumed by the experimenters. It is therefore difficult to interpret the results.

Secondly, Taft (1979) proposes that suffixed words are also accessed by their root morphemes and undergo the same 'affix stripping' analysis as prefixed words. However, if the lexicon (or in this model the peripheral file, see Forster 1976) contains base forms which are found by stripping off the affixes, what happens when suffixation changes the form of the base? For example, when accessing *destruction, -ion* is stripped off, but what base form is accessed, *destruct* or *destroy*? If *destruct* is accessed, the processor gains no efficacy with morphological decomposition because both *destruct* and *destroy* must be stored. If *destroy* is stored, it is not clear how the processor would compute the base from its derived form *destruction*. It can be argued that the affix stripping process is only economical for derived (and inflected) words in which the form of the base has not been changed.

The cohort model (Marslen-Wilson 1980), the logogen model (Morton 1979), and the Taft (1979) model (based on Forster 1976) all appear to require separate entries for morphologically related words which have phonologically different stems (e.g. *erode, erosion*). This class of words corresponds to Level I morphology in Kiparsky's model of lexical morphology and phonology (Kiparsky 1982). The lexical phonology model was not proposed as a processing model, but the proposed linguistic distinction between Level I and Level II morphology appears to be relevant for processing models. Level II morphology includes affixes which do not trigger any phonological processes that affect the root morpheme – e.g. regular inflections (*-s, -ed, -ing*) and derivations (*-ness, un-*). Level I morphology includes irregular inflectional morphemes (e.g. *t* from *keep → kept*) and derivational morphology which triggers phonological processes such as trisyllabic shortening (e.g. *-ity, -ify*). (For a discussion of level-ordered morphology and lexical phonology see Kiparsky 1982 or Mohanan 1982.)

There are some data that lend support to the hypothesis that words with

Level I morphology have separate entries listed in the lexicon, while words with Level II morphology have a single entry. Kemply and Morton (1982) found that pretraining with words with Level II inflections (*looked*, *looking*) facilitated auditory recognition in noise, but pretraining with words with Level I morphology (*knelt*, *kneeling*) did not. In other words, subjects who heard *looked* in a pretraining session recognized *looking* more easily than if they had not previously heard *looked*. However, *kneeling* was not recognized more easily if preceded by *knelt*. These results cannot simply be explained by low level phonetic priming – that is, *looked* primed *looking* because they are more similar phonetically than *knelt* and *kneeling* – because *cooking* did not prime *looking* and *feeling* did not prime *kneeling*. The saliency of the phonetic structure of the first syllable of the word may however be more important than the overall phonetic similarity, which would account for the priming effect of *looked* on *looking* but no-priming effect of *cooking*. The data are, however, suggestive. Within the logogen model this result is explained by assuming that the logogen for *looked* and *looking* corresponds to the root morpheme *look* and is activated when either *looking* or *looked* is heard – thus previous exposure to either form will facilitate later recognition due to the lowering of the logogen threshold for *look*. Two separate independent logogens exist for *kneeling* and *knelt*. Note that in this model the phonological structure, rather than the syntactic or semantic relationship, determines whether words correspond to one logogen or two. The same syntactic/semantic relationship holds between *kneeling* and *knelt* as between *looking* and *looked*.

Furthermore, Job & Sartori (1984) discuss a dyslexic Italian patient who makes many more errors reading regular verb forms (e.g. *mangio*, *mangiamo* 'I, we eat') than reading irregular forms (*vado*, *andiamo* 'I, we go'). This pattern of errors can be explained if exception forms have separate lexical entries and do not require any morphological analysis to be recognized and produced. Regular verbs are more subject to error because they require morphological decomposition, which appears to be impaired in this patient. The patient also makes fewer errors reading pseudoprefixed words which are stored in the lexicon as a single unit than prefixed words which may require morphological analysis. In addition, Kehayia, Caplan and Piggot (1984) found that agrammatic patients had much more difficulty repeating words affixed with Level II morphology (e.g. *goodness*, *worthless*) than words affixed with Level I morphology (e.g. *national*, *continuity*). Again, this result suggests that words with Level I morphology have separate entries listed in the lexicon and can be read without morphological parsing, whereas words containing Level II morphology ('regular' inflections and derivations) have a single entry and require decomposition, which may be impaired with agrammatism.

It is interesting to note that the patients of Kehayia *et al*. (1984) did not exhibit difficulties repeating prefixed words (*unhappy, recount*), suggesting that prefixed words may have separate entries – a result predicted by the cohort model. Interestingly, the cohort model is proposed for spoken word recognition and the Taft & Forster (1975) model is based on visual word recognition data. It is possible that the morphological representation for prefixes is different in the orthographic and phonological components of the lexicon: this would, of course, require an elaboration of the Fromkin addressing model, should this model prove to be a viable one. Obviously, more research comparing auditory and visual word recognition is needed; at this point, however, there is no *a priori* reason to accept or reject such a hypothesis.

The evidence we have presented thus far has argued that words with Level I morphology are listed separately in the lexicon. Two hypotheses exist for how words with Level II morphology are stored and accessed. One possibility we have already discussed is that these words are stored in the lexicon as base forms and require morphological analysis to be recognized and produced (Taft & Forster 1975; Taft 1979). Another hypothesis is that these words are stored in a decomposed form but do not need to be parsed into affixes and bases to be recognized or produced (Burani, Salmaso & Caramazza, 1984; Caramazza *et al*. 1985).

Caramazza *et al*. (1985) propose the addressed morphology model which contains two access procedures for reading morphologically complex words: a morphological parsing address procedure and a whole word address procedure. These two procedures comprise the lexical address system which is distinct from the orthographic input lexicon. The orthographic input lexicon stores words in a morphologically decomposed form with root morphemes represented independently of affixes, although the root morpheme representations include specifications for permissible affixes. The whole word address procedure operates directly on whole words in a passive, logogen-like activation manner. The activated whole word address specifies a morphologically decomposed root morpheme+affix representation in the orthographic input lexicon. The other process, the morphological parsing procedure, operates in parallel with the whole word procedure and also functions by passive activation. Orthographically 'regular' affixed words (Level II morphology) activate and address the individual morphemes that comprise the word. The parsing procedure is assumed to be more complex and slower than the whole word procedure, but is required to read new morphologically complex words. Known words are processed by activation of a whole word entry in the lexical address system which serves to address a morphologically decomposed orthographic lexicon. The addressed morphology model is given in Figure 3.

Evidence for this model comes from an Italian dyslexic patient who was

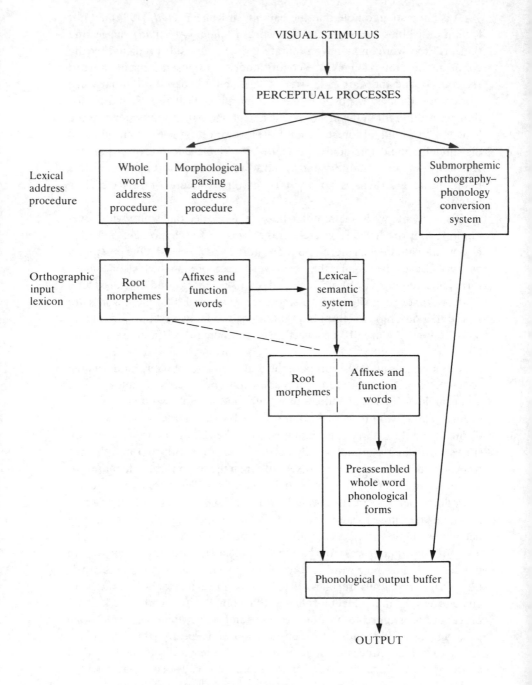

Figure 3. Addressed morphology model (Caramazza *et al*. 1985)

able to read real words and nonwords that could be parsed into a root morpheme plus an illegal suffix (e.g. *chied-iva*: 'to ask' plus an inappropriate suffix *-iva*; an example from English would be *walken*); however, the patient had much more difficulty reading nonwords that could not be parsed this way (e.g. *chiadova*, the English example would be *wolkon*). The patient's performance is explained by hypothesizing that he has an impaired grapheme-to-phoneme conversion system and thus could not read 'non-compositional' nonwords like *chiadova*. However, the morphemic parsing address procedure is still intact, allowing the patient to read 'compositional' nonwords such as *chiediva* by accessing the individual morphemes within the orthographic lexicon. This result cannot be explained by a model which only contained a whole word direct access system since *chiediva* (a nonword due to an illegal combination of root and affix) and *chiadova* (a nonword that does not contain a real root morpheme) must both be processed by a grapheme-to-phoneme conversion process, as neither has a whole word entry. According to such a model both nonword types should be read with an equal number of errors by this patient, and that was not observed.

However, this patient did make more errors reading 'compositional' nonwords (*chiediva*) compared to real words (*chiedeva*). Caramazza *et al.* (1985) hypothesize that these errors are due to an impairment in the assembly procedure for the activated morphological representation. The authors assume that when reading aloud, the output procedure for real words involves the activation of preassembled lexical forms, but reading the 'morphemes' of nonwords involves an assembly process similar to reading any nonword. The nonword does not have a preassembled output form and is signalled in the lexicon as ill-formed by the specifications on the root morpheme. Although the addressed morphology model is very intriguing, the hypotheses are somewhat speculative and much more research is needed before we understand how morphologically complex words are processed.

5.4. **Subcategorization**

Subcategorization information must also be stored in the lexicon, but very little is known about how this information is represented or accessed during speech comprehension and production. For example, we have argued for separate orthographic, phonological, and semantic components within the lexicon – is there a separate component organized by syntactic features or is this information represented within the other components? Speech errors provide evidence that words may be organized by, or at least specified for, their lexical category, since word exchanges almost always occur between words with the same lexical category (Fromkin 1971; Garrett 1980), and words belonging to major grammatical categories exhibit different speech error patterns from words belonging to minor grammatical categories (see section 5.3; Garrett 1980).

The ability to make use of subcategorization information can be impaired with agrammatism: Friederici (1982) showed that agrammatic patients have more difficulty producing subcategorized prepositions (e.g. 'Peter hofft *auf* den Sommer,' 'Peter hopes *for* summer') than non-subcategorized semantically informative prepositions (e.g. 'Peter steht *auf* dem Stuhl,' 'Peter stands *on* the chair'). Interestingly, subcategorization information may be 'available' to these patients as evidenced by their ability to make correct grammaticality judgements for sentences which violate subcategorization restrictions (Linebarger, Schwartz & Saffran 1983). However, more research is required to determine if agrammatic patients have access to subcategorization information but are unable to integrate or utilize it in understanding or producing a sentence. In addition, more research is needed on normal processing to determine when subcategorization information becomes available to a syntactic parser and how it is utilized.

5.5. Semantic representations

Both the logogen model (Morton 1979) and the cohort model (Marslen-Wilson 1980) are 'interactive' models of lexical access in which word recognition is achieved through the interaction of sensory input and contextual (semantic and syntactic) information. In contrast, Forster (1979) and others (Swinney 1979, 1981; Garrett 1978) maintain that lexical access is an autonomous process, operating solely on the basis of sensory information without input from higher order components in the language processing system. In these models context effects occur after lexical access. The nature of the semantic representation stored in the lexicon may differ according to whether an autonomous or interactive access mechanism is adopted. An interactive theory must assume that all information about a word is present in, or at least available to, each entry, since lexical access is argued to be influenced by even minimal semantic cues (Tyler & Wessels 1983).

For example, for the semantic cues in the sentence *The angry crowd threw —— * to be effective in aiding the lexical access of the following word, lexical entries must contain information about whether the entry refers to something that is likely to be thrown by an angry crowd. Interactive models must therefore include a complex inferential system accompanying lexical access in order to explain sentential context effects (Forster 1981). In fact, Marslen-Wilson & Tyler (1980) do suggest that inferential procedures are located with each entry in the lexicon: 'each word would have built into its mental representation not simply a listing of syntactic and semantic properties, but rather sets of procedures for determining which, if any, of the senses of the word were mappable onto the representation of the utterance up to that point' (1980: 31). The logogen model adopts an opposite view in which no semantic information is stored in the lexicon, and all semantic information is represented in a separate cognitive system. Morton & Patterson (1980) state that the cognitive system produces 'the appropriate semantic code from the information transmitted to it by the logogen system' (1980: 91). But what information does the logogen output? Although Morton (1969, 1970) has stated that logogens are defined by their output, the nature of the output is undefined.

Neither the cohort model nor the logogen model appear to make any distinction between lexical semantics and nonlinguistic knowledge. Proponents of an autonomous theory of lexical access have also hypothesized that all meaning-related information about a word is represented in the lexicon (Swinney 1979; Forster 1976), although this assumption is not necessary for an autonomous model, and they do not state what such information includes or how it is represented. A distinction between lexical semantics and other cognitive knowledge is not excluded by this framework. For example, it is possible that lexical meaning is obtained which, in turn, triggers or connects with associated nonlinguistic information stored in other cognitive memory systems.

Again, the modularity of the mind (Fodor 1983) is attested by independent but in some cases interconnecting cognitive systems, both stored and processed separately. A principled distinction between lexical or linguistic semantic knowledge and other cognitive knowledge (e.g. as stored in visual memory, episodic memory etc.) must still be elaborated. That such a distinction exists seems to be unquestionble, as can be seen by the simple example of the difference between knowing the meaning of the word 'water' and knowing that its chemical structure is H_2O. Obviously one can know the first without knowing the second. A modular autonomous lexicon allows such a dissociation, whereas a completely interactive model does not.

Semantic relations between words must also be accounted for in a viable model of the lexicon. Forster (1979) and others have suggested that semantic relations between lexical items are represented by links between words in a network of cross-references. These links are necessary to explain lexical context effects. Meyer and Schvaneveldt (1971) discovered that when a word such as *nurse* is preceded by a semantically related word such as *doctor* lexical decision time (time to decide *nurse* is a word) is faster than when *nurse* is preceded by an unrelated word. One possible mechanism for this result is 'spreading activation' through the links connecting closely associated words, which then facilitates (primes) recognition of the associated words (Collins &

Loftus 1975). Although lexical priming is a context effect, it is entirely internal to the lexicon and thus does not violate the proposed autonomy of the lexicon (Forster 1979).

Speech errors also reveal that words related semantically must be 'net-worked' (see the discussion regarding Figure 2 above, and Volume II, Chapter 7, of this series). The complexities of lexical semantics go beyond the scope of this paper. We simply note that word substitution errors, whether those produced by normals or by aphasics or acquired dyslexics, require that words either be listed in semantic classes, or have close 'addresses,' perhaps on the same 'streets' or in the same 'semantic cities,' or have intricate neural connections the nature of which is now unknown. The following examples reflect this:

(5) Normal speech error word substitutions:
  a. He paid her alimony → he paid her rent
  b. That's a horse of another color → of another race
  c. I better give you a map → . . . a calendar
(6) Deep dyslexic errors (→ = 'read as')
  a. Soccer → football
  b. gnome → pixie
  c. ill → sick
  d. large → big
  e. close → shut
  f. jail → prison

5.6. Summary and conclusions

At the beginning of this chapter we defined the mental lexicon as that component of the grammar in which information about individual words and/ or morphemes is entered, i.e. what a speaker/hearer of a language knows about the form of the entry (its phonology), its structural complexity (its morphology), its meaning (its semantic representation), and its combinatorial properties (its syntactic, categorical properties). We also included its orthographical or spelling representation. This general characterization is not subject to debate. It is obvious that the child or adult learning a language learns vocabulary which permits him/her to produce and comprehend the sentences and utterances of the language and to determine which strings are syntactically and semantically well-formed, an ability which is dependent in some degree on the choice of lexical items. In addition, the speaker can determine which phonological or orthographic strings form single words or morphemes in the language and which are possible but non-occurring nonsense forms. One need not conduct any experiments to conclude that the above information about words must be represented in the lexicon to permit this kind of processing. The questions we have attempted to discuss refer to how such information is represented, and to the structural organization of the lexicon accessed in linguistic performance. While many questions remain unanswered, it is possible to construct a first approximation of a model of the lexicon as follows:

1. Normal and deviant performance data point to a lexicon with independent but interconnected sub-lexicons, each including a specific category of lexical information – at the very least, phonological, semantic and (for literate speakers) orthographic subcomponents. Priming effects and other evidence which indicates the influence of semantic class, orthography, and phonology on each other show that in the normal condition, these subcomponents are networked. In deviant conditions, such as in cases of acquired dyslexia, the connections can be severed.

2. The phonological entries include abstract phonemic representations and may or may not also include systematic phonetic representations. During production, the phonological string, if not already in phonetic representation, must be converted to such and then mapped onto motor commands to produce the physical phonetic output; similarly, in comprehension, the acoustic signal must at some stage be mapped onto phonemic representations which can then be mapped onto their semantic and/or their orthographic representations.

3. The listings in the phonological subcomponent appear to be at least organized by initial segment and syllable (or by serially numbered addresses according to these phonological characteristics). Other organizational structures may also exist, e.g. all monosyllabic, disyllabic words, and/or more frequent words listed together, and/or listings by final segments.

4. To account for one's ability to read and write irregularly spelled words which do not conform to the phonemic–orthographic realization rules, orthographic representations must be listed as well as the regular rules (the latter to account for the ability to read or write new or nonsense forms).

5. Morphologically related words appear to be listed in one entry or in clusters (or again coaddressed); it is not decided as yet whether morphologically complex words are listed by stem followed by affixed forms. Since the complex forms can be decomposed, and since normal and deviant error productions show illegal combinations of occurring bound and free morphemes, individual morphemes must also be entered with morphological rules for their combination, in addition to listing of complex forms. There is evidence supporting the view that words with Level I morphology (which include affixes which trigger phonological changes of the stems) are listed

separately from their stems, distinguishing them from words with Level II morphology (where the root morphemes are not affected by either regular inflection or derivation).

6. Lexical and grammatical morphemes are either marked as such and/or listed in separate parts of the lexicon, as is shown by processing differences. There is support for derived forms being represented in the lexicon, but whether inflected forms are also represented requires further investigation.

7. Subcategorization features of words must be included in the lexicon, but to date there is little evidence to determine whether such information is included as part of the other subcomponent entries or whether there is an additional category component with its own addressing system connecting each entry to its related forms.

8. In the lexical semantic subcomponent, entries are grouped according to semantic class features or postulates, either in the same 'space' or by addresses occurring close together.

9. While the lexicon includes lexical semantic representations, this does not imply inclusion of 'real-world knowledge' – although the lexicon obviously does interact with nonlinguistic information after lexical selection or processing occurs. The fact that cases of agnosia show a dissociation between lexical knowledge and nonlinguistic knowledge suggests that lexical knowledge should be represented separately from nonlinguistic knowledge (Damasio 1985; Newcombe 1985).

The lexicon therefore is a many-splendored and many-faceted thing, highly structured, independent but interdependent in its subcomponents and in its nonlinguistic connections.

REFERENCES

Allport, D. A. & Funnell, E. 1981. Components of the mental lexicon. *Philosophical Transactions of the Royal Society London* B 295: 183–96.
Baker, L. 1974. The lexicon: some psycholinguistic evidence. *UCLA Working Papers in Phonetics* 26.
Beauvois, M. F. & Dérousné, J. 1979. Phonological alexia: three dissociations. *Journal of Neurology, Neurosurgery, and Psychiatry* 42: 1115–24.
Benson, F. 1979. Neurologic correlates of anomia. In H. Whitaker and H. Whitaker (eds.) *Studies in neurolinguistics*, Vol. 4. New York: Academic Press.
Bloomfield, L. 1933. *Language*. New York: Holt.
Browman, C. 1978. Tip of the tongue and slip of the ear: implications for language processing. *UCLA Working Papers in Phonetics* 42.
Brown, R. & McNeill, D. 1966. The tip of the tongue phenomenon. *Journal of Verbal Learning and Verbal Behavior* 5: 325–37.
Buckingham, H. W. 1981. Where do neologisms come from? In J. Brown (ed.) *Jargonaphasia*. New York: Academic Press.
Burani, C., Salmaso, D., & Caramazza, A. 1984. Morphological structure and lexical access. *Visible Language* 4: 348–58.

Caramazza, A., Miceli, G., Silveri, C. & Laudanna, A. 1985. Reading mechanisms and the organization of the lexicon: evidence from acquired dyslexia. *Cognitive Neuropsychology* 2.1: 81–114.

Chomsky, N. & Halle, M. 1968. *The sound pattern of English*. New York: Harper and Row.

Collins, A. M., & Loftus, E. F. 1975. A spreading-activation theory of semantic processing. *Psychological Review* 82: 407–28.

Coltheart, M., Patterson, K. & Marshall, J. 1980. *Deep dyslexia*. London: Routledge & Kegan Paul.

Cutler, A. & Fay, D. 1982. One mental lexicon, phonologically arranged: comments on Hurford's comments. *Linguistic Inquiry* 13: 107–13.

Culter, A., Hawkins, J., & Gilligan, G. 1985. The suffixing preference: a processing explanation. *Linguistics* 2.3: 723–58.

Damasio, A. 1985. Prosopagnosia. *Trends in Neuroscience* 8: 132–5.

Donnenworth-Nolan, S., Tanenhaus, M. & Seidenberg, M. 1981. Multiple code activation in word recognition: evidence from rhyme monitoring. *Journal of Experimental Psychology* 7.3: 170–80.

Fodor, J. 1983. *Modularity of mind*. Cambridge, MA: MIT Press.

Forster, K. 1976. Accessing the mental lexicon. In R. J. Wales & E. Walker (eds.) *New approaches to language mechanisms*. Amsterdam: North–Holland.

Forster, K. 1979. Levels of processing and the structure of the language processor. In W. Cooper & E. Walker (eds.) *Sentence processing: psycholinguistic studies presented to Merrill Garrett*. New Jersey: LEA.

Forster, K. 1981. Priming and the effects of sentence and lexical contests on naming time: evidence for autonomous lexical processing. *Quarterly Journal of Experimental Psychology* 33a: 465–95.

Friederici, A. 1982. Syntactic and semantic processes in aphasic deficits: the availability of prepositions. *Brain and Language* 18: 249–58.

Fromkin, V. 1971. The non-anomalous nature of anomalous utterances. *Language* 47: 27–52.

Fromkin, V. 1973. *Speech errors as linguistic evidence*. The Hague: Mouton.

Fromkin, V. 1977. Putting the empHasis on the wrong sylLaBle. In L. M. Hyman (ed.) *Studies in stress and accent*. Los Angeles: University of Southern California Press.

Fromkin, V. 1980. *Errors in linguistic performance: slips of the tongue, ear, pen, and hand*. London: Academic Press.

Fromkin, V. 1985. Evidence in linguistics. In R. H. Robbins & V. A. Fromkin (eds.) *Linguistics and linguistic evidence*. Newcastle upon Tyne: Grevatt & Grevatt.

Garrett, M. 1978. Word and sentence perception. In R. Held, H. W. Liebowitz & H. L. Teuber (eds.) *Handbook of sensory physiology*, Vol. 8: *Perception*. Berlin: Springer-Verlag.

Garrett, M. 1980. Levels of processing in sentence production. In B. Butterworth (ed.) *Language production*, Vol. 1. New York: Academic Press.

Halle, M. 1985. Speculations about the representation of words in memory. In V. A. Fromkin (ed.) *Phonetic linguistics*. New York: Academic Press.

Henderson, L., Wallis, J., & Knight, D. 1984. Morphemic structure and lexical access. In H. Bouma & D. Bouwhuis (eds.) *Attention and performance*, Vol. 10: *Control of language processes*. New Jersey: LEA.

Humphreys, G., Evett, L. & Taylor, D. 1982. Automatic phonological priming in visual word recognition. *Memory and Cognition* 10.6: 576–90.

Jackson, A. & Morton, J. 1984. Facilitation of auditory word recognition. *Memory and Cognition* 12.6: 568–74.

Job, R. & Sartori, G. 1984. Morphological decomposition: evidence from crossed phonological dyslexia. *The Quarterly Journal of Experimental Psychology* 36a: 435–58.

Kehayia, E., Caplan, D., & Piggot, G. L. 1984. On the repetition of affixes by agrammatic aphasics. *McGill Working Papers in Linguistics* 1.2: 147–56.

Kemply, S. T. & Morton, J. 1982. The effects of priming with regularly and irregularly related words in auditory word recognition. *British Journal of Psychology* 73: 441–54.

Kenyon, J. S. & Knott, T. 1953. *A pronouncing dictionary of American English*. Springfield: G. & C. Merriam Co.

Kiparsky, P. 1982. From cyclic phonology to lexical phonology. In H. van der Hulst & N. Smith (eds.) *The structure of phonological representations*. Dordrecht: Foris.

Ladefoged, P. 1980. What are linguistic sounds? *Language* 56: 485–502.
Linebarger, M., Schwartz, M. & Saffran, E. 1983. Sensitivity to grammatical structure in so-called agrammatic aphasics. *Cognition* 13: 361–92.
McCusker, L. X., Hillinger, M. L., & Bias, R. G. 1981. Phonological recoding and reading. *Psychological Bulletin* 89.2: 217–45.
Marshall, J. & Newcombe, F. 1966. Syntactic and semantic errors in paralexia. *Neuropsychologia* 4: 169–76.
Marshall, J. & Newcombe, F. 1973. Patterns of paralexia. *Journal of Psycholinguistic Research* 2: 175–99.
Marslen-Wilson, W. 1980. Speech understanding as a psychological process. In J. C. Simon (ed.) *Spoken language generation and understanding*. Boston: Reidel.
Marslen-Wilson, W. & Tyler, L. 1980. The temporal structure of spoken language understanding. *Cognition* 18: 1–71.
Marslen-Wilson, W. & Tyler, L. 1981. Central processes in speech understanding. *Philosophical Transactions of the Royal Society London* B295: 317–32.
Marslen-Wilson, W. & Welsh, A. 1978. Processing interactions and lexical access during word recognition in continuous speech. *Cognitive Psychology* 10: 29–63.
Meyer, D. and Schvaneveldt, R. 1971. Facilitation in recognizing pairs of words: evidence of a dependence between retrieval operations. *Journal of Experimental Psychology* 90.2: 227–34.
Mohanan, K. 1982. Lexical phonology. Doctoral dissertation, MIT.
Morton, J. 1969. Interaction of information in word recognition. *Psychology Review* 76: 165–78.
Morton, J. 1970. A functional model of memory. In D. A. Norman (ed.) *Models of human memory*. New York: Academic Press.
Morton, J. 1979. Facilitation in word recognition: experiments causing change in the logogen model. In P. A. Kolers, M. Wrolstad & H. Bouma (eds.) *Processing of visible language*, Vol. 1. New York: Plenum.
Morton, J. 1982. Disintegrating the lexicon: an information processing approach. In J. Mehler, E. Walker & M. Garrett (eds.) *Perspectives on mental representation*. New Jersey: LEA.
Morton, J. & Patterson, K. 1980. A new attempt at an interpretation, or, an attempt at a new interpretation. In Coltheart, Patterson & Marshall 1980.
Newcombe, F. 1985. Neuropsychology of consciousness: human clinical evidence. In D. A. Oakley (ed.) *Brain and mind*. London: Methuen.
Newcombe, F. & Marshall, J. 1985. Sound-by-sound reading and writing. In M. Coltheart, K. Patterson & J. Marshall (eds.) *Surface dyslexia*. London: Erlbaum.
Patterson, K. 1982. The relation between reading and phonological coding: further neuropsychological observations. In A. Ellis (ed.) *Normality and pathology in cognitive functions*. London: Academic Press.
Saffran, E. & Marin, O. 1977. Reading without phonology: evidence from aphasia. *Quarterly Journal of Experimental Psychology* 29: 515–25.
Schwartz, M., Marin, O. & Saffran, E. 1979. Dissociations of language function in dementia: a case study. *Brain and Language* 7: 277–306.
Seidenberg, M. 1985. Constraining models of word recognition. *Cognition* 20: 169–90.
Seidenberg, M. & Tanenhaus, M. 1979. Orthographic effects on rhyme monitoring. *Journal of Experimental Psychology: Human Learning and Memory* 5: 546–54.
Shallice, T. & Warrington, E. 1975. Word recognition in a phonemic dyslexic patient. *Quarterly Journal of Experimental Psychology* 27: 187–99.
Sherzer, J. 1970. Talking backward in Cuna: the sociological reality of phonological descriptions. *Journal of Anthropology* 26: 343–53.
Swinney, D. 1979. Lexical access during sentence comprehension: (re)consideration of context effects. *Journal of Verbal Learning and Verbal Behavior* 18: 645–59.
Swinney, D. 1981. Lexical processing during sentence comprehension: effects of higher order constraints and implications for representation. In T. F. Myers, J. Laver & J. Anderson (eds.) *The cognitive representation of Speech*. Amsterdam/North–Holland.
Taft, M. 1979. Recognition of affixed words and the word frequency effect. *Memory and Cognition* 7.4: 263–72.

Taft, M. 1981. Prefix stripping revisited. *Journal of Verbal Learning and Verbal Behavior* 20: 289–97.

Taft, M. & Forster, K. 1975. Lexical storage and retrieval of prefixed words. *Journal of Verbal Learning and Verbal Behavior* 14: 635–47.

Tyler, L. & Wessels, J. 1983. Quantifying contextual contributions to word-recognition processes. *Perception and Psychophysics* 34.5: 409–20.

6 Where learning begins: initial representations for language learning*

Lila R. Gleitman, Henry Gleitman, Barbara Landau and Eric Wanner

6.0 Introduction

Linguists and psychologists in impressively large numbers have devoted their professional energies to the topic of language learning. This is no surprise. As Bloomfield (1933) put it, 'Language learning is doubtless the greatest intellectual feat any one of us is ever required to perform' (1933: 29). Study of languages and their learning in the years that have intervened since Bloomfield's work have given no cause to diminish our sense of awe that virtually all little children all over the world successfully accomplish this feat. Recently, however, perspectives on just what is learned and how it is learned have changed considerably.

In the view of the structuralist linguists (and many present-day psychologists), acquiring language is a matter of identifying from scratch a linguistic system that might be almost anything at all. Borrowing Bloomfield's words again, 'Features which we think ought to be universal may be absent from the very next language that becomes accessible' (1933: 20), and hence 'The only useful generalizations about language are inductive generalizations' (1933: 29). This view suggests that at bottom learning a language may be no different from other learning feats – for instance, learning to swing a tennis racquet or to recite the Pledge of Allegiance. It is only the sheer size and scope of the problem that elevates language learning to the status of 'greatest' learning feat.

Accepting this perspective, one finding from the language learning literature is perhaps the most startling: deaf youngsters, isolated both from a sign language (because their hearing parents did not know one) and from a spoken language (because they were deaf), invent a rudimentary gesture system that shares many formal and substantive properties with the language of their hearing contemporaries who have been exposed to English (Feldman, Goldin-Meadow & Gleitman 1978; Goldin-Meadow & Feldman

* Section 6.2 of this chapter ('Sound units from speech information') is in part a review and updating of Gleitman & Wanner 1982. We thank the National Foundation, March of Dimes for a grant which supported this work.

150

1979). This language invention seems a more strenuous task than 'merely' acquiring a received language if, as the structuralists seem to assert, a language can be almost anything at all.

However, many recent findings about language learning, as well as comparative studies of the languages of the world (and the linguistic theorizing that they support; see Chomsky 1975, 1980, 1981), suggest that there may be a Universal Grammar after all, that only certain categories and functions can appear in a natural language, and hence that the child need choose only among these biologically prescribed categories and functions in order to learn. The task of inductive learning may be reduced considerably once constrained by this bioprogram.

Let us return to the isolated deaf children from this new perspective. Now it appears that learning a received language is a more difficult task than the deaf children's task in inventing one. Both these tasks are simplified to the same degree, in so far as both learner and inventor are reined in by Universal Grammar. But the inventor of a new language need literally 'learn' little more; he is free, at least up to a point, to choose instances for the categories and functions set by the bioprogram. The child who must learn English or Spanish or Urdu has an additional task: to discover the (partly arbitrary) instantiations of these categories and functions in the exposure language.[1]

The scope of this learning problem – the discovery problem that remains, within the constraints imposed by the bioprogram – is an open empirical question. The task may be a very difficult one (after all, it takes fully five years to learn a language) or a relatively simple one (after all, a language is learned in five short years). But difficult or simple, the discovery procedure for category instances requires stating if there is to be a theory of language learning which explains why the children in France learn French while the children in Greece learn Greek.

In this paper, we focus primarily on a single aspect of the discovery procedure: the machinery that enables the child to detect language-relevant units in the sound stream and in extralinguistic experience, and to represent these appropriately. It is these units (and sequences of them) that constitute what Chomsky (1965) has called 'primary linguistic data,' the base on which learning procedures must operate to acquire the exposure language. As Chomsky has recently put this issue: 'We have to assume that there are some prelinguistic notions which can pick out pieces of the world, say elements of this meaning and of this sound' (1982: 119).

---

[1] We do not mean to underestimate the achievements of the isolated deaf children. They manage to make their invented gesturing transparent to a watcher by selecting iconic items to represent the meaningful words, e.g. downward fluttering fingers to represent 'snow.' The capacities that allow them to do so seem quite exotic. (See the next section of this paper, where we raise – but do not resolve – some issues pertinent to explaining these capacities.)

6.1. **The category discovery problem**

The child's task in learning a language is to pair the (indefinitely many) sounds to the (indefinitely many) meanings. The primary data must be samples of the sounds together with samples of the meanings. But how are the appropriate sound elements and meaning elements to be detected in the world and classified, so as to constitute a representational basis for learning? If the child is free to choose among such potential elements, surely we must expect variability in the rate and character of what is learned. For example, the child who happens to represent certain heard sounds as /r/+/æbit/ and cooccurring meaningful scenes as 'undetached-rabbit-part-scenes' ought to learn English more slowly than the child who represents the sound heard as /ræbit/ and the observed scene as 'a rabbit scene.' Since that variability in learning rate is hardly observed, it must be that there are (biologically or environmentally inevitable) constraints on which such elements the learners construct, given real input.

6.2. **Sound units from speech information**

Our first question is how learners pick out 'pieces of the acoustic–linguistic world' from the sound stream, how they detect and represent the sound. Notoriously, the phones, words, phrases, and sentences of everyday speech run together so complexly that their proper segmentation would appear to be very difficult to accomplish. As one example of the misanalyses that do occur in the course of learning, the 6-year-old child of one of us rendered (in writing) a teacher's command as 'Class be smissed!' How does the learner finally come up with whole words (and phrases, etc.), rather than halves of words or words-and-a-half?

One might guess that caretakers initially present category instances in isolation to improve the infant's chances of detecting them. But, at least in linguistic communities that have been studied carefully, this is not so: maternal speech even to neonates is connected and intonationally natural. Moreover, it is to this connected speech that the infants are naturally responsive. Infants only one month of age will suck more on a nonnutritive nipple for the privilege of hearing intonationally natural connected speech than for hearing speech without these intonational properties (i.e. read essentially as a word list; Mehler *et al.* 1978).

While speech to infants and young children is connected in much the way adult-to-adult speech is, typically it is different from ordinary speech in many other characteristics. Darwin (1877) called this caretaker speech register 'the sweet music of the species,' but language learning investigators more prosaically call it 'motherese.' The motherese utterances are especially short and slow; they contain exaggerated pitch excursions; and pauses occur more reliably at phrase and clause boundaries than they do in speech among adults (Fernald & Simon 1984). Such physical grouping cues have been found to have dramatic effects on learning, at least for adults in the artificial–language learning laboratory.[2] Fernald (in press) showed that 4-month-old infants are more responsive to this special style of speech than to experts' talk, even when the input is just disembodied speech emanating from a loudspeaker, and is the speech of an adult not known to the infant listener: the infants reliably look longer at the loudspeaker when the motherese version is playing.

We can conclude that there is a natural coadaptation at work here, in which the mothers are inclined to provide a particular data base and the babies are inclined to attend particularly to just this. It would be too strong, however, to suppose that motherese input is a requirement for language learning. Its role could be chiefly affective, as Fernald has pointed out. And there exist cultures whose child-rearing practices have the effect of reducing the opportunity to hear this speech style (Schieffelin 1979), not to mention neglected or abused children in American homes. So far as we know these individuals learn to talk all the same.

Most centrally, the maternal input can be useful only to the extent that the learner is prepared by nature to seize upon all and only its linguistically relevant properties. For example, the learner who focusses on detectable – and probably salient – acoustic properties such as the distinction between the absolute pitches of his mother's and father's speech (rather than the relative pitches of a single speaker's speech) is taking a correct step in socialization but a false step in learning a language (see Kuhl 1983 for evidence that infants can avoid this error). So the question of category learning remains to be explained even after it is acknowledged that most children solve the problem in the presence of 'the best possible' input data base.[3]

---

[2] Specifically, Morgan & Newport (1981) and Morgan, Meier & Newport (in press) have shown that adults will induce a phrase-structure description for a miniature language presented without interpretive cues, but only if structural cues to the phrase boundaries are supplied. In their situation, physical cues to phrase groupings such as intonation contour (when sentences were presented orally) or physical closeness of within-phrase items (when sentences were presented visually) were necessary and sufficient for induction of the phrase structures. Infants are surely better language learners than adults; the corpora to which they are exposed are neither miniature nor artificial; and their learning procedures may be different in part from those of adults. Still, these laboratory results indirectly suggest that physical cues to phrase boundaries may be required in the acquisition process. Motherese is probably the ideal data base in this respect at least.

[3] We have remarked that the motherese register is neither necessary nor (in the end) explanatory of language learning. Even so, there is likely to be some surprise that we consider this data base at all, acknowledging that it may play some facilitative role in the normal case. The surprise may arise because we have been identified with a position that casts doubt, in the realm of syntax acquisition, on the usefulness of this special style (see e.g. Newport, Gleitman & Gleitman 1977). What we argued there was that the syntactic forms of motherese are not 'simple' in a way that would support learning. Moreover, our evidence suggested that motherese not only could not, but did not, explain the

We now discuss what is known of the child's preliminary analysis of the wave form. We will conclude that learners are sensitive to physical properties of the speech stream sufficient to provide a rudimentary phrase structure description of heard utterances. Thus if we are correct in our reading of the evidence, bracketed (and partly labeled) clausal representations are available at the initial stage of language learning, and serve as the primary linguistic data which are to be paired with meanings.

6.2.1. Phonetic segments

Infants can and do perform an initial segmentation of the wave form, to derive phonetic segments. For example 2-month-old infants who hear the sound /ba/ contingent on their sucking at a nonnutritive nipple will increase their sucking rate, evidently for the mere pleasure of hearing /ba/ more often. But eventually the infants habituate to this stimulus (their sucking rate decreases). The infants readily dishabituate (suck faster again) if the signal is switched to /pa/ (Eimas *et al.* 1971). And Japanese babies will habituate to /ra/ and then dishabituate to /la/ despite the fact that their Japanese parents recognize only a single liquid consonant (Eimas 1975).

In further detail, these studies have shown that a variety of phonetic distinctions are perceived categorically. That is, within a continuum of physical variation on some dimension, e.g. voice-onset time, the infants show sharp discrimination of variations that can cross phonemic boundaries in human languages; but they show poor discrimination for variations of the same physical magnitude that are always within phonemic boundaries. Thus no learning apparatus appears to be required for an initial segmentation of the acoustic wave into discrete phones. The segmentation has been provided in the nervous system. At this level, then, an objective, highly instrumented sequence of empirical investigations shows that language learners have relevant information in advance about the inventory of possible phonetic elements – they are biologically prepared to pick out useful

---

acquisition of syntax in ways claimed by many other investigators (e.g. Snow 1977; Furrow, Nelson & Benedict 1979). In our studies, rate of learning was not correlated with the extent to which mothers really talked motherese. What we never claimed was that the speech of the mother has no effect on the child's learning. That would be the bizarre idea that some mothers could speak English and, even so, their children might learn French. In the special domain being discussed in the text, we have presented some evidence that motherese may be especially clear in presenting physical cues to linguistic formatives such as the word and the phrase. This acoustic–perceptual property of motherese was in fact correlated with growth rates in the Newport *et al.* studies: closed class items were learned faster if the mother presented them in stressed linguistic environments. But we repeat that, even in this more limited domain, there is no evidence that motherese is absolutely required for learning to take place. What is required are cues to structure in the wave form. These cues are exaggerated in motherese but do appear, albeit in a somewhat murkier form, in expert-to-expert speech. We are interested in asking how the formative-discovery procedure can work, whichever of these data bases the child receives.

haas@linc.

'pieces of the acoustic world' for the sake of language learning. (For a review of this literature, see Jusczyk 1986).[4]

6.2.2. The unit 'word'

The phonetic elements could not exhaust the child's inventory of acoustic–linguistic primitives, for phonetic sequences woefully underdetermine the identification of words (is it *an adult* or *a nuhdult*?), word classes (is *yellow* a noun, verb, or adjective?) and phrases (e.g. *I saw a man eating fish*). The question, then, is whether there are units above and beyond the phonetic distinctive features, physically manifest in the wave form and operative in the child's induction of language structure. We discuss here one such perceptual category that the learner appears to use in extracting the unit *word*: the stressed syllable. (This cannot be the only physical cue usable or used, because stress varies in informativeness over the languages of the world. The position is that there is a small number of physical cues to which the child is specially attentive in the search for the word inside the heard utterance. We concentrate attention on stress because it appears to play a major role in the languages whose acquisition has been studied extensively.)

Suppose for now (we will return to this point) that learners are predisposed to identify a conceptual unit *word*. Slobin (1973) suggested, based on cross-linguistic acquisitional evidence, that they are disposed to identify this unit with particular physical aspects of the wave form, to believe that each wordlike conceptual unit has an 'acoustically salient' and 'isolable' surface expression. Accepting Slobin's perspective, Gleitman & Wanner (1982) proposed that the stressed syllable is this isolable physical unit which learners first identify as the linguistic repository of the word. A first supportive piece of evidence is that, in languages like English, words are first pronounced as their stressed syllables, e.g. 'raff' for *giraffe* and 'e-fant' for *elephant*. Moreover, when the unstressed syllables begin to be uttered, it is often in undifferentiated form (as the syllable schwa for all instances), for example 'əportcard' (*reportcard*). That is, the unstressed syllables are at first not analyzed as fully as the stressed syllables.

Identification of a stressed syllable is a useful heuristic for locating the word formative in the sound stream, but gives no sure cue to where that item begins or ends. The physical cues to word juncture are as likely to be found on unstressed syllables as on stressed ones. So if children are inattentive to unstressed syllables and the subtle junctural information they may contain, they should exhibit some confusion between unstressed word items

[4] Some other animals, including macaques and chinchillas, have been shown to make the same acoustic discriminations (see Kuhl & Miller 1975). This does not migitate the usefulness of these discriminations for human language learners. It only suggests that there must be some other reason why macaques don't acquire English.

and the unstressed syllables of polysyllabic words. Young learners do seem to have this difficulty. Frequently they misanalyze clitic pronouns as the unstressed syllables of preceding words, e.g., 'read-it' and 'have-it,' yielding such utterances as 'Readit ə book' and 'Havit ə cookie.' Getting the unstressed syllables properly bound into the words is a late and lengthy task. As one example, the child mentioned earlier who at 2 years of age said 'əportcard' and 'tape-əcorder,' at 4 years of age asked "Can we go to grandma's repartment house today?" Often, false segmentations are found in much older children (e.g. 'Class be smissed'). Sometimes the problems are intractable for listeners and so the language itself changes (witness such locutions as *a whole nother story* and *spitt'n image* as the modern variant of *the spirit and the image*). Of course this does not mean that there are no physical cues to word segmentation in English (see Nakatani & Dukes 1977; Nakatani & Schaffer 1978). But these cues are subtle and rather unreliable; moreover, by necessity these cues sometimes appear on the relatively disfavored unstressed syllables.

Later stages of speech development lend further weight to the claim that the word and the stressed syllable are perceived by the learner as roughly coextensive. Bellugi (1967) demonstrated that when the elements of the English verb auxiliary make their first appearance in children's speech, the items are in their full (whole syllable), rather than their contracted (subsyllabic), form, e.g. 'I will go' rather than 'I'll go.' This is in contrast to the input corpus in which these items were contracted in over 90% of instances. Evidently, the contracted version of these words fails to be the acoustically salient element the child requires as the sound-stream reflex of *word*, if we take *stressed syllable* to be the appropriate specification of salience.

Further evidence comes from investigations of input effects on learning. Newport, Gleitman & Gleitman (1977) provided correlational evidence that the rate of learning for English verbal auxiliary elements is accelerated in children whose mothers used them proportionally most often in the noncontractable, stressed, sentence-initial position (by asking many yes/no questions, e.g. 'Will you pick up the blocks?'). This result is very reliable, accounting for about 80% of the variance in acquisition rate (see Furrow, Nelson & Benedict 1979, and Landau & Gleitman 1985 for replications of this result). In contrast, the sheer frequency of auxiliary use (ignoring stress and position) is uncorrelated with learning rate. It is reasonable to hypothesize either that initial position favors learning (a prediction that would follow from any theory of learning in which memory is a factor) or that the noncontracted, stressed form favors learning. It is likely that both these properties are relevant to the observed learning effects.

Other properties of children's speech support the stressed-syllable proposal. One of the most striking facts about English speakers' first utterances

is that the functor words are almost entirely absent; hence the speech sounds 'telegraphic' (Brown & Bellugi 1964). To this extent, the child's early linguistic behavior deviates systematically from the environmental model. It is particularly interesting that youngsters learning Russian omit the inflectional affixes that are the main device for marking the thematic roles in that language, adopting instead a word-order strategy that has poor support in the input data (i.e. the speech of their Russian mothers; see Slobin 1966).

The findings just reviewed, taken together, begin to suggest that the child is disposed to select items for early learning based on their acoustic–prosodic properties. Whether the late production of closed class items is, as we have so far suggested, at bottom a perceptual effect is a question to which we will return presently. But first it is necessary to solidify the claim that the learning effects just described are facts attributable to the phonetic substance of the closed class materials. After all, other explanations seem possible. This is because the so-called functors have special semantic and syntactic functions, as well as special prosodic properties. Further evidence suggests that it is the prosodic rather than the semantic–syntactic functions of the closed class that account for the children's early choices.

Consider again Slobin's finding for Russian children. It is impossible to suppose that the functors are omitted from their speech on the grounds that they encode semantically unimportant matters. Surely it is communicatively urgent to distinguish between the do-er and the done-to and, as just stated, the youngest Russian learners do make this semantic distinction, but by means of word ordering, not inflections. No more is it likely that the omission of the functors represents an initial syntactic bias in the child, namely, a bias toward word ordering and against the alternative inflectional marking of thematic roles: Slobin (1982) has shown that Turkish children acquire Turkish inflections very early in life, rather than (like Russian children) passing through an inflectionless word-order stage. The remaining hypothesis is that prosodic–phonological (ultimately, physical) properties of the the functors are what makes them hard to learn: it is their unstressed and subsyllabic character that is hard for the children to detect.[5]

The most striking evidence comes from investigations by Slobin (1982),

---

[5] Another possibility has been suggested by Hyams (1987.) This is that the varying learning rates are attributable to a morphological distinction among these languages. If the bare verb stem can be a whole word, the inflections are first omitted; if the bare stem does not constitute a whole word at all in the exposure language, the words appear with inflections from the beginning. This is a very appealing hypothesis, but unfortunately it does not accord closely enough to the cross-linguistic acquisitional evidence to constitute the whole story. Moreover, Hyams's principle has to be amplified in terms of the stress/nonstress distinction, for even in the languages in which unstressed inflections appear early, they are often at first not differentiated – a single inflected form may be uttered by the child regardless of case, etc., distinctions that underlie the choices among the inflectional morphemes in the exposure language. But Hyams's idea is so plausible that we suspect it may be one factor that will figure in the final explanation of these phenomena.

concerning comprehension among 2- to 4-year-old English, Italian, Serbo-Croatian, and Turkish learners. The Turkish children comprehended Turkish inflectional cues to thematic roles earlier in life than Serbo-Croatian learners comprehended Serbo-Croatian inflectional cues to thematic roles. According to Slobin, the relevant inflectional items in Turkish (though not all Turkish inflectional items) are a full syllable long, are stressed, do not deform the surrounding words phonetically, and do not cliticize. Thus these items are *open class*, not *closed class*, under phonological definitions of this partitioning of the morphological stock (e.g. Kean 1979). The late-comprehended Serbo-Croatian inflectional items are subsyllabic, stressless, and phonetically deformed by adjacent material (phonologically closed class). In sum, these two languages differ according to whether the inflectional cues to the thematic roles are encoded onto isolable stressed syllables. This distinction predicts the differences in learning rate.

In the other two languages investigated by Slobin, English and Italian, the thematic roles are cued primarily by word order, not inflection. Thus, as with Turkish, they do not require the young learner to analyze unstressed grammatical items in order to recover the relational roles. Accordingly, there are no main-effect differences in the rate of the relevant comprehension development between Turkish and these other two languages. Only Serbo-Croatian stands apart, showing a clear delay at each point in development.

Gleitman & Wanner's (1982) reading of this evidence was that a single principle, the advantage of stressed material over unstressed material, accounts for Slobin's main finding. Intriguing new evidence from the acquisition of Quiché Mayan (Pye 1983) is particularly informative in this regard, for in relevant cases Mayan – unlike the other languages just discussed – usually does not confound inflection (and, hence, semantic saliency) with stress. For many verbs in certain syntactic environments, this language stresses inflectional suffixes, while the verb root is unstressed. According to Pye, young learners often pronounce only one of these two syllables; that is, they are forced to make the choice between the semantically salient root and the perceptually salient suffix. They very consistently choose perceptual saliency, pronouncing the inflection and omitting the root. In fact, morpheme boundary and syllable boundary often do not coincide, providing a good testing ground for what it is that children are actually picking up and reproducing of the verb that they hear. According to Pye, the Mayan children reproduce the syllable unit rather than the morpheme unit: they pronounce the whole syllable consisting of the final consonant of the unstressed verb root and the whole terminus, the inflectional suffix.

Summarizing, the cross-linguistic evidence supports the idea that the stressed syllable is highly salient perceptually. Materials encoded on to stressed syllables thus appear in speech early. Stressed verb roots are pronounced early (English, Serbo-Croatian, Turkish, Italian) and unstressed verb roots are often omitted (Mayan). Symmetrically, stressed inflections are pronounced early (Turkish, Mayan) and the unstressed ones are often omitted (English, Serbo-Croatian). In so far as attention to unstressed materials is crucial to recovering the argument structure of utterances, the child will show some comprehension delay (Serbo-Croatian). In so far as the pronunciation of roots is obviously necessary to the adult's comprehension of the child's messages, children's speech in those languages that contain unstressed roots will be hard to understand (Mayan, as noted by Pye).

So far we have regarded the child's early failure to produce and comprehend unstressed items reliably as a perceptual effect, attributable to the lesser saliency of these items as acoustic events. But the facts are really more complex than this. It is unlikely that the unstressed materials are wholly opaque even to the youngest learners – that they do not 'hear' them at all. The low-stressed material is roughly detected from the beginning, but evidently is harder to analyze in detail so as to distinguish one closed class item from the next, and to set word boundaries. As one supportive finding, recall Mehler *et al.*'s demonstration that infants prefer intonationally connected speech to speech which consists of words read as a list. The connected speech contains high- and low-stressed items, of course, and it may well be that their alternation in the sound stream is one of the naturalness factors that the infants pick up. A related effect was found for children between 18 and 30 months by Shipley, Smith & Gleitman (1969). They showed that telegraphic speakers who had never uttered closed class items recognized as odd (refused to respond to) speech from their mothers that excluded the closed class, i.e. they obeyed the command to 'Bring me the book!' more often than they obeyed 'Bring book.' Katz, Baker & MacNamara (1974) showed that 17-month-old children used the presence or absence of determiners as a clue to whether new words were proper nouns (and thus name a particular individual) or common nouns (and thus name some class).[6] Clearly, these children must have detected low-stress segments in the input speech. Moreover, after first words (e.g. 'raff' as the rendition for *giraffe*) children do reproduce the unstressed syllables in the speech they hear, e.g. 'əportcard'; what is missing from speech are the phonetic distinctions among the various unstressed syllables.

The best guess from this fragmentary evidence is that the distinction stress/nonstress provides the learner with a first evidentiary source for parti-

---

[6] This last demonstration, while it shows that the children noted the presence or absence of an unstressed item before the noun (and its semantic implication), does not demonstrate that they were sensitive to the phonetic detail of closed class items. The same holds for the Shipley *et al.* procedure.

tioning the morphological stock in a linguistically relevant way. This partitioning (ultimately, the open/closed class distinction) is observable throughout the acquisition sequence, with the unstressed subcomponent acquired in a late and quasi-independent series of steps (Brown 1973). Moreover, chronologically late learning of a first language as well as features of second language learning show effects of this same distinction, with the unstressed material being forever the last and hardest for older émigrés to acquire (Johnson & Newport 1986; Morgan, Meier & Newport in press). The same or a related distinction also helps to explain properties in other domains of language organization and use, including creolization (Sankoff & LaBerge 1973), speech production (Garrett 1975) and perception (Wanner & Maratsos 1978), language forgetting (Dorian 1978), 'metalinguistic' task performance (Gleitman & Gleitman 1979) including reading acquisition (Rozin & Gleitman 1977), and pathological language dissolution (Kean 1979). Finally, the very basis for the terms *open* and *closed* class is their differential susceptibility to change over time in the life of languages.

The unstressed items are quite well differentiated sometime during the third year of life. At this stage, there may still be production difficulties with the unstressed items over and above any residual perceptual effects. Gerken, Landau & Remez (forthcoming) presented sentences (some produced by real speakers, others synthesized speech signals, so as to control the stress properties) to 2-year-olds to repeat. Some of the sentences were all-English, others contained all-English closed class words but nonsense open class words, some contained all-English open class words but nonsense closed class words, and some were all nonsense. There was an effect on repetition performance, across these conditions, of stress itself: both nonsense and real closed class items were harder to repeat than the stressed real and nonsense items. (See also Blasdell & Jensen 1970 for a related finding.) This may suggest that there is still some perceptual problem with these items. But the overwhelming difficulty was with the real closed class items; nonsense unstressed items made comparatively less trouble. This can only be accounted for by acknowledging that the low-stress items were perceived – and were linguistically analyzed whenever they were real English items. This means that there is something about the syntax and/or semantics of the English closed class that makes trouble even after the problem of perceiving and analyzing them is close to solved.

Summarizing, the physical realization of language categories in the sound stream affects the course of language discovery by the child. The perceptual saliency of stress is one property that supports the early discovery of the (open class) word unit and delays the extraction of distinctions among the low-stress (closed class) elements. The initial partitioning of the input according to the stress distinction is useful for learning because it is well correlated with the morphosyntactic distinctions that must eventually be made between open class and closed class subcomponents of the lexical stock. The effects of this distinction are observable in many aspects of language performance, throughout life. Nonetheless, a cautionary note in the interpretation of the learning effects is struck by recent findings, such as Gerken, Landau & Remez's (forthcoming). Some effects that were initially assigned to perception (and hence would operate to limit the child's effective input) turn out to be output effects when studied in more detail.

6.2.3. **The unit 'phrase'**

If Gleitman & Wanner are correct in their interpretation of the child evidence, the stressed syllable stands out from the rest of the wave form approximately as figure stands out from ground in the analysis of physical space. Although the stressed syllable is by no means equivalent to the mature word form, the evidence suggests that its acoustic correlates (i.e. fundamental frequency, intensity, and duration) are available to the child as a bootstrap into the morphological scheme of the language; specifically, into the distinction between the open and closed class. Evidence from recent studies of adult speech production and perception shows that potential bootstraps exist in the wave form for the phrase unit as well. For example, speech timing, and rise and fall of fundamental frequency are affected by phrase boundaries, and adults are sensitive to these acoustic markers (Klatt 1975, 1976; Klatt & Cooper 1975; Lehista, Olive & Streeter 1976; Streeter 1978). Morgan, Meier and Newport's artificial-language learning experiments (see footnote 2) suggest that adults can and will use this kind of cue to group words together, and thus to induce phrasal patterns in a nonsense language.

These cues are likely to be more reliable, and to be exaggerated, in the special strains of motherese. And there are compelling demonstrations that infants attend to them. Fernald (1984) removed from taped adult-to-adult speech and from motherese all cues to segmental content, leaving only the prosodic information (the resulting signal sounds like the muffled speech heard through the wall to an adjoining hotel room). The infants still preferred the motherese version. The rhythmic and tonal information must be doing the differentiating work. This information, in turn, is correlated with phrase and clause boundaries, as shown by Klatt and other investigators just mentioned. Hirsh Pasek *et al.* (1987) have shown that disruption of the usual phrase-bounding information is noted by prelinguistic children: infants under one year of age are more interested in (look longer at) a loudspeaker producing motherese if that speech is doctored to contain a long (half-

second) pause *between* the subject and predicate phrases than if it is doctored to contain a long pause *within* either the subject or predicate phrase.
These studies taken together provide strong evidence that physical cues to
phrase boundaries are salient to learners well before they speak at all.

One series of investigations with older children (Read & Schreiber 1982)
suggests a continuing reliance on prosodic cues for phrasal identification.
These investigators taught 7-year-olds to play a game in which the children
must listen to a sentence and then repeat some portion of it that corresponds
to one of its major constituents. Children are remarkably successful at this
task, learning to pick out such constituents as surface subject NP with
impressive accuracy. However, they show one curious weakness: if the
subject is only a single monosyllable (e.g. a pronoun or a generic nominal
such as *bees*), children are regularly unable to disentangle it from the rest of
the sentence. Read and Schreiber showed that, of all the many properties of
single word NPs, it is their intonational contour (or lack of one) that
accounts for the difficulty children experience. Unlike longer NPs, single
word phrases are not rendered with falling fundamental frequency and
lengthened final vowel at the close of the phrase. It is this phonological
merging of the single word NP with the following VP that throws the
children for a loop. Apparently phrase boundaries are largely a matter of
intonation for these children, in this task condition at least. They do not
appear to be able to locate these boundaries by syntax alone.

It would be perilous to reason in a straight line from 7-year-olds to 1-
year-olds. Simply because second-graders show heavy reliance upon the
intonational correlates of phrases, it does not necessarily follow that they
began learning phrases as infants through their intonational correlates.
Neither do the studies of infant sensitivity to these properties settle the case
for whether these perceptions play a causal role in the discovery of syntax.
But the evidence just reviewed is certainly suggestive. It is quite possible
that the 7-year-old's heavy reliance on intonation is a remnant of a
dependency formed at the earliest stages of acquisition.

If this is the case, it would have important consequences for the way we
should think about language learning. This is because an infant who is
innately biased to treat intonationally circumscribed utterance segments as
potential phrasal constituents would be at a considerable advantage in discovering the distributional patterns of the exposure language. As an easiest
example, the learner must discover whether specifiers precede or follow
nouns in NPs, for this property varies across languages. A pattern analysis
of English speech which proceeded without prior knowledge of the NP
boundary could not settle this question except with an excruciatingly cum-
bersome, and therefore unrealistic, manipulative procedure (cf. Harris
1951). This is because specifiers do follow rather than precede nouns if a

phrase or clause boundary is crossed (e.g. 'John gave the *boy the* book' and 'Some *men the* boys liked ate tacos').

6.2.4. The unit 'clause'

The child seeking to discover the syntax of the exposure language would also be aided if he or she could find a physical correlate of the notion *clause*. Many crucial properties of the exposure language can be stated only by reference to the clause unit, for example, the interpretation of pronouns and anaphors and the domains of movement transformations (see Lust 1986 for evidence that young children control these abstract linguistic properties). Then there must also be an antecedent procedure for establishing the category *clause*. Recent evidence suggests that there are reliable acoustic cues to clause boundaries in speech, including longer pauses, segmental lengthening, declination of fundamental frequency, and stress marking (Klatt 1975, 1976; Garnica 1977; Cooper & Paccia-Cooper 1980; Jucszyk 1986). There is considerable evidence that adults are sensitive to such cues (e.g. Streeter 1978; Luce & Charles-Luce 1983). This physical marking of the clause boundary can again be expected to be exaggerated in motherese. And again infants have been shown to be responsive to these properties.

One admirable finding from the literature on this topic (Hirsh-Pasek *et al.* in press) adapts Fernald's selective looking measure. Maternal speech (by a stranger to the child) was recorded and doctored by inserting half-second silent intervals either at clause boundaries or at syntactically arbitrary places within the sentence (three words before a clause boundary). Eight-month-old infants were presented with samples of both these kinds of recording and their looking time at the loudspeaker from which the speech emanated was recorded. The infants' clear preference was for the form in which the pauses appeared at the clause boundaries.

The rationale was this: it was assumed for the maternal speech, just as for ordinary speech, that a variety of acoustic cues converge at the clause boundary. The effect of the doctoring was either to maintain this convergence of cues (by inserting pauses at clause boundaries) or to dissociate them (by introducing pauses where the other properties do not ordinarily appear). The findings argue that infants are willing and able to identify these clues to clause units, and expect them to converge on a point in time in input speech.

6.2.5. Sequence and the extraction of the sentential parse

For language to be learned, it is insufficient that children recognize the units in the ways just described. They must also attend to the temporal sequence in which these units appear in the sound stream. For example, the serial ordering of *p*, *a*, and *t* is the requirement for distinguishing the morphemes *pat*, *tap*, and *apt*. Infants have been demonstrated to be sensitive to sequential events in the sound stream: recall Mehler *et al.*'s (1978) finding that 1-month-old infants extract intonational properties over a continuous speech event. Their sucking rate could be increased for speech with natural prosodic and intonational qualities, but not for speech that lacked these properties. Similarly, infants respond to a change of stress in a disyllable (BA-ba versus ba-BA; Spring & Dale 1977). Thus they seem to be picking up information that is displayed across a temporal stream, and is not available by analysis of the wave at single time-points within that stream.

Before they are capable of uttering connected speech, learners appreciate sequential information at the level of words and phrases. Golinkoff *et al.* (in press) showed 17-month-old children – many of whom had never put two words together in an utterance – simultaneous videotapes of two events in which cartoon characters known to the children were interacting. The experimenters demonstrated (again using selective looking as the measure) that the toddlers watching these events attend to the appropriate one depending on whether they simultaneously hear, say, 'Big Bird tickles Cookie Monster' or 'Cookie Monster tickles Big Bird.' That is, these children recognize the order of phrases (or something approximating phrases) within the heard sentence and also understand the semantic significance of the ordering for the propositional interpretation of English speech (see also Slobin & Bever 1982 for cross-linguistic evidence on this topic).

The same attention to sequence is evident early in the development of speech. In a long line of observations beginning with Braine (1963) it has been demonstrated that even the two words of telegraphic speech are ordered, usually in accord with the canonical phrase ordering in the exposure language. For instance, Bloom (1970) showed that American children who can say both 'Mommy throw' and 'Throw ball' do not usually say 'Ball throw' to render the same propositional intent.

It is fair to ask about the essence of the units the children are ordering in their speech, but the answer to this question is not so clear. Some investigators hold that the first sequenced units are such lexical classes as noun and verb, but others believe that they are semantic–relational ones such as agent and patient. Present evidence is too weak to adjudicate these distinct claims about the labeling of word classes in the child's head. But without answering this question, we can still consider the discovery procedure through which the units that are sequenced (whatever their real essence) are derived from the data of experience.

All solutions to this problem somewhere implicate a distributional analysis à la Bloomfield which works by considering the privileges of occurrence of items in heard speech. For example, Maratsos (1982; Maratsos & Chalkley 1980) suggests that the noun class is derived as the items that appear after *the*, etc., and verbs are the ones that appear after *can* and *have* and before *-ed*. This solution has some difficulties. The first is that the child who is to profit from this information must be clever enough to decide that such items as *ed* and *can* are good diagnostic environments for performing the distributional analysis. If the children decided, instead, to compare the distribution of *black* with respect to certain following words (*coal*, *ink*) and *white* to others (*swan*, *snow*), they would extract subcategories of nouns that have little general relevance to the overall language design.

Notice that we have already granted the learners a basis for making the correct choices: to a large extent they can limit the analysis by considering solely the distribution of open class items (the stressed component) to closed class items (the unstressed and subsyllabic ones). In fact, Maratsos's scheme implicitly presupposes such a basis for selecting the units that are to figure in the distributional solution for the major lexical classes. But another difficulty for the envisaged analysis is that its critical use of closed class evidence would lead to many misanalyses (misanalyses which, so far as we know, do not characterize the real learners). For example, *hightail* and *hotfoot* do appear before *ed* and are indeed verbs, but *highhanded*, *bob-tailed*, and *club-footed* meet this *-ed* criterion and all the same are not verbs.

Gleitman and Wanner (1982) proposed certain extensions and revisions of Maratsos's (and, indeed, Bloomfield's) schematism for distributional learning, which may render it more workable. They did so by taking to heart findings we have just reviewed, suggesting that even the youngest children have in hand the apparatus to construct a rough phrase-structure representation of heard sentences. They can bracket the clause into phrases based on prosodic information. Moreover, recent formal demonstrations suggest that phrase labeling can be derived from the bracketings (Levy & Joshi 1978). Finally, they are attentive to the temporal orders in which the units occur. Thus there may be a rudimentary structural analysis of the whole sentence available to learners which they can bring to bear on disentangling the NPs from the VPs and even on the discovery of the semantic values of individual words as they appear within the sentence. For the *hightailed/high-handed* example, potential misanalyses can be avoided by attending to the global properties of the sentential parse. Appearance of *-ed* in the verb phrase identifies a verb item (and so, in this environment *-ed* can signal 'pastness'); but appearance of *-ed* on a morpheme that occurs after *the* and before a noun (e.g. in *the highhanded policeman*) identifies a modifier, and so the interpretation of *-ed* is participial.

To summarize the argument: it is clear that sequential constraints on morphemes hold only up to the phrase boundary. Therefore the child who is to discover these constraints by distributional analysis must have an analysis antecedently in place to set this boundary. After all, phrase-structure descriptions of language are convenient, indeed explanatory, just because they so operate as to express the domains of categorial contingencies, e.g. that *the* is limited in its relative distribution with respect to nouns up to the level of the phrase, and no further. We have reviewed evidence suggesting that the young learner can recover the crucial phrase and clause boundaries by observing the prosodic grouping cues in the utterances heard. The advantage conferred by the phrase-structure representation is that it permits a global description of the sentence so that the values for its morphemes can be assigned in a way that is consistent with the whole sentence.

6.2.6. Discovery of linguistic form: summary and concluding comments

Infants and youngest language learners are attentive to physical aspects of the speech stream that are well correlated (in motherese, and probably all natural speech) with such linguistic units as phonetic segment, word, phrase, and clause; and to sequences of such units as they occur in heard utterances. Taken at its strongest, this evidence suggests that a phrase-structural representation of heard speech is available as the child is just beginning to speak, or earlier. The open class items are identified and placed within this parse structure owing to their realization as perceptually salient stressed syllables (perhaps, early on, the unstressed material is represented as associated 'mush'). The phrase and clause boundaries are given according to other physical grouping cues that we have just discussed. (See also Morgan 1986 for an extensive review and striking new evidence for this 'bracketed input' hypothesis.)

If the analysis just given is correct, it has important consequences for a theory of language learning. For example, it is often supposed that learners receive input in the form of word strings, and must construct the phrases therefrom (see Wexler & Culicover 1980 and Pinker 1984 for interesting proposals taking this perspective). But it may well be that children have information about the phrases as early as – or earlier than! – they have information about the words inside the phrases. After all, the prosodic information about phrase boundaries is far more reliable and obvious than the information about word boundaries. Any investigator (or mother) can adduce tens of child usages that are best interpreted as false word segmentation (e.g. /a nəhdult/ or /əplejəl iyjəns/); but it is very hard to find even anecdotes that are describable as cases of false phrase segmentation. To the extent that phrasal information is physically available and is actually recruited by the learner, the discovery procedure for phrases (given word sequences) can be weakened or dispensed with. The same weakening of a discovery procedure is possible if children know where the clause boundaries are when they set about learning which phrase sequences constitute a whole sentence.

As advertised in the beginning of this chapter we have not discussed the many crucial features of syntax that remain to be discovered after the representational elements have been extracted from the wave form. The fundamental issues on this topic have been laid out by Chomsky in many of his writings, which identify explanation in linguistics with the solution to the learning problem. We cannot in this chapter review the many contributions which, adopting Chomsky's perspective, propose solutions to the discovery of language in terms of quite abstract principles of Universal Grammar. Contributions in this field now go under the name 'learnability theory.' (Most notably, see the foundational work of Wexler and his colleagues, as summarized in Wexler 1982; the collection of articles in Baker & McCarthy 1981; Osherson, Stob & Weinstein 1986; and Borer & Wexler 1987). What we have tried to do here is to ask how learning children populate their world with linguistic categories as instantiated in the language to which they are being exposed. For children who do not recognize these constitutive elements in the wave form could not begin to discover (as one of many examples) whether S or S̄ is a bounding node in the exposure language.

6.3. Primitive interpretive elements

We have just suggested that the infant is well prepared prelinguistically to pick out relevant pieces of sound from the wave forms, as the primitive representational basis for finding the linguistically functioning phones, words, phrases, and clauses; more generally, for extracting a phrase-structural analysis of the speech stream. But since language is a pairing of sounds to their meanings, this is only half the battle. The other half of the representation problem has to do with picking out relevant 'pieces of meaning' from the observation of extralinguistic context.

Here too (just as for the forms), some role may be played by the special character of speech to young children. Caretakers evidently limit the topics of their conversations to those which might be appropriate to the extralinguistic context. As Bruner (1974/5) and others have discussed, speech to infants and young children seems predominantly to concern the 'here and now.' Usually the addressee of the speech is the child listener, and conversation focusses on the identification and manipulation of present objects. Slobin (1975) has argued, from an examination of caretaker speech, that it is accompanied by contextual cues so reliable as to render its interpretation unproblematical in most cases.

These properties of maternal speech may have their source in the caretaker's attempt to get the everyday business of life accomplished (the juice drunk, the toys picked up) by a cognitively and linguistically inadequate listener; still, they may well be helpful for learning. It seems more useful for learning the meaning of *rabbit* to hear this word in the presence of rabbits than in discussions of what one ate in Paris last summer. And the positions and motions of those objects in space, relative to the child, can be informative only in so far as the child is really the addressee. For example, when a child is told to 'Give me the rabbit!' the source and goal positions of the object, relative to the listener, are relevant to the interpretation of *give*, but these spatial interpretations would be irrelevant or misleading if the mother were referring to herself and to nonpresent events, e.g. 'I gave three rabbits to the local zoo last week.'

Further, caretakers' tendency is to speak of whole rabbits rather than their parts, using distinctive deictic structures ('This is a rabbit').[7] And in the rare cases in which the part is selected as the topic, it is usually preceded by mention of the whole, and the whole–part relation is rendered by a possessive (e.g. 'This is a rabbit; these are his ears': Shipley, Kuhn & Madden 1983). So, for meanings just as for forms, the caretakers seem to be providing the clearest information possible.

But again, this does not mitigate the inductive problem for learners unless they are disposed to accept this information in the spirit in which it is given. Speaking of whole rabbits cannot really help the learner who is biased to inspect their pieces or to suppose that they may at the next inspection turn into pillars of salt. If the learners are open minded about how the scene before them is to be represented perceptually and conceptually, surely learning the meanings of words from observation of their instances is impossible. Therefore no one, to our knowledge, has ever assumed that the child's interpretation of the observed world is neutral. At the extreme, the child's hypothesis space could not include the exotic chimeras, disconnected parts, and capriciously transforming objects conjectured by worried philosophers. Significant perceptual (and, perhaps, conceptual) biases underlie babies' organization of the continuously varying, multiply interpretable world (MacNamara 1972; Carey 1982, 1985).

Discovery of these biases and predispositions in the infant must ultimately be relevant to understanding how young children learn the meanings of words in the exposure language (even though there are sure to be

---

[7] Notice that these deictic sentences may be especially useful for the discovery of which word class is which. After all, even the learner who is prepared by nature to think that nouns encode objects and verbs encode acts faces a puzzle when he hears the exposure language, i.e. "The rabbit hops" may be interpreted as encoding an action by an animal – but still /haps/ could be the animal name and /ðəræbit/ could be a present-tense act. The deictic sentence may be useful in this regard because it contains only one unit that refers to the observed world, and occurs in maternal speech independently of whether the object in question is stationary or in motion (see Ninio 1980).

refinements, elaborations, and even discontinuities between infant perceptions and the concept space of 1- and 2-year-old language learners). To the extent that words do describe the world, and are uttered by caretakers in appropriate real-world settings, the child at least partly bootstraps the meanings of words by observing what is actually going on when they are said. How this is accomplished depends on just which 'little pieces of the world' it is possible to extract from the flux of external stimulation.

Studies of infants during the past decade suggest that they are quite well prepared for this task. Perhaps rich and various experiential categories are truly pregiven by nature and can immediately be connected to the task of learning a language. Or perhaps the appropriate experiential categories are derived by learning, based on a very narrow initial vocabulary. But whichever of these alternatives is closer to the truth, one fact is clear: the child has a considerable armentarium for representing the real world by the time this is required for language learning (i.e. at about age 1).

After presenting some findings on this topic, we will turn to the more difficult question of whether the richness of early perceptual representations eases the problem of acquiring a language. Of course we will conclude that the child who must discriminate the conditions of appropriate use for thousands of meaningful words is lucky to have divers representations of the world ready to this task. But familiarly enough, the very latitude of interpretation that perception makes available is potentially a hazard to the learner, for it increases his hypothesis space. Thus the finding of richness in early representations poses its own puzzles for the explanation of word and sentence learning.

6.3.1. Primitive (or close to primitive) perceptual categories

Human infants come richly prepared with means for picking up information about what is going on in their environment – looking, listening, feeling, tasting, and smelling; in fact these different sensory routes appear to be precoordinated for obtaining information from the world (Spelke 1979). Infants evidently impose a great deal of order on the gloriously confusing world that is detectable from these information sources.

To be sure, studies with infants provide only probabilistic data, and it is very often difficult to introduce enough control and parametric variation into experiments to be sure of exactly how to characterize the sources of the small subjects' responses. Another major problem is that there are severe limits on which neonate behaviors can be brought under control in the laboratory: the infants can systematically look at things, suck on nipples, and register observable facial and bodily surprise, and psychologists have to be content to derive whatever they can by manipulating this narrow

169

repertoire. Finally, it is not feasible to perform the experimentation on neonates at the instant they emerge from the womb, and therefore have had no experience of the world. These theoretically ideal subjects are inattentive and fall asleep in the midst of even the shortest experiments. On these grounds (and some grounds of theoretical persuasion) there is controversy about how much of the infancy work is to be interpreted. But we ourselves believe that this literature begins to make the case that infants from the beginning are purposive and highly constrained in their inspection of ongoing things, events, and scenes in the world, in a way that can ultimately be connected to the question of how, a year or so later, they acquire their first words and sentences (for a major review and discussion of the literature on perceptual development, see Gibson & Spelke 1983).

To take a few central examples, infants appear to perceive the world as populated with objects which endure over time (Spelke 1982) and which cannot occupy two positions at the same time (Baillargeon, Spelke & Wasserman 1985). Once the infants have learned about objects, they rapidly come to distinguish among their varying properties, e.g. their rigidity or elasticity (Walker *et al.* 1980; Gibson & Walker 1984), their size (Baillargeon 1986), and even their animacy versus inanimacy (Golinkoff *et al.* 1984). They distinguish between moving and stationary objects in the first few months of life (Ball & Vurpillot 1976). Five-month-olds can interpret sequences of events as connected and notice the motions of objects relative to each other (Lasky & Gogol 1978). They can and do use the perceived layout of surfaces as information about their own position and the positions and movements of other objects relative to their own bodies (Acredolo & Evans 1980; Field 1976).

Below, we flesh out a couple of illustrative cases of infants' perceptual organization: their responsiveness to objects and to numerosity. Thereafter, we will use these examples to ask how early perceptual abilities might be connected to word listening.

6.3.1.1. Objects

An extensive literature converges on the view that infants early perceive the world as furnished with objects, which are unitary, bounded, and persist over time. For example, infants are not surprised when a three-dimensional object in front of a flat surface begins to move toward them, but they register surprise if part of the object in tandem with part of the background starts moving toward them (Spelke 1985). According to Spelke, the infants perceive an object just when they detect a topologically connected arrangement of surfaces that retains its connectedness as it moves. For example, infants under 3 months of age will perceive two adjacent objects as a single unit, even though these vary wildly in color, shape, and size. If the objects are not adjacent, they are perceived as two (Hofsten & Spelke 1985; Kestenbaum, Termine & Spelke in press).

But now consider a partly occluded object, such as a rod whose two ends show out from behind a block. In fact, it may really be two rod fragments – the gap between them may be hidden behind the occluding block. But adults are likely to believe that such a display is really of a single rod whose center is occluded by the block. One might guess, based on the findings just discussed, that infants would draw the opposing conclusion. As seen, the two pieces of the rod are visually separated, and thus seem to qualify on the adjacency criterion as two separate units. Indeed, infants do not seem to make a commitment that the rod is unitary so long as the visual display is a stationary one. They look no longer at succeeding presentations of a complete, nonoccluded rod than at a rod with a gap where the occluder had previously been seen, as if it is no surprise to them whether the occluder concealed one large rod or two smaller ones.

If the two parts of the occluded rod are initially shown to move in tandem behind a stationary block, then the infants appear to conclude that the rod was unitary: after seeing this, they look longer at the rod with the gap, as if they perceive this as a new stimulus. Anthropomorphizing this finding a bit more, the tandem-motion display suggests a single object behind an occluder. The succeeding display of that whole object, occluder removed, is just a new view of an old stimulus, only mildly interesting. But the display of two rod fragments is a wholly new, and therefore more interesting, stimulus. The relevant information for conjecturing a single object, apparently, was that the two visible rod fragments moved interdependently, and independently of the motion of other surfaces in the scene (Kellman & Spelke 1983).

Our adult ways of deciding what is an object are far more refined and various than the youngest infants', of course, involving many more perceptual properties as well as vastly increased knowledge of real-world facts. But once the infants have determined to some degree what the objects are to be, they come to distinguish them according to many properties that are much like our own. When it comes time to decide, say, that a noun label refers to a duck rather than to some of its parts, or to the duck plus the ground on which it stands, it is likely that some of these early available perceptual principles are doing the work in the child's construal of the extralinguistic context.

6.3.1.2. Numerosity

Consider now the concept of numerosity, which eventually must be mapped on to such words as *one*, *two*, and so on. There is an extensive literature which supports (perhaps we should say more modestly 'tends to support') the startling idea that infants are sensitive to numerically relevant information in the environment. For example, 10- to 12-month-olds will habituate to (get bored with, and so look less at) displays which all show three objects, even though the objects themselves are varying across trials. They start to look again when the number of objects in the next display changes (Strauss & Curtis 1981). Even when the items are all different within a trial and the subjects are younger (6 to 8 months of age) they note the difference between two- and three-item displays. Either two or three drumbeats are sounded before the infants see two displays of heterogeneous visual objects, one display consisting of two items, the other of three. A variety of preference measures show that they match the number of drumbeats to the number of visual items (Starkey, Gelman & Spelke 1983). Notice then that the infants can in some circumstances detect and respond to a sameness of numerosity even in the presence of different, changing, visual arrays.

6.3.2. Learning word meanings, given perceptual–interpretive abilities

We have asserted that the learner (roughly) picks out the unit *word* relying on such physical manifestations as the distinction stressed/non-stressed syllable. The vocabulary acquisition literature suggests that the learners map these formal units on to the world in ways that are globally consistent with findings from the infant perception laboratory. Gentner (1982) showed that learners acquire nouns before verbs (roughly, object labels before action labels) and Bloom (1973) showed that they acquired object names before property names (*dog* before *big* or *green*). Nelson (1974) showed that they first acquire names for small moving things in their environment (*duck*) as opposed to large immobile things (*sofa*). Mervis & Crisafi (1978) demonstrated that they acquire 'basic level' terms (*duck*) before superordinates (*animal*) and subordinates (*mallard*). Feldman, Goldin-Meadow & Gleitman (1979) showed that the isolated deaf language-inventors first devised manual equivalents for these same items that are early acquired by children learning English or French.

These findings suggest that factors pertaining to the child's initial conceptions of the world help to explain the course of lexical learning. But there is an orderliness in the acquisition sequence that is not wholly explained by the facts about early percepts and concepts. Particularly, why should object concepts be linguistically encoded earliest since, so far as we know, infants perceive actions and connected events as soon as they perceive objects? (Even more strongly, Spelke contends that part of the very basis for object perception is the behavior of those bodies when in motion.) And why are nouns chosen to label object concepts and verbs to label action concepts? Why not choose some word to be the label for a whole event (proposition)? We discuss now two approaches to these issues. The first speaks to how the child parses situations so as to come up with their presently pertinent foci. The second asks about the contribution of language design to language learning.

6.3.3. Domain specificity in the interpretation of the world

We have just cited experiments that, to a first approximation, suggest that infants are sensitive both to object properties and to numerosity. But they seem to show also that, under specific environmental circumstances, the infants can attend differentially to these aspects of the observed world. For example, in the Starkey *et al.* work, the infants responded to numerosity despite heterogeneity and change in the objects observed. Under many other experimental circumstances, the infants discriminate among the many objects that are treated equivalently in this situation. The puzzle is that the infants are so often correct (i.e. in agreement with the investigators who set up the experiments) in deciding just what properties of the situation to focus upon, among the many possibilities that perception makes available.

The ability to perceive and categorize the observed world differently under varying observational circumstances is surely critical for the acquisition of word and sentence meaning. For example, as Gelman (1986) notes, children are sensitive both to color and to weight. A new property term, say, *gorp*, used in the presence of a heavy red rock thus could allude (*inter alia*) either to its color or to its weight. But if the observed event in which the rock figures 'has to do with' moving it from one place to another, it is reasonable to focus on weight and not color. According to Gelman, that is because weight is relevant to the principles involved in moving objects over space, and color typically is not.

Of course Gelman's perspective does not answer to how word meanings are learned. Rather it suggests that this latter problem be set in a partly new way. The question for meaning acquisition becomes: how does the child (acknowledged to be in possession of rich perceptual and conceptual principles) figure out just what the observed event has to do with, so as to apply the right principles at the right times? She illustrates this situation with a nice example:

On day one I point to these two (duck, pig) and say DUCK, PIG; on day two I point to these two and say YELLOW, PINK; on day three I point to these two and say ONE, TWO. Why wouldn't a beginning language learner think she should call this (duck) DUCK, YELLOW, ONE?

Gelman's learner can marshall evidence from preset perceptual and conceptual domains to generate three hypotheses, all sensible, for labeling the observation of a single yellow duck. But which is the true label in the exposure language for the concept 'duck'? Perception seems to leave too much latitude for the solution to this problem.

Gelman's proposal for a solution draws on two supposed biases or strategies in the child learner. The first is a conjecture from Markman (1986) concerning the child's initial picture of how words map on to the world. Markman's evidence suggests that the child is biased to believe that when a novel word is presented in the context of a novel object, the word refers to that object as a whole. For example, suppose a cup (an old object, with a known name) or a pair of tongs (an unfamiliar object with no name known to the child subject) is presented and called 'pewter.' The children believe that *pewter* is the name for tongs, but not a new name for cups. By default, they assign the new term to the substance (the material) for the case of the cup. It is as though they believe that since the cup object already has a linguistic title (that is, *cup*), a new word used to refer to it must pertain to its other properties. Thus, in Markman's terminology, there is a 'mutual exclusivity' principle operating in acquiring word labels (closely related to the uniqueness principle of linguistic and learnability theory). Each object class (however derived from experience) will have its unique, unchanging, word label. Ducks are not sometimes to be called *aardvark* (though they are sometimes called *Donald* and sometimes called *animal*, a problem to which we will return). Thus the mutual exclusivity principle would predict that the child's first guess is that *two* and *duck* are not synonyms, but are likely to encode different aspects of the observed scene.

The second component of Gelman's solution to the duck/two problem draws on her findings concerning the child's early concept of number and of counting. Gelman and Gallistel (1978) have elucidated basic counting principles and shown that preschoolers have considerable understanding of them. These are well worth reproducing here:

(1) One–one: each and every item in a collection must be uniquely tagged.

(2) Stable order: whenever tags are used, they must be organized in a list that is stably ordered.

(3) Cardinal order: the last tag in a tag sequence represents the cardinal value of the numerosity of the collection.

(4)   Item indifference: any set of entities, no matter their attributes, can be collected together in a count trial.

(5)   Order indifference: the how-to-count principles can be applied to any ordering of the elements in an array.

An ordered list of words is used for counting. Children acquire the count list by memorization, a hard job. But another task the child must confront is to understand that the five principles just listed account for the observed use of these terms. The independence of this task from the memorization of the verbal count sequence was shown by Gelman and Gallistel through a very striking phenomenon: children who have the list wrong (have idiosyncratic count lists, e.g. *One, two, thirteen, five*) observe the count principles in using this list to refer to numerosity. For example, they will assert that all three-item arrays are collections of thirteen, correctly honoring the cardinal order principle. More generally, these investigators have shown that preschool children operate with number tasks (providing the numbers are very small) very systematically and consistently in accordance with the five principles.

Now we are ready to reapproach the duck/two decision. Gelman points out that the use of count terms according to the count principles systematically violates the mutual exclusivity condition that (by Markman's hypothesis) applies to object naming. Two ducks are both to be called *duck*, but one duck (and either one, across count trials) is to be called *one* and the other *two*. Each item is given a different count term, even if each such item is a duck (the one–one principle), and the word *one* can be used to label different objects over trials (the item-indifference and order-indifference principles). There is no physical attribute or attributes that are invariant over the word *two* that will account for its contexts of use, other than the count principles.

Summing up, it is possible to begin to think about the acquisition of such relatively tidy concepts (and terms) as *two* and *duck*, on the assumption that the child learner has some initial principles for organizing the flux of ambient stimulation that is presented to the senses; and maps words on to their meanings as they accord or do not accord with these various principles. The same external stimulations will be differentially labeled, according to which such principles are invoked in using them; and different external stimulations will be labeled identically in so far as they are organized by some single set of these principles.

6.3.4. **Limits on the informativeness of observation: the subset problem in word learning**

The mutual exclusivity or uniqueness principle for assigning labels to object terms really will not work as stated, for – even leaving aside synonyms – the same object is often (in fact, always) provided with more than one name, viz. *animal, duck, Donald Duck*. We would expect that the adult speaker has little difficulty in selecting the level of specificity he or she wants to convey, and so can choose the correct lexical item in each case. And indeed the learner may be preequipped perceptually and conceptually so as to interpret the scene at these various levels of abstraction, and to construct conceptual taxonomies (Keil 1979). But this very latitude makes a mystery of the child's vocabulary acquisition, for how is he or she to know the level encoded by the as yet unknown word? The scene is always the same. For every time there is an observation that satisfies the conditions (whatever these are) for the appropriate use of *duck*, the conditions for the appropriate use of *animal* have been satisfied as well. Similarly, to mention a case to which we will return, *perceive, look, see, eye* (in the sense of 'set eyes on'), *face, orient*, etc. pose the same subset problem.

Gold (1967) addressed a problem that may be analogous to this one. He showed that learners who had to choose between two languages, one of which was a subset of the other, could receive no positive evidence that they had chosen wrong if they happened to conjecture the superset (larger) language. This is because the sentences they would hear, all drawn from the subset, are all members of the superset as well. It has therefore been proposed that learners always hypothesize the smaller (subset) language, i.e. they initially select the most restrictive value for a parameter on which languages vary (Wexler & Manzini 1987).

But the acquisition facts for the lexicon do not allow us to suppose that the child has a solution so simple as choosing the least inclusive possibility. In the end, the learners choose all of them: they learn all the words just mentioned. Moreover, they select neither the most nor the least inclusive level as their initial conjecture. The middle sized, or so-called 'basic level' categories *duck* and *see* are the real first choices of the learners (see Rosch 1978 for the clearest attempts to describe the basic level vocabulary, and its privileged role for both children and adults in various classificatory tasks).[8] This result cannot be written off as a simple consequence of the greater frequency, in speech, of *duck* compared to *mallard* (the subcategory) or

---

[8] We are using *basic level* as a term that describes a variety of classificatory and labeling preferences that have been observed both in adults and in children. But see, e.g., Fodor 1983; Armstrong, Gleitman & Gleitman 1983; Landau & Gleitman 1985, Chapter 9, for some pessimistic discussion, and queries about whether the label 'basic level term' is explanatory or simply names an unsolved, and perhaps unsolvable, problem.

animal (the superordinate), in light of the so-called 'overextension' findings for early lexical development (Rescorla 1980). Sometimes a subordinate term really is the most frequent in the child's environment, for the dog in the house is usually called *Fido* and the man in the house is usually called *Daddy*. But then the young learner may interpret these words as basic level all the same, terming the dog next door *Fido* and the man on the street *Daddy*.

We shall have nothing to say in this paper that contributes to the explanation of preferred levels of categorization by children (or adults for that matter). What is central to the present discussion is that on the one hand, the preferences exist and on the other hand, the word labels for the nonpreferred category levels are finally acquired also. That is, perception and conception allow the same scene to be represented and linguistically described at more than one level. The subset problem assures that different and distinguishable observations of the world when, say, *perceive* or *see* are uttered cannot account in any simple way for how the semantic values of these words are disentangled by the learner.

Landau and Gleitman (1985) studied this problem empirically by considering the sets of verbs learned by a 3-year-old blind child and the extralinguistic information that this child received, pertinent to that learning. This was done by analyzing a series of videotapes of the mother and child interacting, selecting the environments in which these verbs were uttered. (The relevant material was from the period preceding the child's first use of these verbs, i.e. during the learning period for them.) The first analysis conjectured a very limited representational vocabulary in terms of which the child might have reacted to these utterance/situation pairs – thus narrowing the hypothesis space for an inductive learning procedure. (In detail, it was assumed that the child inspected the scenes according to the ways that pertinent objects – whose linguistic labels were known to the child – were located and moving through space when she heard the various verbs; that is, an analysis in terms of sources, paths, and goals.) It was shown that this representational vocabulary was too impoverished to account for all the learning.

The next step was to broaden the representational vocabulary, i.e. hypothesizing that the learner could inspect the situational environment in 'many and divers' ways. But this solution proved to be the other horn of the word-learning dilemma, for it brought the analysis (and the learner) face to face with the subset problem. Particularly, once the child was granted the ability to conceive of scenes as 'contacting,' 'haptically observing,' 'haptically perceiving,' 'amodally perceiving,' etc., it became impossible to state the situational concommitants that allowed her to select (as she did, as shown in comprehension experiments) single interpretations for such words as *touch*, *look*, and *see*. This was because each context in which the child could have haptically perceived (seen) some object was also inevitably one in which she haptically inspected (looked at) and, of course, manually contacted (touched) that object.

We shall return to these findings and a proposal for a solution later in this paper. Here, we have tried to indicate that perception and conception provide too various – and thus too weak – a basis for matching the right words with the right meanings. This problem remains even though it is true that mothers naturally speak to their young children of pertinent objects and events in the ongoing scene (cf. Slobin 1975). Somehow, the evidence from extralinguistic observation must be constrained. As we will now try to show, important constraints derive from the child's natural ('innate') pre-conceptions about language design.

6.3.5. Interpretive biases from language design

Almost all proposals for learning word meaning by observation of the extralinguistic context implicate, implicitly or explicitly, additional principles that derive from language design itself. For instance, Markman's mutual exclusivity (uniqueness) principle, while it alludes to observation, depends as well on how experience maps on to language design in particular, i.e. for object classes at some predefined level, there is to be a single label in the exposure language. A number of findings show that the child's flexibility in interpreting the extralinguistic world is constrained by such pre-existing biases about how that world is to be viewed, *given its linguistic description*.

6.3.5.1. The semantic interpretation of word classes

Earlier, we discussed proposals (Maratsos 1982; Gleitman & Wanner 1982) for how the child discovers the word units and their lexical classifications. Apparently, the children identify these formal classes with distinctive semantic values. Some supportive evidence comes from Markman & Hutchinson 1984 and Waxman & Gelman 1986. These investigators began with the observation that youngsters tend to sort objects according to thematic rather than taxonomic groupings. Shown a poodle replica and asked which other present object 'goes with it,' 2- and 3-year-olds are likely to choose a bone replica rather than a terrier replica. There is nothing incoherent about such a choice: terriers are dogs, but also poodles like bones. The bias can be reversed if the task is changed to focus on the object's label. Suppose the child is told 'This puppet only speaks Japanese and he likes *this dobutso*' (the poodle is shown, and placed near the puppet): 'Give him another

178

dobutso.' The children now are likely to choose the terrier. If the label was a noun, the concept pertains to a taxonomic grouping. Thus the linguistic information acts to narrow down the hypotheses offered by the perception of objects and events.

Such language–concept mappings were investigated by Brown (1957), who showed his child subjects a picture in which, say, spaghetti-like stuff was being poured into a vessel. Some subjects were asked to show *some gorp*, others *a gorp*, and still others *gorping*. The subjects' choices were, respectively, the spaghetti, the vessel, and the action. Evidently, the semantic core of the word classes affects the conjecture about the aspect of the scene in view that is being labeled (for an experimental demonstration with younger children, see Katz, Baker & MacNamara 1974).

.3.5.2. The sentence is the natural repository of propositions

A fascinating line of research, beginning with Bloom's (1970) groundbreaking work on children's spontaneous speech, provides evidence at another level about how children meaningfully interpret the world and map it on to linguistic categories. As we mentioned earlier, from the earliest two-word utterances, the ordering of the component words interpreted against their contexts of use suggests that they are conceived as playing certain thematic roles, such as agent and patient, within a predicate-argument structure (Bowerman 1973; Brown 1973; Bloom, Lightbown & Hood 1975; Braine 1976). Golinkoff *et al.*'s evidence (in press), cited earlier, suggests that even one-word speakers understand the semantic implications of phrase orderings: they realize that 'Cookie Monster tickles Big Bird' means one thing, and that 'Big Bird tickles Cookie Monster' means something quite different. Feldman, Goldin-Meadow and Gleitman (1978) have shown that a similar componential analysis describes the signing of the deaf isolates, for these children too differentiate in their sign order choices depending on the relational roles played by the various nominal gestures. Slobin and Bever (1982) adduced cross-linguistic evidence to support a strong generalization of such findings: learners construct a canonical sentence schema as the preliminary framework for acquisition.

This early linguistic–conceptual organization becomes a bit easier to understand in the light of the evidence just reviewed. Infants understand the connectedness of events in which objects are seen or felt to move, relative to each other, in visual and haptic space. Whatever the precise content of the first relational categories, it seems clear that the child approaches language learning equipped with a propositional interpretation of scenes and events in the world.

The question remains how much this tells us about learning a language.

Lila R. Gleitman, Henry Gleitman, Barbara Landau and Eric Wanner

This depends on whether the categories and forms of natural language are simple with respect to the pre-existing meaning structures. From varying perspectives, a number of authors have assumed that linguistic categories and forms map transparently from the meaning structures, and hence that the bulk of explanatory apparatus – for child learner and for developmental psycholinguist – exists when these categories are isolated and described (e.g. Bates & MacWhinney 1982; Braine & Hardy 1982; Bloom 1973). This view is not unreasonable on the face of it. After all, we previously subscribed to a version of the view that the mapping between words and concepts may be quite direct. The question now is whether the relation between sentences and propositional thought is as straightforward as the relation between words and first concepts may be.

As a first pass at this issue, consider one finding from Feldman *et al.*'s deaf isolates. A distributional–interpretive analysis of these children's rudimentary sentences showed that they gestured a single noun in company with (in construction with) such action gestures as *dance*, two nouns with *hit*, and three with *give*. Moreover, the noun items were sequenced differentially with respect to the action item, roughly according to the thematic roles these items played (i.e. patient first, recipient second). It appears that learners realize that events are to be described linguistically as a predicate–argument structure in which the NPs playing the argument roles are ranged around the verb in systematic ways. Moreover, they realize that *give*, *hit*, and *dance* are concepts that by their logic require a different number of such arguments (i.e. the learners honor the theta criterion). Evidently, for these isolates the mapping between argument structure and sentence structure is quite transparent. Perhaps the youngest learners of real languages also first approach the task by supposing that this transparency condition will hold (for discussion, see Wexler & Culicover 1980; Pinker 1984).

Semantic bootstrapping: syntactic form from meaning

One way of thinking about a discovery procedure that extracts form/meaning relations has been called 'semantic bootstrapping.' Its first premise is the uncontroversial background idea that something about the semantics of various words and structures can be discovered by noticing the real-world contingencies for their use. No one would contest such a view. But its second and more surprising claim is that, once the meanings have been culled from observation, these meanings themselves yield conjectures about linguistic classification (e.g. a word describing an action is probably a verb; different actions imply different syntactic encodings of the verbs that express them; see Bowerman 1973, 1982; Grimshaw 1981; and Pinker 1984 for discussions that adopt this point of view). The viewpoint has been very interestingly outlined and defended by Bowerman, who has collected spon-

180

taneous child syntactic usages that are at variance with those of the surrounding linguistic community.

Bowerman's evidence suggests that children take a strong view of how predicate–argument structure is to be mapped on to sentences at the surface. For example, children who properly say 'John moves the block,' 'The block moves' and 'The baby eats' are sometimes also observed to say – not so properly – 'Don't eat the baby!' when they evidently mean 'Don't feed the baby' (=cause it to eat). The analogy, false in the given case, is evidently from such lexical causatives as *move* and their intransitive (noncausal) alternates. It seems then that, given the meaning as extracted from the observation of events, the child makes a conjecture about syntactic form which amounts to a transparency claim about the relation between argument structures and subcategorization frames. In so far as the exposure language embodies such a relation, the child learner has a productive basis in semantics (derived in turn from observation) for constructing clausal syntax. Of course, in so far as the exposure language deviates from this relation, the child makes errors, as Bowerman showed. Moreover, in so far as meaning cannot fully be derived from observation in the first place owing – among many other things – to the subset problem, there are limits on how far the child can get by adopting this stance.

Syntactic bootstrapping: acquiring meanings from forms

In response to such problems, Landau and Gleitman (1985) developed a verb-learning theory that incorporates the Bowerman–Grimshaw–Pinker insights, but capitalizes on the form–meaning relations in a further way. If there is really a strong correlation between verb syntax and verb meanings – and if Gleitman and Wanner are correct that youngest learners have represented input utterances as parse trees – the learner can make conjectures from form to meaning with only the same trepidation that should apply to his or her conjectures from meaning to form. For example, *gorp* in *John gorps* is unlikely to mean 'bring' because the surface structure contains too few argument positions. Such subcategorization evidence about verb meanings will be particularly useful because the syntactic information from the caretakers is categorical: maternal subcategorization errors are vanishingly rare (Newport 1977; Landau & Gleitman 1985). This contrasts with the probabilistic and degenerate information available from scene inspection.

Landau and Gleitman's first evidence for this hypothesis was an argument by exclusion. They showed that children whose observational conditions differed radically nevertheless achieved closely related meaning representations for the same items: blind learners by age 3, just like sighted learners of the same age, understand that the verbs *look* and *see* describe spatial–perceptual acts and states, and are distinct from the contact term *touch*. For both blind and sighted children, *look* describes the dominant perceptual means for discovering objects in the world, and *see* describes the state that results from such exploration. Thus for the blind, the terms describe haptic exploration and perception, while for the sighted they describe visual exploration and perception. Moreover, blind 3-year-olds understand that these words, applied to sighted others, describe perception that takes place at a distance, that requires line-of-sight orientation, and that is blocked by barriers; that is, they understand much of how these terms apply to the visual experience of others.

The view that word meanings are acquired through extralinguistic observation must be subtle enough to cope with this finding of closely related semantic conjectures from distantly related observational evidence. How is it that the blind child discovers the spatial–perceptual interpretation of these words, and correctly deduces the spatial components of sighted others' *seeing* and *looking*? Surely not from seeing and looking, or from literally observing the seeing and looking of others. Evidently some word meaning acquisition takes place despite impoverishment, or significant change, in the observational evidence.

This problem is of course quite general, extending to sighted children as much as to blind children. The blind learner's manifest competence serves only to dramatize an issue that has always been recognized, but is sometimes submerged in recent thought about the usefulness of observation. Consider the acquisition of the word *know* by sighted children. What is there to observe in the world whenever an individual is said to 'know?' It is wildly implausible to suggest that the learner stores (in a pro tem., hardly organized, fashion) the set of relatively lengthy events and cooccurring lengthy conversations in which *know* (somewhere) appears, to discover the precise real-world contingency for the use of this word. The storage and manipulation problems appear to be hopelessly difficult, especially as one would independently have to store another detailed set of observed scenario–conversation pairs for *think*, *guess*, etc. Discussions of solutions solely in observational terms have certainly lacked specificity. They have usually given little attention to the proliferation of conjectured interpretations of individual scenes that will ensue if learners are allowed great latitude in their representational vocabulary and great ingenuity in reconstructing the interpretation of events. Even a partial theory for extracting interpretation from observed scenes will require a technical and detailed research endeavor in its own right, along the lines suggested by students of perceptual and concept development. This problem cannot be solved, or set aside by investigators of language learning, simply by alluding to the fact that what is said is usually appropriate to the external circumstances in some way.

Some of the real issues that will have to be faced if the observational learning proposal is to achieve detailed support are worth at least listing here. One difficulty is that sometimes the child listener is attending to one thing (say, the cat on the mat) while the parent is speaking of something else altogether ('Time for your nap, dear'). An observational learning theory has to state why the child makes no attempt to pair this observation to that meaning, or must have a procedure for recovering from errors it makes along the way. A second problem has to do with the 'stimulus free' character of even language use that is (in some way) pertinent to ongoing events; there seems no end of pertinent things one could say, given some observed situation. So how is the child to guess which of these alternatives is encoded in the utterance that accompanies the observation? The problem reaches its limit, as we have stated, for words which stand in a class-inclusion relation to each other and differ in no other way. The child who conjectures that *see* means 'perceive' could never experience scenes or events to dissuade her, for every time the caretakers appropriately speak of seeing there will be an event of perceiving taking place. Such problems obtain as strongly for everyday verbs of physical motion, for there is no running without moving, chasing without following, placing without putting, or taking without getting.

Syntactic evidence in utterances heard ought to mitigate these problems significantly. As an example, we will consider the child who by perceptual and conceptual endowment (or by prior learning) is prepared to believe that there is a word in his or her language meaning 'perceive by eye' (or 'by hand' in case the learner is blind). The question is how that learner decides that *see*, rather than *give* or *have*, etc. is the right word in the exposure language for this notion.

To understand how this problem is solved is to bring together many of the strands we have already discussed. We know that the child who is learning verb meanings has already acquired the word labels for many objects and persons: many nouns are learned before verbs begin to be acquired. We also know that speech to the child is predominantly addressed to him or her, and overwhelmingly often concerns the locations, movements, and goals of objects, with known names, in the observable present scene. If the speech is addressed to the child, the object motions relative to his or her own body therefore provide experiential clues to the meaning of the verb in the heard utterance. That is, children can tell if they are the source or the goal of that object motion depending (for one thing) on whether pertinent objects are moving toward or away from them. We know from the infancy perception work that young word learners can understand the scene as such a layout in which there are objects in motion, organized relative to the position of the body. Thus the learner indeed has some observational evidence about the event, but also has linguistic information (the noun labels) about the objects that are participating in that observed event, and are being described in an utterance now heard.

The question is whether, as the semantic bootstrapping hypothesis holds, this information is sufficient to discover that /siy/ means 'see' while /giv/ means 'give.' The problem, in a nutshell, is that while the child observer can notice that objects are in motion, she can also notice that she is perceiving this scenario. And the adult can appropriately refer to either of these aspects in his utterance. He can say 'Do you see the apple?' and 'Can you give me the apple?' in response to the same scene. Indeed, reference to perceptual acts (*listen*, *look*) and states (*hear*, *see*) as they apply to the ongoing scene are frequent in maternal usage – even usage to blind babies.

A solution is available if the learner is equipped with a parse of the heard sentence, can identify the structural positions of the known nouns and unknown verb (*see* or *give*) in that parse, and has a conjecture about the logic of the notions 'see' and 'give.' We have already discussed the evidence. To repeat one theme, even the deaf isolates of Goldin-Meadow know that the language encoding of 'see' and 'give' must be different. Seeing involves an observer's perception of the scene (and hence requires two NPs) while giving involves the transfer of an object between two parties (and hence requires three NPs). A linguistic object (verb) that is to mean 'give' must be one that can appear in parse trees with three argument positions, while a verb that is to mean 'see' can have only two. This is because perception is inalienable and involves no external causal agent to be expressed in a third NP. As we have stated, these strictures derive from the theta criterion: every argument is mapped on to an NP and the number of NPs is limited by the argument structure. More generally, the logic of verb meaning is exhibited in the surface structures. Since different verbs vary in their logic, their surface structures are different too. These surface structures are available for the learner's inspection.

Landau and Gleitman discussed a number of such surface structure derivatives of the meanings of the verbs we are discussing, and showed that the appropriate forms were used by caretakers in their utterances to a young blind child. Many of their claims go well beyond the one–one mapping requirement for NPs on to arguments. As further examples: since (visual and haptic) perception is of both objects and events, a verb meaning 'see' will appear with NP complements and also sentential complements, while a verb meaning 'give' cannot take sentential complements because one cannot transfer events from party to party or from place to place (barring psychokinesis, there is no interpretation of *John looked the ball to Mary*). A verb meaning 'see' pertains to a spatial perception and so should and does appear with a variety of locative prepositions, while 'give' concerns motion to or toward and thus should be, and is, restricted in the locative prepositions it can accept (see Gruber 1968). Landau and Gleitman presented evidence to show that such observational and syntactic evidence provided by a mother of a blind child, *taken together*, was sufficient, in principle, to distinguish the interpretations of the common verbs that this child heard and learned, while neither of these data bases was sufficient by itself.

The hypothesis that children will conjecture verb meanings from subcategorization information has begun to be tested more directly. A recent experiment asked whether children will conjecture new meaning components for known verbs if those verbs are used in new syntactic environments (Naigles, Gleitman & Gleitman 1986). Notice that this question is the converse of Bowerman's question (namely, will children conjecture new syntactic properties for verbs whose meaning is already known?). The answer from the initial experiments seems to be yes. Two- to 4-year-old children were asked to act out (with toys) scenes described by the experimenter, e.g. *The horse comes to the elephant*. But some of the sentences were anomalous, e.g. *The horse brings to the giraffe*. The known verbs were being used in structures which the child surely has not heard. The children by their actions showed that they knew that *come* in *The elephant comes the giraffe to the ark* is to be interpreted as *bring* and that *bring* in *The elephant brings to the giraffe* is to be interpreted as *come*. They understood the semantic significance of adding or subtracting a NP in sentences with motion verbs. This pertains to whether the causal agent of the motion is being expressed.

If results of this kind hold up, this would suggest that verb learning – and indeed vocabulary acquisition in general – proceeds in two directions at once. A child provided by nature with the wherewithal to conceive of perceiving and of moving, and to notice instantiations of such notions in the ongoing scene, has taken the first step to distinguish among such verbs as *give* and *see*; this procedure is sometimes called semantic bootstrapping. But which verb is the adult currently uttering, pertaining to scenes in which both seeing and giving are going on? Crucial clues come from linguistic observation: that is, from observation of the sentences that are being uttered, as represented by their parse trees. These observations have relevance to the extent that the parse trees are reasonably straightforward reflexes of the propositions being encoded. A learning procedure that makes use of this evidence might as well be called syntactic bootstrapping (see Landau & Gleitman 1985 for one idea about how such a procedure could be realized).[9]

[9] Independent evidence is required to document how strong and refined the semantic information in surface structure may be. If the information isn't there, the children can't be using it. Jackendoff (1983)

Both semantic and syntactic bootstrapping are perilous and errorful procedures. Bowerman's children, drawing syntactic conclusions from meaningful overlap, are sometimes wrong. Errors are made in so far as the scenes are multiply interpretable, but also because the form-to-meaning mapping in the exposure language is complex and often inexact. For instance, *exit, enter, reach*, and *touch* do not require prepositional phrase complements in English even though they describe directed motion through space (see Jackendoff 1983). One outcome of this inexact mapping of form on to meaning is errorful learning (e.g. the child may say 'I touched on your arm'). Another is corrective language change (we, but evidently not Shakespeare, find it acceptable to say 'He exited from the stage'). The position we have suggested is that the child to a very satisfactory degree recovers the forms and meanings of the exposure language just because he or she can and does play off the two data bases (the events and the utterances) against each other to derive the best fit between them.

4. Final thoughts

Consider the learner whose innate capacity for language is said to include a 'pro-drop' parameter having to do with the option to omit the subject of the sentence under certain conditions. Learnability theorists point out that the child requires only a little data to set the switch for this parameter of syntactic variation. Hearing an expert say 'Hablo español' may be enough for concluding that the exposure language is a 'pro-drop language (or, from another perspective, hearing an expert say 'There's a horse in the garden' is enough for concluding that the language is *not* pro-drop: Hyams 1987. An acquisition theory couched in these terms is remarkably useful, for by hypothesis a small number of such parameter settings, operating together, will generate the myriad syntactic distinctions at the surface among the natural languages. Thus learning one's native tongue may be just a matter of setting a few switches. Moreover, the data requirements for setting these

---

has provided substantial analyses in these terms, particularly for the verbs of motion; and see Talmy 1983 for further analysis and some cross-language evidence. Fisher, Gleitman & Gleitman (forthcoming) have tried to provide some experimental demonstrations. For a limited set of verbs, they were able to show that a partitioning of the set along semantic lines corresponded to syntactic (subcategorization) distinctions within the set. One group of subjects generated the subcategorization facts about the verbs, by giving judgements of grammaticality for all these items in many syntactic environments. Another group of subjects judged all triads of these verbs, presented without sentential context, for semantic relatedness, by throwing out the semantic outlier. The number of times two verbs stuck together, in the contexts of all the other verbs presented with them, was taken as the measure of 'semantic relatedness.' The semantic space so constructed (either by multi-dimensional scaling or cluster analysis) reflected a number of syntactic distinctions; and the factors (or clusters) derived are usually semantically interpretable (e.g. 'the spatial perception verbs,' 'the interperson cognition verbs'). That is, semantic and syntactic judgements partition the verb set in about the same ways. These findings continue to hold when near synonyms are substituted for the original verb items.

switches appear to be quite modest, as they should be if even the least attentive child is to learn from even the most taciturn caretaker.

But this parameter-setting perspective, important as it is, leaves aside a crucial prior job: the one we have discussed. This is the procedure that assures that the sound wave /abloespanyol/ will be partitioned into a four-morpheme sequence; that the first two of these morphemes will together be identified as the verb; etc. The real learning procedure will be radically different depending on when, during the course of learning, the relevant structural renditions of the wave form become available. Once this representational issue has been described in detail, it is even possible that the descriptions in terms of parameter setting may require some revision.

We have tried to describe what is known about the child's first representations of the sound wave and of the flux of external stimulation. For the wave forms of speech, current evidence suggests that the learner extracts and represents just the right acoustic properties: those that are well correlated with the linguistically functioning formatives, such as phone, word, phrase, and clause. For the interpretations, the evidence suggests that the child is richly endowed with flexible strategies for interpreting the external world as it is presented to the sensorium.

But our major point was that the very flexibility of observation, within the broad bounds established by perception and early conception, poses a new (perhaps we should say 'new new') riddle for induction when taken together with the stimulus-free property of language use. One can't learn the meanings solely from observation, for the child's hypothesis space is too large, and the options open to the adult speaker are too large – there is an almost limitless number of appropriate comments she can make concerning some scene to which her child is attending. Worse, perhaps, the conditions of use give little cue to the level of specificity at which the speaker is describing the scene in view. Similar problems obtain for a procedure that attempts to learn the meanings solely from inspection of the semantically relevant syntactic environments. This is because of the variability, and unreliability, with which surface structures encode predicate–argument structure.

Despite these formidable barriers, the learner achieves knowledge of language that is categorical (or close enough), hardly reflecting the probabilistic and degenerate properties of the two data bases. This is one more way of acknowledging that the discovery procedure for language is not, and should not be confused with, the knowledge that is finally attained or the form in which that final knowledge is represented. The discovery procedure itself can be successful only because it accepts evidence from two imperfect sources, discovering the grammar in their convergence. We have tried to show that children have no aversion to learning the meanings from the forms whilst simultaneously learning the forms from the meanings, for the circularity in this procedure is not vicious. The learners' only desideratum is the simplest statement of these relations.[10]

[10] Terrible as it is to end a chapter, especially so lengthy a one, with a footnote, we cannot forebear from mentioning a further issue. Psychologists reading what has been written here may well complain that we have ended almost where we should have begun. This is by attempting to state the learning mechanism – the one that somehow is to correlate the incoming evidence concerning meanings and forms. We have made a preliminary apology for ignoring such machinery, for we limited the discussion largely to the quest for representational elements. But having raised further issues about the manipulations that are to take place on such elements, a comment at least may be in order. We believe with many linguists of the parameter-setting persuasion that much of language is unlearned in the first place. Beyond that, and once the sounds and meanings have been extracted from the wave forms and the scenes in a principled and closely constrained fashion, we suspect that the correlational–inductive procedure for language learning is similar to or the same as that in other cognitive domains (and so need not be expressed particularly for the subissue of human learning called 'human language learning'). Of course, exactly which words and even structures are heard by particular children in paticular extralinguistic settings is bound to be very variable. This input order has not, so far as it has been investigated, been shown to have particularly systematic effects on the course of acquisition – beyond the obvious fact that some children will learn the word *dinosaur* before *duck*, etc. (see e.g. Gleitman, Newport & Gleitman 1982 for some discussion). It is our bias, perhaps wrong, that such minutiae of a realistic learning procedure are less urgent to state, owing to the known variability in which information is received first, and the known survival of language learning under all these variable circumstances. That is, the course of learning, in so far as it is regular and principled, does not much reside in these details of the input situation.

REFERENCES

Acredolo, L. P. and Evans, D. 1980. Developmental changes in the effects of landmarks on infant spatial behavior. *Developmental Psychology* 16: 312–18.
Armstrong, S., Gleitman, L. R. & Gleitman, H. 1983. What some concepts might not be. *Cognition* 13.3: 263–308.
Baillargeon, R. 1986. Representing the existence and the location of hidden objects: object permanence in 6- and 8-month old infants. *Cognition* 20: 21–42.
Baillargeon, R., Spelke, E. & Wasserman, S. 1985. Object permanence in five-month old infants. *Cognition* 20: 191–208.
Baker, C. L. & McCarthy, J. J. 1981. *The logical problem of language acquisition.* Cambridge, MA: MIT Press.
Ball, W. A. & Vurpillot, E. 1976. Perception of movement in depth in infancy. *L'Année Psychologique* 76: 383–99.
Bates, E. & MacWhinney, B. 1982. Functionalist approaches to grammar. In Wanner & Gleitman 1982.
Bellugi, U. 1967. The acquisition of negation. Doctoral dissertation, Harvard University.
Blasdell, R. & Jensen, P. 1970. Stress and word position as determinants of imitation in first language learners. *Journal of Speech and Hearing Research* 13: 193–202.
Bloom, L. 1970. *Language development: form and function in emerging grammars.* Cambridge, MA: MIT Press.
Bloom, L. 1973. *One word at a time.* The Hague: Mouton.
Bloom, L., Lightbown, P. & Hood, L. 1975. Structure and variation in child language. *Monographs of the Society for Research in Child Development* No. 160.
Bloomfield, L. 1983. *Language.* New York: Holt.
Borer, H. & Wexler, K. 1987. The maturation of syntax. In Roeper and Williams 1987.
Bowerman, M. 1973. Structural relationships in children's utterances: syntactic or semantic? In T. E. Moore (ed.) *Cognitive development and the acquisition of language.* New York: Academic Press.

Bowerman, M. 1982. Reorganizational processes in lexical and syntactic development. In Wanner & Gleitman 1982.

Braine, M. D. S. 1963. The ontogeny of English phrase structure. the first phase. *Language* 39: 1–14.

Braine, M. D. S. 1976. Children's first word combinations. *Monographs of the Society for Research in Child Development* No. 164.

Braine, M. D. S. & Hardy, J. A. 1982. On what case categories there are, why they are, and how they develop: an amalgam of *a priori* considerations, speculations, and evidence from children. In Wanner & Gleitman 1982.

Brown, R. 1957. Linguistic determinism and parts of speech. *Journal of Abnormal and Social Psychology* 55: 1–5.

Brown, R. 1973. *A first language*. Cambridge, MA: Harvard University Press.

Brown, R. & Bellugi, U. 1964. Three processes in the child's acquisition of syntax. *Harvard Educational Review* 34: 133–51.

Bruner, J. S. 1974/5. From communication to language: a psychological perspective. *Cognition* 3: 255–87.

Carey, S. 1982. Semantic development: the state of the art. In Wanner & Gleitman 1982.

Carey, S. 1985. *Conceptual change in childhood*. Cambridge, MA: MIT Press.

Chomsky, N. 1965. *Aspects of the theory of syntax*. Cambridge, MA: MIT Press.

Chomsky, N. 1975. *Reflections on language*. New York: Random House.

Chomsky, N. 1980. *Rules and representations*. New York: Columbia University Press.

Chomsky, N. 1981. *Lectures on government and binding*. Dordrecht: Foris.

Chomsky, N. 1982. *The generative enterprise: a discussion with Riny Huybregts and Henk van Riemsdijk*. Dordrecht: Foris.

Cooper, W. E. & Paccia-Cooper, J. 1980. *Syntax and speech*. Cambridge, MA: Harvard University Press.

Darwin, C. H. 1877. A biographical sketch of a young child. *Kosmos* 1: 367–76.

Dorian, N. 1978. The fate of morphological complexity in language death. *Language* 54.3: 590–609.

Eimas, P. D. 1975. Auditory and phonetic coding of the cues for speech: discrimination of the r–l distinction by young infants. *Perception and Psychophysics* 18: 341–57.

Eimas, P. D., Siqueland, E. R., Jusczyk, P. & Vigorito, J. 1971. Speech perception in infants. *Science* 171: 303–6.

Feldman, H., Goldin-Meadow, S. & Gleitman, L. R. 1978. Beyond Herodotus: the creation of language by linguistically deprived deaf children In A. Lock (ed.) *Action, symbol, and gesture: the emergence of language*. New York: Academic Press.

Fernald, A. 1984. The perceptual and affective salience of mothers' speech to infants. In L. Feagans, C. Garvey & R. Golinkoff (eds.) *The origins and growth of communication*. New Brunswick: Ablex.

Fernald, A. in press. Four-month old infants prefer to listen to Motherese. *Infant Behavior and Development*.

Fernald, A. & Simon, T. 1984. Expanded intonation contours in mothers' speech to newborns. *Developmental Psychology* 20: 104–13.

Field, J. 1976. Relation of young infant's reaching to stimulus distance and solidity. *Child Development* 50: 698–704.

Fisher, C., Gleitman, H. & Gleitman, L. R. 1986. Syntactic–semantic correlations in the organization of English verbs: an experimental investigation. ms.

Fodor, J. A. 1983. *The modularity of mind*. Cambridge, MA: MIT Press.

Furrow, D., Nelson, K. & Benedict, H. 1979. Mothers' speech to children and syntactic development: some simple relationships. *Journal of Child Language* 6: 423–42.

Garnica, O. K. 1977. Some prosodic and paralinguistic features of speech to young children. In C. Snow & C. A. Ferguson (eds.) *Talking to children: language input and acquisition*. Cambridge: Cambridge University Press.

Garrett, M. 1975. The analysis of sentence production. In G. H. Bower (ed.) *The psychology of learning and motivation*, Vol. 9. New York: Academic Press.

Gelman, R. 1986. First principles for structuring acquisition. Presidential address to Division 7, American Psychological Association.

Gelman, R. & Gallistel, C. R. 1978. *The young child's understanding of number: a window on early cognitive development.* Cambridge, MA: Harvard University Press.

Gentner, D. 1982. Why nouns are learned before verbs: linguistic relativity vs. natural partitioning. In S. Kuczaj (ed.) *Language development: language, culture, and cognition.* Hillsdale: Erlbaum.

Gerken, L., Landau, B. & Remez, R. forthcoming. The role of stress in children's early production and perception.

Gibson, E. J. & Spelke, E. 1983. The development of perception. In J. H. Flavell & E. Markman (eds.) *Cognitive development.* Vol. 3 of P. H. Mussen (ed.) *Handbook of cognitive psychology.* New York: Wiley.

Gibson, E. J. & Walker, A. S. 1984. Intermodal perception of substance. *Child Development* 55: 453–60.

Gleitman, L. R. & Gleitman, H. 1979. Language use and language judgment. In C. J. Fillmore, D. Kempler & W. S. Wang (eds.) *Individual differences in language ability and language behavior.* New York: Academic Press.

Gleitman, L. R., Newport, E. L. & Gleitman, H. 1984. The current status of the motherese hypothesis. *Journal of Child Language* 11.1: 43–80.

Gleitman, L. R. & Wanner, E. 1982. Language acquisition: the state of the state of the art. In Wanner & Gleitman 1982.

Gold, E. M. 1967. Language identification in the limit. *Information and Control* 10: 447–74.

Goldin-Meadow, S. & Feldman, H. 1979. The development of language-like communication without a language model. *Science* 197: 401–3.

Golinkoff, R. M., Harding, C. G., Carlson, V. & Sexton, M. E. 1984. The infant's perception of causal events: the distinction between animate and inanimate objects. In L. P. Lipsitt & C. Rovee-Collier (eds.) *Advances in Infancy Research* 3: 145–65.

Golinkoff, R., Hirsh-Pasek, P., Cauley, K. & Gordon, L. in press. The eyes have it: lexical and syntactic comprehension in a new paradigm. *Journal of Child Language.*

Grimshaw, J. 1981. Form, function, and the language acquisition device. In C. L. Baker & J. J. McCarthy, *The logical problem of language acquisition.* Cambridge: MIT Press.

Gruber, J. 1968. Look and see. *Language* 43: 937–47.

Harris, Z. S. 1951. *Methods in structural linguistics.* Chicago: University of Chicago Press.

Hirsh-Pasek, K., Golinkoff, R., Fletcher, A., DeGaspe Beaubien, F. & Cauley, K. 1985. In the beginning: one-word speakers comprehend word order. Paper presented at *Boston Language Conference*, October 1985.

Hirsh-Pasek, K., Kemler-Nelson, D. G., Jusczyk, P. W., Woodward, A., Piwez, J. & Kennedy, L. 1987. The perception of major phrase boundaries by prelinguistic infants. ms.

Hirsh-Pasek, K., Kemler-Nelson, D. G., Jusczyk, P. W., Wright, K. & Druss, B. in press. Clauses are perceptual units for young infants, *Cognition.*

Hofsten, C. von & Spelke, E. S. 1985. Object perception and object-directed looking in infancy. *Journal of Experimental Psychology: General* 114: 198–212.

Hyams, N. 1986. *Language acquisition and the theory of parameters.* Dordrecht: Reidel.

Hyams, N. 1987. The theory of parameters and syntactic development. In Roeper & Williams 1987.

Jackendoff, R. 1983. *Semantics and cognition.* Cambridge, MA: MIT Press.

Johnson, J. & Newport, E. 1986. Critical period effects in second language learning: the influence of maturational state on the acquisition of English as a second language. Speech delivered at the *Boston Child Language Conference*, October 1986.

Jusczyk, P. W. 1979. Infant speech perception: a critical appraisal. In P. D. Eimas & J. L. Miller (eds.) *Perspectives on the study of speech.* Hillsdale: Erlbaum.

Jusczyk, P. W. 1986. A review of speech perception work. In L. Kaufman, J. Thomas & K. Boff (eds.) *Handbook of perception and performance.* New York: Wiley.

Katz, N., Baker, E. & MacNamara, J. 1974. What's in a name? A study of how children learn common and proper names. *Child Development* 45: 469–73.

Kean, M. L. 1979. Agrammatism: a phonological deficit? *Cognition* 7.1: 69–84.

Keil, F. 1979. *Semantic and conceptual development.* Cambridge, MA: Harvard University Press.

Kellman, P. J. & Spelke, E. S. 1983. Perception of partly occluded objects in infancy. *Cognitive Psychology* 15: 483–524.

Kestenbaum, R., Termine, N. & Spelke, E. S. in press. Perception of objects and object boundaries by three-month old infants. *British Journal of Developmental Psychology*.

Klatt, D. H. 1975. Vowel lengthening is syntactically determined in a connected discourse. *Journal of Phonetics* 3: 129–40.

Klatt, D. H. 1976. Linguistic uses of segmental duration in English: acoustic and perceptual evidence. *Journal of the Acoustic Society of America* 59: 1208–21.

Klatt, D. H. & Cooper, W. E. 1975. Perception of segment duration in sentence contexts. In A. Cohen & S. Nooteboom (eds.) *Structure and process in speech perception*. Heidelberg: Springer-Verlag.

Kuhl, P. K. 1983. Perception of auditory equivalence classes for speech by infants. *Infant Behavior and Development* 6: 263–85.

Kuhl, P. K. & Miller, J. D. 1975. Speech perception by the chinchilla: voiced–voiceless distinction in alveolar plosive consonants. *Science* 190: 69–72.

Landau, B. & Gleitman, L. R. 1985. *Language and experience: evidence from the blind child*. Cambridge, MA: Harvard University Press.

Lasky, R. E. & Gogol, W. C. 1978. The perception of relative motion by young infants. *Perception* 7: 617–23.

Lehiste, I., Olive, J. P. & Streeter, L. A. 1976. The role of duration in disambiguating syntactically ambiguous sentences. *Journal of the Acoustical Society of America* 60: 1199–202.

Levy, L. S. & Joshi, A. K. 1978. Skeletal structural descriptions. *Information and Control* 5: 35–45.

Luce, P. A. & Charles-Luce, J. 1983. Contextual effects on the consonant/vowel ratio in speech production. Paper presented at the 105th meeting of the Acoustical Society of America, Cincinatti, May 1983.

Lust, B. 1986. *Studies in the acquisition of anaphora*. Vol. 1: *Defining the constraints*. Dordrecht: Reidel.

MacNamara, J. 1972. Cognitive basis for language learning in infants. *Psychological Review* 79: 1–13.

Maratsos, M. 1982. The child's construction of grammatical categories. In Wanner & Gleitman 1982.

Maratsos, M. & Chalkley, M. A. 1980. The internal language of children's syntax: the ontogenesis and representation of syntactic categories. In K. Nelson (ed.) *Children's language*, Vol. 2. New York: Gardner Press.

Markman, E. 1986. How children constrain the possible meanings of words. In U. Neisser (ed.) *The ecological and intellectual basis of categorization*. Cambridge: Cambridge University Press.

Markman, E. M. & Hutchinson, J. E. 1984. Children's sensitivity to constraints on word meaning: taxonomic versus thematic relations. *Cognitive Psychology* 16.1: 1–27.

Mehler, J., Bertononcini, J., Barriere, M. & Jassik-Gerschenfeld, D. 1978. Infant recognition of mother's voice. *Perception* 7: 491–7.

Mervis, C. B. & Crisafi, M. 1978. Order of acquisition of subordinate, basic, and superordinate level categories. *Child Development* 49.4: 988–98.

Morgan, J. 1986. *From simple input to complex grammar*. Cambridge, MA: MIT Press.

Morgan, J., Meier, R. & Newport, E. in press. Structural packaging in the input to language learning: contributions of intonational and morphological marking of phrases to the acquisition of language. *Cognitive Psychology*.

Morgan, J. & Newport, E. 1981. The role of constituent structure in the induction of an artificial language. *Journal of Verbal Learning and Verbal Behavior* 20: 67–85.

Naigles, L., Gleitman, H. & Gleitman, L. R. 1986. Syntactic boot strapping. ms.

Nakatani, L. & Dukes, K. 1977. Locus of segmental cues for word juncture. *Journal of the Acoustic Society of America* 62.3: 714–24.

Nakatani, L. & Schaffer, J. 1978. Hearing 'words' without words: prosodic cues for word perception. *Journal of the Acoustic Society of America* 63.1: 234–45.

Nelson, K. 1974. Concept, word and sentence: interrelations in acquisition and development. *Psychological Review* 81: 267–85.

Newport, E. L. 1977. Motherese: the speech of mothers to young children. In N. Castellan, D. Pisoni & G. Potts (eds.) *Cognitive theory*, Vol. 2. Hillsdale: Erlbaum.

Newport, E. L., Gleitman, H. & Gleitman, L. R. 1977. Mother, I'd rather do it myself: some effects and non-effects of maternal speech style. In C. E. Snow and C. A. Ferguson (eds.) *Talking to children: language input and acquisition.* Cambridge: Cambridge University Press.

Ninio, A. 1980. Ostensive definition in vocabulary teaching. *Journal of Child Language* 7.3: 565–74.

Osherson, D. N., Stob, M. & Weinstein, S. 1986. *Systems that learn.* Cambridge, MA: MIT Press.

Pinker, S. 1984. *Language learnability and language development.* Cambridge, MA: Harvard University Press.

Pye, C. 1983. Mayan telegraphese: intonational determinants of inflectional development in Quiché Mayan. *Language* 59.3: 583–604.

Read, C. & Schreiber, P. 1982. Why short subjects are harder to find than long ones. In Wanner & Gleitman 1982.

Rescorla, L. 1980. Overextension in early language development. *Journal of Child Language* 7.2: 321–36.

Roeper, T. & Williams, E. (eds.) 1987. *Parameter setting.* Dordrecht: Reidel.

Rosch, E. 1978. Principles of categorization. In E. Rosch & B. Lloyd (eds.) *Cognition and categorization.* Hillsdale: Erlbaum.

Rozin, P. & Gleitman, L. R. 1977. The structure and acquisition of reading, II: The reading process and the acquisition of the alphabetic principle. In A. S. Reber & D. Scarborough (eds.) *Towards a psychology of reading.* Hillsdale: Erlbaum.

Sankoff, G. & LaBerge, S. 1973. On the acquisition of native speakers by a language. *Kivung* 6: 32–47.

Schieffelin, B. 1979. Getting it together: an ethnographic approach to the study of the development of communicative competence. In E. Ochs & B. B. Schieffelin (eds.) *Developmental pragmatics.* New York: Academic Press.

Shipley, E. F., Kuhn, I. F. & Madden, E. C. 1983. Mother's use of superordinate terms. *Journal of Child Language* 10.3: 571–88.

Shipley, E. F., Smith, C. S. & Gleitman, L. R. 1969. A study in the acquisition of language: free responses to commands. *Language* 45: 322–42.

Slobin, D. I. 1966. The acquisition of Russian as a native language. In F. Smith and C. A. Miller (eds.) *The genesis of language.* Cambridge, MA: MIT Press.

Slobin, D. I. 1973. Cognitive prerequisites for the development of grammar. In C. A. Ferguson and D. I. Slobin (eds.) *Studies of child language development.* New York: Holt, Rinehart, & Winston.

Slobin, D. I. 1975. On the nature of talk to children. In E. H. Lenneberg & E. Lenneberg (eds.) *Foundation of language development,* Vol. 1. New York: Academic Press.

Slobin. D. I. 1982. Universal and particular in the acquisition of language. In Wanner & Gleitman 1982.

Slobin, D. I. & Bever, T. G. 1982. Children use canonical sentence schemas: a crosslinguistic study of word order and inflections. *Cognition* 12: 229–65.

Snow, C. E. 1977. Mother's speech research: from input to interaction. In Snow & Ferguson 1977.

Snow, C. E. & Ferguson, C. A. (eds.) 1977. *Talking to children: language input and acquisition.* Cambridge: Cambridge University Press.

Spelke, E. S. 1979. Perceiving bimodally specified events in infancy. *Developmental Psychology* 15: 626–36.

Spelke, E. S. 1982. Perceptual knowledge of objects in infancy. In J. Mehler, E. C. T. Walker & M. Garrett (eds.) *Perspectives on mental representations.* Hillsdale: Erlbaum.

Spelke, E. S. 1985. Perception of unity, persistence, and identity: thoughts on infants' conceptions of objects. In J. Mehler & R. Fox (eds.) *Neonate cognition.* Hillsdale: Erlbaum.

Spring, D. R. & Dale, P. S. 1977. Discrimination of linguistic stress in early infancy. *Journal of Speech and Hearing Research* 20: 224–31.

Starkey, P., Spelke, E. S. & Gelman, R. 1983. Detection of 1–1 correspondences by human infants. *Science* 210: 1033–5.

Strauss, M. S. & Curtis, L. E. 1981. Infant perception of numerosity. *Child Development* 52: 1146–52.

Streeter, L. A. 1978. Acoustic determinants of phrase boundary perception. *Journal of the Acoustic Society of America* 64: 1582–92.

Talmy, L. 1983. How language structures space. In H. Pick & L. Acredolo (eds.) *Spatial orientation: theory, research, and application.* New York: Plenum.

Walker, A. S., Owsley, C. J., Megaw-Nyce, J. S., Gibson, E. J. & Bahrick, L. E. 1980. Detection of elasticity as an invariant property of objects by young infants. *Perception* 9: 713–18.

Wanner, E. & Gleitman, L. R. (eds.) 1982. *Language acquisition: the state of the art.* Cambridge: Cambridge University Press.

Wanner, E. & Maratsos, M. 1978. An ATN approach to comprehension. In M. Halle, J. Bresnan & G. A. Miller (eds.) *Linguistic theory and psychological reality.* Cambridge, MA: MIT Press.

Waxman, S. & Gelman, R. 1986. Preschoolers' use of superordinate relations in classification. *Cognitive Development* 1: 139–56.

Wexler, K. 1982. A principle theory for language acquisition. In Wanner & Gleitman 1982.

Wexler, K. & Culicover, P. 1980. *Formal principles of language acquisition.* Cambridge, MA: MIT Press.

Wexler, K. & Manzini, R. 1987. Parameters and learnability in binding theory. In Roeper & Williams 1987.

7 Second language acquisition

Ellen Broselow

7.0. Introduction

Research on second language acquisition is an especially complicated endeavor.[1] The working out of a complete grammar of a single language is a task of enormous complexity, one that has yet to be completed for any human language. It is all the more daunting, then, to realize that an understanding of all the factors influencing a language learner's performance demands a fairly well-articulated analysis of at least two languages, the native language and the target language. Furthermore, while linguists attempting to describe the grammatical patterns of a single language must deal with the complicating factors of social and regional variation, anyone investigating the acquisition of a foreign language must grapple not only with these but with a host of additional relevant variables: the age at which the learner was exposed to the foreign language; the type of exposure to the foreign language (through formal instruction or outside the classroom); the learner's knowledge of other foreign languages. And while linguists can fairly safely assume that all adult native speakers of a language have reached a particular stage of mastery of the core grammar of that language, learners of a foreign language may have widely varying levels of competence and motivation.

Yet the potential rewards of such study are considerable. The systematic errors of second language learners can provide a valuable source of external evidence to test linguistic theories. For example, where particular error patterns are associated with particular native language backgrounds, we may assume that these errors provide some reflection of the grammatical system of the first language – the sort of evidence which may not be available from evidence internal to the first language. Furthermore, the occurrence of similar error patterns among learners of varying language backgrounds, where such errors are not directly predictable from study of either

[1] A number of people have been very helpful to me in my writing of this chapter, notably Mark Aronoff, Suzanne Flynn, and S. N. Sridhar, and especially Dan Finer.

the native or the target language systems, may provide important insight into universal principles governing language acquisition.[2]

Of course, the question of how human beings acquire a foreign language is an interesting one quite apart from its implications for issues in the description of linguistic knowledge. But a look at the history of research in second language acquisition reveals that, to a large extent, it has been driven by developments in linguistic theory; the questions that researchers in second language acquisition have asked, and the sorts of data that they have identified as significant, have varied as hypotheses concerning language acquisition have evolved. As the linguist's view of language acquisition has moved from the view that language learning involves learning a set of habits to the view that language learning involves the creative construction of a grammar, the focus of second language acquisition studies has shifted from examining the influence of the mother tongue to finding a commonality of error patterns across various language backgrounds and to finding parallels between first and second language acquisition. More recent concentration on formulation of principles of Universal Grammar which constrain the range of hypotheses the child language learner can entertain has led to examination of the role of these principles in second language acquisition. And recent work has begun the task of sorting out the various factors operating in second language acquisition: influence of the native language, developmental factors, and the influence of markedness and universal principles.

This chapter will provide an overview, necessarily brief, of these major trends in second language (L2) acquisition research. The organization is roughly historical. As is inevitable in such a survey, a whole range of important issues and studies have been either ignored or given short shrift, but this neglect is a reflection of lack of space rather than lack of interest.

7.1. Contrastive analysis and creative construction

The structuralist assumption that language learning consists of learning a set of habits implies that the habits of the L1 should interfere with the learning of subsequent languages. It is not surprising, then, that most of the work in L2 research carried out within a structuralist framework focussed on the comparison of the grammatical systems of the first and the second language and on errors that could be attributed to the differences between these two systems. According to the contrastive analysis hypothesis (Fries 1945, Lado 1957, Wardhaugh 1970), an examination of the differences between the first

---

[2] See for example Comrie (1985), who argues that data from second language acquisition may help choose between alternative formulations of the noun phrase accessibility hierarchy, both compatible with the range of facts in native language grammars.

and second languages should allow one to predict or at least explain errors made by second language learners: in areas where the two languages are the same, learning should be facilitated, and where the structure of the L1 and the L2 differ, learners should encounter difficulty due to interference or negative transfer (Carroll 1968). The popularity of this hypothesis in the 1950s and 1960s produced a number of studies, largely pedagogically oriented, comparing some aspect of the structures of two languages. Perhaps the most serious and comprehensive attempt at a contrastive analysis is provided by the volumes by Stockwell and Bowen (1965) and Stockwell, Bowen & Martin (1965) comparing the phonology and the syntax of Spanish and English; these works contain not only a comparison of the surface facts of the two languages, but also an attempt to categorize the types of differences one might find between two linguistic systems, and to rank these types of differences in terms of relative difficulty of acquisition. In general, however, most early contrastive analyses failed to tackle the problems of distinguishing the sorts of differences that were and were not likely to cause problems, and of predicting what form errors would take when the learner was confronted with a second language structure that did not have a direct analogue in the first language. Furthermore, most contrastive studies of this era focussed only on phonology – with good reason, since it was generally in the area of phonology that errors attributable to language transfer were most obvious, and since most structuralist analyses dealt with syntactic patterns superficially if at all.

The generative view of language acquisition as a creative process guided by innate, universal mechanisms brought with it a reaction against the view that the native language is the primary influence on the learning of a second language. The focus of much second language research shifted to errors that could not be explained as transfer of native language structures or rules, errors that often paralleled those made by children acquiring the L2 as their first language. Ervin-Tripp (1974), for example, argued that English-speaking children learning French tend at first to interpret passive sentences in French as active, though they have already mastered the active–passive distinction in English, and Ravem (1968) argued that his Norwegian-speaking children learning English as a second language, like children learning English as their native language, proceeded through a stage of placing the negative marker directly after the subject, though the normal position of the negative is sentence-final in Norwegian. Bailey, Madden & Krashen (1974) found a similar sequence of acquisition of various English morphemes in child L1 and adult L2 acquirers of English. Hatch 1978 contains several additional studies reporting correspondences in the developmental stages of first and second language acquirers, both children and adults.

The reaction against the attempt to ascribe all systematic errors in L2 acquisition to influence of the L1 was given its strongest expression by Dulay and Burt (1974a, b), who concluded, on the basis of their examination of the acquisition of English by Spanish-speaking children, that transfer was simply not a factor in L2 acquisition, at least in syntax. These and similar studies contributed to the view of the language learner's production as the reflection of a coherent system, rather than as a distortion of the second language grammar through interference from the L1. Creative construction, as this view is sometimes called, predicts that we should find the same error patterns occurring in learners despite their L1 backgrounds, and that these patterns should correspond to those of the child acquiring the language. This view brought with it a corresponding change in terminology; researchers began to use the term *error analysis* (Richards 1974) rather than contrastive analysis, and the term *interlanguage* (IL) was suggested by Selinker (1972) to refer to the grammar of the second language learner, a grammar presumably distinct from that of a native speaker of either the L1 or L2, but one which could nonetheless be seen as a coherent system worthy of study in its own right.[3]

But while evidence has accumulated that many of the syntactic errors in L2 acquisition cannot be accounted for as a result of the transfer of L1 patterns, transfer in phonology seems to remain an inescapable fact of life.[4] It might be argued, however, that phonological transfer, manifested in the familiar form of phoneme substitution, is simply a matter of the transfer of motor skills, and therefore of no concern to the linguist interested in cognitive principles. This assumption, though unstated, is a likely factor in the neglect of L2 phonology within a creative construction framework. It is important to note, however, that transfer has been documented not just in the form of transfer of particular patterns of movement of the articulators – that is, in phoneme substitution and application of low level phonetic rules – but in other aspects of phonological organization as well. Thus Mairs (1985) argues that while the errors made by Spanish speakers in stressing English words cannot be explained as direct transfer of Spanish stress rules, these errors result from a more subtle form of transfer: the Spanish learners apply English stress rules, but the syllabic structure which forms the basis of stress assignment is based on Spanish principles of syllabic organization. Furthermore, transfer appears in the learner's perception of the L2 as well as its production. Broselow (1984) provides evidence that the fairly complex rules governing the relationship between phonetic cues, syllable structure, and word structure may be transferred in language learning, leading learners to

---

[3] Competing terms which have not achieved such wide currency, at least in the United States, are 'approximative system' (Nemser 1971) and 'idiosyncratic dialect' (Corder 1971).

[4] See Ioup 1984 for empirical verification of the intuitively correct notion that people can fairly reliably identify the L1 of language learners on the basis of their phonology. Flege (to appear) provides a valuable overview of the literature on transfer in second language phonology.

misparse L2 strings by incorrectly interpreting L2 phonetic cues in terms of the L1 rules. Broselow, Hurtig & Ringen (forthcoming) argue that English speakers' errors in the perception of Chinese tone result from interference from the English grammar of intonation.

Moreover, while transfer may not be so obvious a factor in syntax as in phonology, fairly convincing evidence has been presented that differences in the syntactic structure of the L1 and L2 may in fact influence L2 acquisition. For example, Jansen, Lalleman & Muysken (1981) argue that Turkish and Moroccan guest workers learning Dutch differ in their acquisition of the two possible Dutch word orders; Turkish speakers prefer SOV order while Moroccans prefer SVO order. In each case the preferred order corresponds to the preferred order of the native language. Le Compagnon (1984) argues that French speakers' overgeneralization of the English double object construction with pronoun indirect objects (as in *He explained me the rule*) is an effect of transfer of L1 rules involving pronoun clitics. Flynn (1984) argues that the directionality of branching in a language affects acquisition of complex sentences, with greater difficulty of acquisition associated with differences in directionality in the L1 and L2. And Schachter (1974) claims that transfer may be manifested not in errors but in avoidance of the L2 structures that are most different from corresponding structures in L1. Thus the evidence suggests that L2 acquisition is influenced both by transfer from the L1 and by developmental factors.

7.2. Universals in L2 acquisition

The findings of the creative construction school were useful in establishing that learners' grammars may display structural patterns distinct from those of either the L1 or the L2, and that these patterns may be similar to those revealed in the developing grammars of L1 acquirers. But once this is established, it leads inexorably to the question of why this should be the case: why should particular configurations appear in both L1 and L2 acquisition, even when the grammar of the target language offers no direct evidence for them?

7.2.1. Typologies and markedness

One possible answer to this question is that particular learning strategies, such as overgeneralization or simplification, are involved in both first and second language acquisition (see Adjémian 1976 for discussion). Since these notions are notoriously hard to define, this approach is somewhat resistant to testing. A second approach to this question incorporates the findings of typological work such as that of Greenberg (1963), which sets forth, on the basis of a survey of the surface patterns of a wide variety of languages, implicational relationships holding between various sorts of constructions. Where it can be shown that any language that has construction A will also have construction B, construction A is said to be more marked – rarer, and presumably more difficult to learn – than construction B. The hypothesis that this notion of markedness also plays a role in L2 acquisition has led to interesting results. For example, the noun phrase accessibility hierarchy of Keenan and Comrie (1977) has been argued to be relevant in L2 acquisition of relative clauses. This hierarchy sets out the degree of markedness of relative clauses of various types, ranging from the least marked, in which the relativized element corresponds to the subject of the relative clause (as in *the man who came in*), to the most marked, in which the relative is the object of a comparative (such as *the man whom I am taller than*). It is generally true that a language that allows relativization from a more marked position will allow it on all less marked positions, but not *vice versa*. Gass (1979, 1980, 1984) and Gass & Ard (1985) present evidence that learners find relative clauses involving noun phrases in less marked positions on the hierarchy easier to produce and understand than relatives formed involving noun phrases from more marked positions, even where the L1 allows the marked relatives.[5] And both Gass (1979, 1980, 1984) and Ioup & Kruse (1977) found a tendency for subjects to accept resumptive pronouns (such as *him* in *the man that I saw him*) in English relatives formed on nouns in more marked positions, even where the subjects' L1 does not permit resumptive pronouns. This fact is presumably related to the universally greater likelihood of resumptive pronouns in more highly marked relative clause types.

Once the notion of markedness (as relative difficulty) of certain constructions is accepted, of course, the door is open for a readmission of the notion of language transfer. Eckman (1977) suggests that areas of difficulty in language learning *can* be predicted from contrastive analysis, if such analysis takes into account the relative markedness of the L1 and L2 constructions in question: an L2 structure will be difficult to learn if it is different from the corresponding structure in L1 *and* if it is more marked than the L1 structure. Eckman compares the German speaker's task of learning to produce a word-final voicing contrast in English obstruents (a fairly difficult task) with the English speaker's much easier task of learning to suppress this contrast in German, and argues that while traditional contrastive analysis does not predict any difference in difficulty – since in both

---

[5] However, relatives formed in genitive NPs constituted an exception to this generalization; they were easier for L2 learners than many less marked constructions, suggesting that other factors also play a role.

cases, the learner is faced with a difference between L1 and L2 – the notion of markedness makes just the right predictions. Since maintenance of a voicing contrast between obstruents in word-final position is marked relative to maintenance of this contrast in other positions in the word, English speakers learning German are learning a less marked system, while German speakers learning English must master a more marked system.

Interestingly, however, Eckman's argument, while suggesting the important consequences that a theory of markedness might have for second language research, at the same time illustrates a weakness of this approach. Eckman also discusses the task of learning to produce word-initial *ž* faced by an English speaker learning French. Learning to produce the voiced obstruent *ž* in initial position is much easier than learning to produce final voiced obstruents, a fact that Eckman also ascribes to markedness: since it is more marked for a language to maintain a voicing contrast in final position than in initial position, the English speaker learning French is learning a relatively unmarked system (initial *š* and *ž*). But the two tasks – the English speaker's learning to produce word-initial *ž* and the German speaker's learning to produce word-final voiced obstruents – hardly seem comparable. It makes sense to speak of the German speaker's task as learning to produce a contrast in voicing, since the German speaker must learn to produce the entire series of voiced obstruents. Doing this involves learning to suppress a native language rule, supported by numerous alternations, that systematically neutralizes the opposition between all voiced and voiceless obstruents in final position, turning underlying *b* to *p*, *d* to *t*, and so forth. But an English speaker's learning to produce initial *ž* is not the same sort of task. Though Eckman describes this as learning to produce a contrast between initial *š* and *ž*, the English speaker is not suppressing the tendency to transform initial *ž* into *š*. If anything, English speakers tend to substitute the voiced affricate ǰ, rather than the corresponding voiceless fricative, for *ž*. Thus Eckman might just as well have analyzed the English speaker's task as learning to produce a contrast between initial ǰ and *ž* – a relatively rare contrast, as it happens. On this view, it is not clear how to rank the relative difficulty of the English speaker's and the German speaker's tasks.[6]

Thus, since this view of markedness makes reference solely to the distribution of surface characteristics of the language, and since nothing in the theory tells us which surface features can and cannot be considered to be related, almost any widely distributed feature can be linked in a markedness relation with almost any rare feature. The theory therefore makes possible a number of different analyses of the same facts, with different predictions.

[6] See Broselow 1984 for arguments that the ease with which English speakers learn to produce word-initial *ž* is due to the fact that English has this phoneme syllable-initially, with an arbitrary prohibition restricting the distribution of syllables beginning in *ž* to non-word-initial position.

And since the theory does not recognize a distinction between surface asymmetrical distributions resulting from application of a rule (such as German word-final devoicing) and those reflecting a gap in the distribution of a single phoneme (such as English nonoccurrence of word-initial *ž*), it does not distinguish between very different sorts of learning tasks.

7.2.2. Universal Grammar and parameterized systems

An alternative approach to markedness ties markedness explicitly to a theory of language acquisition. This is the approach developed in recent works such as Chomsky 1980 and 1981. Throughout Chomsky's work, the child's task is presumed to be that of constructing a grammar of the native language based on the incomplete and somewhat misleading data to which the child has access. (The problem of how the child accomplishes this task – the projection problem – is discussed in Baker 1979, Wexler & Culicover 1980, Zobl 1983, and Berwick 1985, among others.) It is assumed in recent work that this task is made possible by the innate principles of Universal Grammar (UG), which define the class of possible human languages and therefore constrain the range of hypotheses that a child can entertain about the structure of its language. UG makes available to the child a set of parameters along with knowledge of possible settings of those parameters. The child presumably starts out with the unmarked value for each parameter, and resets the parameter only when confronted by data incompatible with the unmarked setting. The description of grammars in terms of parameter settings makes an explicit and organic connection between developmental factors in language acquisition and distributional, typological properties of languages. First, since a given parameter setting may induce a constellation of properties, the theory of parameters may serve to predict the simultaneous presence or absence in a language of phenomena which are logically independent but which do in fact seem to be distributionally linked; thus for example a positive setting of the pro-drop parameter (Rizzi 1982) implies both the absence of personal subject pronouns (as in Italian *verrà* 'He will come') and an absence of expletive subjects in sentences like *It's raining*. A fully worked out theory of parameters would constitute a theory of possible variation across languages, and because parameters are presumed to be part of the child's innate equipment, identification of the marked and unmarked values of parameter settings would also constitute a theory of first language acquisition. Here too, markedness may be defined with respect not only to frequency of occurrence in the world's languages but also to acquisition. Much recent work has argued that children do not have access to negative evidence in language acquisition (Baker 1979): that is, children are not often told that particular constructions are ungrammatical, and tend to disregard such admonitions when they are offered. On this assumption, children must start out with the most restrictive parameter settings, those that generate the smallest class of sentences, resetting these parameters only when confronted by positive evidence. The unmarked setting, then, is the setting which generates the most restrictive grammar, and this setting is maintained until the child is exposed to positive evidence suggesting that it is too restrictive for the language being acquired. For example, consider the parameter that determines the domain in which reflexive pronouns may be related to an antecedent (Wexler & Manzini 1987). In English, the domain is the clause,[7] so in a sentence like *John thinks that Bill likes himself*, the reflexive *himself* may refer only to Bill, not to John. In a language like Korean or Japanese, however, the sentence is ambiguous; the reflexive may refer to either John or Bill. Thus English has the more restrictive – and therefore less marked – parameter setting. The assumption that only positive evidence is relevant to L1 acquisition dictates that the English setting is the less marked one – the initial setting – since a child in an English-speaking environment who started out with the more marked Korean setting would never have reason to retreat to the English setting. While the child might never hear an English sentence in which a reflexive had a noun phrase in a higher clause as its antecedent, the child would not be forced to conclude that such a sentence was impossible. A Korean child starting out with the English parameter setting, however – that is, starting out with the assumption that reflexives may be coreferential only with noun phrases in their own clauses – would eventually be exposed to positive evidence contradicting this assumption in the form of sentences containing a reflexive which is coreferential with a noun phrase in a higher clause. Investigation of this view of the acquisition of principles of reflexive binding in L1 acquisition of a variety of languages is currently underway (Wexler & Manzini 1985).[8]

Whether a parameterized theory would account for second language acquisition as well is an open question, but one which is beginning to be explored. It is conceivable that the principles of UG might simply be unavailable to the second language learner, particularly the adult second language learner who has passed what Lenneberg (1967) argued is the critical period for language acquisition, the period during which the child retains the ability to acquire language naturally. Furthermore, classroom L2 learners are certainly exposed to negative evidence (though the extent to which this affects their performance seems to vary). Consideration of these factors might lead to the view that second language acquisition is a very different process from first language acquisition.

[7] More precisely, any category containing a subject.
[8] Investigation of L2 acquisition of reflexives is discussed below.

However, the wealth of evidence accumulated in support of the creative construction hypothesis, revealing parallels between first and second language acquisition, calls into question the view that L2 acquisition and L1 acquisition are completely different enterprises. And if it were true that L2 acquisition proceeds independently of UG principles, we would expect to find interlanguage grammars violating the principles governing other natural languages. Yet, so far as I know, only one candidate has been proposed for an interlanguage rule of a type not found in any native language. This is the rule of 'schwa paragoge' found by Eckman (1981) to operate in the English of native Mandarin speakers. These speakers added a schwa after word-final voiced obstruents, producing forms such as [bigǝ] for 'big.' Eckman argues that no natural language has a rule like schwa paragoge. Such claims are notoriously vulnerable to disconfirmation, which requires only the discovery of one language that has this rule, and though Eckman does not make clear exactly what aspect of the rule makes it unlike any other L1 rule, this claim does seem to be shaky, on several grounds. First, the cautious universalist would like to establish that the inserted schwas do represent true phonological vowels rather than simply forceful release of the consonant. Second, since Eckman did not investigate his subjects' pronunciation of words with internal consonant clusters, the possibility cannot be ruled out that the subjects are actually applying a syllabically conditioned epenthesis rule, a very common type of rule in both L1 and interlanguage grammars (Broselow 1983). But even if the schwa paragoge resists reanalysis as a more familiar rule type, there is at least one language that has a parallel L1 rule inserting a vowel word finally (see Bright 1958 for a discussion of the rule inserting *u* between a consonant and word boundary in Kannada).

Furthermore, there is a growing body of evidence that learners are sensitive to principles of Universal Grammar, even where their native language does not provide direct evidence for the applicability of these principles in particular constructions. Thus Finer and Broselow (1986) present evidence from a pilot study that Korean speakers' interpretation of reflexives in complex sentences does not follow the principles of either English or Korean reflexive binding, but is consistent with the facts of other natural languages. In brief, Korean subjects presented with sentences like the following

(1)   a. John told Bill to paint himself
      b. John thinks that Bill paints himself

showed a greater tendency to interpret the reflexive *himself* as coreferential with *John* in sentences of type a, where the reflexive occurs in an infinitive clause, than in sentences of type b, where the reflexive occurs in a tensed clause. Recall that the equivalent sentences are ambiguous in Korean, both allowing the reflexive to be coreferential with either *John* or *Bill*, while of course in English both allow only *Bill* as the antecedent of *himself*. Thus, the tendency of the Korean learners of English to admit the possibility of coreferentiality between higher noun phrases and reflexives in infinitive clauses more often than between higher noun phrases and reflexives in tensed clauses is not motivated by the facts of either the L1 or the L2, but this asymmetry is consistent with the possible settings of the parameter argued to govern reflexive interpretation: there are languages midway between Korean and English which allow reflexives to take antecedents outside of infinitive clauses but not outside of tensed clauses. However, no language has been discovered that allows the reverse, though such a situation is logically possible. If language learners exhibited the latter pattern of interpretation, we could conclude that their interlanguage grammar violates universal principles; instead, these results are consistent with the hypothesis that the performance of second language learners is governed by possible natural language parameter settings. Similarly, Ritchie (1978) found that Japanese learners of English are sensitive to the proposed universal principle now known as subjacency, which (among other things) prevents rightward movement into a higher clause, as in sentences like * *That it surprised Mary amused Alice that John had left.* Sentences like this were judged ungrammatical by Japanese learners more often than the corresponding version without the movement (*That it surprised Mary that John had left amused Alice*). Since Japanese does not have analogous rightward movement, subjects' judgements were not based on facts of the native language. And finally, Mazurkewich (1984) found that the order of acquisition of English datives by native speakers of French and Inuktitut proceeded in accord with universal principles of markedness: both groups of learners acquired the less marked prepositional phrase complements (*William sent a memo to Isabel*) earlier than the more marked double-NP complements (*William sent Isabel a memo*), despite differences in similar constructions in their first languages.[9]

Other evidence bearing on the importance of universal principles is found in the acquisition of L2 phonology. Altenberg and Vago (1983) found that Hungarians learning English tended to apply unmarked rules, such as the rule devoicing a word-final obstruent, in pronunciation of the target language, though this rule is not part of the grammar of either Hungarian or English.[10] Furthermore, even clearly transfer-based processes may be influenced by universal principles. Various investigations have shown that language learners tend to simplify L2 syllables when these syllables are structurally

[9] See Rutherford 1984 for further discussion of recent work in this area.
[10] English does partially devoice word-final obstruents, but presumably the devoicing displayed by Altenberg and Vago's subjects was significantly greater than that displayed by native speakers of English.

more complex than the syllables of the L1 (Broselow 1983, Sato 1984), and the direction of simplification tends to vary according to the L1, suggesting an effect of transfer. But Tyrone (1980) and, to a lesser extent, Hodne (1985) found that subjects whose native languages had syllables of a complexity roughly equivalent to those of English tended to simplify English syllables to the unmarked CV structure. Thus even syllables of a type that occurs in the L1 were simplified in the direction of less marked syllable types. Furthermore, even where it appears that L2 syllable structure is modified only when it is more complex than L1 syllable structure, the influence of transfer is not sufficient to account for the pattern of syllable modification in L2. Broselow (1983) presents evidence that native speakers of Egyptian and Iraqui Arabic exhibit different patterns of pronunciation of English words beginning in consonant clusters; where Egyptians pronounce *floor*, for example, as [filor], the Iraqi pronunciation is [iflor]. Broselow traces this difference to a difference in L1 patterns of epenthesis: Egyptians insert a vowel to the right of an otherwise unsyllabifiable consonant, while Iraqis insert a vowel to the left of the consonant. However, Egyptians deviate from this pattern in one class of words, those beginning in s-stop clusters, which are produced with the epenthetic vowel before the *s*: [istadi] for 'study.' The differential treatment of clusters consisting of *s* plus an obstruent, on one hand, and of an obstruent plus a sonorant, on the other, is quite widespread across L1 backgrounds, as well as in L1 acquisition, and is unquestionably related to the universal principles governing the structure of syllables. Elements in the syllable tend universally to be arranged so that sounds of decreasing sonority are further from the nucleus of the syllable; thus, at the beginning of a syllable, stops (the least sonorous elements) should precede the more sonorous fricatives, which should in turn precede the even more sonorous liquids. Initial s-stop clusters provide the only violation of this principle in English syllable onsets, and this, along with other evidence, has been used to argue for the treatment of s-stop clusters as single units at some level of representation (Selkirk 1982); such units are therefore not capable of being divided by epenthesis. Learners are presumably constrained by the sonority principle to analyze all clusters that violate the sonority hierarchy as complex segments.

The evidence is convincing, then, that universal principles, along with language transfer, do play some role in L2 acquisition. Given this, there are a number of plausible hypotheses available concerning the way in which that acquisition proceeds. One hypothesis is that one learns a second language in exactly the same way as the first, by beginning with the unmarked parameter settings and resetting parameters only when confronted with L2 data demanding a marked setting; this is the hypothesis most compatible with the creative construction approach. Alternatively, it might be hypothesized that the learner approaches the L2 with the parameter settings of the L1, and is forced to reset these where they differ in the two languages. Some evidence for this position is presented in White 1985b, where it is argued that at least some of her subjects had carried over their L1 setting for the parameter determining the bounding nodes for subjacency, though others – slightly more than half – had successfully reset this parameter to the L2 value. And while this question has not been treated explicitly in the domain of phonology, much in the acquisition of L2 phonology could probably be described in this way. For example, Eimas (1985) reports on a series of experiments suggesting that infants perceive sounds taken from a continuum of VOT (voicing onset time) values categorically, and that these categories correspond to the largest range of phoneme categories into which that continuum is divided in any human language. Monolingual adults, on the other hand, seem to perceive the same range of sounds in terms of the phoneme categories of their native language. Thus, infants in all linguistic environments are able to perceive the three stop phonemes of Thai (voiceless aspirated, voiceless unaspirated, and voiced), while adults whose native language divides this continuum into only two categories have trouble distinguishing three distinct ranges of sounds. This evidence suggests that in perception of phoneme categories, at least, second language learners start out with the set of phoneme boundaries defined by their native language – potentially defined by the L1 parameter settings – rather than the set of categories available to infants.

The assumption that parameter setting (or resetting) is a part of L2 acquisition makes interesting predictions; for example, it predicts that where a cluster of structural properties represent the effect of a single parameter setting, all the related properties should be acquired at once. White (1985a), in an examination of the effects of the pro-drop parameter, did find a connection between the acquisition of several different pro-drop phenomena in the L2. In addition, as Flynn's chapter in Volume II of this series and White (1985b, c, d) point out, a parameterized system provides the possibility of a framework in which comparison of L1 and L2 settings can be used to predict the nature and occurrence of transfer and developmental effects; differences in markedness of the L2 and L2 settings would be expected to have different consequences in acquisition. (The reader is referred to Flynn 1984, 1985 to appear, Mazurkewich 1984 and White 1985c for theories of the effects of various parameter settings on L2 acquisition.)

7.3. Directions for future research

The parameterized approach to linguistic description outlined in the preceding section has the potential to provide a framework in which the competing trends of past decades – the focus on the influence of L1 and the focus on the commonality of interlanguage patterns across L1 backgrounds – may find a place in a comprehensive theory of second language acquisition. L2 acquisition, it seems, has felt the need for such a framework. Much of the work in the field has consisted of papers refining terminology and outlining or reviewing basic assumptions, and the percentage of papers presenting new data and relating the data to current hypotheses has been relatively small in comparison to the percentage of such papers in other areas of linguistics. This situation is no doubt due in part to the overwhelming difficulties, discussed earlier, of collecting reliable L2 data, but perhaps may also be connected to the lack of a well-articulated theory of second language acquisition broad enough to accommodate the range of factors influencing the language learner. It is to be hoped that such a theory is now beginning to emerge.

The serious investigation of L2 facts within a rigorous linguistic theory should benefit not only L2 acquisition but theoretical linguistics as well. Work in language acquisition, particularly L2 acquisition, has often been viewed as a branch of 'applied linguistics,' in which the constructs of theoretical linguistics are applied to a new set of data. On this view, the L2 researcher takes the set of rules, parameters, or some other theoretical construct proposed by the linguist and investigates their relevance to L2 acquisition. But this role of consumer is not an appropriate one for L2 researchers. The hypotheses of linguistic theory are constantly undergoing revision in the face of new data, and L2 research can provide one important source of such data.

REFERENCES

Adjémian, C. 1976. On the nature of interlanguage systems. *Language Learning* 26: 297–320.
Altenberg, E. & Vago, R. 1983. Theoretical implications of an error analysis of second language phonology production. *Language Learning* 33: 427–47.
Bailey, N., Madden, C. & Krashen, S. 1974. Is there a 'natural sequence' in adult second language learning? *Language Learning* 24: 125–43.
Baker, C. L. 1979. Syntactic theory and the projection problem. *Linguistic Inquiry* 10: 533–82.
Berwick, R. 1985. *The acquisition of syntactic knowledge*. Cambridge, MA: MIT Press.
Bright, W. 1958. *An outline of coloquial Kannada*. Poona: R. Cambray & Co.
Broselow, E. 1983. Nonobvious transfer: on predicting epenthesis errors. In Gass & Selinker 1983.
Broselow, E. 1984. An investigation of transfer in second language phonology. *IRAL* 22: 253–69.
Broselow, E., Hurtig, R. & Ringen, C. to appear. The perception of second language prosody. In G. Ioup & S. Weinberger (eds.) *Interlanguage phonology*. Rowley: Newbury House.
Carroll, J. 1968. Contrastive linguistics and interference theory. In J. Alatis (ed.) *Report of the nineteenth annual round table meeting on linguistics and language studies*. Washington: Georgetown University Press.
Chomsky, N. 1980. *Rules and representations*. New York: Columbia University Press.
Chomsky, N. 1981. *Lectures on government and binding*. Dordrecht: Foris.
Comrie, B. 1985. Why linguists need language acquirers. In Rutherford 1985.
Corder, S. 1971. Idiosyncratic dialects and error analysis. *IRAL* 9: 147–59.

Dulay, H. & Burt, M. 1974a. Natural sequences in child second language acquisition. *Language Learning* 24: 37–53.

Dulay, H. & Burt, M. 1974b. A new perspective on the creative construction process in child second language acquisition. *Language Learning* 24: 253–78.

Eckman, F. 1977. Markedness and the contrastive analysis hypothesis. *Language Learning* 27: 315–30.

Eckman, F. 1981. On the naturalness of interlanguage phonological rules. *Language Learning* 31: 195–216.

Eckman, F., Bell, L. & Nelson, D. (eds.) 1984. *Universals in second language acquisition.* Rowley: Newbury House.

Eimas, P. 1985. The perception of speech in early infancy. *Scientific American* 252: 46–52.

Ervin-Tripp, S. 1974. Is second language learning like the first? *TESOL Quarterly* 8: 111–28.

Finer, D. & Broselow, E. 1986. Second language acquisition of reflexive binding. In *Proceedings of the Sixteenth Annual Meeting of the Northeastern Linguistics Society.* Distributed by the Graduate Linguistics Student Association. Amherst: University of Massachusetts.

Flege, J. to apear. The production and perception of foreign languages. In H. Winitz (series ed.) *Human communication and its disorders*, Vol. 1. New York: Ablex.

Flynn, S. 1984. A universal in L2 acquisition based on a PBD typology. In F. Eckman, L. Bell, and D. Nelsons (eds.) 1984.

Flynn, S. 1985. Principled theories of second language acquisition. *Studies in Second Language Acquisition* 7: 99–107.

Flynn, S. to appear. Adult L2 acquisition: resetting the parameters of Universal Grammar. Dordrecht: Reidel.

Fries, C. 1945. *Teaching and learning English as a foreign language.* Ann Arbor: University of Michigan Press.

Gass, S. 1979. Language transfer and universal grammatical relations. *Language Learning* 29: 327–44.

Gass, S. 1980. An investigation of syntactic transfer in adult second language learners. In Krashen & Scarcella 1980.

Gass, S. 1984. A review of interlanguage syntax: language transfer and language universals. *Language Learning* 34: 115–131.

Gass, S. & Ard, J. 1985. Second language acquisition and the ontology of language universals. In Rutherford 1985.

Gass, S. & Selinker, L. (eds.) 1983. *Language transfer in language learning.* Rowley: Newbury House.

Greenberg, J. 1963. *Universals of language.* Cambridge, MA: MIT Press.

Hatch, E. 1978. *Second language acquisition.* Rowley: Newbury House.

Hodne, B. 1985. Yet another look at interlanguage phonology: the modification of English syllable structure by native speakers of Polish. *Language Learning* 35: 405–17.

Ioup, G. 1984. Is there a structural foreign accent? A comparison of syntactic and phonological errors in second language acquisition. *Language Learning* 34: 1–17.

Ioup, G. & Kruse, A. 1977. Interference versus structural complexity as a predictor of second language relative clause acquisition. In H. Brown, C. Yorio and R. Crymes (eds.) *On TESOL 77.* Washington: Georgetown University Press.

Jansen, B., Lalleman, J. & Muysken, P. 1981. The alternation hypothesis: acquisition of Dutch word order by Turkish and Moroccan foreign workers. *Language Learning* 31: 315–36.

Keenan, E. & Comrie, B. 1977. Noun phrase accessibility and universal grammar. *Linguistic Inquiry* 8: 63–100.

Krashen, S. & Scarcella, R. (eds.) 1980. *Issues in second language research.* Rowley: Newbury House.

Lado, R. 1957. *Linguistics across cultures.* Ann Arbor: University of Michigan Press.

Le Compagnon, B. 1984. Interference and overgeneralization in second language learning: the acquisition of English dative verbs by native speakers of French. *Language Learning* 34: 39–67.

Lenneberg, E. 1967. *Biological foundations of language.* New York: Wiley.

Mairs, J. 1985. Stress assignment in interlanguage phonology: an analysis of the stress system of Spanish speakers learning English. ms.

Mazurkewich, I. 1984. The acquisition of the dative alternation by second language learners and linguistic theory. *Language Learning* 34: 91–110.

Nemser, W. 1971. Approximative systems of foreign language learners. *IRAL* 9: 114–24.

Ravem, R. 1968. Language acquisition in a second language environment. *IRAL* 6: 175–85.

Richards, J. 1974. A non-contrastive approach to error analysis. In J. Richards (ed.) *Error analysis*. London: Longman.

Ritchie, W. 1978. The right-roof constraint in adult second language. In W. Ritchie (ed.) *Second language acquisition research*. New York: Academic Press.

Rizzi, L. 1982. *Issues in Italian syntax*. Dordrecht: Foris.

Rutherford, W. 1984. Description and explanation in interlanguage syntax: state of the art. *Language Learning* 34: 127–55.

Rutherford, W. (ed.) 1985. *Language universals and second language acquisition*. Amsterdam: John Benjamins.

Sato, C. 1984. Phonological processes in second language acquisition: another look at interlanguage syllable structure. *Language Learning* 34: 43–57.

Schachter, J. 1974. An error in error analysis. *Language Learning* 24: 205–14.

Selinker, L. 1972. Interlanguage. *IRAL* 10: 209–31.

Selkirk, L. 1982. The syllable. In H. van der Hulst & N. Smith (eds.) *The structure of phonological representations*, Vol. 2. Dordrecht: Foris.

Stockwell, R. & Bowen, J. 1965. *The sounds of English and Spanish*. The Contrastive Culture Series. Chicago: University of Chicago Press.

Stockwell, R., Bowen, J. & Martin, J. 1965. *The grammatical structures of English and Spanish*. Chicago: University of Chicago Press.

Tyrone, E. 1980. Some influences on the structure of interlanguage phonology. *IRAL* 18: 139–52.

Wardhaugh, R. 1970. The contrastive analysis hypothesis. *TESOL Quarterly* 4: 123–30.

Wexler, K. & Culicover, P. 1980. *Formal principles of language acquisition*. Cambridge, MA: MIT Press.

Wexler, K. & Manzini, R. 1987. Parameters and learnability in binding theory. In T. Roeper and E. Williams (eds.) *Parameter setting*. Dordrecht: Reidel.

White, L. 1985a. The pro-drop parameter in adult second language acquisition. *Language Learning* 35: 47–63.

White, L. 1985b. The acquisition of parameterized grammars: subjacency in second language acquisition. *Second Language Research* 1: 1–17.

White, L. 1985c. Universal grammar as a source of explanation in second language acquisition. In B. Wheatley *et al.* (eds.) *Current approaches to second language acquisition: proceedings of the 1984 University of Wisconsin-Milwaukee linguistics symposium*. Distributed by the Indiana University Linguistics Club.

White, L. 1985d. Island effects in second language acquisition. Paper delivered at MIT Conference on Second Language Acquisition and Linguistic Theory.

Zobl, H. 1983. Markedness and the projection problem. *Language Learning* 33: 293–313.

8 Neurolinguistics: an overview of language–brain relations in aphasia*

Sheila E. Blumstein

8.0 Introduction

The past fifteen years have seen an increasing interest by linguists in the field of neurolinguistics. Broadly construed, neurolinguistics is the study of language and brain relations. Its primary goal is understanding and explicating the neurological bases for language and speech, and the nature of the mechanisms and processes implicated in language use. Roman Jakobson was probably the first linguist to realize the potential importance of such a field of study – not only for the contributions that linguistics might make towards understanding the nature of language deficits subsequent to brain damage, but also for the unique insights provided by such 'experiments in nature,' insights which might inform linguistic theory as well as offer a testing ground for theoretical linguistic assumptions (Jakobson 1971). Jakobson focussed his attention on the adult aphasias, particularly addressing the primitives and structural properties of language, their hierarchy and organization (Jakobson 1968, 1971). He provided one of the first indications that language dissolution indeed reflects structural principles inherent in the language system. In other words, the organizational framework of the language system breaks down in lawful ways, lawful only if certain assumptions are made about the nature of the primitives and structural principles of the linguistic system.

In this chapter, I will review the major issues in the field of neurolinguistics, particularly with respect to the study of language impairments in adult aphasia. Adult aphasia is of particular interest because the language impairments of these patients reflect the impairment of premorbidly normal language and cognitive systems. Thus, the organization of language, cognition, and the interaction of these two systems can be assumed to be similar to normal adults prior to brain insult.

Much as linguistics research has been guided by considerations of the structural levels of the linguistic grammar as phonetics, phonology, lexicon,

* This research was supported in part by Grant NS22282 to Brown University and Grant NS06209 to the Boston University School of Medicine.

syntax and semantics, so have linguistic investigations of aphasia. In particular, studies have largely attempted to determine whether impairments at a particular level of representation can best exemplify the nature of the language deficit, and within a particular level, whether particular structural principles provide an explanatory basis for the language patterns of the patient. For example, much research has focussed on whether the language comprehension impairments of Wernicke's aphasics reflect a deficit in phonological processing, and in particular, in 'phonemic hearing' (Luria 1966; Blumstein, Baker & Goodglass 1977; Baker, Blumstein & Goodglass 1981). This deficit is characterized by an inability to perceive the phonological attributes of words correctly. As a result, words which are distinguished by minimal phonological contrasts may be misperceived. For example, the word *bee* might be misperceived as *pea* or *D*. Nevertheless, although patients may show deficits affecting predominantly one language level, there are virtually no patients who seem to have a selective deficit in one component of the grammar with the remainder of the linguistic system intact. While Wernicke's aphasics do show impaired phonological processing, they also show syntactic and lexical deficits that affect both language input and output (Lesser 1978). Similarly, although a characteristic feature of many Broca's aphasics is agrammatism (Goodglass 1968; Zurif *et al.* 1974; Saffran, Schwartz & Marin 1980; Schwartz, Saffran & Marin 1980; Grodzinsky 1984), these patients also display phonetic and phonological deficits (see Blumstein 1981) as well as lexical processing impairments (Milberg, Blumstein & Dworetzky 1986). The full range of language impairments of agrammatic patients cannot then be accounted for in terms of a selective syntactic deficit. That is not to say that these patients do not have a syntactic deficit, but clearly other impairments at other linguistic levels are implicated as well.

The last few years of research has seen a reconsideration of a number of these issues, but with respect to whether language impairments in aphasia reflect processing deficits affecting access to the components of the grammar, rather than deficits in the components themselves. In this view, the structural components are relatively intact, but access to them is impaired. Such hypotheses have been proposed to account for dichotomies in performance on language tasks which seem to require access to the same structural component of the grammar. For example, comprehension of syntactic structures and grammatical judgements both seem to require spared syntactic knowledge, and yet given the same array of sentences varying in particular syntactic structures, agrammatic aphasics seem to show relatively spared abilities in grammatical judgements tasks in the context of relatively impaired abilities in syntactic comprehension tasks (Linebarger, Schwartz & Saffran 1983). Similarly, Wernicke's aphasics show a relatively intact semantic organization of the lexicon in a lexical decision task, and yet cannot judge whether semantically similar words go together (Milberg & Blumstein 1981; Blumstein, Milberg & Shrier 1982; Milberg *et al*. 1987). I will consider these issues in detail below, particularly with respect to lexical and syntactic processing. Suffice it to say that consideration of the possibility that processing routines in language use are impaired in aphasia may provide a basis for explaining why the language deficits seem to cut simultaneously across various components of the grammar.

Consideration of aphasia as a deficit in the components of the grammar, or in the processes involved in accessing these components, speaks directly to the issue of the modularity of language. Throughout the history of aphasia, various forms of modularity theories have been postulated (see Head 1926, and Fodor 1983 for a review). Broadly speaking, evidence clearly supports the view that language is modular, in that it is an autonomous system which is (within limits) functionally and neurologically distinct from other higher cortical functions. Dissociations have been found between language and cognition in certain patients where language is impaired, but cognitive tasks seem to be preserved (Tissot, Lhermitte & Ducarne 1963; Zangwill 1964). Similarly, some demented patients may show severe cognitive deficits in the face of relatively spared language abilities (Irigaray 1967). Studies of brain-damaged patients also suggest that mathematical, musical, and artistic abilities are dissociated from language (Gardner 1983).

Nevertheless, considerably stronger claims have been made about the modularity of language. In particular, in some versions of the modularity hypothesis it has been postulated that language consists of submodules that are functionally autonomous. Each of these modules has its own vocabulary and operations, and a restricted domain of analysis and processing (Garrett 1979; Forster 1979; Fodor 1983). These submodules include lexical, syntactic, semantic, and message levels. Moreover, these submodules can 'speak' to each other only in very particular ways. Namely, for a module to be functionally autonomous, it must operate only on input from lower level systems or modules, and its operation cannot be affected by the output of other modules which are downstream from it (see Forster 1979; Fodor 1983; Tanenhaus, Carlson & Seidenberg 1985 for detailed discussions). To date, there is only one study in aphasia that speaks directly to this stronger form of the modularity hypothesis (Swinney *et al*. 1986), and I will consider it in the section on the lexicon. Nevertheless, it is unlikely that the submodules of language have a direct instantiation in localized areas of the brain. While discrete brain lesions produce different patterns of language impairment (Geschwind 1965; Goodglass & Kaplan 1983), as discussed above, they do not produce selective deficits in one component of the grammar to the exclusion of other components. Moreover, as I will discuss later on in this chapter, similar hierarchies of breakdown have been noted across patients with very different lesion sites and clinical syndromes. Thus, the mapping of discrete neurological structures to linguistic functions or language modules is not very promising.

For purposes of exposition, I will review the nature of language deficits with respect to particular components of the grammar. In particular, I will focus on the phonological (including phonetic), lexical and syntactic (including morphological) components. Consideration of possible processing impairments will be addressed as they relate to particular components of the grammar.

Before discussing research on language deficits in aphasia, it is worthwhile noting the different types of language impairments encountered in aphasia. For approximately 90% of right-handers, the left hemisphere is dominant for language. Brain damage within the left hemisphere will have different effects depending upon the site and extent of the lesion. While there have been recent challenges to the reliability of classification schemas in aphasia, and more importantly, concern about whether such schemas provide the bases from which language impairments may be studied to elucidate a theory of language (Caramazza 1984; Schwartz 1984; Badecker & Caramazza 1985), it goes without saying that a broad array of language behaviors is impaired in very particular ways as a function of different areas of brain damage. These constellations of language behavior constitute the aphasia syndromes. Perhaps the two aphasia syndromes which have received the most attention in neurolinguistic investigations are Broca's and Wernicke's aphasia.

Broca's aphasia is best characterized as an expressive disorder of speech/ language. Auditory language comprehension, while not perfect, is relatively spared compared to the severe speech output disorder of these patients. There are several manifestations of this output disorder. First, speech production, i.e. the articulation and melody of speech, is impaired. Second, it is nonfluent; the patient's speech output is slow and labored. Third, it is often agrammatic. Productive agrammatism is characterized by the loss or substitution of grammatical words such as 'the,' 'is,' as well as grammatical inflectional endings such as plural and past tense. Syntactic structures are generally limited to simple sentences with few embeddings and dependent clauses. In the most severe cases, the patient's speech production is reduced to nominals like 'boy,' 'cookie,' 'running'. In such cases, it is difficult to determine if the patient is agrammatic since there is insufficient language production to judge whether grammatical formatives and syntactic structures are compromised. As to other language abilities, naming an object to confrontation is generally fair to good, and repetition of language is usually good or better than spontaneous speech output.

The syndrome of Wernicke's aphasia is characterized by both language input and language output impairments. Auditory language comprehension is severely impaired. Speech output is fluent and well articulated. Grammatical structures seem relatively intact. However, the semantic content of the output is severely compromised. Language is empty, often difficult to understand, with the overuse of high frequency, low content words such as 'thing,' 'it,' 'be,' 'have,' 'this.' In addition, literal paraphasias (sound substitution errors) and verbal paraphasias (word substitution errors) occur in speech output. There are some Wernicke's patients who also produce neologisms or 'jargon.' Another frequent characteristic of this disorder is 'logorrhea' or a press for speech, whereby patients, even in a conversational setting, seem to be compelled to talk on and on without stopping. Other associated language impairments include a moderate to severe naming deficit and a severe repetition disorder.

The syndromes of Broca's and Wernicke's aphasia are only two of a fairly large number of aphasia syndromes which occur subsequent to brain damage in the left language-dominant hemisphere. It is beyond the scope of this paper to review all of these syndromes. Nevertheless, they represent a broad array of interesting patterns of impairments, from repetition deficits to reading and writing impairments to selective sparing of repetition in the face of impaired speech production and comprehension (cf. Goodglass & Kaplan 1983). Such impairments provide a unique challenge and opportunity for studying language–brain relations.

8.1. Phonology

8.1.1. Speech production

Speech research has attempted to understand the nature of the phonetic and phonological impairments of aphasics and has attempted to determine the extent to which such impairments contribute to the language production and comprehension impairments of these patients. Linguistic theory makes a clear distinction between phonetics and phonology, and the facts of aphasia support such a distinction, particularly in the investigation of speech production deficits. It is the case that nearly all aphasics, regardless of clinical type of aphasia, manifest some phonological difficulties in speech output. While a broad array of phonological errors may occur, they can be reduced to four descriptive categories (Blumstein 1973): phoneme substitution errors in which one phoneme is substituted for another, e.g. *teams*→[kimz]; simplification errors in which a phoneme or syllable is deleted, e.g. *green*→[gin]; addition errors in which an extra phoneme or syllable is added, e.g. *see*→[sti]; and environment errors in which a particular phoneme occurs that can be accounted for by the influence of the surrounding phonological context. These environment errors include metatheses, e.g. *degrees*→[gədriz], and progressive and regressive assimilations, e.g. *championships*→[čæčɪnšɪps] and *Crete*→[trit], respectively.

There have been a number of studies exploring the phonological patterns of aphasic errors. And while some differences emerge across clinical types of aphasia, the differences are often subtle, and they occur only in some experimental tasks and not in others (Trost & Canter 1974; Martin *et al.* 1975; Nespoulous *et al.* 1984; Canter, Trost & Burns 1985). The stability of these patterns is evidenced by their occurrence among different phonological systems of varying languages: French (Bouman & Grunbaum 1925; Lecours & Lhermitte 1969), German (Bouman & Grunbaum 1925; Goldstein 1948), English (Blumstein 1973; Green 1969), Turkish (Peuser & Fittschen 1977), Russian (Luria 1966), and Finnish (Niemi, Koivuselka-Sallinen & Hanninen 1985).

Analyses of the four error types described above reveal some interesting insights into the organization of the phonological system in aphasic patients. First, while the particular occurrence of a phoneme substitution error cannot be predicted, the direction of such errors can be. There is a systematic relation between target phoneme and phoneme substitution errors with the predominance of errors involving the substitution of a single distinctive feature. Moreover, a hierarchy of features can be derived with the most stable feature contrasts representing the major classificatory features, consonants and vowels, and the least stable representing either the manner feature [continuant] or the place feature [compact] (Blumstein 1973).

The importance of syllable structure at the level of phonological planning, and ultimately articulatory programming, is reflected by the rarity of forms produced by aphasic patients that violate the phonotactic or morpheme structure constraints of the language. Even the phonological structure of jargon produced by Wernicke's aphasics respect such constraints (Green 1969; Brown 1981).

Turning to the other error types, analysis of simplification errors reveals a general tendency to simplify syllable structures to the canonical CV. Thus, clusters tend to be reduced, and syllable-final consonants tend to be deleted. Addition errors also reflect this tendency with a preponderance of such errors changing a marked syllable structure V to the unmarked canonical form CV, e.g. *army*→[ǰarmi].

And finally, assimilation errors provide further insights into the size of the planning units in speech production. In particular, both progressive and regressive assimilations occur within a word and across word boundaries. For those that occur within words, the contaminating and assimilated phoneme are generally separated by a distance of only one syllable. In contrast, assimilation errors across word boundaries are characterized by a parallel structure relation. Basically, the assimilated phoneme has the same structural position in the word as the contaminating phoneme. If the contaminating phoneme is in word-initial position, so is the assimilated phoneme, e.g. *history books*→[bɪstri bʊks]. If the contaminating phoneme is in final position, the assimilated phoneme is too, e.g. *was not*→[wət nat]. The pattern of the assimilation errors within words indicates that the unit of articulatory programming must be larger than a single syllable. However, it is clear from the pattern of assimilation errors between words that articulatory programming is not simply a concatenation of individual syllables independent of the properties of the grammar. Rather, even at the level of articulatory planning and programming, information concerning word boundaries and lexical structure seems to be maintained.

As this brief review has shown, phonological errors in aphasia reflect patterns consistent with the view that the underlying phonological system of the patient is still governed by structural principles intrinsic to the phonology of language in general as well as to the particular language affected. Nevertheless, there is another source of errors which indicates that articulatory implementations of these phonological patterns may be impaired in some patients. In particular, anterior aphasics, including Broca's aphasics, often display phonetic impairments. It is particularly the presence of these phonetic impairments which dissociate the speech patterns of Broca's aphasics from those of Wernicke's aphasics.

Investigations of the phonetic patterns of speech have primarily used acoustic measurements of the speech produced by these patients to infer the nature of their impairments (see Alajouanine, Ombredane & Durand 1939; Lehiste 1968; Kent & Rosenbek 1983). More direct measures of articulation using fiberoptics (Itoh, Sasanuma & Ushijima 1979), computer controlled x-ray microbeams (Itoh *et al.* 1980), and electromyography (Shankweiler, Harris & Taylor 1968) have also been made. The conclusions drawn across of all these methodologies have been remarkably consistent. In particular, they suggest that Broca's aphasics have an articulatory coordination or articulatory timing deficit, affecting in particular the timing relation between two independent articulators. For example, it has been shown that voice-onset time, VOT, an acoustic parameter reflecting the timing relation between the release of a stop consonant and the onset of glottal pulsing or voicing and a critical attribute to the voiced–voiceless distinction, is significantly impaired in Broca's aphasia. These patterns emerge not only in English and Japanese, for which VOT serves to distinguish voiced and voiceless phonetic categories (Blumstein *et al.* 1977b, 1980; Freeman, Sands & Harris 1978; Itoh *et al.* 1982; Shewan, Leeper & Booth 1984). They also emerge in Thai, for which VOT serves as a three-category distinction among pre-voiced VOT ([b]), short lag VOT ([p]), and voiceless aspirated VOT ([pʰ]) stops (Gandour & Dardarananda 1984a). Similarly, the timing relation between the closure of the velum and release of a stop, which cues the contrast between nasals and stops, is also impaired in Broca's aphasia (Itoh *et al*. 1979).

Nevertheless, it is not clear whether the timing disorder of Broca's aphasia is a pervasive one affecting all phonetic categories. While the absolute durations of vowels seems to be impaired in Broca's aphasia (Collins, Rosenbek & Wertz 1978; Ryalls 1981; Duffy & Gawle 1984) and the resulting vowel durations seem to compromise the contrast between voiced and voiceless stops in final position, e.g. *beat* versus *bead* (Duffy & Gawle 1984; Tuller 1984), intrinsic vowel duration differences seem to be maintained in English, e.g. *bead* versus *bid*, and phonemic length seems to be preserved in Thai (Gandour & Dardarananda 1984b). Further, absolute durations of fricative noise and the contextual factors affecting noise durations of both voiced and voiceless fricatives seem to be relatively spared (Harmes *et al*. 1984).

Although a timing disorder is clearly implicated in the speech production of Broca's aphasics, acoustic analyses of the spectral characteristics of stop consonants suggest that these patients seem to be able to get their vocal tract into the appropriate configuration for place of articulation in stop consonants (Shinn & Blumstein 1983). Moreover, these patients also show relatively normal coarticulation effects in the transitions between consonants and vowels (Katz 1986a), although these effects might be somewhat delayed in time (Ziegler & von Cramon 1985).

The dichotomy between Broca's and Wernicke's aphasia in speech production thus rests predominantly on the distinction between phonetic and phonological impairments. Nevertheless, it is worth noting that while Wernicke's aphasics do not evidence the severe articulatory implementation disorders of the Broca's aphasics, several studies have shown a subtle phonetic impairment. This impairment may have minimal perceptual effects, but suggests that even posterior lesions have an effect on articulatory implementation (see Blumstein *et al*. 1980; Ryalls 1984; Duffy & Gawle 1984).

8.1.2. Speech perception

Studies on speech perception in aphasia have focussed primarily on the extent to which speech perception deficits might underlie or significantly contribute to auditory comprehension deficits. A subsidiary but relevant question, which has also been investigated, is whether the basis for speech perception failures is primarily auditory in nature. In this view, speech perception and auditory comprehension deficits are a secondary consequence of a nonlinguistic auditory processing impairment.

Perhaps the only study that has shown a systematic relation between auditory perception ability and language comprehension in aphasia has been that of Tallal and Newcombe (1978). They focussed on the auditory perception of rapidly changing acoustic information in both nonverbal and verbal stimuli. For nonverbal stimuli, they explored the ability of patients to determine the temporal order of two complex tones separated by various interstimulus intervals. For the speech stimuli, they focussed on the perception of place of articulation, and in particular on the rapidly moving formant transitions signalling this contrast. Their results showed impairments in both the verbal and nonverbal stimuli. Moreover, for the speech stimuli, they demonstrated that lengthening the duration of the formant transitions from 40 to 80 msec resulted in improved performance for three out of the six aphasic subjects tested.

Nevertheless, several recent studies have failed to show systematic improvement in either labeling or discrimination of place of articulation with extended formant transitions in a large group of aphasic patients (Blumstein *et al.* 1984; Reidel & Studdert-Kennedy 1985). Moreover, dissociations have been shown between the perception of place of articulation and non-speech auditory analogues varying in onset frequency and duration of formant transitions (Blumstein *et al.* 1984). And while a number of studies have shown that brain-damaged patients demonstrate increased thresholds for determining temporal order between two events in both the auditory and visual modalities (Efron 1963; Swisher & Hirsh 1972), these findings are not restricted to aphasic patients. Thus, auditory deficits do not seem to provide the basis for speech perception deficits in aphasia.

Studies exploring potential speech perception deficits have focussed primarily on the perception of phonemic or segmental contrasts. Results have shown that aphasics do evidence deficits in processing segmental contrasts in tasks requiring them to determine if two naturally spoken real words or nonsense syllables are the same or different, e.g. *bait* versus *date* or [beip] versus [deip], or to point to an appropriate picture of an auditorily presented target word given a picture array containing phonologically similar words, e.g. target *pea* with pictures of a pea, 'T,' key (Blumstein *et al.* 1977a; Jauhiainen & Nuutila 1977; Miceli *et al.* 1978, 1980; Baker, Blumstein & Goodglass 1981). In terms of the feature relations of the consonants, subjects are more likely to make discrimination errors when the test stimuli contrast by a single feature than when they contrast by two or more features (Blumstein *et al.* 1977a; Miceli *et al.* 1978; Baker, Blumstein & Goodglass 1981; Sasanuma, Tatsumi & Fujisaki 1976). Further, discrimination errors are more common on place contrasts than on voicing contrasts (Blumstein *et al.* 1977a; Miceli *et al.* 1978; Baker *et al.* 1981).

Further studies have explored aphasic patients' sensitivity to the acoustic parameters contributing to phonetic contrasts and in particular have investigated whether aphasic patients show categorical perception. Categorical perception is a phenomenon that is largely, although not exclusively, limited to speech stimuli (Liberman *et al.* 1967). If normal listeners are presented with a continuum of stimuli in which the endpoint stimuli contain acoustic parameters appropriate to two different phonetic categories, and the remaining stimuli vary in equal steps along a particular acoustic dimension, a very particular relation obtains between their ability to label and discriminate the stimuli. Namely, subjects perceive the stimuli as belonging to discrete categories and show a fairly sharp change in the identification of the categories at a particular stimulus along the continuum. When asked to discriminate the stimuli, they discriminate at a high level of accuracy only those stimuli which they label as two different phonetic categories. Those stimuli labeled as members of the same phonetic category are discriminated only slightly better than chance.

The studies exploring categorical perception in aphasia have focussed on two phonetic dimensions – voicing (Basso, Casati & Vignolo 1977; Blumstein *et al.* 1977b; Gandour & Dardarananda 1982) and place of articulation (Blumstein *et al.* 1984). For voicing, the acoustic dimension varied was voice-onset time, and for place of articulation, the dimensions varied were the frequency of the formant transitions appropriate for [b], [d], [g], and the presence or absence of a burst preceding the transitions. Results showed that if an aphasic patient could perform either of the two tasks (labeling or discrimination), it was the discrimination task. Most importantly, the discrimination functions were generally similar in shape and cross-over boundaries to those of normals.

The fact that no perceptual shifts were obtained for the discrimination and labeling functions compared to normals, and that the discrimination functions remained stable even in those patients who could not label the stimuli, underscores the stability of the categorical perception phenomenon in the face of brain damage to the language area. Perhaps more importantly, they suggest that aphasic patients may not have a deficit specific to the perception of the categories of speech *per se*, as they do perceive the acoustic dimensions relating to phonetic categories in a similar fashion to normals. Rather, they have a deficit in the perception of the categories of speech as these categories are *used* in relation to higher order language processing, and in particular, as speech processing relates to lexical processing. After all, the perception of a lexical item requires a stable auditory–

phonetic representation. The failure of aphasics to maintain a stable 'label' for phonetic categories in the segmental identification task may reflect a tenuous link between the sounds of speech and their meaning representation.

Nevertheless, while aphasic patients clearly show some speech perception deficits, a number of studies that have compared speech perception abilities with auditory comprehension have failed to show any systematic or strong correlations (Jauhiainen & Nuutila 1977; Basso, Casati & Vignolo 1977; Blumstein *et al.* 1977a; Miceli *et al.* 1980; Boller 1978; Lesser 1978). Thus, speech perception deficits, while contributing to auditory comprehension deficits, do not seem to provide the primary basis for auditory language comprehension failures.

8.2. Lexicon

One of the least localizing characteristics and yet most common clinical attributes in aphasia is a naming deficit. Such a deficit is operationally defined as an inability or inconsistency in giving the appropriate name for an object, an action, and so on, upon confrontation. This deficit may also manifest itself in word difficulty (i.e. groping for the appropriate word), semantic paraphasias (i.e. word substitutions), or empty speech (i.e. use of such nonspecific words as 'thing,' 'be') in the patient's spontaneous speech output.

Results from numerous studies have indicated that several important attributes contribute to the evocation of a name: the frequency of a word (Howes 1964; Rochford & Williams 1962), its concreteness, its picturability or imageability (Goodglass, Hyde & Blumstein 1969), and its operativity, i.e. the number of sensory modalities contributing to the concept of a word (Gardner 1973). All aphasics seem to be sensitive to these characteristics. However, as important a role as they may play in the success or failure to name, they do not provide an indication of the nature of the naming deficit in aphasia.

Three possible bases for anomia have been addressed in the literature. The first is that naming deficits reflect a low level modality-specific deficit. That is, the word to be named is not perceived appropriately, and, as a consequence, the subject cannot name it. The second is that naming deficits reflect an impairment in the lexical or semantic structure of the words themselves. Such altered semantic structures would affect the patient's ability not only to name on confrontation, but also to understand language. The third is that naming deficits reflect a lexical access or retrieval problem. In this view, the lexical entry is basically intact, but the processes involved in lexical access are in themselves impaired.

On the basis of the clinical behavior of aphasic patients, it is impossible to determine the basis for their deficit. Nevertheless, a summary of such behavior provides some insights into the nature of their disorder. A patient who is unable to name a particular object in one context or at one time may be able to do so at another. Further, the patient who has failed to name or has misnamed an object may recognize the appropriate name of the object when it is offered. Having failed to name an object, the patient may nonetheless say what the object is used for, and so for *pencil*, may say 'to write.' Interestingly, the patient may be able to provide the generic properties of the word, such as the letter it begins with or the number of syllables it contains, despite an inability to evoke the appropriate name (Barton 1971; Goodglass *et al*. 1976). Finally, the patient who misnames an item may often substitute a word in the same semantic field (Weigl & Bierwish 1970) or a word that is a semantic associate to the target (Rinnert & Whitaker 1973). For example, the patient may say 'pencil' for *pen*, 'sofa' for *chair*, mother for *wife*.

Evidence that anomia in the classical aphasias is not a modality-specific deficit is provided in a study by Goodglass, Barton & Kaplan (1968). In this study, patients were asked to name objects to touch, smell, sound, and sight. Both correct responses and latency of response were measured. Results indicated that all patients and normal controls demonstrated a similar hierarchy in naming proficiency in relation to modality, with the visual modality being the easiest, then the auditory, tactile, and finally the olfactory modality the hardest. Thus, selective modality-specific impairments could not account for the performance of these patients.

Probably the most common view is that naming deficits, and in particular, the auditory comprehension deficits of Wernicke's aphasics, reflect a deficit at the level of lexical representation, and, in particular, an impairment of the lexical or semantic structure of lexical entries. Goodglass & Baker (1976) and Grober *et al*. (1980) used a task in which aphasic patients were shown pictures of objects that were to be matched (via yes/no responses) to auditorily presented category names (e.g. a picture of an apple matched to the auditorily presented word 'fruit'). The test words to be matched varied in the type of semantic associations to the target word – functional associates (e.g. 'eat'), superordinates (e.g. 'fruit'), attributes (e.g. 'red'), or no match (e.g. 'animal'). Results showed that posterior or Wernicke's aphasics showed a different hierarchy for association categories than either normals or aphasics with good comprehension (primarily Broca's aphasics). Further, the words for which the patients showed difficulty indicating semantic relations were also those they could not name (Goodglass & Baker 1976). These results were attributed to a 'reduction' in semantic fields or a deficit in the structure of the patient's lexical knowledge.

Similar conclusions were drawn by Zurif *et al*. (1974), who explored patients' subjective judgements about 'what words go best together.' Subjects were asked to group the two words of a set of three that went best together. The words used (*mother*, *wife*, *cook*, *partner*, *knight*, *husband*, *shark*, *trout*, *dog*, *tiger*, *turtle*, *crocodile*) varied along several semantic dimensions. Results showed that normals grouped the words along these dimensions. In contrast, Wernicke's aphasics produced random clusters of words. The authors concluded that at least part of the word finding problem in Wernicke's aphasia is rooted in the disruption of stored semantic information.

Several recent studies, however, have questioned these claims. Using an adaptation of a procedure developed by Meyer & Schvaneveldt (1971), aphasic patients were asked to make lexical decisions about words and nonwords. In each case, the target word to be judged (e.g. *dog*) was preceded by a prime that was semantically related (e.g. *cat–dog*), unrelated (e.g. *table–dog*), or neutral (e.g. *glub–dog*) with respect to the prime. Normal subjects show semantic facilitation in such a lexical decision task. That is, they show a faster lexical decision reaction time to a word which is preceded by a semantically related prime word compared to a semantically unrelated or neutral prime. Although slower in making lexical decisions than normals or Broca's aphasics, Wernicke's show semantic facilitation in a lexical decision task. These results are obtained whether the stimuli are presented visually (Milberg & Blumstein 1981) or auditorily (Blumstein, Milberg & Shrier 1982), whether pairs of high semantic associates (Milberg & Blumstein 1981; Blumstein *et al.* 1982) or triplets containing polysemous words are used (Milberg, Blumstein & Dworetzky 1986), or whether the lexical decision is made on each word (Milberg & Blumstein 1981) or on the last word of each trial (Blumstein *et al.* 1982; Milberg *et al.* 1986). These semantic facilitation effects are observed even when patients are unable to reliably perform a metalinguistic task requiring them to judge whether two words are related or not. For example, patients are given the same real word pairs as in the lexical decision task and are asked to determine whether *cat–dog* or *table–dog* are related. Wernicke's aphasics often perform very poorly and even randomly on such tasks. Thus, despite severe auditory comprehension deficits and an inability to overtly judge the semantic values of words, Wernicke's aphasics display a sensitivity to semantically associated words as well as to semantically ambiguous words.

Surprisingly, the results for Broca's aphasics are less clear cut. Although they appear to show semantic facilitation to highly associated words presented auditorily (Blumstein *et al.* 1982), they do not show such effects consistently to words presented visually (Milberg & Blumstein 1981). Moreover, while they show semantic facilitation to polysemous words when presented in pairs (Katz 1986b), they fail to do so when these words are presented in word triplets (Milberg *et al.* 1986). Nevertheless, in contrast to Wernicke's aphasics, Broca's aphasics have little difficulty making meta-linguistic semantic judgements.

The apparent dichotomy in performance between Broca's and Wernicke's aphasics, on the one hand, and the consistent semantic facili-tation effects displayed by Wernicke's aphasics, on the other, decrease the likelihood that the lexical deficits in aphasia can be characterized in terms of an impairment in the lexicon *per se* or in its structure, and increase the likelihood that the deficits lie in one of the many processing operations required for lexical access.

Recent claims have emerged in the study of lexical processing in normals that there are two distinct types of processing contributing to lexical access. Both processes are based, in part, on the assumption that semantic memory or the mental lexicon is represented as a network of lexical entries organized in terms of shared semantic features or attributes. In this view, accessing a lexical item with a particular meaning automatically reduces the threshold for all of those words sharing semantic properties with the lexical item. The more closely related the words, the more likely it is that they will be 'excited' and the lower their threshold of activity will be. Although this process occurs in real time, it is assumed to be very rapid, of short duration, and to be virtually unlimited in capacity. Further, the initiation and termina-tion of this process is assumed not to be under the voluntary control of the subject. On the basis of these characteristics, this process has been called automatic (Shriffin & Schneider 1977; Laberge & Samuels 1974).

The second process involved in lexical access is less consistently labeled in the literature, but it is defined by the fact that it is under that subject's voluntary control (either consciously or unconsciously), is slow, is of relatively long duration, and is limited in capacity (Shiffrin & Schneider 1977). The second process is called strategic or controlled processing. Con-trolled processing is also involved in lexical access, but it is influenced by the subject's expectancies and attentional demands. Any paradigm asking the subject to retrieve a word, make a semantic judgement, or perform a metalinguistic task requiring accessing knowledge of semantic features would require controlled processing.

The results of the lexical decision experiments with aphasics may be characterized in terms of these two processes. Wernicke's aphasics show consistent evidence of semantic facilitation in the lexical decision task, but do not appear to be able to analyze word meaning in a simple semantic judgement task. Therefore, they seem to be able to access word meanings automatically, and yet are unable to use knowledge of rules about semantic features or semantic relations. For Broca's aphasics, results are less clear cut. The lack of consistent priming effects suggests that lexical access based on automatic processing may be impaired. However, these patients appear to have little difficulty analyzing word meaning using controlled processing routines.

Some recent research in online processing during sentence comprehension is consistent with the view that agrammatic aphasics have a lexical processing deficit. The import of these findings is that they suggest that while Broca's aphasics have a lexical processing impairment, the nature of their deficit is consistent with a modular view of language, and, in particular, with the view that lexical access is at some level of processing autonomous or independent of the influence of contextual information.

Onifer and Swinney (1981) studying lexical access in normal subjects, examined the time course of semantic facilitation and the influence of sentence context in a cross-modal lexical decision task. In this task, subjects were presented with an auditorily presented sentence. During the presentation of the sentence, a string of letters was presented visually to the subjects for a word–nonword judgement. Stimuli consisted of sentences with biasing contexts and with ambiguous words embedded in these contexts, e.g. 'the man saw several spiders, roaches, and other *bugs1* in the 2corner of the room.' The target strings for lexical decision were presented immediately after the ambiguous word (time 1) or three syllables downstream (time 2). The real word targets were related to one of the meanings of the ambiguous word e.g. *ant*, *spy*, or they were unrelated to either meaning of the ambiguous word. Results with normals showed that at time 1 there was semantic facilitation or priming for both interpretations of the ambiguous words, despite the fact that the context biased the listener towards only one interpretation. Such priming occurred whether the biasing context was towards the more or less frequent meaning of the ambiguous word. At time 2, however, only the contextually relevant interpretation of the ambiguous word was primed (in this example *ant*). Thus, all meanings of words seem to be accessed and contextual information seems to have its effect upon lexical processing only following such access.

Swinney *et al.* (1986) investigated some of these issues in agrammatic Broca's aphasics and Wernicke's aphasics by exploring semantic facilitation effects to ambiguous words when the target word was presented immediately after the ambiguous word (time 1). Similar to normals, Wernicke's aphasics showed priming to both meanings of the ambiguous word, irrespective of the biasing context. In contrast, Broca's aphasics showed semantic facilitation only to the most frequent meaning of the ambiguous word *regardless* of the biasing context. Thus, while Broca's aphasics clearly show an impairment in accessing word meanings from the lexicon, such access seems to be autonomous in that it is not affected by sentence context, which in theory operates 'downstream' from lexical access itself.

8.3. Syntax

As indicated earlier, there are many Broca's aphasics whose primary clinical characteristic is productive agrammatism. In productive agrammatism, grammatical markers of the language seem to be selectively affected. In addition, as we will discuss below, the full range of syntactic structures used by these patients is also severely restricted. Investigations of agrammatism in English-speaking subjects suggest that grammatical markers such as inflections and plurals, and grammatical words such as articles, verb modals, and prepositions, are lost or are used inconsistently. However, analyses of agrammatic patients in languages other than English indicate that grammatical markers are dropped *only* if the subsequent string constitutes an allowable word in the language (see Grodzinsky 1984). Thus, in infixing languages like Hebrew, the patient does not produce the phonologically ungrammatical skeletal root in the absence of grammatical inflections, e.g. *[ktb] 'write' for [katab] 'he wrote,' nor does the patient produce a phonologically permissible jargon string maintaining the root with a series of vowels infixed in the string. Instead the patient produces a fully inflected form which may be inappropriate to the context, and which seems to reflect a reduction in the markedness of the particular inflectional ending, e.g. for past tense producing present tense (LaPointe 1985). Similarly, in an inflected language like German, the patient does not produce a phonologically unallowable verb form consisting solely of a verb stem, e.g. [singe] 'he sings'→*[sing]. Rather, the patient produces an inflected form which again seems to be generally less marked grammatically. As a result, inflected verbs are often produced as infinitives by these patients.

One of the most interesting findings in the study of agrammatism across languages is the similarity of the agrammatic patterns. In particular, whether a language is agglutinative as in Japanese or inflected as in German or Russian, it is the grammatical markers which seem to be selectively affected (Panse & Shimoyama 1973; Luria 1966; Peuser & Fittschen 1977). Thus, the grammatical structures of human language seem to be subserved by similar neural substrates despite different surface instantiations of such structure. Interestingly, even aphasic deaf signers display agrammatism with damage to similar neural structures as those implicated in agrammatic hearing subjects (Bellugi, Poizner & Klima in press).

Productive agrammatism is usually accompanied by a severe restriction on the syntactic structures of sentences. The occurrence of embedded sentences, complementizers, and relative clauses, or complex phrases in which several adjectives precede a noun, is rare. Further, in severe cases of agrammatism, even the domain of a simple sentence is limited to either an NP or VP with the juxtaposition of an NP–VP occurring only on occasion (Goodglass *et al.* 1972; Gleason *et al.* 1975).

225

Consistent with these findings are results of the acoustic analysis of speech prosody in Broca's aphasics. In particular, Danly and Shapiro (1982) found that although Broca's aphasics showed F_0 declination, i.e. a decrease in the fundamental frequency peaks over the course of an utterance, it was present only over shorter domains than normal. Moreover, these patients did not show evidence of utterance-final segment lengthening. These researchers interpret their results to indicate that Broca's aphasics' prosodic disorder does not result from articulatory difficulties, but is a manifestation of an underlying linguistic disturbance, one relating to sentence planning.

The failure of agrammatic patients to produce syntactically correct sentences seems not to reflect a loss of the conceptual basis for these structures, since patients use alternate strategies to produce sentences with equivalent meaning (Goodglass *et al.* 1972; Gleason *et al.* 1975). For example, the intensifier *very* in *very cold* is replaced by the reduplicated form *cold cold*; comparative forms such as *the boy is taller than the girl* are realized as two independent simple sentences – *the boy is tall, the girl is not*; tense markers as in *he will go* are realized by adverbial forms such as *tomorrow, he go*, and so on.

While it has generally been considered that agrammatic aphasics display primarily an output disorder, more recent research has shown that they have comprehension impairments as well, and further, that the impairments may be primarily grammatical in nature. Zurif, Caramazza and Myerson (1972) investigated the linguistic intuitions of agrammatic patients by asking them to judge how words in a written sentence 'go best together.' Results from normal subjects show that they cluster words in terms of the syntactic relations of the words and basically produce a surface phrase-structure configuration. In contrast, Broca's aphasics cluster content words together and group articles and function words on a random basis. Moreover, Goodglass (1968) showed that the comprehension of sentences which turns on understanding grammatical markers, e.g. *the deer runs* versus *the deer run*, is also compromised in Broca's aphasics.

Further studies have shown that the comprehension deficit in these patients goes well beyond processing function words and grammatical markers. Rather, the processing of syntactic structures is also affected. Particularly vulnerable are embedded subject and object relatives (particularly object relatives), object cleft sentences, and reversible passives (Zurif & Caramazza 1976; Caplan, Baker & Dehaut 1985; Blumstein, Dworetzky & Engen 1986). Even simple reversible active declarative sentences may be poorly understood, e.g. *the boy chases the girl* (Schwartz, Saffran & Marin 1980).

The failure to understand such sentences seems to reflect a syntactic impairment and not a limitation on integrating linguistic/semantic information. If syntactically embedded sentences such as *the man greeted by his wife was smoking a pipe* are 'expanded' to two conjoined propositions such as *the man was greeted by his wife, and he was smoking a pipe*, then Broca's comprehension performance is significantly improved (Goodglass *et al.* 1979). Thus, it does not seem to be the amount of linguistic information in the sentence which is at the basis of the comprehension deficit of these patients, but rather the syntactic structure of the sentences themselves.

Since most agrammatic aphasics evidence both a language production and a language comprehension problem (but cf. Miceli *et al.* 1983; Kolk 1983), it has been suggested that the basis of the deficit is a central one reflecting an impairment at a particular linguistic level of representation. There is considerable debate in the literature, however, about the nature of this impairment, and in particular, about which level of representation is impaired – phonological, lexical, or syntactic. Kean (1980) has proposed that agrammatic aphasics have a phonological deficit selectively affecting nonphonological words or clitics (which are not stressed) and sparing phonological words (which are stressed). In contrast, several researchers propose that the impairment in agrammatism is a lexical one, affecting in particular the closed class (or function word) vocabulary (Bradley, Garrett & Zurif 1980; Zurif, Caramazza & Myerson 1972; Friederici 1985; but cf. Gordon & Caramazza 1982, 1983). In this view, there is an impairment in accessing the closed class vocabulary and ultimately using this vocabulary as input to the parser. Finally, several different hypotheses have been proposed implicating a central syntactic deficit as the basis for agrammatism (Berndt & Caramazza 1980; Caramazza *et al.* 1981; Saffran, Schwartz & Marin 1980; Schwartz, Saffran & Marin 1980). Different claims have been made for the structural basis of this syntactic disorder. One of the most detailed accounts is that of Grodzinsky (1984, 1986; Grodzinsky, Swinney & Zurif 1985), who suggests that agrammatism turns on a structural impairment in the assignment of thematic roles due to the failure to coindex empty categories or *traces* with their antecedents. In contrast, Caplan (Caplan, Baker & Dehaut 1985; Caplan & Futter 1986) argues that syntactic structure is 'simplified' for agrammatic patients and that these structures are analyzed for meaning in terms of a linear rather than a hierarchical grouping of major lexical categories.

While the above hypotheses differ, they all share the assumption that agrammatism reflects a structural impairment. Recently, it has been suggested that agrammatism reflects instead a processing impairment. This hypothesis stems from converging evidence using several different experimental paradigms. One of the first such experiments explored agrammatic patients' abilities to make grammatical judgements (Linebarger, Schwartz & Saffran 1983). Four Broca's aphasics who were agrammatic in both production and comprehension were asked to judge the grammaticality of a series of sentences violating 10 types of syntactic structures, e.g. gapless relatives: *he shut the window that the door was open*; subcategorization: *the girls laughed the clown*; empty elements: *my father knew they would give the job to*; tag questions: *the box fell, didn't he*. These patients performed surprisingly well at 82% correct. This relatively spared ability in the face of grammatical comprehension and production deficits suggested to Linebarger and her colleagues that agrammatic aphasics have an intact syntactic representation. However, they have a processing impairment affecting the 'mapping' of syntactic structures on to their appropriate semantic interpretations.

Results consistent with this view have been shown in several online processing tasks exploring aphasic patients' sensitivity to morphological constraints. In a lexical decision task, normal subjects show faster reaction times to real words preceded by grammatically appropriate strings than they do to real words preceded by grammatically inappropriate strings. These results obtain when the preceding string is either a single word (e.g. *is–going* versus *would–going*) or an incomplete phrase (e.g. *the boy is–going* versus *the boy could–going*), and occurs for target words containing derivational as well as inflectional affixes (Goodman, McClelland & Gibbs 1981; Lukatela *et al.* 1983; Wright & Garrett 1984). These results show that syntactic constraints can and do affect lexical access. Agrammatic aphasics, however, fail to show such effects. In particular, they fail to show faster reaction times to a verb form marked for tense or aspect (present, past, progressive), e.g. *going*, when it is preceded by an appropriate modal, e.g. *is–going*, compared to when it is preceded by an inappropriate modal, e.g. *could–going*, or inappropriate part of speech, e.g. *very–going*.

In a recent study, Baum (1986) directly compared agrammatic patients' performance on grammaticality judgement tasks with a lexical decision task using the same stimuli. In one condition, subjects were required to make a grammatical judgement on a sentence, and in another condition, they were required to make a lexical decision on the last word of that sentence, e.g. 'at 6 o'clock he came to *dinner*' versus 'at 6 o'clock he came *dinner*.' Overall, results were consistent with those reported earlier. In particular, unlike normal controls, agrammatic patients did not show faster reaction times in a lexical decision task when the sentence was grammatical compared to when it was ungrammatical. Nevertheless, these same patients generally were able to make grammatical judgements, although not as well as those reported by Linebarger *et al.* (1983).

Baum's results are of particular interest in that she correlated performance of her subjects on the grammaticality judgement and lexical decision tasks. For normals, she found no correlation. These results are consistent with the view that lexical decisions and grammaticality judgements tap different processing routines – with the lexical decision task, an online task, invoking largely automatic processing, and the grammaticality judgement task, an offline task, invoking largely controlled processing. In contrast to normals, agrammatic patients showed a significant correlation between the two tasks. These results suggest that performance on the two tasks is related and that the patients are invoking similar processing routines in performing these two tasks. As discussed in the previous section, these findings support the hypothesis that Broca's aphasics display a processing deficit particularly affecting automatic processing, while leaving controlled processing relatively spared.

While the major focus on syntactic deficits in aphasia has been on agrammatism in Broca's aphasia, grammatical deficits are not restricted to these patients. Investigations of the speech production of Wernicke's aphasics indicate that these patients often show paragrammatism or the juxtaposition of inappropriate grammatical phrases, e.g. *I saw him to the boy*. Moreover, they seem to use a restricted range of syntactic structures in their speech output (Gleason *et al.* 1980). Consistent with these findings are the results of the acoustic analysis of speech prosody in Wernicke's aphasics (Danly, Cooper & Shapiro 1983). While to the ear, patients seem to have normal prosody, acoustic analyses reveal some subtle impairments. In particular, unlike normals, Wernicke's aphasics show increased use of F_0 rises within a sentence, more frequent F_0 resetting in shorter sentences and at minor syntactic boundaries, and a failure to use F_0 to signal differences between syntactic boundaries whose constituent structures are different. These impairments suggest that these patients have a deficit in sentence production strategies and in the use of syntactic structures.

With respect to language comprehension, Wernicke's aphasics also show syntactic impairments, and in fact many studies have shown that while Wernicke's aphasics are more impaired than Broca's aphasics, the two groups show similar patterns of performance. These studies have varied a number of critical dimensions including morphological endings, syntactic structures, syntactic complexity, and real-world plausibility (Goodglass 1968; Parisi & Pizzamiglio 1970; Shewan & Canter 1971; Shewan 1976; Lesser 1978; Caplan, Baker & Dehaut 1985; Goodglass & Menn 1985).

What is not clear, however, is whether these patterns of performance reflect impairments to similar underlying mechanisms. Several researchers (Caplan, Baker & Dehaut 1985; Goodglass & Menn 1985) have taken this view and have suggested that the syntactic deficit of Wernicke's aphasia is not different in kind from that of Broca's aphasia. Nevertheless, these conclusions may be premature. First, several studies have demonstrated dissociations in patterns of performance on syntactic comprehension tasks between Broca's and Wernicke's aphasics (Goodglass, Gleason & Hyde 1970; Von Stockert 1972; Zurif & Caramazza 1976; Goodglass *et al.* 1979; Blumstein *et al.* 1983). Second, although different types of aphasics may display similar patterns of performance, it is not clear whether impairments in the same underlying mechanisms are responsible for these common patterns. As discussed in the previous section, processing dichotomies have been shown between Broca's and Wernicke's aphasics in lexical access, and similar dichotomies may well emerge for Broca's and Wernicke's aphasia in online tasks exploring syntactic processing. Preliminary results to that effect have been shown by Milberg *et al.* (1985). Unlike Broca's aphasics, Wernicke's aphasics show sensitivity to the morphological structure of words by demonstrating faster reaction times in a lexical decision task to a verb (e.g. *going*) preceded by a grammatically appropriate auxiliary (e.g. *is*) than an inappropriate auxiliary (e.g. *could*). Moreover, while Broca's aphasics can make fairly consistent grammatical judgements, Wernicke's aphasics fail to do so (Milberg *et al.* 1985; Baum 1986). Thus, a similar hierarchy of breakdown shown in tasks investigating sentence comprehension may result from impairments to different underlying mechanisms or processes.

8.4. Conclusion

This chapter has attempted to provide an overview of the field of neurolinguistics. Neurolinguistics is a broad field of study necessitating a multidisciplinary approach to language and brain function. In this chapter, we have restricted our focus to language breakdown in the adult aphasias. However, there are many other areas of critical importance which are subsumed within neurolinguistics, including language disabilities in children, dyslexia, and the dementias, to name a few.

While the study of the adult aphasias is only one small part of the study of neurolinguistics, it provides a potentially important source for such study. The study of aphasia suggested that language is independent (within limits) of cognition, that it is organized into sub-systems similar in kind to components of the grammar proposed in linguistic theory, and that while these sub-systems have their own vocabulary, structure, and operating characteristics, they probably do not have a direct instantiation in localized areas of the brain. More recent research has challenged the view that the structure of the linguistic components themselves is affected in aphasia, but rather suggests that the processing operations affecting access to and communication between these components are impaired.

The investigation of aphasia of necessity underscores the critical role of the left hemisphere in normal language processing. However, it is worth noting that the right hemisphere also seems to play a role. Although the right hemisphere seems to have only a primitive linguistic ability, its primary contribution to normal language processing seems to be with respect to the pragmatic and narrative of discourse properties of language (Gardner *et al.* 1983; Brownell *et al.* 1986). Thus, severe right-hemisphere damaged patients often show difficulties in integrating facts presented in individual propositions into a larger coherent framework. For example, while recalling individual facts of a story, they are unable to infer what is likely to happen based on the facts of the story, to judge which events in a narrative are plausible or implausible, or to infer the moral of a story. Thus, normal language processing seems to require the integration of the functions of both the right and left hemisphere. A great deal more research is necessary to explicate the nature of this interaction and the mechanisms contributing to what appears to be the 'unitary' basis of language communication.

REFERENCES

Alajouanine, T., Ombredane, A. & Durand, M. 1939. *Le syndrôme de la désintegration phonétique dans l'aphasie.* Paris: Masson.
Badecker, W. & Caramazza, A. 1985. On considerations of method and theory governing the use of clinical categories in neurolinguistics and cognitive neuropsychology: the case against agrammatism. *Cognition* 38: 97–125.
Baker, E., Blumstein, S. E. & Goodglass, H. 1981. Interaction between phonological and semantic factors in auditory comprehension. *Neuropsychologia* 19: 1–16.
Barton, M. 1971. Recall of generic properties of words in aphasic patients. *Cortex* 7: 73–82.
Basso, A., Casati, G. & Vignolo, L. A. 1977. Phonemic identification defects in aphasia. *Cortex* 13: 84–95.
Baum, S. 1986. Syntactic processing in aphasia. Doctoral dissertation, Brown University.
Bellugi, U., Poizner, H. & Klima, E. S. in press. *What the hands reveal about the brain.* Cambridge, MA: MIT Press.
Berndt, R. S. & Caramazza, A. 1981. Syntactic aspects of aphasia. In M. T. Sarno (ed.) *Acquired aphasia.* New York: Academic Press.
Blumstein, S. E. 1973. *A phonological investigation of aphasic speech.* The Hague: Mouton.
Blumstein, S. E. 1981. Phonological aspects of aphasia. In M. T. Sarno (ed.) *Acquired aphasia.* New York: Academic Press.
Blumstein, S. E., Baker, E. & Goodglass, H. 1977a. Phonological factors in auditory comprehension in aphasia. *Neuropsychologia* 15: 19–30.
Blumstein, S. E., Cooper, W. E., Goodglass, H., Statlender, S. & Gottlieb, J. 1980. Production deficits in aphasia: a voice-onset time analysis. *Brain and Language* 9: 153–70.
Blumstein, S. E., Cooper, W. E., Zurif, E. & Caramazza, A. 1977b. The perception and production of voice-onset time in aphasia. *Neuropsychologia* 15: 371–83.
Blumstein, S., Dworetzky, B. & Engen, E. 1986. Auditory comprehension of syntactic structures in aphasia. Under editorial review.
Blumstein, S. E., Goodglass, H., Statlender, S. & Biber, C. 1983. Comprehension strategies determining reference in aphasia: a study of reflexivization. *Brain and Language* 18: 115–27.
Blumstein, S., Milberg, W. & Shrier, R. 1982. Semantic processing in aphasia: evidence from an auditory lexical decision task. *Brain and Language* 17: 301–15.
Blumstein, S. E., Tartter, V. C., Nigro, G. & Statlender, S. 1984. Acoustic cues for the perception of place of articulation in aphasia. *Brain and Language* 22: 128–49.
Boller, F. 1978. Comprehension disorders in aphasia: a historical review. *Brain and Language* 5: 149–65.

Bouman, L. & Grunbaum, A. 1925. Experimentell-psychologische Untersuchungen zur Aphasie und Paraphasie. *Zeitschrift für gesamte Neurologie und Psychiatrie* 96: 481–538.

Bradley, D. C., Garrett, M. E. & Zurif, E. B. 1980. Syntactic deficits in Broca's aphasia. In D. Caplan (ed.) *Biological studies of mental processes.* Cambridge, MA: MIT Press.

Brown, J. (ed.) 1981. *Jargonaphasia.* New York: Academic Press.

Brownell, H., Potter, H. H., Bihrle, A. M. & Gardner, H. 1986. Inference deficits in right brain-damaged patients. *Brain and Language* 27: 310–22.

Canter, G. J., Trost, J. E. & Burns, M. S. 1985. Contrasting speech patterns in apraxia of speech and phonemic paraphasia. *Brain and Language* 24: 204–22.

Caplan, D., Baker, C. & Dehaut, F. 1985. Syntactic determinants of sentence comprehension in aphasia. *Cognition* 21: 117–75.

Caplan, D. & Futter, C. 1986. Assignment of thematic roles to nouns in sentence comprehension by an agrammatic patient. *Brain & Language* 27: 117–34.

Caramazza, A. 1984. The logic of neuropsychological research and the problem of patient classification in aphasia. *Brain and Language* 21: 9–20.

Caramazza, A., Berndt, R. S., Basili, A. & Koller, J. 1981. Syntactic processing deficits in aphasia. *Cortex* 17: 333–48.

Caramazza, A. & Zurif, E. B. 1976. Dissociation of algorithmic and heuristic processes in language comprehension: evidence from aphasia. *Brain and Language* 3: 572–82.

Collins, M., Rosenbek, J. C. & Wertz, R. T. 1983. Spectrographic analysis of vowel and word duration in apraxia of speech. *Journal of Speech and Hearing Research* 26: 224–30.

Danly, M., Cooper, W. E. & Shapiro, B. 1983. Fundamental frequency, language processing and linguistic structure in Wernicke's aphasia. *Brain and Language* 19: 1–24.

Danly, M. & Shapiro, B. 1982. Speech prosody in Broca's aphasia. *Brain and Language* 16: 171–90.

Duffy, J. R. & Gawle, C. A. 1984. Apraxic speakers' vowel duration in consonant–vowel–consonant syllables. In J. C. Rosenbek, M. R. McNeil & A. E. Aronson (eds.) *Apraxia of speech: physiology, acoustics, linguistics, management.* San Diego: College-Hill Press.

Efron, R. 1963. Temporal perception, aphasia, and déjà vu. *Brain* 86: 403–23.

Fodor, J. A. 1983. *The modularity of mind.* Cambridge, MA: MIT Press.

Forster, K. I. 1979. Levels of processing and the structure of the language processor. In W. E. Cooper & E. C. T. Walker (eds.) *Sentence processing.* New York: Erlbaum.

Freeman, F. J., Sands, E. S. & Harris, K. S. 1978. Temporal coordination of phonation and articulation in a case of verbal apraxia: a voice-onset time study. *Brain and Language* 6: 106–11.

Friederici, A. 1985. Levels of processing and vocabulary types: evidence from on-line comprehension in normals and agrammatics. *Cognition* 19: 133–66.

Gandour, J. & Dardarananda, R. 1982. Voice onset time in aphasia: Thai, ı: perception. *Brain and Language* 17: 24–33.

Gandour, J. & Dardarananda, R. 1984a. Voice onset time in aphasia: Thai, ıı: production. *Brain and Language* 23: 177–205.

Gandour, J. & Dardarananda, R. 1984b. Prosodic disturbance in aphasia: vowel length in Thai. *Brain and Language* 23: 206–24.

Gardner, H. 1973. The contribution of operativity to naming capacity in aphasic patients. *Neuropsychologia* 11: 213–20.

Gardner, H. 1983. *Frames of mind: the theory of multiple intelligences.* New York: Basic Books.

Gardner, H., Brownell, H. H., Wapner, W. & Michelow, D. 1983. Missing the point: the role of the right hemisphere in the processing of complex linguistic materials. In E. Perecman (ed.) *Cognitive processes in the right hemisphere.* New York: Academic Press.

Garrett, M. 1979. Levels of processing in sentence production. In B. Butterworth (ed.) *Language production.* London: Academic Press.

Geschwind, N. 1965. Disconnexion syndromes in animals and man. *Brain* 88: 237–94, 585–644.

Gleason, J. B., Goodglass, H., Green, E., Ackerman, N. & Hyde, M. 1975. The retrieval of syntax in Broca's aphasia. *Brain and Language* 2: 451–71.

Gleason, J. B., Goodglass, H., Obler, L., Green, E., Hyde, M. R. & Weintraub, S. 1980. Narrative strategies of aphasic and normal speaking subjects. *Journal of Speech and Hearing Research* 23: 370–83.

Goldstein, K. 1948. *Language and language disturbances.* New York: Grune & Stratton.

Goodglass, H. 1968. Studies on the grammar of aphasics. In S. Rosenberg & J. H. Koplin (eds.) *Developments in applied psycholinguistic research.* New York: Macmillan.

Goodglass, H. & Baker, E. 1976. Semantic field, naming, and auditory comprehension in aphasia. *Brain and Language* 3: 359–74.

Goodglass, H., Barton, M. & Kaplan, E. 1968. Sensory modality and object naming in aphasia. *Journal of Speech and Hearing Research* 11: 488–96.

Goodglass, H., Blumstein, S. E., Gleason, J. B., Hyde, M. R., Green, E. & Statlender, S. 1979. The effect of syntactic encoding on sentence comprehension in aphasia. *Brain and Language* 7: 201–9.

Goodglass, H., Gleason, J., Bernholtz, N. A. & Hyde, M. R. 1972. Some linguistic structures in the speech of a Broca's aphasic. *Cortex* 8: 191–212.

Goodglass, H., Gleason, J. B. & Hyde, M. R. 1970. Some dimensions of auditory language comprehension in aphasia. *Journal of Speech and Hearing Research* 13: 595–606.

Goodglass, H., Hyde, M. R., Blumstein, S. 1969. Frequency, picturability, and availability of nouns in aphasia. *Cortex* 5: 104–19.

Goodglass, H. & Kaplan, E. 1983. *The assessment of aphasia and related disorders.* Philadelphia: Lea & Febiger.

Goodglass, H., Kaplan, E., Weintraub, S. & Ackerman, N. 1976. The 'tip-of-the-tongue' phenomenon in aphasia. *Cortex* 12: 145–53.

Goodglass, H. & Menn, L. 1985. Is agrammatism a unitary phenomenon? In M. L. Kean (ed.) *Agrammatism.* New York: Academic Press.

Goodman, G. O., McClelland, J. L. & Gibbs, R. W. 1981. The role of syntactic context in word recognition. *Memory and Cognition* 9: 580–6.

Gordon, B. & Caramazza, A. 1982. Lexical decision for open- and closed-class words: failure to replicate differential frequency sensitivity. *Brain and Language* 15: 143–60.

Gordon, B. & Caramazza, A. 1983. Closed- and open-class lexical access in agrammatic and fluent aphasics. *Brain and Language* 19: 335–45.

Green, E. 1969. Phonological and grammatical aspects of jargon in an aphasic patient: a case study. *Language and Speech* 12: 103–18.

Grober, E., Perecman, E., Kellar, L. & Brown, J. 1980. Lexical knowledge in anterior and posterior aphasics. *Brain and Language* 10: 318–30.

Grodzinsky, Y. 1984. The syntactic characterization of agrammatism. *Cognition* 16: 99–120.

Grodzinsky, Y. 1986. Language deficits and the theory of syntax. *Brain and Language* 27: 135–59.

Grodzinsky, Y., Swinney, D. & Zurif, E. 1985. Agrammatism: structural deficits and antecedent processing disruptions. In M. L. Kean (ed.) *Agrammatism.* New York: Academic Press.

Harmes, S., Daniloff, R. G., Hoffman, P. R., Lewis, J., Kramer, M. B. & Absher, R. 1984. Temporal and articulatory control of fricative articulation by speakers with Broca's aphasia. *Journal of Phonetics* 12: 367–85.

Head, H. 1926. *Aphasia and kindred disorders of speech*, Vol. 2. Cambridge: Cambridge University Press.

Howes, D. 1964. Application of the word frequency concept to aphasia. In A. V. S. DeReuck & M. O'Connor (eds.) *Disorders of language.* London: Churchill.

Irigaray, L. 1967. Approche psycholinguistique de langage des déments. *Neuropsychologia* 5: 25–32.

Itoh, M., Sasanuma, S., Hirose, H., Yoshioka, H. & Ushijima, T. 1980. Abnormal articulatory dynamics in a patient with apraxia of speech. *Brain and Language* 11: 66–75.

Itoh, M., Sasanuma, S., Tatsumi, I. F., Murakami, S., Fukusako, Y. & Suzuki, T. 1982. Voice onset time characteristics in apraxia of speech. *Brain and Language* 17: 193–210.

Itoh, M., Sasanuma, S. & Ushijima, T. 1979. Velar movements during speech in a patient with apraxia of speech. *Brain and Language* 7: 227–39.

Jakobson, R. 1968. *Child language, aphasia, and phonological universals.* Trans. by A. R. Keiler. The Hague: Mouton.

Jakobson, R. 1971. *Studies on child language and aphasia.* The Hague: Mouton.

Jauhiainen, T. & Nuutila, A. 1977. Auditory perception of speech and speech sounds in recent and recovered cases of aphasia. *Brain and Language* 4: 572–9.

Katz, W. 1986a. An acoustic and perceptual investigation of co-articulation in aphasia. Doctoral dissertation, Brown University.

Katz, W. 1986b. An investigation of lexical ambiguity in Broca's aphasics using an auditory lexical priming technique. Under editorial review.

Kean, M. L. 1980. Grammatical representations and the description of language processing. In D. Caplan (ed.) *Biological studies of mental processes.* Cambridge, MA: MIT Press.

Kent, R. D. & Rosenbek, J. C. 1983. Acoustic patterns of apraxia of speech. *Journal of Speech and Hearing Research* 26: 231–49.

Kolk, H. 1983. Agrammatic processing of word order. Paper presented at the Academy of Aphasia, Minneapolis.

LaBerge, D. & Samuels, S. J. 1974. Towards a theory of automatic information processing in reading. *Cognitive Psychology* 6: 293–323.

LaPointe, S. G. 1985. A theory of verb form use in the speech of agrammatic aphasics. *Brain and Language* 24: 100–55.

Lecours, A. R. & Lhermitte, F. 1969. Phonemic paraphasias: linguistic structures and tentative hypotheses. *Cortex* 5: 193–228.

Lehiste, I. 1968. *Some acoustic characteristics of dysarthria.* Switzerland: Biblioteca Phonetica.

Lesser, R. 1978. *Linguistic investigations of aphasia.* London: Arnold.

Liberman, A. M., Cooper, F. S., Shankweiler, D. P. & Studdert-Kennedy, M. 1967. Perception of the speech code. *Psychological Review* 74: 431–61.

Linebarger, M., Schwartz, M. & Saffran, E. 1983. Sensitivity to grammatical structure in so-called agrammatic aphasics. *Cognition* 13: 361–92.

Lukatela, G., Kostic, A., Feldman, L. B. & Turvey, M. T. 1983. Grammatical priming of inflected nouns. *Memory and Cognition* 11: 59–63.

Luria, A. R. 1966. *Higher cortical functions in man.* New York: Basic Books.

Martin, A. D., Wasserman, N. H., Gilden, L. & West, J. 1975. A process model of repetition in aphasia: an investigation of phonological and morphological interactions in aphasic error performance. *Brain and Language* 2: 434–50.

Meyer, D. E. & Schvaneveldt, R. W. 1971. Facilitation in recognizing pairs of words: evidence of a dependence between retrieval operations. *Journal of Experimental Psychology* 90: 227–34.

Miceli, G., Caltagirone, C., Gainotti, C. & Payer-Rigo, R. 1978. Discrimination of voice versus place contrasts in aphasia. *Brain and Language* 6: 47–51.

Miceli, G., Gainotti, G., Caltagirone, C. & Masullo, C. 1980. Some aspects of phonological impairment in aphasia. *Brain and Language* 11: 159–69.

Miceli, G., Mazzucchi, A., Menn, L. & Goodglass, H. 1983. Contrasting cases of Italian agrammatic aphasia without comprehension disorder. *Brain and Language* 19: 65–97.

Milberg, W. & Blumstein, S. E. 1981. Lexical decision and aphasia: evidence for semantic processing. *Brain and Language* 14: 371–85.

Milberg, W., Blumstein, S. E. & Dworetzky, B. 1985. Sensitivity to morphological constraints in Broca's and Wernicke's aphasics: a double dissociation of syntactic judgement and syntactic facilitation in a lexical decision task. Paper presented at the Academy of Aphasia, Pittsburgh.

Milberg, W., Blumstein, S. E. & Dworetzky, B. 1987. Processing of lexical ambiguities in aphasia. *Brain and Language* 31: 138–50.

Nespoulous, J. L., Joanette, Y., Beland, S., Caplan, D. & Lecours, A. R. 1984. Production deficits in Broca's and conduction aphasia: repetition vs. reading. Paper presented at Symposium of Motor and Sensory Language Processing, Montreal.

Niemi, J., Koivuselka-Sallinen, P. & Hanninen, R. 1985. Phoneme errors in Broca's aphasia: three Finnish cases. *Brain and Language* 26: 28–48.

Onifer, W. & Swinney, D. A. 1981. Accessing lexical ambiguities during sentence comprehension: effects of frequency of meaning and contextual bias. *Memory and Cognition* 9: 225–36.

Panse, F. & Shimoyama, T. 1973. On the effects of aphasic disturbance in Japanese: agrammatism and paragrammatism. In H. Goodglass & S. Blumstein (eds.) *Psycholinguistics and aphasia.* Baltimore: Johns Hopkins University Press.

Parisi, D. & Pizzamiglio, L. 1970. Syntactic comprehension in aphasia. *Cortex* 6: 204–15.

Peuser, G. & Fittschen, M. 1977. On the universality of language dissolution: the case of a Turkish aphasic. *Brain and Language* 4: 196–207.

Reidel, K. & Studdert-Kennedy, M. 1985. Extending formant transitions may not improve aphasics' perception of stop consonant place of articulation. *Brain and Language* 24: 223–32.

Rinnert, C. & Whitaker, H. A. 1973. Semantic confusions by aphasic patients. *Cortex* 9: 56–81.

Rochford, G. & Williams, M. 1962. Studies in the development and breakdown in the use of names, IV: The effects of word frequency. *Journal of Neurology, Neurosurgery, and Psychiatry* 28: 407–13.

Ryalls, J. H. 1981. Motor aphasia: acoustic correlates of phonetic disintegration in vowels. *Neuropsychologia* 19: 365–74.

Ryalls, J. H. 1984. An acoustic investigation of vowel production in aphasia. Doctoral dissertation, Brown University.

Saffran, E. M., Schwartz, M. F. & Marin, O. S. M. 1980. The word order problem in agrammatism, II: Production. *Brain and Language* 10: 263–80.

Sasanuma, S., Tatsumi, I. F. & Fujisaki, H. 1976. Discrimination of phonemes and word accent types in Japanese aphasic patients. *XVIth International Congress of Logopedics and Phoniatrics:* 403–8.

Schwartz, M. 1984. What the classical aphasia categories can't do for us, and why. *Brain and Language* 21: 3–8.

Schwartz, M. F., Saffran, E. M. & Marin, O. S. M. 1980. The word order problem in agrammatism, I: Comprehension. *Brain and Language* 10: 249–63.

Shankweiler, D. P., Harris, K. S. & Taylor, M. L. 1968. Electromyographic study of articulation in aphasia. *Archives of Physical Medicine and Rehabilitation* 49: 1–8.

Shewan, C. M. 1976. Error patterns in auditory comprehension of adult aphasics. *Cortex* 12: 325–36.

Shewan, C. M. & Canter, C. J. 1971. Effects of vocabulary, syntax, and sentence length on auditory comprehension in aphasic patients. *Cortex* 7: 209–26.

Shewan, C. M., Leeper, H. A. & Booth, J. C. 1984. An analysis of voice onset time (VOT) in aphasic and normal subjects. In J. Rosenbek, M. McNeil & A. Aronson (eds.) *Apraxia of speech: physiology, acoustics, linguistics, management.* San Diego: College-Hill Press.

Shiffrin, R. M. & Schneider, W. 1977. Controlled and automatic human information processing, II: Perceptual learning, automatic attending and a general theory. *Psychological Review* 84: 127–90.

Shinn, P. & Blumstein, S. E. 1983. Phonetic disintegration in aphasia: acoustic analysis of spectral characteristics for place of articulation. *Brain and Language* 20: 90–114.

Swinney, D., Zurif, E. B., Rosenberg, B. & Nicol, J. 1986. Lexical processing during sentence comprehension in agrammatic and Wernicke's aphasics: a real-time analysis. ms.

Swisher, L. & Hirsh, I. J. 1972. Brain damage and the ordering of two temporally successive stimuli. *Neuropsychologia* 10: 137–52.

Tallal, P. & Newcombe, F. 1978. Impairment of auditory perception and language comprehension in dysphasia. *Brain and Language* 5: 13–24.

Tanenhaus, M. K., Carlson, G. N. & Seidenberg, M. S. 1985. Do listeners compute linguistic representations? In D. Dowty, L. Kartunnen & A. Zwicky (eds.) *Natural language parsing: psychological, computational and theoretical perspectives.* Cambridge: Cambridge University Press.

Tissot, R., Lhermitte, F. & Ducarne, B. 1963. Etat intellectuel des aphasiques. *L'Encephale* 52: 285–320.

Trost, J. E. & Canter, G. J. 1974. Apraxia of speech in patients with Broca's aphasia: a study of phoneme production accuracy and error patterns. *Brain and Language* 1: 63–79.

Tuller, B. 1984. On categorizing speech errors. *Neuropsychologia* 22: 547–58.

Von Stockert, T. R. 1972. Recognition of syntactic structure in aphasic patients. *Cortex* 8: 323–34.

Weigl, E. & Bierwisch, M. 1970. Neuropsychology and linguistics: topics of common research. *Foundations of Language* 6: 1–18.

Wright, B. & Garrett, M. 1984. Lexical decision in sentences: effects of syntactic structure. *Memory and Cognition* 12: 31–45.

Zangwill, O. L. 1964. Intelligence in aphasia. In A. V. S. de Reuck and M. O'Connor (eds.) *Disorders of language.* London: Churchill.

Ziegler, W. & von Cramon, D. 1985. Anticipatory co-articulation in a patient with apraxia of speech. *Brain and Language* 26: 117–30.

Zurif, E. B. & Caramazza, A. 1976. Psycholinguistic structures in aphasia: studies in syntax and semantics. In H. Whitaker & H. Whitaker (eds.) *Studies in neurolinguistics*, Vol. 1. New York: Academic Press.

Zurif, E. B., Caramazza, A. & Myerson, R. 1972. Grammatical judgements of agrammatic aphasics. *Neuropsychologia* 10: 405–17.

Zurif, E. B., Caramazza, A., Myerson, R. & Galvin, J. 1974. Semantic feature representations for normal and aphasic language. *Brain and Language* 1: 167–87.

9 The biological basis for language*

David Caplan

The physical substrate responsible for the representation and processing of human language is the human brain; more specifically, certain portions of telencephalic cortex and possibly some subcortical structures. Though the cerebral hemisphere which is responsible for language varies in different subgroups of the adult human population, the area responsible for language is thought to be relatively circumscribed within the relevant hemisphere in the normal adult human population. The existence of a restricted neocortical area responsible for language is known as the *localization* of language functions; the location of this area within one telencephalic hemisphere is known as the *lateralization* of language functions. Many authorities believe that localization of function extends to *subcomponents* of a language processing mechanism, and a variety of theories of the further extent of localization of language functions has been proposed. Similarly, many workers believe that aspects of the language system can be differentially lateralized. This chapter will present a review of the concepts of localization and lateralization of language functions, focussing upon the identification of the 'language areas' of the brain, their internal organization with respect to language functions, and the genetic and environmental determinants of their location and internal organization.

Both clinical and experimental studies of aphasia indicate that the neocortex surrounding the Sylvian fissure is responsible for many language functions. Clinical evidence to this effect consists of large-scale studies of pathological and radiological correlates of aphasias, which show that permanent aphasias arise after lesions in this area (Luria 1947; Russell & Espir 1961). Experimental studies take several forms. Electrical stimulation of very small areas of this cortex during neurosurgical procedures produces impairments in language performances during the duration of the stimulation (Penfield & Roberts 1959; Ojemann 1983). Recording of electrical responses to language stimuli and electrical events in telencephalon before

* This paper was prepared while the author was the recipient of a Chercheur-Boursier Senior Award, Level 1, from the Fonds de Recherche en Santé du Québec.

and during speech also tends to confirm the importance of this region in language functions (Neville, Kutus & Schmidt 1982), though the exact location of a generator of electrical potentials is hard to infer from the surface location of a potential (Picton & Stuss 1984). However, these same sources of evidence also have suggested that other telencephalic structures play a role in language functioning in the normal adult brain. There are, therefore, two aspects to the question of the localization of language functions: 'gross' location – the question of whether language functions are carried out exclusively in perisylvian association cortex – and 'narrow' localization – the question of whether and how subcomponents of a language processing system are localized within portions of this cortex.

On first glance, recent discoveries would seem to demonstrate that language functions are not grossly localized to the perisylvian cortex. Observations of the language abilities of patients with non-perisylvian lesions in the dominant hemisphere, such as lesions of the thalamic nuclei (Mohr, Walters & Duncan 1975), the caudate nucleus (Damasio *et al.* 1982), white matter structures surrounding these subcortical grey matter areas (Naeser & Hayward 1978), and the supplementary motor cortex (Masdeu, Schoene & Funkenstein 1978), have documented language deficits. Electrical stimulation of dominant thalamic and perithalamic structures leads to interference with some language functions (Ojemann 1983), and stimulation of the dominant supplementary motor cortex leads to speech arrest (Penfield & Roberts 1959). Metabolic scanning has shown that there is often subcortical hypometabolism in the case of strokes whose CT loci appear to be uniquely cortical (Metter *et al.* 1985). All these results have been taken as indications that structures outside the dominant perisylvian cortex, but within the dominant hemisphere, are involved in normal language functioning in the intact brain. The non-dominant hemisphere is capable of some language functions, as judged by studies in callosally sectioned patients (Zaidel & Peters 1981), dichotic listening and half-field tachistoscopic experiments in normals (Bryden 1982), and studies of recovery from aphasia after brain injury (Kinsbourne 1971). Studies of the language abilities of patients with non-dominant hemisphere injuries also reveal deficits in some language functions (see below), suggesting that the non-dominant hemisphere is actively involved in language functioning in the intact brain, even in individuals whose language functions are expected to be completely lateralized to one hemisphere (right-handed individuals from right-handed families). This has suggested to some workers that language processing goes on in many areas of the brain in all adult humans (Damasio & Geschwind 1984).

Despite these discoveries, it is possible that what may be termed 'core' language processing is carried out exclusively in the dominant perisylvian cortex. Roughly speaking, we may consider those processes which recognize the form of the words and sentences of an utterance and assign a literal meaning to these elements as 'core' language functions; conversely, on the expressive side, 'core' language functions are those which select, structure, and produce the formal codes of these lexical, morphological, and sentential elements. It is reasonable to divide language structures into these 'core' elements, which constitute the essential forms and semantic values conveyed by the language code, and other aspects of language, such as discourse structure, inferences, etc., which interact with these aspects of language. This division roughly corresponds to distinctions made in current linguistic theory, which is mainly restricted to what we are calling 'core' aspects of language. It may yet be that this division is mistaken, but it is not unmotivated in the present state of knowledge.

Some of the language functions which are impaired following non-perisylvian dominant-hemisphere injuries do not fall into these core areas of language processing. They include the ability to make inferences and structure texts, and to recognize emotional tones of voice, which is impaired following non-dominant hemisphere lesions (Winner & Gardner 1977; Heilman, Scholes & Watson 1975), and to initiate and modulate phonation in utterances, which is impaired following dominant supplementary motor area lesions (Masdeu, Schoene & Funkenstein 1978). In other instances, though core language processing functions are impaired following lesions in other brain areas, there may be physiological impairment in the dominant perisylvian cortex associated with the responsible injuries. Lesions in locations deep within the dominant hemisphere which are found on CT scans may be accompanied by physiological impairments in the overlying cortex. This is especially true in vascular cases, which constitute the majority of such lesions in which an aphasia has been documented, since the middle cerebral artery and its branches supply all these structures (Bladin & Berkovic 1984). The fact that the aphasic symptoms found following injury to any non-perisylvian structure in the dominant hemisphere are transient also weakens the argument that these areas are normally involved in language processing; at the least, it indicates that their functions (if any) are quite rapidly taken over by other brain areas. It is true that patients with non-dominant hemisphere lesions have been shown to have mild impairments in some 'core' language functions (Joanette *et al.* 1983), but these impairments are very slight and may reflect general impairments in all intellectual functions attendant upon any form of telencephalic injury – some sort of 'capacity limitation' showing up in language (the studies showing these mild impairments did not report performances on control nonlinguistic tasks, nor did they contrast right hemisphere lesions with equivalent non-perisylvian left-hemisphere lesions). Finally, studies showing that the non-dominant hemisphere can accomplish several core tasks when surgically isolated from the dominant hemisphere, or when presented with a linguistic stimulus in a half-field or dichotic task, do not show that this hemisphere actually accomplishes these functions when connected to its homologue and when linguistic stimuli are presented to both. In short, the case that core language processing occurs outside the dominant perisylvian cortex is far from established. The strongest position is that 'gross' localization is correct: that core language functions are accomplished solely in perisylvian association cortex.

What of 'narrow' localization of subcomponents of the system devoted to core language processing? The basic, traditional, neurolinguistic model pertaining to the function neuroanatomy of the perisylvian cortex maintains that narrow localization of language processing subcomponents exists. Figure 1 represents the basic 'connectionist' model of language processing and its relationship to areas within the dominant perisylvian cortex. According to this model, the permanent representations for the sounds of words are stored in Wernicke's area, the association cortex of the second temporal gyrus. These auditory representations are accessed following auditory presentation of language stimuli. They, in turn, evoke the concepts associated with words in the 'concept center.' According to Lichtheim (1885), the concept center is diffusely represented within association cortex. Accessing the phonological representation of words and the subsequent concepts associated with these representations constitutes the function of comprehension of auditory language. In spoken language production, concepts access the

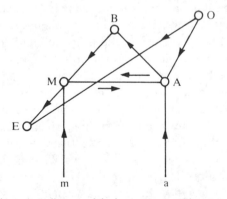

Figure 1. A diagram of the language processing system, according to Lichtheim. A represents the 'storehouse for the auditory form of words,' located in Wernicke's area (temporal association cortex). M represents the motor speech planning center, located in Broca's area in frontal lobe. B represents the 'concept center,' located diffusely in association cortex. O and E are centers responsible for reading and writing respectively (not discussed in the present text). Arrows indicate direction of information flow between centers. For details of the operation of this system, see accompanying text.

phonological representations of words in Wernicke's area, which are then transmitted to the motor programming areas for speech in Broca's area, the association cortex of the *pars triangularis* and *opercularis* of the third frontal gyrus and possibly that of the Rolandic (frontal) operculum. Simultaneously, according to Lichtheim (1885), the concept center activates Broca's area. The proper execution of the speech act depends upon Broca's area receiving input from both these different cortical areas, each conveying different types of linguistically relevant representations. This model was depicted schematically by Lichtheim (1885), as represented in Figure 1. The connectionist model of language representation and processing in the brain was revived by Geschwind (1965) and his colleagues, and has achieved considerable popularity in the past two decades in North America. The basic model of the representation of language in dominant perisylvian cortex proposed by Geschwind and his colleagues differs little from that proposed by Wernicke (1874), Lichtheim (1885), and the other nineteenth-century connectionists. These historical origins of the theory are acknowledged. The major innovation proposed by Geschwind is in the location of one aspect of the concept center. Geschwind (1965) proposed that the inferior parietal lobule – the supra-marginal and angular gyri – is the location at which the fibers projecting from somathestetic, visual, and auditory association cortices all converge, and that, as a consequence of this convergence, associations between word sounds and the sensory properties of objects can be established in this area. Geschwind argued that the establishment of these associations is a prerequisite for the ability to name objects. Aside from this innovation, the revised modern version of connectionist psycholinguistic and neurolinguistic models does not substantially change the earlier theory. A recent review of the 'neural basis for language' (Damasio & Geschwind 1984) reiterates this theory.

The principal evidence in favor of this model is the occurrence of specific syndromes of language disorders which can be accounted for by lesions of these centers and the connections between them. A disturbance in Broca's area leads to 'Broca's aphasia,' a severe expressive language disturbance without concomitant disturbances of auditory comprehension first described by Broca (1861). A disturbance of Wernicke's area leads to the combination of fluent paraphasic speech and auditory comprehension disturbances first described by Wernicke (1874). A lesion of the input pathway to Wernicke's area leads to pure word deafness, in which spontaneous speech is normal but comprehension and repetition are disturbed. A lesion in the outflow pathway from Broca's area leads to pure anarthria or dysarthria, in which both repetition and spontaneous speech are misarticulated but comprehension is preserved. The difference between Broca's aphasia and pure dysarthria relates to the role of Broca's area in writing – Broca's area is thought to be involved in planning stages for written language, and therefore Broca's aphasia is accompanied by an agraphia while dysarthria is not – and to the fact that the speech of the Broca's aphasic is 'reduced' in some way(s), while that of the pure dysarthric patient is only misarticulated. A lesion between the concept center and Broca's area leads to 'transcortical motor aphasia,' in which spontaneous speech is abnormal, as in Broca's aphasia, because of the failure of the concept center to provide its input to Broca's area, but repetition is intact. A lesion of the pathway between the concept center and Wernicke's area leads to 'transcortical sensory aphasia,' a comprehension disturbance without a disturbance of repetition. Finally, a lesion of the pathway connecting Wernicke's and Broca's area leads to a disturbance in spontaneous speech and repetition similar to that seen in Wernicke's aphasia without a disturbance in auditory comprehension, termed 'conduction aphasia.' All of these syndromes were alleged to have been discovered in relatively pure form by Lichtheim (1885), and to have resulted from lesions in the appropriate cortical and subcortical areas of the brain. Benson and Geschwind (1975), Damasio and Geschwind (1984), Benson (1979), Kertesz (1979), and many other contemporary researchers claim these syndromes exist, and base a model of the functional neuroanatomy of perisylvian cortex upon their existence. These models are all closely related versions of the Wernicke–Lichtheim 'connectionist' model.

The Wernicke–Lichtheim analysis has been subject to considerable criticism, both 'internal' and 'external.' 'External' criticisms hold that the phenomena described in these theories are not the principal language-related functions which should be modeled, either in normalcy or in pathological states. Classical objections of this 'external' sort were raised by Jackson (1874), Marie (1906), Head (1926), Goldstein (1948), and many other workers. These critics argued that features such as motivational state and level of arousal influence language performance and need to be incorporated into models of psycholinguistic function and of the neural basis for language. In line with my concern to restrict my discussion to core aspects of language processing, I shall not focus on these objections. Rather, I shall be concerned with internal objections, which consist of arguments that the proposed psycholinguistic account of language functions and/or its neural basis is either incomplete or inaccurate.

These criticisms date from the earliest post-connectionist writings. For instance, Freud (1891) pointed out that the occurrence of an alexia with Broca's aphasia was common and could not be accounted for by any natural extension of the Wernicke–Lichtheim model. The documentation of anomias without disturbances of single word auditory comprehension entailed that the pathway from the concept center to Wernicke's area must be separate from that in the opposite direction. A similar conclusion can be reached from the presence of transcortical sensory aphasia without anomia: patients with transcortical sensory aphasia have disturbances of auditory word comprehension due to a lesion affecting the pathway connecting the concept center and Wernicke's area, but need not have either anomia or a disturbance of the sound pattern of words in speech production. In general, the relationship between the concept center and Wernicke's area was unspecified in the classical literature, both at the level of the psycholinguistic mechanisms involved and in terms of its neurological location. The latter is not surprising given the fact that the concept center itself never received a clear anatomical locus in the classical literature. The modern revision of connectionism has been subject to the same sort of criticisms as the earlier versions, though they have not always been presented in this perspective. For instance, the claim made in a paper by Kinsbourne (1972) on 'conduction aphasia' that there is a direct psychological (and neural) connection between a 'visual word center' and the speech mechanism contradicts one aspect of the classical and contemporary view, that the process of reading aloud necessarily involves the identification of 'sound patterns' of words.

Recent internal criticisms of this theory have raised additional points. The first problem raised in the modern literature is that each of the classic aphasic syndromes consists of a variety of different symptoms. For instance, the expressive speech disorder in 'Broca's aphasia' consists of various combinations of symptoms – dysarthria, apraxia of speech, agrammatism – which can be found in this syndrome. 'Wernicke's aphasia' has numerous forms, including paragrammatism, phonologically based phonemic paraphasias, morphological errors, anomia, and others. The disturbance in repetition found in conduction aphasia has been shown to have at least two sources, one in disturbances of short-term memory and one in disturbances of single word production (Shallice & Warrington 1977). The multiplicity of symptoms within a given syndrome points to the need for a much more detailed linguistic and psycholinguistic description of aphasic performances. The number of different symptoms found within a syndrome also leads to serious questions about the homogeneity of patients who are considered to have a single syndrome. Schwartz (1984) calls this the problem of the 'polytypicality' of clinical syndromes. In the extreme, one patient called 'Broca's aphasic' may have no symptoms in common with another patient with the same label. Functional–anatomical correlations based upon the location of lesions underlying these classical syndromes therefore cannot lead to the discovery of the neural basis of the individual components of psycholinguistic function.

A second recently cited problem with classical syndromes is that many linguistic disturbances occur in more than one syndrome. As with the first

David Caplan

problem, this leads to difficulties in classifying patients. Patients who show only these language disturbances – such as anomia and the production of phonemic paraphasias in spontaneous speech – cannot be unequivocally classified into a single aphasic syndrome. In fact, most studies attempting to classify patients into the traditional clinical groups of patients on the basis of clinical observations have failed to classify a significant number of patients unequivocally. Again, clinical–pathological correlations based upon the classical clinical syndromes may be misleading with respect to the neural basis of isolated components of the language processing system, since many cases are excluded. Moreover, the existence of these unclassifiable cases raises doubts about the adequacy of the connectionist model.

These problems with localization of function on the basis of the lesions correlated with the classical aphasic syndromes point to a fundamental limitation in classical aphasiological work. This limitation is a consequence of the nature of the descriptions of aphasic syndromes and symptoms found in classical work and its contemporary revival. As increasing attention has been paid to linguistic structures and their abnormalities and attempts have been made to incorporate observations on aphasic patients into models of language processing, both the problem of the fractionation of the syndromes into small functional components and that of the overlap of functional disturbances across the classical syndromes have become increasingly apparent.

The most widespread approach to these challenges to classical and modern connectionism has been for theorists to extend the notion of localization of function to a greater number of components of a language processing mechanism, through correlation of deficits in these smaller processing units with lesion sites in aphasic cases. The work of Luria (1947, 1972) is probably best known as an example of this approach, but that of many other researchers also falls into this category (e.g. Brown 1982).

Luria's neurolinguistic model recognizes a number of subcomponents of a language processor. These subcomponents are often those identified in the classical connectionist theory, reformulated in terms provided by linguistic, psycholinguistic, and philosophical models of language. For instance, Wernicke's 'store-house for the sounds of words' becomes a mechanism for phonemic discrimination and recognition in Luria's model. The set of processes grouped together as 'the faculty for articulate speech' is subdivided into processes related to retrieval of the logical content of a sentence, those responsible for its syntactic form, and others. In Luria's model, each subcomponent of a language-processing device acts in a variety of language functions. For instance, the phonemic discrimination/identification mechanism is involved in naming, repetition, and spontaneous speech, as well as comprehension. The result is that any language act draws upon the entirety

244

of the perisylvian language-related cortex, since these components of the language processor are localized in various areas of this cortex. Moreover, Luria's model of language functions includes nonlinguistic, regulatory, processes such as an attention-focussing and an attention-switching device. These components are localized in areas of the brain outside the language zone, such as pre-frontal association cortex. These brain areas are therefore also involved in language performances, though not necessarily in the construction of linguistic form itself.

Luria represents his model as a combination of what he takes to be the best features of the connectionist, localizationist and anti-connectionist holist approaches. The division of language functions into subcomponents is taken from the former approach and is extended. These subcomponents are then localized. In this sense, Luria is more of a detail localizationist than any of the connectionist predecessors he recognizes. On the other hand, Luria is impressed with the contribution of large areas of telencephalon, if not the entire telencephalon, to individual language performances. Though he disagrees with notions such as 'mass action' and Gestalt psychological concepts advocated by many holist theorists, he incorporates the idea of the widespread utilization of cortex in language performances through the inclusion of nonlinguistic attentional and motivational functions in the accomplishment of language activity. Luria believes in the localization of these nonlinguistic capacities, as well as of more strictly linguistic components of a language processor. In this sense, he is an extreme localizationist, with a more complex model of the processing components and control mechanisms which are involved in the performance of particular linguistic tasks than many of his connectionist predecessors had.

A somewhat similar view is held by Brown (1982). Brown's theory incorporates the notion of a heirarchy of representational levels and processing stages in language-related tasks. For instance, Brown claims that speech production involves two separate processes: the construction of a sound pattern and the construction of lexical content. The former is carried out in an anterior set of neural structures, and the latter in a posterior set. The anterior set begins by the construction of an intonation contour, and eventually produces the articulatory gestures responsible for individual speech sounds. The posterior sequence first involves the neural elaboration of a semantic message, and then proceeds to the selection of individual words through inhibition of related but inappropriate lexical items, and finally specifies the abstract phonological values for individual words. In both cases, the earliest stages of these processes involve less advanced limbic cortex of both hemispheres; the intermediate stages involve neocortical association areas; and the final stages involve focal motor or sensory cortex. Brown cites Sanides (1970) in support of the view that these cortical areas represent progressive phylogenetic developments. Like Luria, Brown recognizes a number of stages of language processing, each related to specific language structures, which are each carried out in specific cortical areas. Because of the large number of processing components, the system relies upon a larger area of brain than is specified in the classical or contemporary connectionist models.

Both Luria's and Brown's models – and many more of this sort – are subject to a variety of criticisms. One is that all of these authors show at least ambivalence, if not disregard, for truly detailed linguistic and psycholinguistic theories, so that the linguistic representations and processing stages specified in these theories suffer from being more or less impressionistic and none of these theories specifies enough representational types or processing stages; many of the syndromes and symptoms which are correlated with lesion sites, such as Brown's early processing stages or Luria's stage of 'inner speech,' are still too vague and too large. Even in cases where these models incorporate processing mechanisms which do seem to be candidates for natural kinds within a processing model of language, the data regarding the neural basis for these components provided by these researchers is impressionistic and scanty.

These criticisms could, of course, be further incentives to develop and provide empirical support for yet more detailed narrow localization models, with increasingly smaller components of the language-processing system being related to areas of the perisylvian cortex. However, there is reason to believe that, if it exists, narrow localization cannot have some of the features which all of the theories we have reviewed ascribe to it. All the theories we have reviewed which postulate narrow localization of components of the language processing system share two features. First, they all claim that, ignoring the issue of lateralization, the localization of components of the language system is the same in all normal adults. Second, they all derive the specific functions of the sub-areas of language-related cortex from the relationship of these sub-areas to motor and sensory areas of the brain. For instance, Geschwind (1965) relates the language functions of the inferior parietal lobe to its connections, as noted above, not to its intrinsic elements and organization, indicating that pre-frontal cortex, which does not have similar connections, has no language functions despite its equally advanced structural character. Similarly, Luria (1947) explicitly derives the particular role of areas of cortex in language from the role of adjacent cortex in motor and sensory function. These features of existing theories ignore the nature of many language-processing components, and are inconsistent with a number of findings regarding the variability of localization of language-processing components.

Though some parts of a language processor must interact with processes which are responsible for sensory registration of events in the world – such as the auditory registration of sounds – and with others responsible for the execution of actions – such as the operation of the speech musculature – a large number of components of a language processor are devoted to operations affecting abstract representations of the language code. These operations consist of the interconversion of linguistic representations. There is no reason to believe that these 'central' stages of language processing have any similarity to processes related to nonlinguistic sensory and motor functions, or are in any way derived from these functions. Thus, the pragmatic inference that areas of cortex devoted to language derive their specific language functions from their connections to sensory and motor association cortex (Wernicke 1874; Geschwind 1965), or from their adjacency to such cortex (Luria 1947; Brown 1982) is, at best, relevant to the interface between a language processor and sensory and motor systems and not to many central stages of language processing of interest to linguists and psycholinguists.

In fact, the pragmatic inference just mentioned has been questioned by many investigators. Lashley (1937), for one, doubted the need and advantage of the juxtaposition of any particular part of cortex with any other part as the basis for the determination of the functions of the first cortical area in question, on the basis of the observation that the entire cortex is so densely interconnected that adjacency of cortical areas need have no computational advantage (see Marshall 1980, for similar questions). Some gross observations about the motor system disprove the necessity of proximity and direct connectivity for functional relatedness. For instance, some motor neurons project axons for over a meter to achieve direct synapses on lower motor neurons – an indication that mono-synaptic connections between control – and execution-devoted neurons need not be physically close. Other neurons involved in motor function – Purkinje cells in the cerebellum – synapse in deep cerebellar nuclei, from which other neurons project to thalamus (sometimes through a second synapse in the red nucleus), from which other neurons project to pre-frontal lobe, before a series of intra-cortical neurons relay cerebellar influences to motor cortex. Despite this multi-synaptic system, cerebellar influence on action is marked. The role of adjacency and direct connectivity in determining functional systems is, therefore, an empirical matter and some systems do not show these features.

Recent studies have shown that the language functions accomplished by areas of cortex are also not due to the juxtaposition of that cortex to sensory or motor association cortex. For instance, if there is a single language-processing component whose neural locus has been related to the proximity of that site to a sensory area of the brain by virtually every localizationist researcher, it is the function of phoneme discrimination and identification, which is traditionally claimed to be located in association cortex of the dominant temporal lobe adjacent to Heschl's gyrus. However, in careful large-scale studies, Blumstein *et al.* (1977) and Basso, Casati & Vignolo (1977) have found that phonemic discrimination is impaired with lesions throughout the perisylvian cortex. Thus even in the domain of language processes which may be conceived of as interfaces between central language functions and sensory (and motor) systems, there is very little reason to believe that areas of brain have the language functions they do because of their connections or adjacency to sensory and/or motor cortex.

Recent studies have also raised major problems for the first postulate of the localizationist theories we have reviewed – that narrow localization, when it exists, is identical across all adult members of the human species. Caplan, Baker & Dehaut (1985) found that lesions confined to any single lobe within the dominant perisylvian cortex could produce the entire range of degrees of impairment in the comprehension of syntactic structures observed in an unselected aphasic population, from no impairment to total inability to accomplish this task, ranging through all intermediate degrees of deficit. The fact that some lesions confined to a single lobe give rise to severe or total impairment of this function implies that, for some individuals, syntactic comprehension is carried out in a single lobe; that is, it is narrowly localized. The fact that these severe impairments arise following lesions in single lobes rules out the possibility that the perisylvian cortex is 'equipotential' for language, in Lashley's (1950) sense. The fact that the lobe associated with these severe impairments varies across the population, however, indicates that this narrow localization is not the same for all adults. In addition, the fact that any lobe can be lesioned without affecting syntactic comprehension at all rules out any theory based upon 'mass action' (Lashley 1950) as the neural basis for language. These results suggest that different areas within the perisylvian cortex are capable of supporting particular aspects of language functions within particular individuals. The notion of localization of function applies, but in a rather different sense than theorists have so far considered. A particular function may be narrowly localized in an individual in a particular area of perisylvian dominant cortex, localized equally narrowly in another area in another individual, and carried out in a much larger area of perisylvian cortex in a third. The only constraint seems to be that core language processes are accomplished in this area of neocortex.

An important feature of recent research is the finding that sociological and environmental factors play no role in the determination of the neural basis for language. There is no indication that processing components are differently localized in languages with different structures, or in the brains of patients who have mastered particular forms of representation such as orthographies (i.e. are literate) (Damasio *et al.* 1976). These findings apply both to the localization and to the lateralization of language functions and strongly suggest that internal organic factors, possibly entirely genetic, determine the location of processing subcomponents of the language system within a specified area of the human brain. Caplan, Baker & Dehaut (1985) found no correlation between age or sex and degree of impairment of syntactic comprehension, nor any interaction between these factors, lesion site, and degree of impairment. These findings suggest that genetic factors determine the location of processing subcomponents of the language system within a specified area of the human brain, independently of these other factors.

This concept of localization of language functions may be termed 'local genetic equipotentiality' of a specified cortical area for language. According to this concept, the genetic program specifies that the perisylvian cortex will accomplish language functions. The genetic program must also specify which particular areas of this cortex accomplish particular functions in an individual, but a considerable amount of variation occurs with respect to how much and which part of perisylvian cortex is devoted to a particular language function in each individual. The particular claim of localizationist theorists that language-processing components are invariant with respect to their narrow cortical loci is too strong a version of narrow localization.

Recent studies have begun to document the particular anatomical features of the area of the brain responsible for human language. Some have been known for some time. Geschwind (1965) points to the particular connectivity of the inferior parietal association cortex as a critical feature of the organization of cortex responsible for aspects of lexical semantics, as we have seen. The general development of this area of cortex in terms of its degree of myelinization and the nature of its cellular organization (advanced association isocortex) have also been cited as anatomical features of this cortex which are related to its ability to sustain human language. More recently, histological features of this cortex have also been described, which seem to distinguish areas within this cortex from other areas which are not related to language. For instance, Galaburda (1982) describes vacuoles in the association cortex of the *pars triangularis* of the third frontal convulution which disappear once the tertiary sulcus separating this area of the cortex from the frontal operculum is passed.

Clearly there are far too few neuroanatomical and neurohistological studies of the language areas of the brain for us to be sure of their significance. As Marshall (1980) comments, our knowledge of the actual physical structures in the language cortex is the least well-developed area of our knowledge regarding the neural basis for language. There are, in fact, many questions that can be raised about the facts currently at our disposal. All of the features of cortex cited above are found in both the dominant and non-dominant hemisphere, yet language is a function of one hemisphere in the vast majority of humans. These features alone are therefore not sufficient to explain the lateralization of language functions. (We shall consider the question of the relative size of these areas of cortex below.) The detailed functional – structural correlations of these features of cortex is unknown. To say the least, some of the histological features which have recently been discovered in the language zones are not transparently related to language functions. The vacuoles described by Galaburda (1982), for instance, are largely filled with excretory products of intracellular metabolism and their relationship to the information-processing capacities of the cells in which they are found is far from clear.

The second striking feature of the neural basis for language is the lateralization of language functions. Close to 99% of right-handed adults are 'left-hemisphere dominant' for language, in the sense that they show permanent aphasias following left-hemisphere perisylvian damage and mild, if any, language disturbances following right-hemisphere damage (Luria 1947). (For the significance of abnormalities on language batteries following right-hemisphere damage see above.) Wada testing has confirmed this percentage (Branch, Miller & Rasmussen 1964). Although the data is controversial, some researchers who have access to callosally sectioned patients argue that their data supports a similar percentage of left-hemisphere language dominance in this population (Gazzaniga, Smylie & Baynes 1984).

Despite this overwhelming trend for the left hemisphere to be responsible for language functions in the right-handed population, it is clear that the right hemisphere of the adult can also support language functions. One percent of right-handed subjects, without familial sinistrality, show so-called crossed dextral aphasia; that is, permanent aphasia following a right-hemisphere lesion. Moreover, the percentage of left-hemisphere-dominant subjects varies in different adult subpopulations. The left-handed population, and right-handed individuals in whose family there are left-handers, are far less prone to the development of permanent aphasia following left-hemisphere lesions than purely right-handed individuals with no familial sinistrality (Luria 1947). Up to one-third of left-handed individuals in left-handed families are right-hemisphere-dominant for language, in the sense that lesions in the right hemisphere produce permanent aphasias and lesions in the left hemisphere act similarly to right-hemisphere lesions in the right-handed familially dextral population, or show a so-called 'mixed' pattern of dominance, according to which lesions to neither hemisphere cause long-lasting aphasias (Milner, Branch & Rasmussen 1966).

These statistics strongly suggest that the hemisphere that is dominant for language is determined through the action of a gene (or genes) which is physically close to, but separable from, the gene(s) determining handedness. The data are consistent with a model of the genetic determination of hemispheric dominance for language, according to which most alleles of the responsible portion of the genome contain both the gene for right-handedness and that for left-hemisphere language dominance, but some alleles exist in which these two genes are separate. Moreover, the data suggest that there is both a gene or genes coding for left-hemisphere language functioning and one or more genes coding for right-hemisphere language functioning, the former being 'dominant,' in the genetic sense, over the latter. The inheritance of genes coding for right-hemisphere language must be linked to the inheritance of genes coding for left-handedness, although as the evidence of the rare cross dextral aphasic indicates, the two genetic pools are separable.

A second feature of the genetic basis for language lateralization can be inferred from the observation that aphasias following unilateral hemispheric lesions are milder and less long-lasting in the non-right-handed population. One reasonable account for this finding is that subcomponents of the language system are separately lateralized in these subjects. For instance, a function such as phonemic discrimination may be left-hemisphere based and a function such as syntactic comprehension right-hemisphere based in these subjects. Lesions to a single hemisphere would then occasion a less complete and damaging interference with language functions than in a person all of whose language-processing components are in a lesioned hemisphere. The only other possible reason for the mild nature of aphasia following unilateral cerebral injury in this population is that 'computing space' is available in both hemispheres in this population, but not in the purely right-handed population. The exact profile of impairments following unilateral injury in non-right-handers has not yet been studied in sufficient detail to distinguish these possibilities. Assuming separate lateralization of language-processing subcomponents, the implication would be that genetic mechanisms code for the lateralization of individual subcomponents of the language-processing system.

Though nothing is known of the exact genetic structures responsible for the lateralization of the language system as a whole (or its subcomponents, or computational space), something is now known about features of the cortex which may be the physical basis for lateralization of language features. After a century of widespread belief that the two cerebral hemispheres were symmetrical from side to side, Geschwind and Levitsky (1970) clearly showed that the *planum temporale* was significantly larger on the left side in about 89% of an unselected series of human brains. Further work has shown that this difference in part reflects differences in the size of particular cortical areas, such as Tpt, which can be up to seven times larger on the left than on the right (Galaburda *et al*. 1982). A variety of radiological features suggesting asymmetry between hemispheres have also been found (Lemay & Culebras 1972). Researchers who have discovered these findings claim that they are related to the lateralization of language to the left hemisphere in right-handers. The notion is that the language regions of the left hemisphere are larger than their homologues on the right.

Though these observations are suggestive, their significance is as yet not entirely clear. For one thing, there are too many cases of larger right-hemisphere language regions than left-hemisphere language regions in the Geschwind and Levitsky (1970) series, compared to the incidence of aphasia following right-hemisphere lesions. Even assuming that some of the 11% of brains which showed larger *planum temporale* on the right were those of left-handed individuals, there are up to 5% too many brains with a larger *planum temporale* on the right than on the left to correlate with the incidence of left-hemisphere dominance for language in the right-handed population. Some studies have found that some areas of the brain that are responsible for language are larger on the right than on the left (Wade, Clark & Hamm 1975). Though the cerebral asymmetries are important neurological discoveries that may be related to the functional asymmetries of the hemispheres, their exact significance is as yet undetermined and the simplest possible notion – that 'bigger is better' – is likely to prove too simplistic.

To summarize the analyses presented in this paper, I have reviewed available data regarding the neurological and genetic basis for language. The picture that emerges is that core language functions are the responsibility of a relatively small area of human neocortex – association cortex located around the Sylvian fissure. As far as is known this area subserves language regardless of the language spoken, the method of instruction, the number of languages spoken, the literacy of a subject, or any other environmental variable. The location of language in this area of cortex thus seems to be entirely determined by internal organic factors. Whether the genome codes for the language role of this area directly, by specifying certain features of the neurones and of their organization in this area, or does so indirectly, by influencing one of a number of internal organic factors which affect the nature of this area (Geschwind & Galaburda 1984), is as yet unknown. Whatever the responsible organic mechanisms, they are ultimately genetic and seem to be uninfluenced by the phenomenological environment.

The expression of the genetic program with respect to the neural substrate for language does, however, allow for some variability. Earlier theories of language representation in the brain narrowly localized sub-components of the language-processing system within areas of the perisylvian cortex identically across all adult members of the human species. To a large extent, subcomponents of the language-processing system were thought to be localized in cortex adjacent to specialized sensory or motor cortex and to be located in these regions because of the relationship of language cortex to sensory and motor regions of the brain. More recent studies suggest that while this may be true of the distal execution and early sensory registration components of a language-processing device, the representation of the abstract aspects of the language code and of the interfaces between language processing and motor and sensory functions are not tied to particular areas of the perisylvian cortex in this way. Rather, it appears that subcomponents of the language processing mechanism can be located in any one of the lobes of the perisylvian cortex or in several of these lobes and may be localized differently in different individuals. This variability of the localization of subcomponents of a language-processing system also seems to be genetically determined.

The second variable feature of the neural basis for language is the lateralization of language functions. The genome codes for the location for most language functions in one hemisphere, usually the left. This coding is tied to the coding for handedness. It is unclear whether lateralization is influenced by genetic sex or changes with advancing age, but the degree of lateralization for language is apparently unaffected by environmental factors. Whether asymmetries in the size of the cortical areas responsible for language are the physical basis for lateralization is as yet unclear, though recent work suggests that this may be the case.

The overall picture which presently emerges regarding the biological basis for language is one which recognizes a great degree of genetic determination of the location of the neural substrate responsible for language functions. There is some degree of variability in the narrow localization and lateralization of subcomponents of the language-processing system, and this variability seems to represent variable expression of the genome. Data presently available regarding the biological basis for language is thus in keeping with a strong nativist position regarding the physical mechanisms underlying human language capacities.

REFERENCES

Basso, A., Casati, G. & Vignolo, L. A. 1977. Phoneme discrimination defects in aphasia. *Cortex* 13: 94–5.
Benson, D. F. 1979. *Aphasia alexia agraphia*. New York: Churchill Livingstone.
Benson, D. F. & Geschwind, N. 1975. Aphasia and related disturbances. In A. Baker & H. Baker (eds.) *Clinical neurology*. New York: Harper & Row.
Bladin, P. F. & Berkovic, S. F. 1984. Strolatocapsular infarction: large infarcts in the lenticulostriate arterial territory. *Neurology* 34: 1423–30.

David Caplan

Blumstein, S. E., Cooper, W. E., Zurit, E. & Caramazza, A. 1977. The perception and production of voice-onset time in aphasia. *Neuropsychologia* 15: 128–49.

Branch, C., Milner, B. & Rasmussen, T. 1964. Intracortical sodium amytal for lateralization of cerebral speech dominance. *Journal of Neurosurgery* 21: 399–407.

Brown, J. 1982. Hierarchy and evolution in neurolinguistics. In M. Arbib, D. Caplan & J. C. Marshall (eds) *Neural models of language processes*. New York: Academic Press.

Broca, P. 1861. Remarques sur le siège de la faculté du langage articulé. *Bulletin de la Société de l'Anthropologie* 6: 330–57.

Bryden, M. P. 1982. *Laterality*. New York: Academic Press.

Caplan, D., Baker, C. & Defaut, F. 1985. Syntactic determinants of sentence comprehension in aphasia. *Cognition* 21: 117–75.

Damasio, A. R., Costro-Caldas, A., Grosso, A. & Ferro, F. M. 1976. Brain specialization for language does not depend on literacy. *Archives of Neurology* 33: 300–10.

Damasio, A. R., Damasio, W., Rizzo, M., Varney, N. & Gersh, F. 1982. Aphasia with non-hemorrhagic lesions in the basal ganglia and interal capsule. *Archives of Neurology* 39: 15–20.

Damasio, A. R. & Geschwind, N. 1984. The neural basis of language. *Annual Review of Neuroscience* 7:127–47.

Freud, S. 1891. *On aphasia*. Vienna: Deuticke.

Galaburda, A. M. 1982. Histology, architectonics, and asymmetry of language areas. In M. Arbib, D. Caplan & J. C. Marshall (eds.) *Neural models of language processes*. New York: Academic Press.

Galaburda, A. M., LeMay, M., Kemper, T. L. & Geschwind, N. 1978. Right–left asymmetries in the brain. *Science* 199: 852–6.

Gazzaniga, M. S., Smylie, C. S. & Baynes, K. 1984. Profiles of right hemisphere language and speech following brain bisection. *Brain and Language* 22: 206–20.

Geschwind, N. 1965. Disconnection syndromes in animal and man. *Brain* 88: 237–94.

Geschwind, N. & Galaburda, A. M. 1985. Cerebral lateralization: biological mechanisms, associations and pathology: a hypothesis and a program for research. *Archives of Neurology* 42: 428–59.

Geschwind, N. & Levitsky, W. 1968. Human brain: left–right asymmetries in temporal speech region. *Science* 161: 186–7.

Goldstein, K. 1948. *Language and language disturbances*. New York: Grune & Stratton.

Head, M. 1926. *Aphasia and kindred disorders of speech*. New York: Macmillan.

Heilman, K. M., Scholes, R. & Watson, R. T. 1975. Auditory affective agnosia. *Journal of Neurology, Neurosurgery and Psychiatry* 38: 69.

Jackson, J. M. 1874. On the nature and duality of the brain. *Medical Press and Circular* 1: 19–41.

Joanette, Y., Lecours, P. R., Lepage, Y. & Lamoureux, M. 1983. Language in right-handers with right hemisphere lesions: a preliminary study including anatomical, genetic and social factors. *Brain and Language* 20: 217–48.

Kertesz, A. 1979. *Aphasia and associated disorders: taxonomy, localization and recovery*. New York: Grune & Stratton.

Kinsbourne, M. 1971. The minor hemisphere or a source of aphasic speech. *Transactions of the American Neurological Society* 96: 141–5.

Kinsbourne, M. 1972. Behavioural analysis of the repetition deficit in conduction aphasia. *Neurology* 22: 1126–32.

Lashley, K. S. 1937. Functional determinants of cerebral localization. *Archives of Neurology and Psychiatry* 38: 371:87.

Lashley, K. S. 1950. In search of the engram. *Symposia of the Society for Experimental Biology* 4: 454–82.

Lemay, M. & Culebras, A. 1972. Human brain: morphological differences in the hemispheres demonstrable by acarotid angiography. *New England Journal of Medicine* 287: 168–70.

Lichtheim, L. 1885. On aphasia. *Brain* 7: 433–84.

Luria, A. R. 1947. *Traumatic aphasia*. English translation: The Hague: Mouton (1970).

Luria, A. R. 1972. *The working brain*. New York: Basic Books.

Marie, P. 1906. La troisième convolution frontale ne joue aucun rôle spécial dans la fonction du langage. *Semaine Médicale* 26: 241–70.

Marshall, J. C. 1980. On the biology of language acquisition. In D. Caplan. (ed.) *Biological studies of mental processes*. Cambridge, MA: MIT Press.

Masdeu, J. C., Schoene, W. C. & Funkenstein, M. D. 1978. Aphasia following infarction of the left supplementary motor area. *Neurology* 28: 1220–3.

Metter, E. J., Sepulveda, C. A., Jackson, C. A., Mazziotta, J. C., Benson, D. F., Hanson, W. R., Riege, W. K. & Phelps, M. E. 1985. Relationship of temporal–parietal lesions and distant glucose metabolic changes in the head of the caudate nucleus in aphasic patients. *Neurology* 35: 120.

Milner, B., Branch, C. & Rasmussen, T. 1966. Evidence for bilateral speech representation in some non-right-handers, *T.A.N.A.* 91: 306.

Mohr, J. D., Walters, W. C. & Duncan, G. W. 1975. Thalamic hemorrhage and aphasia. *Brain and Language* 2: 3–17.

Naeser, M. A. and Hayward, R. W. 1978. Lesion localization in aphasia with cranial computed tomography and the B.D.A.E. *Neurology* 28: 545–51.

Neville, M. J., Kutus, M. & Schmidt, A. 1982. Event-related potentials studies of cerebral specialization during reading I: studies of normal adults. *Brain and Language* 16: 300–15.

Ojemann, G. A. 1983. Brain organization for language from the perspective of electrical stimulation mapping. *Behavioural and Brain Sciences* 6: 189–230.

Penfield, W. & Roberts, L. 1959. Speech and brain mechanism. Princeton: Princeton University Press.

Picton, T. & Stuss, D. 1984. Event related potentials in the study of language: a critical review. In D. Caplan, A. R. Lecours & A. Smith (eds.) *Biological perspectives on language*. Cambridge, MA: M.I.T. Press.

Russell, W. R. & Espir, M. L. E. 1961. *Traumatic aphasia*. Oxford: Oxford University Press.

Sanides, F. 1970. Functional architecture of motor and sensory cortices in primates in the light of a new concept of neocortex evolution. In C. Nobock and W. Montagna (eds.) *Advances in primatology*. New York: Appleton-Century-Crofts.

Schwartz, M. 1984. What the classical aphasic syndromes don't tell us, and why. *Brain and Language* 21: 479–91.

Shallice, T. & Warrington, E. K. 1977. Auditory–verbal short-term memory impairment and conduction aphasia. *Brain and Language* 4: 479–91.

Wada, J., Clark, A. & Hamm, A. 1975. Cerebral hemisphere asymmetry in humans. *Archives of Neurology* 32: 239–46

Wernicke, C. 1874. *The aphasic symptom complex. A psychological study on a neurological basis*. Breslau: Kohn and Weigert. Reprinted in translation in R. S. Cohen & M. W. Wartocsky (eds.) *Boston studies in the philosophy of science*, Vol. 4. Boston: Reidel.

Winner, E. & Gardner, M. 1977. The comprehension of metaphor in brain-damaged patients. *Brain* 100: 719–27.

Zaidel, E. & Peters, A. M. 1981. Phonological encoding and ideographic reading by the disconnected right hemisphere. *Brain and Language* 14: 205–34.

10 Linguistics and speech–language pathology*

Catherine A. Jackson

10.0. Introduction

This chapter will discuss the relationship between a classically theoretical discipline and a traditionally clinical one, the former being linguistics and the latter being speech–language pathology. The historical differences in the goals of these two fields make it difficult to assess what they share in terms of theory and methodology. Both fields concern themselves with how language is normally acquired, represented, and processed. Individuals with disorders of language are studied by researchers from both disciplines. However, the different concerns of each discipline have often led to misunderstanding and a lack of cooperative research between the fields.

In attempting to bridge the gap between the fields, this chapter will focus on the ways in which linguistic knowledge has affected clinical practice in speech–language pathology. To do this, it will also be necessary to discuss the ways in which the fields have differed in their views of language and language disorders. First, some general background is given on the field of communicative disorders. Second, several specific populations studied by both speech–language pathologists and linguists are discussed, and what is known about the linguistic abilities of these groups is reviewed. The third section describes some of the clinical methodology used with language-disordered individuals, and focusses on how linguistic theory has and should affect clinical work. Finally, the ways in which clinical data may be relevant to linguistic theory are discussed.

10.1. Background on communicative disorders

Speech–language pathology and audiology together comprise the academic area known as communicative disorders, audiology being the branch of the field dealing with hearing and hearing impairment. The field of communicative disorders has its origins in the early 1900s, when 'speech correction-

* Thanks are due to Victoria Fromkin and Daniel Kempler for helpful comments and criticisms of this paper.

ists' worked primarily with individuals who stuttered, or who had a hearing loss, articulation difficulty or disorder secondary to brain damage. In the 1920s the American Academy of Speech Correction was founded (West 1966), the precursor of the current American Speech–Language Hearing Association (or ASHA). Wood (1971) defined the focus of the modern discipline as 'the study and treatment of functional and organic speech defects and disorders.' A more common statement of the goals of the field might be the evaluation and treatment of disorders of communication. ASHA defines a communicative disorder as 'an impairment in the ability to (1) receive and/or process a symbol system, (2) represent concepts or symbol systems, and/or (3) transmit and use symbol systems' (1982). Thus, the definition includes disorders of hearing, language, and speech which are either developmental or acquired. Perkins (1977) defined the field as an 'applied interdisciplinary behavioral science,' emphasizing 'the study of disordered oral communication as well as the clinical practice to which academic knowledge is applied.'

It is interesting to note that speech pathologists have not always been officially engaged in clinical work with language-disordered individuals, although even in early texts sections were devoted to helping the child who is 'hesitant to talk' or who is having difficulty learning vocabulary, and information on normal 'speech development' was commonly included. In 1979 ASHA officially changed its name (if not the acronym) from the American Speech and Hearing Association to the American Speech–Language Hearing Association, reflecting the shift of the field towards recognition and treatment of language as well as speech disorders.

ASHA requires that anyone who desires national certification as a speech–language pathologist fulfill a number of requirements, including academic requirements. The academic requirements are somewhat eclectic, reflecting the historical relationship of communicative disorders to psychology, medicine, and education. For example, twelve semester hours in courses on 'basic communicative processes' are required. These units may be comprised of linguistics courses, such as acoustic and articulatory phonetics. However, the requirement may also be satisfied by many other types of courses, such as courses in anatomy and physiology, or in verbal learning and verbal behavior. Undergraduates typically take a course in phonetics, and courses in the anatomy of the speech mechanism and in speech/language development. This leaves only one additional course needed to satisfy the above requirement. At the graduate level, coursework on language disorders is typically included in the curriculum, e.g. courses on adult aphasia, language disorders in school-aged children, and evaluation and treatment of speech and language disorders. Thus, while academic preparation in the field includes courses on language development, disordered language, and clinical methodology for the assessment or remediation of language disorders, it does not *necessarily* include much study of linguistics.

Additional coursework in specific areas, clinical practicum, passing a national exam and completion of 9 months supervised clinical experience after completion of graduate work round out the requirements for national certification as a speech–language pathologist or audiologist.

10.2. Language-disordered populations: clinical versus theoretical findings

Linguists have begun to turn to language-impaired populations as a source of neurolinguistic and psycholinguistic data relevant to the investigation of a variety of theoretical claims. In the following sections three language-impaired populations are discussed, both in terms of what is known about the language profiles of individuals in the various diagnostic groups, and the differences in the issues of concern to the speech–language pathologist as opposed to the linguist.

10.2.1. Adult aphasia

Current linguistic theory has increasingly focussed on the biological bases of language and the genetic basis of linguistic principles constituting Universal Grammar (UG). An increasingly common view is that syntax develops via domain-specific learning principles, and is supported in the adult via the language-dedicated areas of the brain, typically located in the left hemisphere. Data from adults with injury to specific sites within the left hemisphere have been important to linguistic theory as (a) evidence for the autonomy of grammar from other cognitive abilities, and (more recently) (b) evidence for a deficit which can be characterized along lines consistent with current grammatical theory (e.g. the notion of 'breakdown compatibility': Grodzinsky 1986; see also Kean 1978 and Caplan 1983).

Speech–language pathologists, on the other hand, are concerned with collecting a wide variety of data to be used in (a) determining the type and pattern of communicative deficit relevant to differential diagnosis of various neuropathologies necessary for prognostic and remediation reasons, (b) measuring often subtle changes in communicative behavior over time to determine improvement, (c) determining appropriate rehabilitative or compensatory programs for the patient, and (d) carrying out such therapeutic programs (including actual contact hours in therapy as well as coordinating other aspects of patient care and educational concerns, conferencing with parents, spouses, teachers, physicians, nurses and therapists, etc.) Thus, clinical concerns dictate the necessity of collecting and utilizing much information in addition to the kind of data relevant to linguistic theory. The exact characterization of a syntactic or phonological deficit may at a given point in time be secondary or even irrelevant to concerns of how a patient will communicate functionally with his or her family (see section 10.3.2.2).

The differences between clinical and theoretical characterizations of the disorder of the aphasic individual are exemplified in the use of the classical syndrome accounts used by the speech–language pathologist and members of the medical community. The use of the classical aphasia syndromes as descriptive terms is common in the aphasia literature; however, it remains an open question as to whether descriptions of patients as having aphasia of Broca's type or Wernicke's type reflect differences in the language impairment suffered by any given patient. Research in the 1970s began to redefine traditional dichotomies of aphasia based on syndrome or type (e.g. of nonfluent aphasia/good comprehension of language versus fluent aphasia/ poor comprehension of language). Evidence was found that even the nonfluent or agrammatic aphasic individual had deficits in comprehension of certain syntactic structures (e.g. Caramazza & Zurif 1976). Current research suggests that the clinical categories do not, in fact, correspond in a direct way to the type of linguistic impairment demonstrated by the patient (Goodglass & Menn 1985; Heeschen 1985), highlighting the need for research on the language abilities of these individuals across diagnostic categories.

10.2.2. Language disorders in children

While language-disordered children have not been the object of linguistic research to the same degree as adult aphasic patients, they do comprise a significant portion of the speech–language pathologist's caseload (particularly for those clinicians working in the schools). The prevalence of language disorders in children has been estimated to be approximately 8.4% of the population (Silva 1980). Disorders of language can be a primary disorder, as in the group of children variously identified as having 'specific language impairment,' 'developmental aphasia' (Benton 1964) or simply as 'language disordered' (Rees 1973). Language disorders can also occur secondarily to mental retardation, autism, or hearing impairment, the latter to be considered separately in the next section. This section will discuss what is known about children with specific language impairment.

The definition of this population is largely one of exclusion: that is, an impairment of one or more areas of linguistic development in the absence of other impairments, including any impairment of nonverbal intelligence (American Psychiatric Association 1980). The definition is somewhat problematic in that at least some of these children often perform below age-level

259

expectations in other, nonlinguistic areas: i.e. on Piagetian tasks of symbolic abilities (e.g. Kamhi 1981), in measures of motor development and coordination (e.g. King, Jones & Lasky 1982), and in measures of auditory processing skills (Tallal & Piercy 1973, 1975). It is also somewhat unclear as to the extent to which primary language disorders are related to a (presumed) central nervous system etiology.

Wetherby (1985) describes four subclassifications of primary language disorders relevant here: developmental phonological disorders, developmental apraxia of speech, developmental aphasia, and developmental dyslexia, noting that these are not mutually exclusive categories, and further, that a child's diagnosis may change over time. Phonological disorders, or what used to be known as functional articulation disorders (reflecting the shift towards terms drawn from linguistics), are described by Shriberg and Kwiatkowski (1982) as impairment in knowledge and use of phonological rules. However, there is continued controversy as to whether this disorder can be separated from that of developmental apraxia, a deficit in the volitional control of the articulators in producing speech movements (Williams, Ingham & Rosenthal 1981). Developmental aphasia is characterized by an impairment or production of spoken language (as opposed to the deficit of written language in dyslexia), with most children described as having a syntactic type of language disorder (Ludlow 1980). There are, however, few details about the actual character of the linguistic impairment, as is the case with adults. What is known is that language-impaired children, while appearing to acquire grammatical structures in roughly the same developmental sequence as nonimpaired children, tend to have a protracted rate of acquisition, a disparity in their performance on comprehension versus production tasks, and persistence of early-learned forms alongside later-mastered forms (Johnston & Schery 1976; Leonard 1982).

Research on language-disordered children is relevant to a number of questions concerning the language acquisition process. In particular, cases with a clearly defined neurological basis are relevant to neurolinguistic investigations of the nature of the relationship between the brain and knowledge of language. If the proposed neurological substrate is damaged, what are the consequences for acquisition/knowledge of key linguistic principles? The ways in which a developing grammar can be damaged, and what the long-term linguistic consequences of a specific language impairment might be, are as yet unknown, and are only beginning to be investigated.

10.2.3. The hearing impaired

The hearing impaired are of interest to linguists for several reasons. First, children with a hearing impairment are faced with the task of learning a spoken language on the basis of degenerative input, allowing us to test the relative role of well-formed input in models of language acquisition. Second, deaf individuals often have as their native language a natural human signed language, such as American Sign Language, the study of which allows linguists to test the influence of the modality of a language on its structure, and to determine the linguistic universals which exist for human languages whether the language is spoken or signed.

The hearing impaired have also long been the focus of the speech–language pathologist (and audiologist). In tandem with deaf educators, the obvious goal in remediation has been to improve speech intelligibility and oral and written language abilities relative to the hearing-impaired child's hearing peers. However, the training provided by educators and therapists has met with less than desirable success, and the education of this group of individuals is complicated by the holy war of oral–aural educators versus those who advocate intervention with some form of sign language.

Research on the spoken language proficiency of the hearing impaired, like that of the two previously discussed populations, gives only tantalizing hints of their linguistic knowledge. (This discussion will be limited to the skills of the hearing impaired with the spoken language of their environment, as those using a signed language are simply using a different linguistic system.) Indeed, evaluating their linguistic knowledge is difficult to do without using tasks which require considerable speechreading (lipreading) ability (Geers & Moog 1978), making utilization of tasks of written language common. McKay & Vernon (1971), Swisher (1976), and Quigley & King (1982) all reviewed a variety of studies, finding that many, if not most, deaf children do not reach a fourth-grade proficiency level in written language (English) abilities assessed by standardized tests of reading and writing. Most are evaluated as having unintelligible speech as well. It is important to note that these are children who were still involved in special education, and most of whom were orally educated (educated within the model which emphasizes use of residual hearing, speech reading, and acquisition of spoken English). Like language-impaired children, the hearing impaired tend to show protracted acquisition of syntax (Presnell 1973), but with an overall sequence of acquisition similar to their hearing peers. There appears to be better performance on 'simpler' than on 'complex' grammatical constructions (e.g. on simple active declarative sentences versus passives, negatives, or negative passives, Swisher 1976). Finally, while acquisition of morphology may also be slow, there is some indication that inflectional morphology is more difficult for the hearing-impaired child than derivational morphology (Cooper 1967).

Research to date on all of the populations discussed above can be viewed as an attempt to describe the language performance of impaired individuals, and then compare them to normals. Thus, in the case of the language-impaired and hearing-impaired children, we know that they are delayed in acquiring specific aspects of language. What we do not have is a linguistic characterization of their deficit, of the aspects of their grammar that are missing or different from that of their peers. This is the type of question which must be addressed by linguistic research and which could have great potential for those clinically involved with these populations as well.

10.3. Clinical methodology

In this section some of the issues concerning the framework for clinical work in speech–language pathology will be discussed, along with the ways in which clinical evaluation of a patient's abilities can and should differ from the data collection concerns of the linguistic researcher. Also included will be a discussion of views on the methodology which has characterized assessment and therapy with language-impaired populations, and the areas in which the lack of a clear and appropriate theoretical framework has affected the field.

10.3.1. Assessment / evaluation

The initial task to be faced in the clinical setting is to evaluate the present speech and language abilities of the individual requesting service. The most obvious method for collecting data on linguistic abilities utilized in everyday situations is to collect naturalistic language samples, such as the longitudinal samples which have comprised the data bases for countless studies of child language. Analysis of spontaneous samples have been used in speech–language pathology for a long time, and as models of acquisition have changed, the analyses used by clinicians have likewise changed. The analyses have evolved from simple measures of mean length of response (McCarthy 1954) or mean length of utterance (Brown 1973) to more comprehensive analyses of the structure, meaning, and function of patients' utterances (e.g. Tyack & Gottsleben 1974; Crystal, Fletcher & Garman 1976; Miller 1981). However, the practical demands of clinical work can sometimes make such initial longitudinal data collection impractical. Even short samples, as desirable as they might be, are often not included in assessment: Kilburg (1982) notes that although most clinicians might want an analyzed spontaneous speech sample to utilize in working with their cases, less than one-third of those surveyed actually used this methodology. It is possible that the increasing availability of computer software designed to aid in analyzing language samples may ameliorate this problem somewhat, e.g. Miller and Chapman's *Systematic analysis of language transcripts (SALT)*, 1983. Language samples as included in the initial assessment of an individual are also problematic in terms of their variability depending on the communicators and the physical surroundings, affecting the 'representativeness' of the data collected (Gallagher 1983).

Another procedure (commonly used by linguistic researchers) to determine the grammatical knowledge of a given individual is the elicitation of grammaticality judgements. Unfortunately, this is often inappropriate or impossible to use with language-impaired populations. In fact, this technique appears to be ineffective even with nonimpaired children until at least the age of 5 when metalinguistic judgement skills seem to develop (Gleitman, Gleitman & Shipley 1972). Its use with adult language-impaired individuals is often difficult at best, although Linebarger, Schwartz & Saffran (1982) report success using this methodology with agrammatic aphasics, a population often thought to demonstrate poor metalinguistic abilities.

The procedures used by speech–language pathologists to assess the linguistic abilities of children and adults may not include the analyses of spontaneous speech and the grammaticality judgement procedures which linguists have relied on in fieldwork or grammar construction. However, there are other types of tasks (such as comprehension tasks) which are common to both. It is important to note that the type and extent of the data to be collected can vary greatly depending on the clinical setting and the purpose of the evaluation. Evaluative procedures can have a variety of functions in the clinical setting: screening, diagnosis and prognosis, evaluation of specific sets of abilities relevant to designing or evaluating remediation or teaching programs, and evaluation of a given set of abilities relevant to nonimpaired peers. Thus, the evaluation may stress the functional communicative abilities of given individuals rather than a descriptive analysis of their syntactic or phonological knowledge.

Most popular by far in clinical evaluations are the norm-referenced tests: those standarized tests which evaluate a subject's performance relative to some peer group. For children, such tests often yield age scores or other derived scores such as percentiles, stanines, standard scores, or quotients. Advantages to these tests lie in the fact that they are usually highly standardized and reliable. Their greatest strength lies in their usefulness in identifying the presence or absence of a problem. However, they are often misused to try to determine the nature of a language disorder, to determine goals for clinical teaching, or to measure progress in language therapy (Kelly & Rice 1986). Standardized tests are also used with adults to yield a percentile, such as on the *Porch index of communicative abilities (PICA;* Porch 1967), which compares the performance of patients with others who also have aphasia. A quotient (scaling performance as is done on intelligence tests) is another possible type of score, as is the case on the *Western aphasia battery (WAB;* Kertesz 1982).

In addition to outright misuse of standardized tests, there are several other problems in interpreting their results. First, as McCauley and Swisher (1984) note, many of the popular tests of language and articulation used with preschool children fail to demonstrate the very psychometric characteristics which are supposedly their strong suit: for example, they fail to demonstrate adequate empirical evidence of reliability and validity. Second, many tests of 'language' depend crucially on a subject's nonlinguistic abilities as well. Tests for preschoolers tap behaviors as diverse as imitation of play with blocks (*The sequenced inventory of communicative development;* Hedrick, Prather & Tobin 1975), general academic-related knowledge such as ability to name colors (*The preschool language scale;* Zimmerman, Steiner & Evatt 1969), and counting and gesturing (*The Houston test for language development;* Crabtree 1963). Some tests rely primarily on an informant interview, e.g. asking the parent about the child's abilities, rather than on actually evaluating the child's behavior directly (as on the *Receptive–expressive emergent language scale;* Bzoch & League 1971). Use of standardized tests with adults is also problematic for similar reasons: tasks are included which are not necessarily linguistic in nature, such as those requiring production of gestures (*PICA*) and those involving written language skills (e.g. on the *PICA* and the *WAB,* to name but two commonly used tests). Many of the tests used with language-impaired adults do not necessarily evaluate language abilities in isolation, such as those which evaluate general communicative competence, including compensatory communicative strategies (*Functional communication profile, FCP;* Sarno 1969). The problem with these tests is not, of course, that they measure a variety of communicative behaviors; rather, that they are too often accepted as being specific indices of language abilities.

Up to this point the discussion has focussed on the inadequacy of the language assessment procedures and tests which are available to the clinician. However, there *are* assessment procedures which have been based on the methodology and findings of linguistic and psycholinguistic research, and which more narrowly define the behaviors to be considered in evaluating 'language.' Many of these procedures are found in the area of child language, where the clinical goal is a comparison of a child's development to normal abilities at a given point in time. Instruments for assessment of adults, while they may briefly focus on the extent to which performance is determined to be 'non-normal,' emphasize the particular profile of preserved and impaired abilities and/or the extent to which compensatory strategies must be implemented for the patient.

Evaluation of phonological development is an example of an area which has been influenced by the methods used in linguistics to describe non-impaired language. This area also exemplifies how advances in theoretical characterizations have led to changes in clinical methodology. Historically, assessment of phoneme production in children has been based on the 'articulation' or motor speech production abilities of the child. Articulation tests typically had a picture-naming format eliciting production of single words. Eventually the importance of the phonetic environment was recognized, leading to testing phoneme production in a variety of phonetic contexts (as on *The deep test of articulation*; McDonald 1964). More recently, assessment of speech sound production has included a distinctive feature analysis of the child's pattern of misarticulation (McReynolds & Engman 1975) and an analysis of the error patterns of the child in terms of rule-governed phonological processes which appear in the speech of nonimpaired children, e.g. the assessment procedures of Shriberg & Kwiatkowski (1980), Weiner (1977), Hodson (1980) and Ingram (1981).

Many of the available measures of morphosyntax also attempt to relate a child's performance to the stages and patterns of development observed in nonimpaired children. For example, the language sampling procedures of Tyack and Gottsleben (1974) compare syntactic development to the developmental levels noted by Morehead & Ingram (1973), as well as to more specific developmental sequences, e.g. the patterns expected in the acquisition of negation described by Klima & Bellugi (1966). Unfortunately, the majority of tests which evaluate grammatical knowledge either (a) test comprehension or production of a given type of structure insufficiently (one or two trials); (b) are not designed to evaluate the grammatical knowledge of older children (those past the age of 4 or 5), and/or (c) do not clearly test grammatical knowledge separately from other types of linguistic knowledge. *The Curtiss–Yamada comprehensive evaluation of language* (in press) is a test which promises to fill this gap.

10.3.2. **Therapy / treatment**

Both the linguist and the clinician must evaluate and analyze their data. At this point, however, the concerns of speech–language pathologists are unique and clearly clinical: they must begin to devise the plan of therapy or treatment which will most benefit the individual with the disorder. The clinician is confronted with a dilemma: the need to provide immediate treatment for individuals with language disorders by drawing upon theory which is constantly and rapidly changing. As Nespoulous & Lecours (1984) point out, 'Aphasiology and neurolinguistics can wait for better models; aphasics cannot.'

10.3.2.1. Childhood disorders

The study of language acquisition has been characterized by the shifting popularity of theoretical positions, and remediation programs for language-impaired children reflect this unstable theoretical base. As major theories viewed the course of normal acquisition, so did they dictate what intervention programs should accomplish. The psychological theory of behaviorism which was prominent in the 1950s (Skinner 1957) emphasized language as a learned *behavior* which can be described and accounted for without reference to the mind or cognitive functions. Intervention programs emphasized the role of the environment in changing behavior, and aimed to shape new behaviors and increase frequency of desired old behaviors. They often focussed on increasing production of certain lexical items or of particular grammatical morphemes.Typical of these approaches are the programs of Guess, Sailor and Baer (1974), Kent (1972) and Lovaas, Berberich, Perloff & Schaffer (1966).

Several more recent approaches to the study of child language have influenced the course of clinical intervention. In the 1960s, the popularity of Chomsky (1965) and of transformational syntax led to research which emphasized the specific syntactic differences between normal and language-impaired children. Programs were then designed which replaced those emphasizing the shaping of memorized, prototypical production with those teaching productive rules of syntax and morphology, e.g. Fygetakis and Gray (1970), Miller & Yoder (1974), Waryas & Stremel-Campbell (1978), and Zwitman & Sonderman (1979). The 1970s brought popularity to semantically based child grammars (e.g. Bloom 1970; Bowerman 1973), and thus emerged remediation programs which emphasized the semantic relations posited to underlie children's utterances (e.g. McDonald & Blott 1974; Lahey & Bloom 1977). The most recent trend in remediation programs has been in the area of pragmatics, with programs emphasizing the child's ability to use and respond to language as a communicative tool in a variety of situations (Hart & Rogers-Warren 1978; Bloom & Lahey 1978).

10.3.2.2. Remediation of adult disorders

As language acquisition research has shaped intervention programs for children, so has neurolinguistic research influenced the remediation methods used with adults with language disorders. The work done with adults is more strongly affiliated with medical models of treatment, as adult language disorders often clearly present a specific neurological pathology, typically brain damage.

Efforts to treat aphasia have been increasingly developed since World

War II. Initial treatment focussed on stimulation of the aphasic individual, relying on nonspecific stimulation via the patient's general environment. Since the beginning of these efforts, remediation for adults with neurogenic language disorders has been based on various linguistic or neuropsychological explanations for the patterns of language disturbance in these individuals. For example, Jakobson's (1956) linguistic regression hypothesis led to therapy in which developmental patterns of language development were modeled in reverse. Therapy thus focussed on teaching patients their lost first language. Specific or direct stimulation approaches to therapy (Schuell, Jenkins & Jimenez-Pabon 1964) were based on the premise that linguistic knowledge is not lost in aphasia, but that the aphasic individual is faced with a disruption of the processing abilities through which linguistic knowledge is accessed. Direct stimulation was supposed to facilitate or strengthen the recovery of these neurolinguistic processes. The clinician aimed to elicit a high rate of successful responses during a given therapy session under increasingly complex situations. The influence of behaviorism was not limited to the treatment of childhood disorders: programmed instruction (e.g. LaPointe 1978) emphasized modification of behavior through operant procedures, with the patient advancing through a number of very specific behavioral objectives to reach certain long-range goals.

More recent advances in therapy include melodic intonation therapy (Sparks, Helm & Albert 1974), in which the aphasic individual with severely impaired verbal expression is taught to utter sentences with a particular melodic intonation pattern. This approach draws heavily on the literature implicating the right hemisphere in the processing of prosody, the right hemisphere typically being intact in the case of aphasia. Other recent approaches include teaching alternative modes of communication, such as gesture (e.g. *Amer-Ind* system; Skelly 1979), and programs emphasizing functional communication skills (Aten, Caligiuri & Holland, 1982). Group therapy for socialization purposes and programmed instruction using computer technology are also common.

One of the most important research questions for speech pathologists regarding aphasia concerns the extent to which therapy can found to be efficacious for recovery. In most cases, a certain amount of 'spontaneous recovery' can be expected within the first several months following the onset of the neuropathology (Darley 1972). Some initial research in this area found no significant difference between treated and untreated groups (e.g. Sarno, Silverman & Sands 1970). However, most recent reports indicate better recovery (as measured by standardized tests) for those groups receiving treatment (e.g. Shewan & Kertesz 1984).

In summary, therapeutic paradigms in speech–language pathology have been based to some extent on linguistic theory and research. There are several problems with the organization and application of therapeutic models in general which deserve mention at this point. First, there is a general confusion between methodological techniques and the theoretical goals dictated by different theoretical positions. As Craig (1983) notes, a particular theoretical position may be relevant to one or the other or both of these considerations. Behaviorism in particular has left its mark on clinical methodology in spite of more recent theoretical positions on what the theoretical framework for invention ought to be. For example, Bricker and Bricker (1970) emphasize Piagetian sensori-motor cognitive skills as pre-requisite to linguistic development, but use methodology more typical of behaviorism. Fygetakis and Gray (1970) also used behavioral techniques despite their generative syntactic views of language. This continued reliance on behaviorism and operant conditioning has led to the continued emphasis in therapy on frequency of behavior, use of repeated trials of measurement instead of teaching or remediation, and success of therapy evaluated only in terms of measurable behavioral objectives. Second, and perhaps most important, is the problem of how information about normal language is relevant to cases of disorder. While theory may dictate how grammar is best described and accounted for, it does not indicate how a course of intervention for individuals in which the normal mechanisms supporting linguistic knowledge have been permanently altered. Finally, it should be mentioned that, regardless of the methodological model involved, it is difficult to evaluate the success or failure of a particular remediation program. There are few studies which actually measure the extent to which a particular ability taught or invoked in therapy is maintained over time, either in the therapy session itself or in real-life communicative situations.

10.4. Evidence and linguistic theory

Up to this point, I have focussed on the extent to which speech–language pathology has or has not benefited from linguistic theory. An equally inter-esting question is whether linguistics can benefit from the study of the language-disordered populations which speech pathologists routinely encounter, and from the data which the clinician has access to.

First, as mentioned earlier, the data are relevant to issues of the rela-tionship between the brain and language, both in development and in the mature state. Volumes of research on adults with aphasia have documented the linguistic impairment which occurs in cases of left- but not right-hemi-sphere damage, clearly implicating the special role of sites within the left hemisphere in processing language. Analogous data on focal cortical damage in strokes in children have been less forthcoming, although the recent work of Aram, Ekelman, Rose and Whitaker (1985) suggests that early focal damage to the left hemisphere critically impinges on acquisition of syntax as well as affecting mature syntactic knowledge.

Second, such data are also relevant to the current debate on the autonomy or modularity of cognitive systems. Proponents of modular views of cognitive organization view human cognition as, at least in part, modular in nature, with certain major components operating according to specific and unique principles (Fodor 1983). Principles of syntactic knowledge are viewed as being nonderivable from other cognitive domains, and as operating autonomously. Neurolinguistic data are relevant to this debate; to the extent to which separable deficits are found in one component or another of language, the data will support claims that grammatical knowledge is modular.

Finally, such data constitute a source of evidence with which to evaluate the claims of linguistic theory. We should recall that biological data are but one source of evidence relevant to the evaluation of linguistic theory (Fromkin 1985), and, as Mehler, Morton & Jusczyk (1984) argue, as such are no more important than any other type of data. There is, however, a wealth of data from a variety of populations which has yet to be addressed to the claims of linguistic theory, and it should not be ignored.

One of the areas in which speech–language pathologists can readily contribute to our knowledge of the patterns of language breakdown is in the area of case studies. Single-case studies have been the backbone of research attempting to find a relationship between brain and behavior since the work of Broca (1861) and Wernicke (1874). Group studies which compare behavior of some pathological group to that of controls have increased since the 1950s, reflecting the increasing influence of psychology on the study of cognitive deficits. However, given the difficulties in conducting group studies (in particular, the difficulty in finding a truly heterogenous group of brain-damaged individuals), the case study continues to occupy a legitimate and important place in evaluating theory. As Marshall & Newcombe (1984) note: 'the theoretical significance (in the nonstatistical sense) of a clinical datum is not logically linked to the number of patients in whom that datum can be observed.' If a particular theory makes a claim about the isolability of a given component of language, and thus, about an isolated deficit in this component, documentation of a single case should be sufficient to support or refute such a claim, unless it can be shown that the particular case is truly aberrant. Speech–language pathologists, as well as neurospsychologists and physicians, are in contact with great numbers of patients, allowing them to select those patients who seem particularly worthy of further study. They are likely to have the necessary interdisciplinary information which also might bring to light a particularly important or interesting case (such as the neurological data which confirms the site of lesion). Finally, they must essentially perform a case study on each patient in their efforts to determine changes in status, and appropriate remediation goals. They often have the opportunity to see a patient on a regular basis over a long period of time, and are able to collect a wealth of data on the particular cluster of abilities and deficits they observe in an important case. This stands in contrast to the more typical research methodology in which a few sessions (or even a single session) are used to collect data. Given the variability of performance which clinicians know and expect from language-impaired individuals, they may be able to collect data which avoid the gross under- or over-representation of a patient's linguistic abilities due to nonlinguistic performance factors.

Thus, while there are differences which remain and which perhaps should remain between clinical disciplines such as speech–language pathology on the one hand and linguistics on the other, a common goal can be found: to better understand the patterns of linguistic behavior found in individuals with language disorders. The collaboration of clinicians and theoreticians cannot but help to advance our understanding of language and speech, important to both linguistic theory and clinical methodology.

REFERENCES

American Psychiatric Association. 1980. *Diagnostic and statistical manual of mental disorders* (3rd edn). Washington: American Psychiatric Association.

American Speech–Language Hearing Association Committee on Language, Speech and Hearing in the schools. 1982. Definitions: communicative disorders and variations. *ASHA* 24: 949–50.

Aram, D., Ekelman, B., Rose, R. & Whitaker, H. 1985. Verbal and cognitive sequelae following unilateral lesions acquired in early childhood. *Journal of Clinical and Experimental Neuropsychology* 7: 55–78.

Aten, J. L., Caligiuri, M. P. & Holland, A. L. 1982. The efficacy of functional communication therapy for chronic aphasic patients. *Journal of Speech and Hearing Disorders* 47: 93–6.

Benton, A. 1964. Developmental aphasia and brain damage. *Cortex* 1: 40–52.

Bloom, L. 1970. *Language development: form and function in emerging grammars*. Cambridge, MA: MIT Press.

Bloom, L. & Lahey, M. 1978. *Language development and language disorders*. New York: Wiley.

Bowerman, M. 1973. Structural relationships in children's utterances: syntactic or semantic? In T. Moore (ed.) *Cognitive development and the acquisition of language*. New York: Academic Press.

Bricker, W. & Bricker, D. 1970. An early language training strategy. In R. Schiefelbusch and L. Lloyd (eds.) *Language perspectives: acquisition, retardation, and intervention*. Baltimore: University Park Press.

Broca, P. 1961. Nouvelle observation d'aphémie produite par une lésion de la moitié postérieure des deuxième et troisième circonvolutions frontales. *Bulletin de la Société Anatomique de Paris* 3: 398–407.

Brown, R. 1973. *A first language: the early stages*. Cambridge, MA: Harvard University Press.

Bzoch, K. R. and League, R. 1971. *Receptive–expressive emergent language scale (REEL)*. Gainsville: Tree of Life Press.

Caplan, D. 1983. Syntactic competence in agrammatism. In M. Studdert-Kennedy (ed.) *Psychobiology of language*. Cambridge, MA: MIT Press.

270

Caramazza, A. & Zurif, E. 1976. Dissociation of algorithmic and heuristic processes: evidence from aphasia. *Brain and Language* 3: 572–82.

Chomsky, N. 1965. *Aspects of the theory of syntax*. Cambridge, MA: MIT Press.

Cooper, R. L. 1967. The ability of deaf and hearing children to apply morphological rules. *Journal of Speech and Hearing Research* 10: 77–86.

Crabtree, M. 1963. *The Houston test for language development*. Houston: The Houston Test Company.

Craig, H. 1983. Applications of pragmatic language models for intervention. In T. Gallagher and C. Prutting (eds.) *Pragmatic assessment and intervention issues in language*. San Diego: College-Hill Press.

Crystal, D., Fletcher, P. & Garman, M. 1976. The grammatical analysis of language disability: a procedure for assessment and remediation. Studies in language disability and remediation, Vol. 1. London: Arnold.

Curtiss, S. & Yamada, J. in press. *The Curtiss–Yamada comprehensive language evaluation (CYCLE)*. Psycholing Inc.

Darley, F. 1972. The efficacy of language rehabilitation in aphasia. *Journal of Speech and Hearing Disorders* 37: 2–21.

Fodor, J. A. 1983. *The modularity of mind*. Cambridge, MA: MIT Press.

Fromkin, V. A. 1985. Evidence in linguistics. In R. H. Robins & V. A. Fromkin (eds.) *Linguistics and linguistic evidence*. Newcastle upon Tyne: Grevatt & Grevatt.

Fygetakis, L. & Gray, B. 1970. Programmed conditioning of linguistic competence. *Behavior Research and Therapy* 8: 153–63.

Gallagher, T. M. 1983. Pre-assessment: a procedure for accommodating language use variability. In T. M. Gallagher & C. A. Prutting (eds.) *Pragmatic assessment and intervention issues in language*. San Diego: College-Hill Press.

Geers, A. E. & Moog, J. S. 1978. Syntactic maturity of spontaneous speech and elicited imitations of hearing-impaired children. *Journal of Speech and Hearing Disorders* 43: 380–91.

Gleitman, L., Gleitman, H. & Shipley, E. 1972. The emergence of the child as grammarian. *Cognition* 1: 137–64.

Goodglass, H. & Menn, L. 1985. Is agrammatism a unitary phenomenon? In M.-L. Kean (ed.) *Agrammatism*. New York: Academic Press.

Grodzinsky Y. 1986. Cognitive deficits, their proper description and its theoretical relevance. *Brain and Language* 27: 178–91.

Guess, D., Sailor, W. & Baer, D. 1974. To teach language to retarded children. In R. L. Schiefelbusch & L. L. Lloyd (eds.) *Language perspectives: acquisition, retardation and intervention*. Baltimore: University Park Press.

Hart, B. & Rogers-Warren, A. 1978. A milieu approach to teaching language. In R. L. Schiefelbusch (ed.) *Language intervention strategies*. Baltimore: University Park Press.

Hedrick, D., Prather, E. & Tobin, A. 1975. *The sequenced inventory of communicative development (SICD)*. Seattle: University of Washington Press.

Heeschen, C. 1985. Agrammatism versus paragrammatism: a fictitious opposition. In M.-L. Kean (ed.) *Agrammatism*. New York: Academic Press.

Hodson, B. 1980. *The assessment of phonological processes*. Danville: Interstate Publishers and Printers.

Ingram, D. 1981. *Procedures for the phonological analysis of children's language*. Baltimore: University Park Press.

Jakobson, R. 1956. Two aspects of language and two types of aphasic disturbances. In R. Jakobson & M. Halle *Fundamentals of language*. The Hague: Mouton.

Johnston, J. & Schery, T. 1976. The use of grammatical morphemes by children with communication disorders. In D. Morehead & A. Morehead (eds.) *Normal and deficient child language*. Baltimore: University Park Press.

Kamhi, A. 1981. Nonlinguistic symbolic and conceptual abilities of language-impaired and normally developing children. *Journal of Speech and Hearing Research* 24: 446–53.

Kean, M.-L. 1978. The linguistic interpretation of aphasic syndrome. In E. Walker (ed.) *Explorations in the biology of language*. Montgomery: Bradford.

Kelly, D. J. and Rice, M. L. 1986. A strategy for language assessment of young children: a combination of two approaches. *Language, Speech, and Hearing Services in Schools* 17: 83–94.

271

Kent, L. R. 1972. A language acquisition program for the retarded. In J. E. McClean, D. Yoder & R. L. Schiefelbusch (eds.) *Language intervention with the retarded*. Baltimore: University Park Press.

Kertesz, A. 1982. *The Western aphasia battery*. New York: Grune & Stratton.

Kilburg, G. 1982. The assessment of emerging communication. *Communication Disorders* 7: 87–101.

King, R., Jones, C. & Lasky, E. 1982. In retrospect: a fifteen year follow-up report of speech–language disordered children. *Language, Speech and Hearing Services in Schools* 13: 24–32.

Klima, E. & Bellugi, U. 1966. Syntactic regularities in the speech of children. In J. Lyons and R. J. Wales (eds.) *Psycholinguistic papers*. Edinburgh: Edinburgh University Press.

Lahey, M. and Bloom, M. 1977. Planning a first lexicon: which words to teach first. *Journal of Speech and Hearing Disorders* 42: 340–50.

LaPointe, L. L. 1978. Aphasia therapy: some principles and strategies for treatment. In D. F. Johns (ed.) *Clinical management of neurogenic communicative disorders*. Boston: Little, Brown.

Leonard, L. 1982. The nature of specific language impairment. In S. Rosenberg (ed.) *Handbook of applied psycholinguistics: major thrusts of research and theory*. Hillsdale: Erlbaum.

Linebarger, M. L., Schwartz, M. F. & Saffran, E. M. 1976. Sensitivity to grammatical structure in so-called agrammatic aphasics. *Cognition* 13: 361–92.

Lovaas, O. I., Berberich, J. P., Perloff, B. F. & Schaffer, B. 1966. Acquisition of imitative speech by schizophrenic children. *Science* 151: 705–7.

Ludlow, C. 1980. Children's language disorders: recent research advances. *Annals of Neurology* 7: 497–507.

McCarthy, D. 1954. Language development in children. In L. Carmichael (ed.) *Manual of child psychology*. New York: Wiley.

McCauley, R. J. & Swisher, L. 1984. Psychometric review of language and articulation tests for preschool children. *Journal of Speech and Hearing Disorders* 49: 34–42.

McDonald, E. T. 1964. *A deep test of articulation: picture form and sentence form*. Pittsburgh: Stanwix House.

McDonald, J. D. & Blott, J. P. 1974. Environmental language intervention: the rationale for a diagnostic and training strategy through rules, context and generalization. *Journal of Speech and Hearing Disorders* 39: 244–56.

McKay, E. and Vernon, M. 1971. *They grow in silence*. Silver Spring: National Association for the Deaf.

McReynolds, L. and Engman, D. 1975. *Distinctive feature analysis of misarticulations*. Baltimore: University Park Press.

Marshall, J. & Newcombe, F. 1984. Putative problems and pure progress in neuropsychological single-case studies. *Journal of Clinical Neuropsychology* 6: 65–70.

Mehler, J., Morton, J. & Jusczyk, P. 1984. On reducing language to biology. *Cognitive Psychology* 1: 83–116.

Miller, J. 1981. *Assessing language production in children: experimental procedures*. Baltimore: University Park Press.

Miller, J. & Chapman, R. 1983. *Systematic analysis of language transcripts (SALT)*. Madison, Wisconsin: University of Wisconsin Language Analysis Laboratory.

Miller, J. & Yoder, D. 1972. A syntax teaching program. In J. McLean, D. E. Yoder & R. Schiefelbusch (eds.) *Language intervention with the retarded: developing strategies*. Baltimore: University Park Press.

Morehead, D. & Ingram, D. 1973. Development of base syntax in normal and linguistically deviant children. *Journal of Speech and Hearing Research* 16: 330–52.

Nespoulous, J. -L. & Lecours, A. R. 1984. Clinical description of aphasia: linguistic aspects. In D. Caplan, A. R. Lecours & A. Smith (eds.) *Biological perspectives on language*. Cambridge, MA: MIT Press.

Perkins, W. 1977. *Speech pathology: an applied behavioral science*. Saint Louis: C. V. Mosby.

Porch, B. E. 1967. *The Porch Index of Communicative Abilities*. Palo Alto: Consulting Psychologists Press.

Presnell, L. 1973. Hearing-impaired children's comprehension and production of syntax in oral language. *Journal of Speech and Hearing Research* 16: 12–21.

Quigley, S., and King, C. 1982. The language development of deaf children and youth. In S.

Rosenberg (ed.) *Handbook of applied psycholinguistics: major thrusts of research and theory*. Hillsdale: Erlbaum.

Rees, N. 1973. Auditory processing factors in language disorders: the view from Procrustes' bed. *Journal of Speech and Hearing Disorders* 38: 304–15.

Sarno, M. T. 1969. *Functional Communication Profile (FCP)*. New York: Institute of Rehabilitative Medicine, New York University Medical Center.

Sarno, M., Silverman, M. & Sands, E. 1970. Speech therapy and language recovery in severe aphasia. *Journal of Speech and Hearing Research* 13: 607–23.

Schuell, H., Jenkins, J. J. & Jimenez-Pabon, E. 1964. *Aphasia in adults: diagnosis, prognosis and treatment*. New York: Harper & Row.

Shewan, C. & Kertesz, A. 1984. Effects of speech and language treatment on recovery from aphasia. *Brain and Language* 23: 272–99.

Shriberg, L. & Kwiatkowski, J. 1980. *Natural process analysis*. New York: Wiley.

Shriberg, L. & Kwiatkowski, J. 1982. Phonological disorders I; a diagnostic classification system. *Journal of Speech and Hearing Disorders* 47: 226–41.

Silva, P. 1980. The prevalence, stability and significance of developmental language delay in preschool children. *Developmental Medicine and Child Neurology* 22: 768–77.

Skelly, M. 1979. *Ameri-Ind gestural code*. New York: Elsevier.

Skinner, B. F. 1957. *Verbal behavior*. New York: Appleton-Century-Crofts.

Sparks, R., Helm, N. & Albert, M. 1974. Aphasia rehabilitation resulting from melodic intonation therapy. *Cortex* 10: 303–16.

Swisher, L. 1976. Performance of the oral deaf. In H. Whitaker & H. Whitaker (eds.) *Current trends in neurolinguistics*. New York: Academic Press.

Tallal, P. & Piercy, M. 1973. Developmental aphasia: impaired rate of nonverbal processing as a function of sensory modality. *Neuropsychologia* 11: 389–98.

Tallal, P. & Piercy, M. 1975. Developmental aphasia: the perception of brief vowels and extended stop consonants. *Neuropsychologia* 13: 69–74.

Tyack, D. & Gottsleben, R. 1974. *Language sampling, analysis and training*. Palo Alto: Consulting Psychologists Press.

Waryas, C. & Stremel-Campbell, K. 1978. Grammatical training for the language-delayed child. In R. Schiefelbush (ed.) *Language intervention strategies*. Baltimore: University Park Press.

Weiner, F. 1977. *Phonological process analysis*. Baltimore: University Park Press.

Wernicke, C. 1874. *Der aphasische Symptomenkomplex*. Breslau: Cohn & Weigert.

West, R. 1966. A historical review of the American literature in speech pathology. In R. W. Rieber & R. S. Brubaker (eds.) *Speech pathology: an international study of the science*. Amsterdam: North–Holland.

Wetherby, A. M. 1985. Speech and language disorders in children – an overview. In J. K. Darby (ed.) *Speech and language evaluation in neurology: childhood disorders*. New York: Grune & Stratton.

Williams, R., Ingham, R. & Rosenthal, J. 1981. A further analysis for developmental apraxia of speech in children with defective articulation. *Journal of Speech and Hearing Research* 244: 496–505.

Wood, K. 1971. Terminology and nomenclature. In L. E. Travis (ed.) *Handbook of speech pathology and audiology*. New York: Appleton-Century-Crofts.

Zimmerman, I. R., Steiner, V. G. & Evatt, R. L. 1969. *The preschool language scale*. Columbus: Charles E. Merrill.

Zwitman, D. & Sonderman, J. 1979. A syntax program designed to present base linguistic structures to language-disordered children. *Journal of Communication Disorders* 12: 323–37.

273

11 The evolution of human communicative behavior

William Orr Dingwall

> the capacity to communicate by symbols and syntax does lie within the ape's grasp. Many zoologists now doubt the existence of an unbridgeable linguistic chasm between animals and man.
>
> (Wilson 1978: 26)

> It seems reasonable to assume that evolution of the language faculty was a development specific to the human species long after it separated from other primates.
>
> (Chomsky 1979: 36)

11.0. Introduction

There are two classes of nontrivial questions in science: those that are in principle answerable and those that are not. Most questions discussed in this volume belong to the former category, although one might argue that some, such as the instantiation of language in the brain, may lie beyond our rational powers (cf. Chomsky 1968: 78–9). The question addressed in this chapter, however, belongs to the second category, and that being the case, one might reasonably ask why consider it at all. Indeed, as is well known, the Société de Linguistique de Paris passed a by-law in 1866 banning all consideration of the origin of language.

If there were no framework available for investigating the evolution of complex behaviors such as human communication, and furthermore, if we lacked any empirical data base relevant to such an investigation, we might indeed be inclined to support what Stam (1976) refers to as the 'annihilation of the question.' However, as can be seen from Table 1, we do not lack data upon which to base our investigations. Indeed, the availability of such empirical data has led to a recrudescence of interest in the evolution of human communicative behavior (see Wescott 1974; Harnad, Steklis & Lancaster 1976; Hockett 1978; Steklis & Raleigh 1979; Dingwall 1979a; Snowdon, Brown & Peterson 1982; Calvin 1983; de Luce & Wilder 1983). Furthermore, biology provides us with a framework, viz. *the synthetic theory of evolution*, which can aid us in gaining probable answers to questions involved in the evolution of human communicative behavior. Moreover, since in the case of most nontrivial questions in science which are in principle answerable, the answers available are only more or less probable, the gulf between such questions and those dealt with in this chapter is not quite as vast as might first appear.

Table 1. *New sources of evidence relevant to the evolution of human communicative behavior*

1. rapidly expanding fossil evidence coupled with increased ability to date it accurately
2. reconstructions of the brain, as well as peripheral structures, based on fossil evidence
3. increased data from the neurosciences
   a. comparative neurological studies
   b. neurolinguistic studies
   c. research in experimental phonetics and hearing and speech sciences
   d. the rapid advance in neuro-imaging techniques (CAT, NMR, SPECT for example)
4. biochemical studies of the relatedness of animal species
5. studies of nonhuman primates in the wild and in the laboratory leading to increased knowledge of their complex behaviors in general and their communicative behavior in particular
6. studies of signing and nonverbal communicative behavior in general in human and non-human primates
7. renewed research on the effects of isolation on the development of communicative behavior
8. increasing knowledge of the normal ontogenesis of language in humans
9. studies of vocal learning in nonprimates, particularly birds
10. investigation of the graphic behavior of early hominids
11. research on language universals
12. increased understanding of linguistic structures and their complexity
13. research on pidgins and creoles

Why be interested in questions such as the evolution of human communicative behavior? First of all, we harbor an inherent curiosity about our origin and evolution just as we do in the case of the origin and evolution of life and of the universe. One cannot gaze upon the fossilized remains of our hominid ancestors without queries as to all aspects of their being. There is an additional reason, however, for being interested in this question. In the course of our investigations, we may well accrue data of relevance to those questions which are in principle answerable.

We are charged by the editor of this Survey with reviewing the issues, results, debates, unsolved problems and prospects of our topic. In attempting to fulfill this charge, I shall range my discussion under the following general headings:

- evolutionary framework
- behavioral systems
- peripheral structures
- central control and processing systems

Under each one of these rubrics, I shall attempt to provide an overview of recent research. Because of space contraints, overlap with topics addressed in this and other volumes, and because some areas have evinced greater advances, in my opinion, than others, all rubrics will not be treated in equal detail.

William Orr Dingwall

11.1. Evolutionary framework

> The doctrine of continuity is too well established for it to be
> permissible to me to suppose that any complex natural phenomenon
> comes into existence suddenly, and without being preceded by simpler
> modifications . . . (Huxley 1917: 236)

The modern, synthetic theory of evolution derives from a melding of the views of Darwin (1859) with those of modern geneticists. This theory seeks to account for changes that take place within populations of plants and animals over time (*phylogeny*). The individuals making up such populations at any given moment display wide variability in both *phenotype* (morphology and behavior) and *genotype* (the sum of inherited genetic material). The phenotype variance observed is determined by the variance in the genotype plus the variance in the environment, as well as their interaction. This fact may be expressed mathematically as: $\sigma^2 p = \sigma^2 g + \sigma^2 e + \sigma^2 ge$ (see Murphy 1973; Whalen 1971). There are thus two main factors involved in evolution: *variation* created by random factors and a *filter*, whose properties are determined by factors that may be subsumed under the rubric of *natural selection*, which maintains or alters distributions of characteristics in certain ways.

Recent work in *molecular biology* indicates that the rate of phenotypic change cannot be wholly explained by the rate of accumulation of point mutations. The latter rate remains constant across species while the former does not (Wilson 1985). This discrepancy can be partially accounted for by maintenance versus rapid change of environmental factors. Thus, the lamp shell, *Lingula*, which lives in a deep-sea environment, has changed very little in over 500 million years. Other factors which may be involved are changes in *regulatory gene* mutation which controls the course of development of specific genes. A second factor may involve the effects of the internal environment, so to speak, created by an *increase in brain size* which leads to cultural change through imitative learning.

Both of these latter factors may have been important in hominid evolution. Gould (1977) has recently revived the theory that humans may have evolved some of their characteristics by a retardation of developmental processes (*neoteny*). The rapid increase in the size of the hominid brain is thus explained by the carrying over of a rapid fetal brain growth into the post-natal period in contrast to the nonhuman primate pattern. This view ties in with another recent theory advanced by Gould and his colleagues (Eldredge & Gould 1972) that evolution does not proceed in general by the gradual accumulation of changes, as Darwin thought, but by relatively brief periods of rapid change followed by long periods of stasis (*punctuated equilibrium*)

276

(cf. also Stanley 1981 and Eldredge & Tattersall 1982 for discussions of hominid evolution within this theoretical framework).

Our knowledge of the hominid fossil record has been expanding rapidly of late (see Johanson & Edey 1981 and Leakey 1981 for recent reviews). As Figure 1 shows, fossils have been discovered that date from at least 4 million years ago. There also exist fragments such as the Ngorora molar that may be of even earlier origin. Note also that several species of hominids appear to have inhabited the earth during the same time spans. Finally, as the skull sizes in this figure graphically indicate, there is a relatively gradual increase in brain size up to late *H. erectus* when rapid growth begins.

At the same time as we have learned more about the fossil record, molecular biology has been providing us with biochemical indices of related-ness among animals and perhaps even a 'biological clock' capable of dating the divergences of populations (see Goodman, Tashian & Tashian 1976 for a review as well as Gould 1985). A major finding has been the remarkable genetic similarity that exists between humans and the great apes, particularly the chimpanzee (Yunis, Sawyer & Durham 1980). The differences on a number of measures are so small that researchers have been hard put to account for phenotypic differences (King & Wilson 1975). Whereas previously physical anthropologists have set the time of separation of the human and African ape stocks as long ago as 50 million years, molecular biologists have argued for a date of separation as recent as 5–10 million years (Wilson & Sarich 1969). Thus, whereas the biochemical data has had the effect of pushing the date of the ape/man split forward in time, more and more fossil discoveries have pushed back the date of the emergence of man.

1.1.1. The concept of behavioral homology

The two eminent scholars cited at the outset of this chapter, appraised presumably of exactly the same body of evidence, are clearly in sharp disagreement. Even though both have adopted a rather extreme position in favor of the genetic determination of behavior – a position which, one might feel, should unite them on the question of the continuity of communicative behavior between us and our closest primate relatives – it is clear they could not be more opposed.

Chomsky adopts a *discontinuity theory* first put forth by Descartes and supported by Lenneberg (1967) and later Fodor, Bever & Garrett (1974). It has two aspects: (a) the universal features of language are *species-specific*, i.e., unique to humans, and (b) the structures that subserve language are assumed to be *task-specific*. These specificities are logically independent, so that all possible combinations of them are imaginable and have been argued by philosophers, linguists and psychologists (see Dingwall 1975).

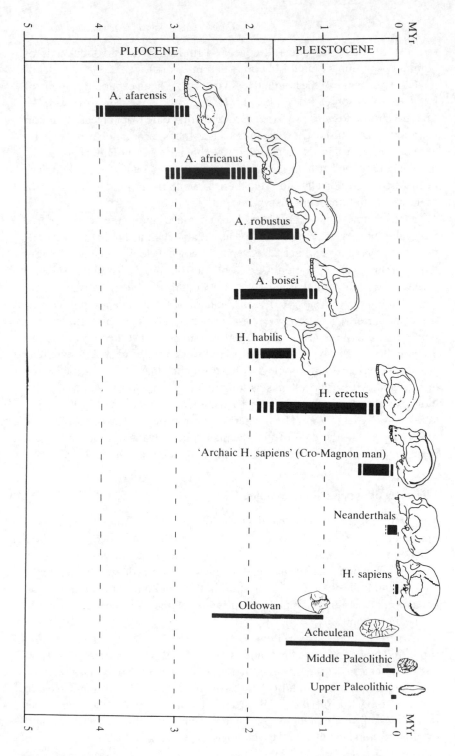

MYr

PLIOCENE   PLEISTOCENE

A. afarensis

A. africanus

A. robustus

A. boisei

H. habilis

H. erectus

'Archaic H. sapiens' (Cro-Magnon man)

Neanderthals

H. sapiens

Oldowan

Acheulean

Middle Paleolithic

Upper Paleolithic

MYr

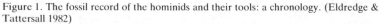

Figure 1. The fossil record of the hominids and their tools: a chronology. (Eldredge & Tattersall 1982)

Wilson (1978), on the other hand, adopts a view, shared by many biologists, which may be termed the *continuity theory*. It too has two aspects. It can hold either (a) that animals need only acquire a bit more of a trait they already possess, say general intelligence or volitional control of the vocal tract, in order to approximate to human linguistic abilities or (b) that such abilities are acquired within the primate order by gradual accretion of traits some of which were not possessed earlier. Darwin appears to have embraced the first version, while Huxley appears to defend the second (cf. the quotation that heads this section). The second, *accretion hypothesis*, will be adopted in this chapter as a working principle. In the words of Stephen Toulmin (1971: 378) this stance

> interprets the language capacity as something which developed in the
> hominid precursors of modern man by the gradual accumulation of
> physiological and behavioral changes which were advantageous, in
> part for 'proto-linguistic' reasons, in part for non-linguistic reasons.
> The physiological changes that were progressively selected in this way
> were associated behaviorally, first with the emergence of a partial
> language function, and eventually with a full language function.

On the evidence available, it seems most unlikely that human communicative behavior suddenly arose in our hominid ancestors by some one-shot genetic saltation. It is equally unlikely that, given their genetic proximity to us, the great apes would evince no aspect of this complex behavior. What is much more likely is that such a behavior developed gradually over time by the process known as *mosaic evolution*, with structures subserving various aspects of the behavior not evolving at the same rate (see Wind 1983). The process of *preadaptation*, whereby some mutations and genotypes may become advantageous as an aspect of a behavior complex that did not prevail in the original selective situation, may also be involved (Lieberman 1984). As we shall see later, the sharp contrast between the discontinuity and continuity theories is blurred in part by considering a broad rather than narrow view of what constitutes human communicative behavior.

The evolutionary framework I propose to utilize in this chapter was probably first set forth by Darwin (1872) in his monograph on the expression of emotions in man and animals. In this work, he sought to demonstrate how one might glean insights into the origins and development of human emotional expressions via the study of closely related species, particularly non-human primates. He, in effect, extended the methods of comparative anatomy to behavior, retaining the insight that behaviors require structural correlates. This program for the establishment of *behavioral homologies* has been clarified and extended recently in a number of papers (see e.g. Hodos 1976). Basically, what is being proposed is that behaviors that are similar in closely related species, that can be related to structures showing a high degree of concordance in a number of parameters, and that could – together with their structural correlates – be traced back to a common ancestor, may be considered homologous. Structural correlates refer, as they did in Darwin's work, to peripheral structures such as peripheral nerves, muscles, bones, and structures of the central nervous system. Some of the possible relationships that have been documented among these variables are illustrated in Figure 2. As this figure shows, there are behaviors that, while similar, cannot be related to a common ancestor. These are termed *behavioral homoplasies*, and include *parallelism* (Figure 2B), *convergence* (Figure 2C) as well as *mimicry, chance similarity*, and *analogy*.

A number of guidelines (heuristics) have been proposed by Hodos and others for the investigation of behavioral homologies. Some of the more important are listed below.

1. The most convincing examples of behavioral homology involve behaviors that are uniquely observed in closely related species. Species that make up a so-called *scala naturae* form a discontinuous sequence. Thus, for example, comparisons of rats, cats, and monkeys are meaningless for the establishment of behavioral homologies.

2. Behaviors, in order to be considered homologous, must be mediated by both peripheral and central structures that can be shown to be homologous.

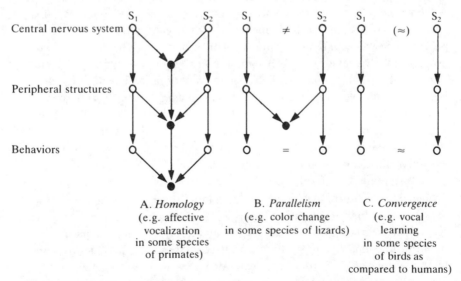

A. *Homology*
(e.g. affective
vocalization
in some species
of primates)

B. *Parallelism*
(e.g. color change
in some species of lizards)

C. *Convergence*
(e.g. vocal
learning
in some species
of birds as
compared to humans)

Figure 2. Three instances of similar or identical behaviors – only one of which can be traced back to a stipulated common ancestor. (S_1=species$_1$; white circles refer to structures or behaviors in extant forms; black circles refer to reconstructed structures or behaviors in common ancestors.) For further discussion of the processes illustrated in this figure, see Dingwall 1979; Hodos 1976; Nottebohm 1975. (Dingwall 1980)

3. One must avoid the circularity of employing behavior to establish taxonomies and then using such similarity in behavior as evidence of behavioral homology. The widest possible evidence for genetic relationships must be used.

4. In comparing acquired behavior across species, the maximum ability to perform the behavior should be the common reference point.

5. The ontogeny of behaviors, together with their mediating structures, can be an important clue in establishing behavioral homologies (see Campbell & Hodos 1970; Scovel 1972; Parker & Gibson 1979).

Figure 3 provides a graphic representation of the basic concept of homology. Black circles indicate homologous features; circles and crosses, nonhomologous features developed after the period of common ancestry. Such features would, of course, be species-specific.

The following three sections will explore those factors involved in establishing behavioral homologies, viz. the behavior itself, the peripheral structures that are directly involved in input and output of the behavior, and finally the central nervous system structures involved in the control and processing of the behavior.

11.2. Behavioral systems

> The defect that hinders communication between them and us, why may it not be on our part as well as theirs? (Montaigne)

11.2.1. Communicative behavior

In biology, models of behaviors such as communication are typically presented in the form of hierarchial input/output systems. Such a model is presented in panel A of Figure 4, together with a listing of memory components that may be involved at each stage (panel B). I have discussed this model in great detail in earlier publications (Dingwall 1978, 1980) and shall confine myself here to a brief summary of its salient points. It is proposed that three basic transductions are involved in communicative behavior. The first (T_1), labeled *cognition*, involves the capacity of the brain of an organism to deal with a variety of concepts which may be either simple or complex. One cannot at present judge whether an animal is in command of a particular concept unless the animal signals it in some manner. This involves linking the concept with a neurological state that mediates either its production or recognition. T_2, labeled *coding* involves this linkage between an abstract conceptual system and an equally abstract sensori-motor representation which is only imperfectly reflected in the various stages of its production and recognition. This is,

281

William Orr Dingwall

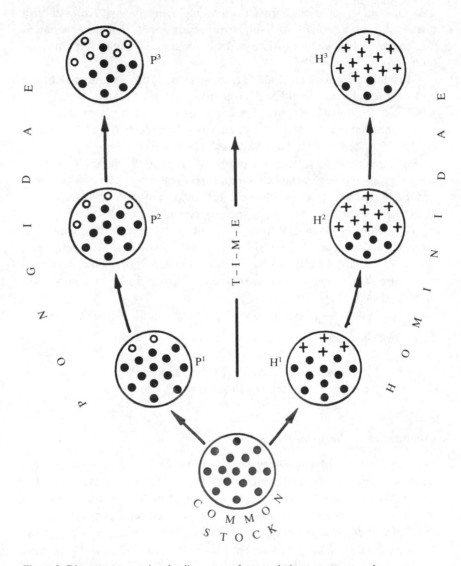

Figure 3. Diagram representing the divergence of two evolutionary sequences, the
Pongidae (great apes) and the *Hominidae* (modern and extinct man). The two
sequences inherit a common ancestry – characters of common inheritance (black
circles). As the lines diverge, each one acquires its own distinctive features or
characters of independent acquisition (species-specific characteristics); those distinctive
of the hominid line are represented by crosses and those of the pongid line by white
circles. (Dingwall 1979b)

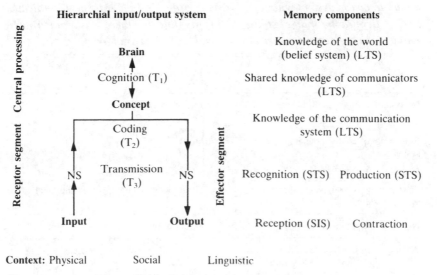

Figure 4. Aspects of a general biological model of the communicative behavior of primates. (T_1=transduction$_i$; LTS=long-term store; STS=short-term store; SIS=sensory information store; NS=neurological state.) (Dingwall 1980)

of course, the transduction in human communication behavior that is generally considered the principal concern of theoretical linguistics. The nature of this transduction need not have always been as complex as it appears to be in human communication (see Table 2). The third transduction component (T_3), which I term *transmission*, involves the process of signal production and detection. Note that T_3 is neutral as to input/output modality. Table 3 provides an extensive listing of the modalities that man and other primates are capable of using.

This model, it will be noted, is quite similar to modular models advanced by Franz Josef Gall, Chomsky (1980) and particularly Fodor (1983). In the latter's framework, cognition (T_1) is not domain-specific (i.e. is not tied to any particular domain such as language, music, mathematics, etc.). It is also not modular in that it is not encapsulated (i.e. it has access to the general belief systems of the organism). Coding (T_2), however, *is* domain-specific (i.e., in this instance, specifically tied to language) and is modular. Finally, transmission (T_3) is an input/output system consisting of domain-specific transducers.

As in Fodor's system, it is clear that each of the three transductions in Figure 4 are independent of each other and can be dissociated (see Dingwall 1980 for evidence to this effect). Furthermore, there is ample psychological as well as neurological evidence that production and comprehension involve

Table 2. *Some of the changes involved in moving towards a more efficient communication system within the primate order. All the transitions indicated are gradient rather than absolute. (*It is possible that there was an intermediate stage where gesture rather than speech was foregrounded.)*

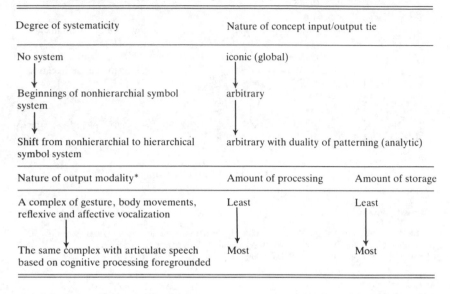

Degree of systematicity	Nature of concept input/output tie	
No system	iconic (global)	
↓	↓	
Beginnings of nonhierarchial symbol system	arbitrary	
↓	↓	
Shift from nonhierarchial to hierarchical symbol system	arbitrary with duality of patterning (analytic)	

Nature of output modality*	Amount of processing	Amount of storage
A complex of gesture, body movements, reflexive and affective vocalization	Least	Least
↓	↓	↓
The same complex with articulate speech based on cognitive processing foregrounded	Most	Most

quite different processes. Finally, it should be evident that human communicative behavior is characterized by a vast conglomeration of skills that are acquired and lost in a mosaic fashion. It is highly improbable that so complex a behavior emerged full blown at some point in hominid evolution.

11.2.2. Naturalistic and experimental studies of general complex behavior of the great apes

In relatively recent times we have begun to amass accurate and detailed descriptions of great ape behavior in the wild (Lawick-Goodall 1971, 1976; Bourne & Cohen 1975; Galdikas-Brindamour 1975; Goodall 1986). I shall not describe the results of these studies in detail, as I believe they are well known by now, but I shall provide a précis. If one constructs a list of man's putatively unique behavior patterns, one finds that almost without exception these have precursors in the behavior of the great apes (cf. Lawick-Goodall & Hamburg 1974; Lawick-Goodall 1976). The great apes display *tool use and construction, cooperative hunting and food sharing, nest construction, territoriality, bipedal locomotion, and social organization.* All of these behaviors may have been channeled in the hominid direction by some environmental change, such as a shift in habitat from woodland to savanna. This does appear

Table 3. *Primate communication systems: input/output modalities, media, and signal types. (Asterisks mark signal types presumed unique to human communication*

Input/output modality	Medium	Signal types

ear/vocal tract (±articulation)	acoustic	prosodic feature
		  pitch
		  pause
		  loudness
		  tempo
		  *segmental features
		  consonants
		  vowel
		voice qualifiers
		affective vocalization
		  laughter
		  cries
		  groans etc.
		vegetative sounds
		  cough
		  sneeze etc.
		  *whistling

ear/hand		clapping finger-snapping drumming
eye/body	visual	body posture body movements proxemics spatial orientation piloerection

eye/hand–arm		hand gestures
		  sign languages
		  *finger-spelling etc.
		writing
		  *phonemic
		  *morphophonemic
		  *syllabic
		  ideographic
		  plastic cutouts etc.

eye/face		facial expression *lip-reading
cutaneous (usually hand/hand)	tactile	*braille writing grooming touching *petting
nose/body	chemical	body odor *perfume

to have occurred early in hominid evolution. Furthermore, as Wilson (1985) suggests, increase in brain size may result in new selection pressures that lead to fixation of mutations in a population. This interaction of factors is schematized in Figure 5.

Experimental studies of complex behaviors in the great apes leave little doubt that if cognitive abilities (T_1) alone could assure human-like communicative behavior, it should be manifest. *General learning, self-recognition, symbolic play, 'art', insight learning, counting, maze running, relationship problems, categorization, cross-modal transfer, and even the construction of australopithecine-like tools* (Wright 1978) do not lie beyond the abilities of the great apes (cf. Dingwall 1979a).

11.2.3. Naturalistic and experimental studies of communicative behavior in non-human primates

Primate communication in both nonhuman primates and man involves a complex, partially redundant, multichannel system (see Table 3). Visual, tactile, olfactory, and auditory input modalities are involved. *Gestures* employed in the wild by chimpanzees are remarkably similar to those seen in humans. *Facial expressions* are also very similar to emotional expressions in humans and may indeed be tied to related neurological control (Myers 1972). *Vocalizations* are limited in number, tied to a particular time and place, appear to be triggered by a small set of emotional stimuli, appear to be the product of an essentially closed genetic program (see Mayr 1974) and do not evince duality of patterning. In sum, it should be evident that nonhuman primate vocalization in the wild is not homologous with human speech, but rather with certain aspects of human paralanguage. It is true that some nonhuman primates tie their calls to specific external stimuli, but it is by no means clear that they have volitional control over such cries, i.e. that they differ from human paralinguistic phenomena (see Steklis 1985 for a recent review). Finally, it should be noted that there is no evidence of vocal learning in nonhuman primates of the type demonstrated in altricial song birds (see Nottebohm 1984 for a recent review). Moreover, there is a lack of early vocalization paralleling cooing and babbling in the human child.

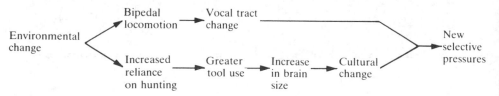

Figure 5. Factors involved in the channeling of nonhuman primate behaviors in the hominid direction.

It is clearly the experimental studies of nonhuman primate communicative behavior that have sparked the most interest in the evolution of human communicative behavior. It should not come as a surprise, given the facts of vocalization in the wild, that it is extremely difficult to condition nonhuman primates to phonate (Sutton *et al.* 1973). Their weak voluntary control over phonation shows itself in their inability to suppress spontaneous vocalization. A chimp cleverly managing to steal some choice bit of food invariably gives himself away by the utterance of noisy food grunts. Attempts to reach great apes to articulate have invariably ended in failure. The Hayes (1951) had the greatest success: four words after $6\frac{1}{2}$ years of training. Observing the film of their chimp Viki's efforts at articulation should be sufficient to convince anyone of nonhuman primates' inability to produce articulate speech. As we shall see, there are clear neurological and vocal tract differences between nonhuman primates and man that account for this inability.

While speech represents a species-specific trait (Dingwall 1975) that appears to have developed relatively late in the hominid line, auditory processing may have evolved much earlier. All researchers who have worked with chimpanzees and other great apes report evidence of auditory language processing (Kellogg 1968; Hayes & Hayes 1951). Recently, using more controlled experiments, considerable auditory processing ability for spoken English has been demonstrated in *Pan paniscus* (the pygmy chimpanzee) 'Kanzi' (Savage-Rumbaugh *et al.* 1985).

As long ago as 1661, Samuel Pepys suggested that, if apes could not be taught to speak, perhaps they could be taught to express themselves by means of manual gestures. It was indeed the realization that the film of Viki's efforts at articulate communication could be understood without sound – in terms of gestures alone – that initially encouraged the Gardners to undertake their research in teaching American Sign Language (ASL) to chimpanzees. After their considerable success with Washoe, a number of research projects employing the visual–manual modality sprang up. A listing of the major projects is presented in Table 4. Only the productive vocabulary of the subjects is listed in the general results column. Stringent requirements for evidence of productive acquisition undoubtedly lead to underestimation of the subjects' abilities. As in the case of children, recognition vocabulary may be as much as twice as productive vocabulary.

Although the aims, training procedures and symbol systems used differ considerably from one project to another, with one exception to be discussed below, the results of language training are remarkably similar.

The large size of the ape-language vocabularies, coupled with the fact that individual lexical items are generalized in their reference, makes it appear unlikely that apes are simply learning conditioned associations between symbol and referent. Nevertheless as Sue Savage-Rumbaugh has pointed out

287

Table 4. *Major studies of the great apes' communicative abilities (visual–manual input/output modality)*

Projects: principal investigator(s) and representative publications	Name, species, age (at onset of study), and sex of subjects	Communication system	General results as reported by investigators
1. Beatrice and Allen Gardner (1969, 1971, 1974a, 1974b, 1975a, 1975b, 1984, 1985)	Washoe (chimp., f., 8–14 mths)	ASL	160 signs; considerable syntactic ability
	Moja (f.), Pili (f.), Tatu (f.), Dar (m.) (all chimps, acquired within a few days of birth)	ASL	Signing generally equivalent to that reported for children of comparable age
2. Ann and David Premack (1970, 1971a, 1971b, 1972, 1976a, 1976b, 1978, 1983)	Sarah (chimp., f., 6 yrs)	Plastic symbols	130 signs; considerable cognitive and syntactic abilities
	Work started with two additional chimps: Elizabeth (f., 5 yrs) and Peony (f., 5 yrs)		
3. Roger Fouts (1972, 1973, 1974a, 1974b, 1975a, 1975b, 1976, 1983, 1984)	Washoe (chimp., f., 33–39 mths)+numerous other chimps and one orang.	ASL	Varying sign vocabularies and syntactic abilities
4. Duane Rumbaugh and Sue Savage-Rumbaugh (1973, 1974, 1976, 1977, 1978a, 1978b, 1980a, 1980b, 1984, 1985)	Lana	Yerkish	100 lexigrams plus considerable syntactic ability
	Sherman and Austin (chimps, m., 4½ yrs)		Considerable naming abilities demonstrated
	Kanzi (pygmy chimp., m., 6 mths)		Spontaneous acquisition of signs; comprehension of spoken English
5. Maurice Temerlin (1975)	Lucy (chimp., f., 1 mth)	ASL	102 signs; considerable syntactic ability
6. H Terrace (1976, 1979, 1984)	Nim (chimp., m., 1 mth)	ASL	125 signs; little true syntactic ability
7. F. Patterson (1978, 1981)	Koko (gorilla, f., 1 yr)	ASL	375 signs; considerable syntactic ability
8. H. L. Miles (1978, 1983)	Chantek (orang, m., 1 yr)	ASL	100 signs; considerable syntactac ability

288

in a number of papers, this possibility cannot be ruled out *a priori*. Lexical usage in human language involves linkage between a symbol and a concept rather than a referent. The Rumbaughs have been able to demonstrate the conceptual use of symbols in a number of tasks. In one of the most elaborate of these, chimps demonstrated the ability to use lexigrams to ask one another for tools needed to extricate food from a container (Savage-Rumbaugh, Rumbaugh & Boyson 1978). Only one chimp knew where the food was and what tool (money, straw, stick, etc.) was needed to obtain it. Symbol usage was necessary for such cooperative behavior, because when the chimps were prevented from using lexigrams, their accuracy dropped from 92% to 10% even though they could freely vocalize and gesture to each other.

A recent critique of the ape-language studies is that many of their results can be explained on the basis of unintentional cuing. Just as Wilhelm von Osten unintentionally cued his horse, Clever Hans, in his hoof-tapping responses, so ape-language researchers may have cued their subjects in their signing (Sebeok & Rosenthal 1981). Comparative psychologists are acutely aware of cuing phenomena, and many, such as the Gardners and the Rumbaughs, employ appropriate double-blind procedures in testing symbol acquisition. The fact that their results differ so little from projects where such procedures are not stringently adhered to indicates that cuing does not play an important role in vocabulary learning. Also it has been pointed out that signing behavior is much more difficult to cue inadvertently than hoof-tapping.

As noted above, the ape-language projects have generally reported comparable results, with one exception, Project Nim. In early reports this was not the case, but when the principal investigator, H. S. Terrace, reexamined video tapes of Nim's signing behavior, he reached conclusions that are at variance with those of other projects. He found that Nim's signing behavior was in no way comparable with developing communicative abilities in children. It lacked creativity and spontaneity; it was repetitious and involved extensive imitation of teachers' signing. Mean length of utterance did not increase and was not related to maximum length of utterance, as is the case with children. Finally, expansions of Nim's teachers' utterances were rare, and turn-taking behavior in conversations differed from that observed in children (Terrace 1984).

I believe it would be a mistake to generalize from Terrace's findings, as some have precipitously done. First of all, chimps, like human beings, differ markedly in their abilities. Furthermore, it is becoming clear that there are differences among species of apes in their communicative abilities (see Miles 1983; Savage-Rumbaugh *et al*. 1985). The training procedures employed by Terrace differed markedly from those of other projects (Gardner 1981). Finally, the criteria used to judge Nim's accomplishments would exclude many children from demonstrating linguistic competence (Lieberman 1984).

In a recent address, Duane Rumbaugh (1985) summarized the great apes' communicative behavior as follows:

(1)   they can learn words spontaneously, efficiently, and they can use them referentially for things not present;
(2)   they can learn words from one another;
(3)   they can learn to use their words to coordinate their joint activities and tell one another things otherwise not known;
(4)   they can learn rules for ordering their words;
(5)   they do make comments;
(6)   they announce their intended actions;
(7)   they are spontaneous and not necessarily subject to imitation in their signs and not necessarily poor turn-takers in conversation;
(8)   they are communicative and know what they are about.

I was privileged to visit the Yerkes Project some years ago for two weeks, and my personal observations are in accord with the above views. Given the demonstrated cognitive abilities of the great apes, it would be astonishing if they were incapable of mastering some aspects of human language. Syntax, like articulation, may be beyond their capabilities. It is possible that they, like the Broca's aphasic, can combine lexical items following semantic but not syntactic constraints (see Parisi 1983). This question has not as yet been carefully explored.

11.2.4. A note on brain damage and gestural abilities

It is probably fair to say that the vast majority of researchers into the origin and evolution of human communicative behavior accept some version of Hewes's gestural origin theory (Hewes 1976; de Grolier 1983). It is not claimed that this was the sole modality employed – all the modalities listed in Table 3 were operative – only that this modality was the first to come under completely volitional control.

There is increasing evidence that sign-language breakdown in deaf signers with acquired aphasia parallels that of language breakdown in hearing aphasics and is a sequela of left-hemisphere damage. If we turn from deaf signers who have become aphasic to patients who have been taught gestural systems subsequent to brain injury, the results are somewhat different.

There are four major theories that have been put forth to explain gestural deficits following brain damage. Such deficits have been viewed as part of a cognitive impairment of 'the abstract attitude' (Goldstein 1948), as part of a general asymbolia (Finkelnberg 1870), as part of a generalized apractic disturbance (Liepmann 1908) and, finally, as a modality-specific disturbance (Varney 1982). In a recent doctoral dissertation examining in detail the comprehension, imitation and production of American Indian Signs (a system of gestural communication designed to be more iconic and thus transparent than ASL) (Skelly 1979), in aphasics, considerable support for the modality model was found. The comprehension tasks correlated most highly with reading ability, while the production tasks correlated most highly with performance on an apraxia battery; neither comprehension nor production was significantly correlated to performance on a standard aphasia battery (Rao 1985). Chomsky (1979) has suggested that various populations, such as feral children, left-hemispherectomized patients, and aphasics, may not be in total possession of a language faculty (T_2). Rather, he speculates, these populations rely heavily on their conceptual systems (T_1) for communication. The great apes may lack a language faculty altogether, as Chomsky suggests, or evince a very rudimentary form of such a faculty. It seems likely, because of the great complexity of this faculty, that it, like speech, may have developed in a mosaic fashion within the hominid line over a considerable span of time. (Lieberman 1984: 326 suggests a tandem development of speech and syntax in hominids.) As we have seen, gesture involves an input–output modality (T_3) in the great apes that is already in place and can be used to some degree for communication. It thus seems plausible that gesture may have been utilized for communication in conjunction with primitive forms of vocalization by early members of the hominid line, as Hewes suggests.

11.3. Peripheral structures

> the primate pharynx and airway are preadapted for speech-like
> vocalizations ever since the origins of the anthropoids.
>
> (Wind 1983: 17)

The role played by peripheral structures in the evolution of speech has been a subject of much dispute in the past and continues to be so today. There is also continuing argument over the locus of crucial change. Does it lie in the peripheral structures or in the central control and processing systems?

11.3.1. The vocal tract

Human speech can be characterized in terms of a *source* and a *filter*. The source is provided by the lungs, which produce an airstream which causes the vocal folds of the larynx to vibrate. The laryngeal tone is then filtered through a number of resonators, two of which, the pharyngeal and oral cavities, can be altered in shape by so-called articulators. The complex chain of events is diagrammed in Figure 6.

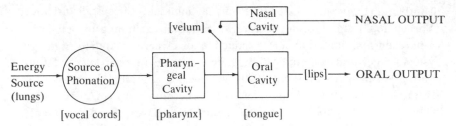

Figure 6. The basic components of the human vocal tract. (Boxes represent resonators; square brackets enclose articulators.) (Dingwall 1979b)

When we compare the vocal tracts of anthropoid apes and modern man, we do find a number of differences. Some of these are clear even in the grossly simplified representation in Figure 7. One of the most striking and potentially important differences that one observes is the position of the larynx. In the chimpanzee, it is positioned quite high with its superior margin at the level of the second cervical vertebra. In contrast, in the human the superior margin is, on the average, at the third cervical vertebra (C_3) in women and the fourth (C_4) in men. The position of the larynx in modern man is the culmination of a gradual process of descent in the primate order as a whole. Thus apes have a lower larynx position than monkeys (see Fink 1975).

As a result of the descent of the larynx in man, the epiglottis no longer interacts with the soft palate to allow the oral cavity to be closed off while breathing through the nose. The epiglottis, which is high and wider in its

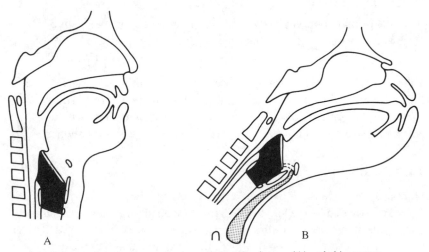

Figure 7. Scheme of the resonant tube in sagittal section in man (A) and chimpanzee (B). The black field is the laryngeal cavity, and the dotted field is the laryngeal sac. (Dingwall 1979b).

292

upper portion in the chimpanzee, is capable of sealing off the inlet to the larynx while swallowing; this is no longer the case in man.

Many of the changes in the relations among the structures of the vocal tract may be the result of upright posture. Chimpanzees often adopt such a posture and this tendency increases in the hominid line. The pelvic bones of the earliest known hominid fossils, now classified as *A. afarensis*, indicate that upright posture and locomotion was the norm.

Another set of changes that may have played a role in our vocal tract configuration involves the facial region. There has been a gradual recession of the jaws in hominid line, a definitive chin has developed and the so-called simian shelf at the base of the jaw has disappeared, allowing for greater tongue mobility.

The tongue in nonhuman primates is flatter and thinner than in man. It is supplied with muscle spindles that may play a role in feedback during articulation in humans (Smith 1973) and is capable of assuming a large number of positions. Nevertheless, according to Bastian (1965) and others, the tongue remains relatively immobile during the production of calls. If this is true, it is the locus of the qualitative distinction between man and non-human primates in articulation mentioned earlier, and deserves careful study using electromyography and ultrasound.

Examination of Figure 7 reveals another major difference, viz. the presence of the laryngeal air sac. These sacs are present in all great apes. They are connected to the laryngeal ventricles via a structure known as the *appendix*. It is now felt that they may serve as a resonator and amplifier, selectively emphasizing the fundamental frequency of calls at the expense of higher harmonics (see Gautier 1971).

There are a number of differences in the structure of the larynx in anthropoid apes compared to man. The thyrohyoid is shorter. The cricoid is funnel-shaped rather than round. There is an internal cricothyroid muscle lacking in man. The hyoid bone is larger and its corpus is hollowed out and cupped. The true and false vocal folds can be articulated separately in the chimpanzee. The sharp, cusp-like edges of the vocal folds, which probably play an important role in preventing air from entering the lungs during brachiation, are not present in man. On the other hand, the lateral thyroarytenoid muscle sends offshoots to the medial portion of the vocalis muscle in humans, allowing for finer regulation, while in nonhuman primates it runs only along the base (Jürgens & Ploog 1976).

While chimpanzees vocalize during both exhalation and inhalation (Jordan 1971), the latter pulmonic airstream mechanism is not employed in normal human speech (Ladefoged 1971).

This catalogue of anatomical and physiological differences clearly indicates that the vocal tract structures in the great apes are at best *fractionally homologous* with those of man in terms of their role in vocalization. This lack of homology becomes even more evident when the control of these structures is examined.

11.3.1.1. Lieberman's theory of the evolution of speech

Making use of many of the facts recounted in the previous section, Philip Lieberman has advanced a most intriguing theory concerning the evolution of efficiency in vocal communication in hominids. The bases of this theory have been summarized in two publications (Lieberman 1975, 1984). Although the latter survey is somewhat more ambitious than the former, Lieberman's basic views have not changed appreciably. I have reviewed Lieberman theory at length (Dingwall 1977, 1979a; also Locke 1986). A brief summary of these reviews is presented in this section.

First of all, Lieberman examines the acoustic characteristics of the vocalizations of nonhuman primates, human infants, and adult humans. Since the vocal tracts of the former two groups are quite similar, it is not surprising that he finds their vocalizations similar. Neither group appears to move the tongue while vocalizing. The output of the larynx is less periodic, and they appear incapable of producing certain vocalic sounds such as [i u a] which play a central role in Lieberman's theory.

The vocal tracts of nonhuman primates and infants constitute what Lieberman terms *the standard supralaryngeal vocal tract* characteristic of all terrestrial animals save humans (see Figure 7). The fact that human infants display such a vocal tract configuration clearly indicates that in this feature, adults are not neotenous, as Lieberman correctly points out.

Employing reconstructions of the vocal tracts of various hominid fossils provided by the anatomists Crelin and, more recently, Laitman (Lieberman, Crelin & Klatt 1972; Laitman 1983), Lieberman is in a position to compare these vocal tracts with those of extant nonhuman and human primates. Having available the size and shape of these various vocal tracts, Lieberman can also determine, via computer modeling, their phonetic capabilities. Anthropoid apes, Australopithecines, *Homo habilis* and some members of *H. erectus*, as well as so-called 'classic' Neanderthals such as La Ferrasie and La Chapelle-aux-Saints, were found to have deficient phonetic inventories when compared with other fossil hominids often classified as Neanderthal (e.g. Broken Hill and Es-Skhūl) and Cro-Magnon man (cf. Figure 1). In particular, none was able to produce the so-called *point vowels*: [i u a].

These point vowels, Lieberman holds, following Stevens (1972), are crucial for efficient, rapid vocal communication. They are presumed to be *acoustically stable*, so that sloppy articulation does not distort them as easily as other vowels. Two of the vowels, [i u], are also claimed to be *determinate*, by which Lieberman means they allow a hearer to arrive at an estimate of the size of the speaker's vocal tract. This is important, as Lieberman subscribes to the motor theory of speech perception which postulates that covert articulation mediates speech perception. Citing work that demonstrates property detectors in various species matched to their vocal output, Lieberman seems to imply that the human auditory system might be similarly matched to the vocalizations that can be produced by the human vocal tract. It is also important that the point vowels are maximally distinct both articulatorily and acoustically. Finally, Lieberman notes that these vowels occur allophonically in all languages, as indeed one might expect given their remarkable characteristics.

It is important to point out that Lieberman is not claiming that communication via the auditory–vocal channel would be impossible in the absence of these vowels – only that it would be less efficient.

While I find myself in general agreement with Lieberman's overall approach to the evolution of human communication behavior, I find his theory of the evolution of speech flawed in both its assumptions and its methodology. I shall state my own and others' critical comments in the form of a list:

1. [a] may be acoustically stable for relatively large changes in articulation [i] and [u] are not (Gay 1974; Ladefoged 1978);

2. [i] and [u] do not appear to be determinate (Shankweiler *et al.* 1975; Verbrugge *et al.* 1974);

3. the assumption that one needs to know the size of a given vocal tract to perceive speech sounds accurately is questionable in light of the very considerable evidence against the motor theory of speech perception as well as the fact that infants, nonhuman primates and even chinchillas perceive speech in a linguistic mode without any prior knowledge of the articulations involved in the production of such sounds;

4. infants at one month of age with a cranial base angle outside (greater than) the adult range still did not produce any of the point vowels (George 1978). Basicranial flexion is one of the criteria that Lieberman uses to reconstruct fossil vocal tracts (Laitman 1983). Yet in this instance, as George points out, 'there is a lag between the time of vocal tract development and the use of its capacity' (George 1978: 93);

5. not only are the details as to how fossil hominid vocal tracts are reconstructed far from clear, but the resulting reconstructions have been severely criticized as untenable by a number of anatomists (Falk 1975; DuBrul 1977; 1979);

6. finally, as I have pointed out, although a given computer model of a vocal tract, no matter how accurately reconstructed, fails to produce certain sounds, it does not necessarily follow that the owner of the vocal tract could not produce

these sounds (see Ladefoged 1978). Humans with gross deformities of the vocal tract, as well as those with major portions of the tract, such as the larynx or tongue, removed, are capable of producing comprehensible speech (LeMay 1975; Drachman 1969), as are birds with a vocal apparatus radically different from that of humans (Klatt & Stefanski 1974).

11.3.2. The ear

There is much less controversy surrounding the structure of the ear of anthropoid apes and its capacity for auditory processing. Unlike the vocal tract, the structure of the chimpanzee ear does not differ markedly from that of modern man. House *et al.* (1964) found only slight differences in the angle of the tympanic membrane and in the slope of the auditory canal. The oval and round windows, as well as the cochlea, occupy positions similar to those in man. The number of coils and fine structure of the Organ of Corti were found to be identical to those in humans. Also the innervation is identical.

The auditory thresholds of the chimpanzee are very similar to man's, but are generally below his except at 4096 Hz. Chimpanzees do evince a greater sensitivity to higher frequencies than man. Masterton, Hefner & Ravizza (1968) note that there is a trend toward extension of the range of optimum sensitivity to lower frequencies (below 1 kHz) and a reduction in the range of optimum sensitivity in the high frequency range (above 20 kHz) in primate phylogeny. Temporal discrimination does not differ from man's; sound localization, however, appears to be far superior. It appears that the ability of nonhuman primates to resolve differences in frequency are inferior to those in man (Stebbins 1970).

11.3.2.1. Neurological feature detectors

Neurological feature detectors have been defined as organizational configurations of the sensory nervous system that are highly sensitive to certain parameters of complex stimuli (Abbs & Sussman 1971). Evidence for such detectors in the auditory and visual systems of a wide range of animals has been collected. The methodology employed to identify feature detectors in nonhuman animals involves (1) the identification of biologically significant stimulus–response relationships and (2) determination of those aspects of the stimulus that are minimally necessary to evoke the response. These first two steps are similar to those applied by Haskins Laboratories in the isolation of the acoustic cues for human speech sounds. The final step is (3) the application of similar testing procedures to responses of both the peripheral and central nervous systems (see Brown 1975).

Feature detectors may be tuned for the rapid identification of predators' sound emissions. Thus, the moth's auditory system contains neurons that fire only when stimulated in the 17–100 kHz range, which matches the ultrasonic sonar pulses utilized by bats to detect prey. Feature detectors may also be matched to species-specific auditory or visual signals. Thus, for example, Wollberg & Newman (1972) have recently demonstrated that the auditory cortex of the squirrel monkey may be crucially involved in the analysis of species-typical vocalizations.

There is now a considerable body of evidence that such feature detectors may exist in human infants and adults for various parameters of speech sounds. These detectors appear to be in part pretuned to process sounds in a linguistic manner (see Eimas 1984 for a review of these studies). It is now evident that these detectors are amenable to modification in humans. This 'tuning process' has also been observed in the vocal learning of birds (Nottebohm 1975).

Not only nonhuman primates, but also animals as distinct from man as chinchillas can discriminate human speech sounds reliably. Dewson & Cowey (1969) taught monkeys (*Macaca*) to discriminate two human vowel sounds, [i] and [u], even in the presence of masking noise. They found that discrimination is retained even when stimuli are presented by different speakers. Such *perceptual constancy* has also been observed in chinchillas and dogs (Burdick & Miller 1975; Baru 1975).

Sinnott (1974) and Sinnott, Moody and Stebbins (1974) have shown that Old World monkeys (*Macaca* and *Cercopithecus*) can learn to discriminate between CV syllables, [ba] and [da], whether spoken or synthesized. However, when several synthetic speech sounds were equally spaced along a continuum between these two syllables and presented for discrimination, the monkeys failed to demonstrate categorical perception.

Morse and Snowdon (1975) found a somewhat similar effect. Using heart rate as a measure, they presented stimuli from the place of articulation continuum [bae – dae – gae] to eight rhesus monkeys. Each subject received a between-category, a within-category and a no-shift stimulus in counter-balanced order. Their results indicated that monkeys are better able to discriminate between two stimuli that fall in separate human perceptual categories than between acoustically different stimuli within such a category. Still, the within-category condition differed reliably from the control (no-shift) condition.

Pisoni (1971) has demonstrated that under certain conditions requiring minimal memory load, e.g. an AX versus ABX paradigm, human subjects can make within-category discriminations. This finding has led to the hypothesis that humans possess both an auditory and phonetic short-term memory. Speech sounds are briefly stored in auditory memory before being passed on to phonetic memory upon processing. Morse (1976) tentatively suggests that rhesus monkeys' within-category discrimination may mean they lack a phonetic short-term memory.

Using an avoidance task, Waters and Wilson (1976) obtained a result very similar to Morse and Snowden's on the voice-onset time continuum. Kuhl and Padden (1982, 1983) have also recently demonstrated enhanced discriminability at phonetic boundaries for voicing and place features in macaques.

In discussing their most recent results, Kuhl and Padden (1983) summarize the above data in terms of three possible theoretical stances on the question of the potential role of auditory constraints on the evolution of speech. These are:

> (1) audition did not provide a strong selective pressure, independent of articulation, on the choice of a phonetic inventory, (2) audition provided an independent pressure, but one that served to *initially structure* rather than *solely determine* the selection of the inventory and (3) audition *per se* directed the selection of the inventory by providing a set of 'natural classes' for auditory stimuli that the articulatory mechanism evolved to achieve (italics in original). (Kuhl & Padden 1983: 1009)

Kuhl and Padden feel the first view is least plausible in light of the above evidence, that the second is consistent with this evidence, and that the third should not be ruled out.

11.4. Central control and processing systems (the central nervous system)

> All brains of primates seem to be models of each other. In fact, no new structure *per se* is found in man's brain that is not found in the brain of other primates. (Noback & Moskowitz 1963: 133)

It will be recalled that in order to establish behavioral homologies, we require similarities in behavior in closely related species that can be related to structures showing a high degree of concordance. We have now reviewed many behaviors felt to be relevant to the evolution of human communication, as well as the peripheral structures that subserve some of these behaviors. As noted in the quotation at the beginning of this section, the brain, which is responsible for central control and processing, is a highly conservative organ. As one example, it is well known that the middle ear ossicles in mammals are derived from the jaw bones of earlier vertebrates. Nevertheless, the muscles attached to two of these ossicles, the stapedius and tensor tympani, are still innervated by the same cranial nerves, viz. the facial (vii) and trigeminal (v) respectively (Hildebrand 1982).

Because of its conservative nature, the reader who has followed the discussion thus far is in a good position to predict, in general terms, aspects of hominoid brain evolution relevant to the evolution of human communicative behavior. Our brief review of general complex behaviors in the great apes reveals what is probably a quantitative rather than qualitative difference between them and the hominids in general cognitive abilities (T_1). This is manifest, *inter alia*, in the great apes' humanlike lexical abilities. There is also considerable overlap between man's affective (paralinguistic) communication system and nonhuman primate communicative behavior in the wild. As regards coding (T_2), there is, as we have seen, considerable debate as to whether this transduction is present in some primitive form or lacking altogether. Neither syntax nor phonotactics has been convincingly demonstrated. When we turn to transmission (T_3) we find, on the output side, phonation, which is innate and largely nonvolitional, coupled with volitional manual control capable of signaling concepts. There is no evidence of articulatory capacity. On the input side, there is some evidence of preadaptation for the processing of speech sounds.

What might the above data lead us to expect in terms of brain evolution in primates? Two trends appear likely: (1) an increase in the size of extant neural structures concerned with higher mental functions (T_1) and (2) an elaboration of structures in terms of cytoarchitecture and connectivity to accommodate a nonaffective, volitional auditory–vocal–input–output modality (T_3) and more complex coding of concepts (T_2). Note that, following the principle of conservation, neither of these trends envisions the creation of new neural structures; both, however, will lead to an increase in relative brain size. This trend will probably be heightened by the need for additional storage and information-processing capacity entailed by an ever more efficient communication system.

Comparative studies of the primate brain generally involve two basic procedures: (1) *descriptive* or *anatomical* and (2) *experimental* or *physiological*. In seeking to determine whether the trends predicted above are in fact in evidence, I shall survey the results of each of these two types of investigation.

11.4.1. Descriptive procedures

Many animals have a much larger brain size than humans. An adult male beaked whale (*Ziphius cavirostris*), for example, may have a brain weight of 2940 grams – more than twice that of modern man. What is required is not an absolute measure of brain weight but a relative one. Brain weight and body weight are correlated, although this correlation decreases with increasing body size, probably due to changes in the genetic control of brain and body weight during development (Riska & Atchley 1985). Because of this fact, when we measure the relation of brain weight to body weight in a large number of animals, small-sized mammals, such as the squirrel monkey, outrank man. Thus, in addition, it appears that a reference point is needed with which to compare brain weights for a given species.

Following the maxim that the most revealing comparisons are those among closely related species, I prefer Passingham's use of the great apes as a reference point (see Figure 8). When this is done, we see that all fossil hominids greatly exceed the expected values for great apes of equal body weights (see Passingham & Ettlinger 1974). Note that it is not true, as claimed by Lenneberg (1967), that nanocephalic dwarfs capable of some speech and language ability are within the geat ape range (cf. Figure 8, Point D). Perhaps

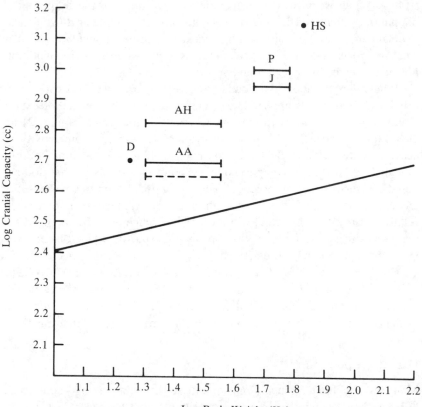

Figure 8. Regression line for cranial capacity on body weight for the pongids. Log cranial capacity=2.17+0.24×log body weight (kg). Data for pongids from A. H. Schultz (personal communication). D=Dwarf, AA=*Australopithecus africanus*, AH=*Australopithecus habilis*, J=*Homo erectus erectus* (Java), P=*Homo erectus pekinensis* (Peking), HS=*Homo sapiens sapiens*. Continuous line for AA is for cranial capacity as estimated by Tobias (1971), and dotted line is for cranial capacity as estimated by Holloway (1972). (Dingwall 1979)

such cases can be regarded as providing some evidence, however meager, for the degree of encephalization minimally necessary to subserve speech.

Speech represents the ultimate in the tendency towards elaboration of neural structures controling fine motor movements and their coordination which Tilney & Riley (1928) termed *neokinesis*. Darley (1975) has calculated that at least 140,000 neuromuscular events per second are required for speech production. Passingham (1982) notes that some areas of the primate brain have expanded more than others. The cerebellum and the neocortex have shown the greatest development in the human brain. In the latter structure, *agranular cortex* (motor and premotor cortex) has shown greater development than *koniocortex* (sensory cortex). In addition to these motor structures, there has been even greater increase in *eulaminate cortex* which includes the association areas that are known to play an important role in speech and language (Brodmann areas: 44, 45, 22, 37, 39, and 40). All of the above increases are based on indices showing how many times larger is each area of a human's brain compared with the values for a nonhuman primate of the same body weight. It should be noted, however, that these increases are those that would be expected in the primate with the same brain size as ours (see Hahn, Jensen & Dubck 1979 for a recent review of the evolution of brain size).

Using counts of cells in thalamic nuclei of a range of nonhuman primates including anthropoid apes, Armstrong (1982) delimits three sets of nuclei which she classifies as conservative, allometrically expected and divergent. The latter set, which contains many more nerve cells in humans than in nonhuman primates, is made up of the *anterior principal* and *lateral dorsal*; both nuclei are intimately related to the limbic system (see also Crosson 1984).

In keeping with the conservative nature of the primate brain, it should come as no surprise that all of the neocortical areas associated with speech and language functions have been identified in terms of cytoarchitecture in nonhuman primates. At one time, Geschwind (1965) isolated the *angular gyrus* (39) as being crucial for language function because of its putative role in cross-modal transfer. He presumed that direct transfer of learning from one modality to another without limbic mediation was unique to man. When such transfer was demonstrated in apes, he was forced to revise his views (Geschwind 1970). In fact, this area exists in terms of cytoarchitecture in nonhuman primates (Passingham 1973) and also evinces the same polymodal connectivity as in humans (Pandya & Kuypers 1969).

After Broca proposed that the third frontal convolution (F_3) was the seat of articulate speech in the human brain, several investigators sought to convince him that F_3 was lacking in nonhuman primates. Broca steadfastly refused to accept this conclusion even while remarking that if it were correct it

William Orr Dingwall

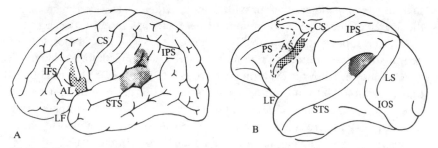

Figure 9. Diagram of the cerebral convexity in man (A) and monkey (B) to show the topographic distribution of areas Tpt (crosshatched) and 44 (closed circles). Note the extension of Tpt to the parietal lobe in man. Also note the shift of area 44 toward the frontal operculum from monkey to man. The similar relationship of 44 to an anterior sulcus in both species suggests homology for the ascending limb of the Sylvian fissure in man (AL) and the inferior limb of the arcuate sulcus in the monkey (AS). Other abbreviations: CS, central sulcus; IFS, inferior frontal sulcus; IOS, inferior occipital sulcus; IPS, intraparietal sulcus; LF, lateral (Sylvian) fissure; LS, lunate sulcus; PS, principal sulcus; STS, superior temporal sulcus. (Galaburda & Pandya 1982)

would please him very much (see Dingwall 1980b: 22–4). It turns out that as usual Broca was correct, as Galaburda & Pandya (1982) have recently identified an area homologous in cytoarchitecture to *Broca's area* (44, 45) in rhesus monkeys. In addition, they have also identified the homolog of *Wernicke's area* (Tpt: a portion of Brodmann area 22) in the same species (cf. Figure 9). There are some slight differences in cytoarchitecture as well as more striking differences in relative size and areal topography.

The neurologist Jerzy Konorski (1967) claimed that the *arcuate fasciculus*, the bundle of fibers connecting Broca's and Wernicke's areas, was not present in the chimpanzee brain, and that this accounted for the lack of vocal learning in this species (and other nonhuman primates). Employing auto-radiographic tract-tracing techniques, however, Galaburda & Pandya (1982) were able to confirm this tract's existence in the rhesus monkey. As Figure 10 shows, the course of the tract under the insula differs from the opercular course in humans, but it exists nonetheless.

Finally, since Geschwind & Levitsky's (1968) demonstration of a marked asymmetry in the *planum temporale* (cytoarchitecturally part of Wernicke's area) of humans, favoring the left hemisphere, there has been a resurgence of interest in hemispheric asymmetries (see Geschwind & Galaburda 1985: 435–6 for an exhaustive listing of these in the human brain). These asymmetries are also manifest in the brains of some species of nonhuman primates. Wada *et al.* (1975) studied the brains of 20 rhesus monkeys and 11 baboons and failed to find an asymmetry. Asymmetries comparable to those in the human brain do appear to exist, however, in the great apes. Yeni-Komshian & Benson (1976) measured the length of the Sylvian fissure in rhesus,

302

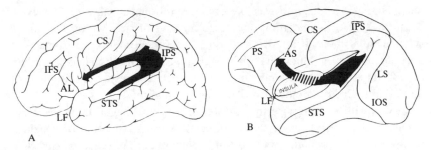

Figure 10. Diagram of the cerebral convexity in man (A) and monkey (B) to show the origin, course, and termination of the fiber pathway connecting areas Tpt and 44. In man this pathway forms a portion of the arcuate sulcus, which is only partially shown in the diagram to show primarily the superior temporal gyrus origins. The pathway becomes a compact bundle only in the operculum (see text) and terminates in the subcentral and opercularis portions of the frontal operculum (arrow). In the rhesus monkey radioactively labeled tracer in area Tpt results in labeled fibers and terminations along the course of the arrow shown, passing beneath the insula (interrupted) and terminating in the caudal bank of the inferior limb of the arcuate sulcus corresponding to area 44. For abbreviations see Figure 9 legend. (Galaburda & Pandya 1982)

chimpanzee and human brains (N=25 for each species). They found no significant asymmetries in monkeys but did in chimpanzees and humans. If the so-called *principle of proper mass* (see Jerison 1973) can be said to apply, then these asymmetries in the great apes may indicate a preadaptation, possibly in the auditory realm, towards the type of processing that characterizes human speech. Recently, Scheibel *et al.* (1985) have demonstrated significant differences in the dendritic patterns of neurons in Broca's area on the left and its homolog on the right in humans. It is not known as yet if such a difference is present in nonhuman species (see Glick 1985 for a recent review of cerebral lateralization in nonhuman species; also Dunaif-Hattis 1984).

11.4.2. Experimental procedures

The experimental literature on the primate brain, even if one confines oneself to its comparative aspects, is vast and its review is beyond the scope of this chapter. (See Dingwall 1981 for bibliography; for reviews see Harnad, Steklis & Lancaster 1976; Steklis & Raleigh 1979; Oakley & Plotkin 1979; Passingham 1982; Macphail 1982; Oakley 1985.)

In my opinion, the most significant advances in this area relevant to the topic of this chapter, have been made by the members of the Max Planck Institute for Psychiatry in Munich. Prior to the research of this group, the common wisdom in physical anthropology, and neuroscience in general, was that nonhuman primate vocalization was under the direct control of the limbic system (Campbell 1976; Robinson 1976). This made sense, since it was felt that such vocalization was essentially emotional in nature. However, because electrical stimulation of a large number of sites within the limbic system results in vocalization as well as various other emotional responses, it does not necessarily follow that this system is *directly involved* in call production. Chimps like to be tickled, and they laugh in response, but this does not mean that their ribs are the control center for laughter.

It was with this premise that the Munich Group began their research. Jürgens (1976, 1979), using self-induced electrical stimulation of vocalization-producing sites in the brains of squirrel monkeys (*Saimiri sciureus*), was able to determine which sites were highly correlated with motivational changes (either positive or negative) and which were neutral in this regard. He assumed that it was the latter group that represents *primary vocalization areas*. These sites and their interconnections are displayed in Figure 11.

The most caudal vocalization area (iv) consists of the *nucleus ambiguus*, the nucleus in the medulla that contains the motor neurons for cranial nerves (ix, x, xi) which are involved in phonation as well as pharyngeal constriction and nasalization in humans. In addition, for control of articulation, one must consider cranial nerve nuclei v (jaw movement) and vii (lip movement) at the level of the pons and xii (tongue movement) at the level of the medulla. Damage to these areas produce various forms of flaccid dysarthria in humans; in the monkey, damage to the n. ambiguus results in disturbances or elimination of phonation.

The next level (iii) in the vocalization circuit consists of the caudal *periaqueductal gray* and adjacent tegmentum in the midbrain. This area constitutes the most archaic vocalization center in the vertebrate brain. Electrical stimulation of this area in animals ranging from amphibians to higher primates produces species-typical calls. Jürgens & Pratt (1979) have demonstrated direct connections between this area and the n. ambiguus. Damage to this area in humans produces absolute mutism with retained ability to communicate via gesture (Botex & Barbeau 1971; Larson 1985).

At the next level (ii) two separate structures are apparently involved: *anterior cingular cortex* and the *supplementary motor area*. The Munich Group has demonstrated that the former area is necessary for the volitional initiation of *conditioned* vocalization, but not for the production of innate calls. This area is directly connected with the periaqueductal gray, and it receives direct projections from the cortical larynx area. Bilateral damage to this area in humans results in akinetic mutism. The recovery pattern from this state is of interest in that speech returns before phonation (*aphonic whispering*) (Brown & Perecman 1985). This may be the case because the lateral cortical areas responsible for articulation in humans are spared. On the other hand, if the lateral cortical areas alone are involved, producing apraxia of speech, phonation returns before speech (Itoh & Sasanawa 1984).

The evolution of human communicative behavior

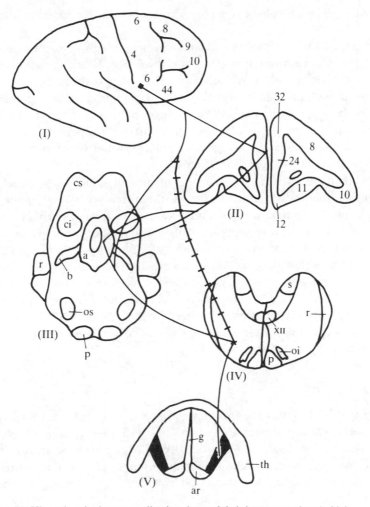

Figure 11. Hierarchy of primary vocalization sites and their interconnections in higher primates. I. cortical larynx area, II. anterior cingular cortex, III. periaqueductal gray, IV. nucleus ambiguus, V. vocal folds. (Ploog & Jürgens 1980)

Only the anterior portion of the supplementary motor area is involved in phonation in the squirrel monkey. The entire area is involved in speech. Penfield & Roberts (1959) produced prolonged vowel vocalizations through electrical stimulation of this area. Damage to this area produces akinetic mutism in humans which gradually resolves into transcortical motor aphasia (Brown & Perecman 1985). Because this area shows an increase in cerebral blood flow not only before voluntary movements of the vocal tract and limbs but even during imagination of such movements, it may be involved in

305

planning complex volitional motor sequences (see Kirzinger & Jürgens 1982).

It appears that control of nonhuman primate vocalization terminates at level II and does not, as is true in humans, involve the lateral surface of either the left or right neocortex. Ablations of the homologs of the language areas in monkeys, both unilaterally and bilaterally, fail to produce any appreciable effects on vocalization (Myers 1976; Kirzinger & Jürgens 1982). It is interesting to note that there is no direct projection from the cortical larynx area to the motoneurons of the n. ambiguus in monkeys, while there is in man. Once again we have an example of *neokinesis*.

While there is thus no evidence that the homologs of human speech and language areas on the lateral surface of the neocortex play a role in non-human primate *production* communication, there is considerable evidence for their role in *receptive* behavior. Ablation of auditory cortex in monkeys results in loss of ability to discriminate learned auditory patterns and human speech sounds (Dewson *et al.* 1969; Hupfer, Jürgens & Ploog 1977). There is even some evidence, based on a monaural discrimination task producing a REA and recent lesion studies, of cerebral lateralization in the processing of species-specific calls (Petersen 1978; Heffner & Heffner 1984). See also Morse 1987 for electrophysiological evidence for categorical perception in rhesus monkeys paralleling that in humans.

11.4.3. Summary

In sum, it is clear that the two trends we predicted for brain evolution in primates relative to the control and processing of communication are borne out. Human communicative behavior, like other complex behaviors, is the culmination of mosaic evolution within the primate order. There is no reason to postulate the *de novo* creation of this behavior in its entirety within the hominid line.

REFERENCES

Abbs, J. H. & Sussman, H. M. 1971. Neurophysiological feature detectors and speech perception: a discussion of theoretical implications. *Journal of Speech and Hearing Research* 14: 23–36.
Armstrong, E. 1982. Mosaic evolution in the primate brain: differences and similarities in the hominoid thalamus. In E. Armstrong & D. Falk (eds.) *Primate brain evolution*. New York: Plenum Press.
Baru, A. V. 1975. Discrimination of synthesized vowels [a] and [i] with varying parameters in dog. In G. Fant & M. Tatham (eds.) *Auditory analysis and perception of speech*. New York: Academic Press.
Bastian, J. 1965. Primate signaling systems and human languages. In I. Devore (ed.) *Primate behavior: field studies of monkeys and apes*. New York: Holt, Rinehart & Winston.

Botez, M. I. & Barbeau, A. 1971. Role of subcortical structures, and particularly the thalamus, in the mechanisms of speech and language. *International Journal of Neurology* 8: 300–20.

Bourne, G. & Cohen, M. 1975. *The gentle giants: the gorilla story*. New York: Putnam's Sons.

Brown, J. L. 1975. *The evolution of behavior*. New York: Norton.

Brown, J. W. & Perecman, E. 1985. Neurological basis of language processing. In J. K. Darby (ed.) *Speech and language evaluation in neurology: adult disorders*. Orlando: Grune & Stratton.

Burdick, C. & Miller, J. Speech perception by the chinchilla: discrimination of sustained /a/ and /i/. *Journal of the Acoustical Society of America* 58: 415–27.

Calvin, W. H. 1983. *The throwing madonna*. New York: McGraw-Hill.

Campbell, B. G. 1976. The physical basis of language use in primates. In M. J. Leaf (ed.) *Frontiers in anthropology*. New York: Van Nostrand.

Campbell, C. B. G. & Hodos, W. 1970. The concept of homology and the evolution of the nervous system. *Brain, Behavior and Evolution* 3: 353–67.

Chomsky, N. 1968. *Language and mind*. New York: Harcourt, Brace & World.

Chomsky, N. 1979. Human language and other semiotic systems. *Semiotica* 25: 31–44.

Chomsky, N. 1980. Rules and representations. *The Behavioral and Brain Sciences* 3: 1–61.

Crosson, B. 1984. Role of the dominant thalamus in language: a review. *Psychological Bulletin* 96: 491–517.

Darley, F. L., Aronson, A. E. & Brown, J. R. 1975. *Motor speech disorders*. Philadelphia: Saunders.

Darwin, C. 1859. *The origin of species*. New York: Atheneum.

Darwin, C. 1872. *The expression of the emotions in man and animals*. Chicago: University of Chicago Press.

Dewson, J. & Cowey, A. 1969. Discrimination of auditory sequences by monkeys. *Nature* 222: 695–7.

Dingwall, W. O. 1975. The species-specificity of speech. In D. Dato (ed.) *Developmental psycholinguistics: theory and applications*. Washington: Georgetown University Press.

Dingwall, W. O. 1977. Review: *On the origins of language* (Lieberman). *Lingua* 43: 280–92.

Dingwall, W. O. 1978. Human communicative behavior: a biological model. *Die Neueren Sprachen* 3/4: 269–99.

Dingwall, W. O. 1979a. The evolution of human communication systems. In H. Whitaker & H. A. Whitaker (eds.) *Studies in neurolinguistics*. New York: Academic Press.

Dingwall, W. O. 1979b. Reconstruction of the Parker/Gibson 'model'. *The Behavioral and Brain Sciences* 2: 383–4.

Dingwall, W. O. 1980a. Human communicative behavior: a biological model. In I. Rauch & G. F. Carr (eds.) *The signifying animal*. Bloomington: Indiana University Press.

Dingwall, W. O. 1980b. Broca's contributions to physical anthropology relating to the brain and its functions. *Working Papers in Biocommunication* 1: 1–28.

Dingwall, W. O. 1981. *Language and the brain: a bibliography and guide*. New York: Garland.

Drachman, G. 1969. Adaptation in the speech tract. In R. Binnick (ed.) *Papers from the 5th regional meeting of the Chicago Linguistic Society*, 314–29. Chicago: University of Chicago Press.

Du Brul, L. 1977. Origins of the speech apparatus. *Brain and Language* 4: 365–81.

Du Brul, L. 1979. Poor old Neanderthal Man. *Brain and Language* 8: 251–7.

Dunaif-Hattis, J. 1984. *Doubling the brain: on the evolution of brain lateralization and its implications for language*. New York: Lang.

Eimas, P. 1984. Infant competence and the acquisition of language. In D. Caplan, A. Lecours & A. Smith (eds.) *Biological perspectives on language*. Cambridge, MA: MIT Press.

Eldredge, N. & Gould, S. J. 1972. Punctuated equilibria: an alternative to phyletic gradualism. In T. Schopf (ed.) *Models of paleobiology*. San Francisco: Freeman, Cooper & Co.

Eldredge, N. & Tattersal, I. 1982. *The myths of human evolution*. New York: Columbia University Press.

Falk, D. 1975. Comparative anatomy of the larynx in man and the chimpanzee: implications for language in Neanderthal. *American Journal of Physical Anthropology* 43: 123–32.

Fink, B. R. 1975. *The human larynx: a functional study*. New York: Raven.

Finkelnberg, F. 1870. Aphasia as asymbolia (Trans. by R. Duffy & B. Liles). *Journal of Speech and Hearing Disorders* 44: 156–68.

Fodor, J. A. 1983. *The modularity of mind*. Cambridge, MA: MIT Press.
Fodor, J. A., Bever, T. G. & Garrett, M. F. 1974. *The psychology of language*. New York: McGraw-Hill.
Fouts, R. S. 1972. Use of guidance in teaching sign language to a chimpanzee. *Journal of Comparative and Physiological Psychology* 80: 515–22.
Fouts, R. S. 1973. Acquisition and testing of gestural signs in four young chimpanzees. *Science* 180: 978–80.
Fouts, R. S. 1974a. Language: origins, definitions and chimpanzees. *Journal of Human Evolution* 3: 475–82.
Fouts, R. S. 1974b. Talking with chimpanzees. *Science Year*: 34–49. Chicago: Field Enterprises.
Fouts R. S. 1975a. Communication with chimpanzees. In I. Eibl-Eibesfeldt & G. Kurth (eds.) *Hominisation und Verhalten*. Stuttgart: Gustav Fischer-Verlag.
Fouts, R. S. 1975b. Capacities for language in Great Apes. In R. H. Tuttle (ed.) *Socioecology and psychology of primates*. The Hague: Mouton.
Fouts, R. S. 1976. Discussion paper: comparison of sign language projects and implications for language origins. *Annals of the New York Academy of Sciences* 280: 589–91.
Fouts, R. S. 1983. Chimpanzee language and elephant tails: a theoretical synthesis. In J. de Luce & H. T. Wilder (eds.) *Language in primates*. New York: Springer-Verlag.
Fouts, R. S., Fouts, D. H. & Schoenfeld, D. 1984. Sign language conversational interaction between chimpanzees. *Sign Language Studies* 42: 1–12.
Galaburda, A. M. & Pandya, D. N. 1982. Role of architectonics and connections in the study of primate brain evolution. In. E. Armstrong & D. Falk (eds.) *Primate brain evolution: methods and concepts*. New York: Plenum.
Galdikas-Brindamour, B. 1975. Orangutans, Indonesia's 'People of the forest'. *National Geographic* 148: 444–73.
Gardner, B. & Gardner, R. 1971. Two-way communication with an infant chimpanzee. In A. Schrier & F. Stollnitz (eds.) *Behavior of nonhuman primates*. New York: Academic Press.
Gardner, B. & Gardner R. 1974a. Comparing the early utterances of child and chimpanzee. In A. Pick (ed.) *Minnesota symposium on child psychology*, Vol. 8. Minneapolis: University of Minnesota Press.
Gardner, B. & Gardner, R. 1974b. Teaching sign language to a chimpanzee, vii: Use of order in sign combinations. *Bulletin of the Psychonomic Society* 4: 264.
Gardner, B. & Gardner, R. 1975b. Evidence for sentence constituents in the early utterances of child and chimpanzee. *Journal of Experimental Psychology* 104: 244–67.
Gardner, B. & Gardner, R. 1985. Signs of intelligence in cross-fostered chimpanzees. *Philosophical Transaction of the Royal Society London* B308: 159–76.
Gardner, R. & Gardner, B. 1969. Teaching sign language to a chimpanzee. *Science* 165: 664–72.
Gardner, R. & Gardner, B. 1975a. Early signs of language in child and chimpanzee. *Science* 187: 752–3.
Gardner, R. & Gardner, B. 1984. A vocabulary test for chimpanzees (*Pan troglodytes*). *Journal of Comparative Psychology* 96: 381–404.
Gautier, J. P. 1971. Etude morphologique et fonctionnelle des annexes extralaryngées des Cercopithecinae; liaison avec les cris d'espacement. *Biologia Gabonica* 7: 229–67.
Gay, T. 1974. A cinefluorographic study of vowel production. *Journal of Phonetics* 2: 255–66.
George, S. L. 1978. The relationship between cranial base angle morphology and infant vocalization. Doctoral dissertation, University of Connecticut.
Geschwind, N. 1965. The problem of language in relation to the phylogenetic development of the brain. *Sistema Nervosa* 17: 411–19.
Geschwind, N. 1970. Intermodal equivalence of stimuli in apes. *Science* 168: 1249.
Geschwind, N. & Galaburda, A. M. 1985. Cerebral lateralization. *Archives of Neurology* 42: 428–654.
Geschwind, N. & Levitsky, W. 1968. Human brain: left–right asymmetries in temporal speech region. *Science* 161: 186–7.
Glick, S. D. (ed.) 1985. *Cerebral lateralization in nonhuman species*. New York: Academic Press.
Goldstein, K. 1948. *Language and language disturbances*. New York: Grune & Stratton.
Goodall, J. 1986. *The chimpanzees of Gombe: patterns of behavior*. Cambridge, MA: Belknap Press.

Goodman, M., Tashian, R. E. & Tashian, J. H. (eds.). 1976. *Molecular anthropology: genes and proteins in the evolutionary ascent of the primates*. New York: Plenum.

Gould, S. J. 1977. *Ontogeny and phylogeny*. Cambridge, MA: Harvard University Press.

Gould, S. J. 1985. A clock of evolution. *Natural History* 4: 12–25.

Greenfield, P. M. & Savage-Rumbaugh, E. S. 1984. Perceived variability and symbol use: a common language-cognition interface in children and chimpanzees (*Pan troglodytes*). *Journal of Comparative Psychology* 2: 201–18.

Grolier, E. de 1983. *Glossogenetics: the origin and evolution of language*. New York: Harvard Academic Press.

Hahn, M. E., Jensen, C. & Dubek, B. C. (eds.) 1979. *Development and evolution of brain size*. New York: Academic Press.

Harnad, S., Steklis, H. & Lancaster, J. (eds.) 1976. Origins and evolution of language and speech. *Annals of the New York Academy of Sciences* 280.

Hayes, K. & Hayes, C. 1951. The intellectual development of a home-raised chimpanzee. *Proceedings of the American Philosophical Society* 95: 105–9.

Heffner, H. E. & Heffner, R. S. 1984. Temporal lobe lesions and perception of species-specific vocalizations in macaques. *Science* 226: 75–6.

Hewes, G. W 1976. The current status of the gestural theory of language origin. *Annals of the New York Academy of Sciences* 280: 482–504.

Hildebrand, M. 1982. *Analysis of vertebrate structure*. New York: Wiley.

Hockett, C. F. 1978. In search of Jove's Brow. *American Speech* 53: 243–313.

Hodos, W. 1976. The concept of homology and the evolution of behavior. In R. B. Masterton, W. Hodos & H. Jerison (eds.) *Evolution, brain and behavior: persistent problems*. New York: Wiley.

Holloway, R. L. 1972. Australopithecine endocasts, brain evolution in the hominoidea, and a model of hominid evolution. In R. Tuttle (ed.) *The functional and evolutionary biology of primates*. Chicago: Aldine.

House, E., Pansky, B., Jacobs, M. & Wagner, B. 1964. The ear of the chimpanzee. *Technical Report 64–1*, Air Force Research Laboratories. New Mexico: Holloman Air Force Base.

Hupfer, K., Jürgens, U. & Ploog, D. 1977. The effect of superior temporal lesions on the recognition of species-specific calls in the squirrel monkey. *Experimental Brain Research* 30: 75–87.

Huxley, T. H. 1917. *Methods and results: essays*. New York: Appleton & Co.

Itoh, M. & Sasanawa, S. 1984. Articulation movements in apraxia of speech. In J. Rosenbeck, M. R. McNeil & A. E. Aronson (eds.) *Apraxia of speech*. San Diego: College-Hill Press.

Jerison, H. J. 1973. *Evolution of the brain and intelligence*. New York: Academic Press.

Johanson, D. C. & Edey, M. A. 1981. *Lucy: the beginnings of humankind*. New York: Simon & Schuster.

Jordan, J. 1971. Studies on the structure of the organ of voice and vocalization in chimpanzees. *Folia morphologica (Warsaw)* 30: 97–126; 222–48; 323–40.

Jürgens, U. 1976. Reinforcing concomitants of electrically elicited vocalizations. *Experimental Brain Research* 26: 203–14.

Jürgens, U. 1979. Neural control of vocalization in nonhuman primates. In H. Steklis & M. Raleigh (eds.) *Neurobiology of social communication in primates*. New York: Academic Press.

Jürgens, U. & Ploog, D. 1976. Zur Evolution der Stimme. *Archiv für Psychiatrie und Nervenkrankheiten* 222: 117–37.

Jürgens, U. & Pratt, R. 1979. Role of the periaqueductal grey in vocal expression of emotion. *Brain Research* 167: 367–78.

Kellogg, W. N. 1968. Communication and language in the home-raised chimpanzee. *Science* 162: 423–7.

King, M. & Wilson, A. 1975. Evolution at two levels in humans and chimpanzees. *Science* 188: 107–16.

Kirzinger, A. & Jürgens, U. 1982. Cortical lesion effects and vocalization in the squirrel monkey. *Brain Research* 233: 299–315.

Klatt, D. H. & Stefanski, R. A. 1974. How does a mynah bird imitate human speech? *Journal of the Acoustical Society of America* 55: 822–32.

Konorski, J. 1967. *Integrative activity of the brain*. Chicago: University of Chicago Press.

Kuhl, P. K. & Padden, D. M. 1982. Enhanced discriminability at the phonetic boundaries for the voicing feature in macaques. *Perception and Psychophysics* 32: 542–50.
Kuhl, P. K. & Padden, D. M. 1983. Enhanced discriminability at the phonetic boundaries for the place feature in macaques. *Journal of the Acoustical Society of America* 73: 1003–10.
Ladefoged, P. 1971. *Preliminaries to linguistic phonetics*. Chicago: University of Chicago Press.
Ladefoged, P. 1978. Review: *Speech physiology and acoustic phonetics* (Lieberman). *Language* 54: 920–2.
Laitman, J. T. 1983. The evolution of the hominid upper respiratory system and implications for the origin of speech. Grolier 1983.
Larson, C. 1985. The midbrain periaqueductal gray: a brainstem structure involved in vocalization. *Journal of Speech and Hearing Research* 28: 241–9.
Lawick-Goodall, J. 1971. *In the shadow of man*. Boston: Houghton Mifflin Co.
Lawick-Goodall, J. 1976. Continuities between chimpanzee and human behavior. In G. Isaac & E. McCown (eds.) *Human origins*. Menlo Park: Benjamin.
Lawick-Goodall, J. & Hamburg, D. 1974. Chimpanzee behavior as a model for the behavior of early man. In D. Hamburg & K. Brodie (eds.) *American handbook of psychiatry*, Vol. 6. New York: Basic Books.
Leakey, R. E. 1981. *The making of mankind*. New York: Dutton.
LeMay, M. 1975. The language capabilities of Neanderthal man. *American Journal of Physical Anthropology* 42: 9–14.
Lenneberg, E. H. 1967. *Biological foundations of language*. New York: Wiley.
Lieberman, P. 1975. *On the origins of language*. New York: Macmillan.
Lieberman, P. 1984. *The biology and evolution of language*. Cambridge, MA: Harvard University Press.
Lieberman, P., Crelin, E. S. & Klatt, D. H. 1972. Phonetic ability and related anatomy of the newborn and adult human, Neanderthal man, and the chimpanzee. *American Anthropologist* 74: 287–307.
Liepmann, H. 1908. *Drei Aufsätze aus dem Apraxiebebiet*. Berlin: S. Karger.
Locke, J. 1986. Review: *The Biology and education of language* (Lieberman). ASHA 28.9: 73–4.
de Luce, J. & Wilder, H. T. (eds.) 1983. *Language in primates*. New York: Springer-Verlag.
Macphail, E. M. 1982. *Brain and intelligence in vertebrate*. Oxford: Clarendon Press.
Masterton, B., Hefner, H. & Ravizza, R. 1968. The evolution of human hearing. *Journal of the Acoustic Society of America* 45: 966–85.
Mayr, E. 1974. Behavior programs and evolutionary strategies. *American Scientist* 62: 650–9.
Miles, H. L. 1978. Language acquisition in apes and children. In F. Peng (ed.) *Sign language and language acquisition in man and ape.*. Boulder: Westview Press.
Miles, H. L. 1983. Apes and language: the search for communicative competence. In J. de Luce & H. T. Wilder (eds.) *Language in primates*. New York: Springer-Verlag.
Morse, P. A. 1976. Speech perception in the human infant and rhesus monkey. *Annals of the New York Academy of Sciences* 280: 694–707.
Morse, P. A., Molfese, D., Laughlier, N., Linville, S. & Wetzel, F. 1987. Categorical perception for voicing contrasts in normal and lead-treated rhesus monkeys: electrophysiological indices. *Brain and Language* 30: 63–80.
Morse, P. A. & Snowden, C. 1975. An investigation of categorical speech discrimination by rhesus monkey. *Perception and Psychophysics* 17: 9–16.
Murphy, R. 1973. Genetic correlates of behavior. In G. Bermant (ed.) *Perspectives on animal behavior*. Glenview: Scott, Foresman.
Myers, R. 1972. Role of prefrontal and anterior temporal cortex in social behavior and affect in monkeys. *Acta Neurobiologiae Experimentalis* 32: 567–79.
Myers, R. 1976. Comparative neurology of vocalization and speech: proof of a dichotomy. *Annals of the New York Academy of Sciences* 280: 745–57.
Noback, C. & Moskowitz, N. 1962. Structural and functional correlates of 'encephalization' in the primate brain. *Annals of the New York Academy of Sciences* 102: 210–18.
Noback, C. R. & Moskowitz, N. 1983. The primate nervous system: functional and structural aspects in phylogeny. In J. Buettner-Janush (ed.) *Evolutionary and genetic biology of primates*, Vol. 1. New York: Academic Press.
Nottebohm, F. 1975. A zoologist's view of some language phenomena with particular emphasis

on vocal learning. In E. H. Lenneberg & E. Lenneberg (eds.) *Foundations of language development*. New York: Academic Press.

Nottebohm, F. 1984. Vocal learning and its possible relation to replaceable synapses and neurons. In D. Caplan, A. Lecours & A. Smith (eds.) *Biological perspectives on language*. Cambridge, MA: MIT Press.

Oakley, D. A. (ed.) 1985. *Brain and mind*. London: Methuen.

Oakley, D. A. & Plotkin, H. C. (eds.) 1979. *Brain, behavior and evolution*. London: Methuen.

Pandya, D. & Kuypers, H. 1969. Cortico-cortical connections in the rhesus monkey. *Brain Research* 13: 13–36.

Parisi, D. 1983. A three-stage model of language evolution: from pantomime to syntax. In de Grolier 1983.

Parker, S. T. & Gibson, K. R. 1979. A developmental model for the evolution of language and intelligence in early hominids. *The Behavioral and Brain Sciences* 2: 367–407.

Passingham, R. E. 1973. Anatomical differences between the neocortex of man and other primates. *Brain, Behavior and Evolution* 7: 337–59.

Passingham, R. E. 1982. *The human primate*. San Francisco: Freeman.

Passingham, R. E. & Ettlinger, G. 1974. A comparison of cortical functions in man and other primates. *International Review of Neurobiology* 16: 233–99.

Patterson, F. G. 1978. Linguistic capabilities of a lowland gorilla. In F. Peng (ed.) *Sign language acquisition in man and ape*. Boulder: Westview Press.

Patterson, F. G. & Linden, E. 1981. *The education of Koko*. New York: Holt, Rinehart & Winston.

Penfield, W. & Roberts, L. 1959. *Speech and brain-mechanisms*. Princeton: Princeton University Press.

Petersen, M. R. 1978. The perception of species-specific vocalizations by old world monkeys. Doctoral dissertation, University of Michigan.

Pisoni, D. B. 1971. On the nature of categorical perception of speech sounds. Doctoral dissertation, University of Michigan.

Ploog, D. & Jürgens, U. 1980. Vocal behavior of nonhuman primates and man. In S. A. Carson, E. Carson & J. A. Alexander (eds.) *Ethology of nonverbal communication in mental health*. New York: Pergamon.

Premack, A. 1976. *Why chimps can read*. New York: Harper & Row.

Premack, A. & Premack, D. 1972. Teaching language to an ape. *Scientific American* 227.4: 92–9.

Premack, D. 1970. The education of Sarah: a chimp learns the language. *Psychology Today* 4.4: 55–8.

Premack, D. 1971a. Language in chimpanzee? *Science* 172: 808–22.

Premack, D. 1971b. On the assessment of language competence in the chimpanzee. In A. Schier & F. Stollnitz (eds.) *Behavior of nonhuman primates*. New York: Academic Press.

Premack, D. 1976. *Intelligence in ape and man*. New York: Wiley.

Premack, D. & Premack, A. 1983. *The mind of an ape*. New York: W. W. Norton.

Premack, D. & Woodruff, G. 1978. Does the chimpanzee have a theory of mind? *The Behavioral and Brain Sciences* 1: 515–26; 616–29.

Rao, P. 1985. An investigation into the neuropsychological bases of gesture. Doctoral dissertation, University of Maryland.

Riska, B. & Atchley, W. 1985. Genetics of growth predicts patterns of brain-size evolution. *Science* 229: 668–71.

Robinson, B. W. 1976. Limbic influences on human speech. *New York Academy of Sciences* 280: 761–71.

Rumbaugh, D. (ed.) 1977. *Language learning by a chimpanzee: the Lana project*. New York: Academic Press.

Rumbaugh, D. 1985. Comparative psychology: patterns in adaptation. In A. M. Rogers & C. J. Scheirer (eds.) *The S. Stanley Hall lecture series*, Vol. 5. Washington: American Psychological Association.

Rumbaugh, D. & Gill, T. 1976. Language and the acquisition of language-type skills by a chimpanzee (*Pan*). *Annals of the New York Academy of Sciences* 270: 90–123.

Rumbaugh, D., Gill, T. & von Glasersfeld, E. 1973. Reading and sentence competition by a chimpanzee. *Science* 182: 731–33.

311

Rumbaugh, D. & Savage-Rumbaugh, S. 1978. Chimpanzee language research: status and potential. *Behavior Research Methods and Instrumentation* 10: 119–31.

Rumbaugh, D., von Glasersfeld, E., Warner, H., Pisani, P. & Gill, T. 1975. Lana (chimpanzee) learning language: a progress report. *Brain and Language* 1: 205–12.

Savage-Rumbaugh, S., Rumbaugh, D. & Boyson, S. 1978. Linguistically mediated tool use and exchange by chimpanzees (*Pan troglodytes*). *The Behavioral and Brain Sciences* 1: 539–54; 614–16.

Savage-Rumbaugh, S., Rumbaugh, D., Smith, S. & Lawson, J. 1980. Reference: the linguistic essential. *Science* 210: 922–5.

Savage-Rumbaugh, S., Sevcik, R., Rumbaugh, D. M. & Rubert, E. 1985. The capacity of animals to acquire language: do species differences have anything to say to us? *Philosophical Transactions of the Royal Society London* B308: 177–85.

Scheibel, A. B., Paul, L. A., Forsythe, A. B., Tomiyasu, U., Wechsler, A., Kao, A. & Slotnick, J. 1985. Dendritic organization of the anterior speech area. *Experimental Neurology* 87: 109–117.

Schovel, T. 1972. Does language ontogeny recapitulate language phylogeny? In H. G. Lunt (ed.) *Proceedings of the Ninth International Congress of Linguistics* The Hague: Mouton.

Sebeok, T. & Rosenthal, R. 1981. *The Clever Hans phenomenon: communication with horses, whales, apes, and people.* New York: The New York Academy of Sciences.

Shankweiler, D., Strange, W. & Verbrugge, R. 1975. Speech and the problem of perceptual constancy. Haskins Laboratories Research Reports SR–42/43: 117–45.

Sinnott, J. 1974. A comparison of speech sound discrimination in humans and monkeys. Doctoral dissertation, University of Michigan.

Sinnott, J., Moody, D. & Stebbins, W. 1974. A comparison of speech sound discrimination in man and monkey. *Journal of the Acoustical Society of America* 55: 462.

Skelly, M. 1979. *Amer-Ind gestural code based on universal American Indian hand talk.* New York: Elsevier.

Smith, T. S. 1973. Review: *The muscle spindle and neural control of the tongue* (Bowman). *Journal of Phonetics* 1: 171–9.

Snowdon, C. T., Brown, C. H. & Petersen, M. R. (eds.) 1982. *Primate communication.* Cambridge: Cambridge University Press.

Stam, J. 1976. *Inquiries into the origin of language: the fate of a question.* New York: Harper & Row.

Stanley, S. M. 1981. *The new evolutionary timetable.* New York: Basic Books.

Stebbins, W. 1970. Studies of hearing and hearing loss in the monkey. In E. Stebbins (ed.) *Animal psychophysics.* New York: Appleton-Century-Crofts.

Steklis, H. D. 1985. Primate communication, comparative neurology, and the origin of language re-examined. *Journal of Human Evolution* 14: 157–73.

Steklis, H. D. & Raleigh, M. J. (eds.) *Neurobiology of social communication in primates. An evolutionary perspective.* New York: Academic Press.

Stevens, K. N. 1972. The quantal nature of speech. In E. David & P. Denes (eds.) *Human communication.* New York: McGraw-Hill.

Sutton, D., Larson, C., Taylor, E. & Lindeman, R. 1973. Vocalization in rhesus monkeys: conditionability. *Brain Research* 52: 225–31.

Temerlin, M. K. 1975. *Lucy: growing up human, a chimpanzee daughter in a psychotherapist's family.* Palo Alto: Science and Behavior Books.

Terrace, H. 1979. *Nim: a chimpanzee who learned sign language.* New York: Knopf.

Terrace, H. 1984. 'Language' in apes. In R. Harre & V. Reynolds (eds.) *The meaning of primate signals.* Cambridge: Cambridge University Press.

Terrace, H., Petitto, L. & Bever, T. 1976. Project Nim: progress reports I and II. MS.

Tilney, F. & Riley, H. 1928. *The brain from ape to man.* New York: Hoeber.

Tobias, P. V. 1971. *The brain in hominid evolution.* New York: Columbia University Press.

Toulmin, S. 1971. Brain and language: a commentary. *Synthèse* 22: 369–95.

Varney, N. R. 1982. Pantomime recognition deficit in aphasia: implications for the concept of asymbolia. *Brain and Language* 15: 32–9.

Verbrugge, R., Strange, W. & Shankweiler, D. What in formation enables a listener to map a talker's vowel space? *Haskins Laboratories Research Reports* SR–37/38: 199–208.

Wada, J., Clark, R. & Hamm, A. 1975. Cerebral hemispheric asymmetry in humans. *Archives of Neurology* 32: 239–46.

Waters, R. S. & Wilson, W. A. 1976. Speech perception by rhesus monkeys: the voicing distinction in synthesized labial and velar stop consonants. *Perception and Psychophysics* 19: 285–9.

Wescott, R. (ed.) 1974. *Language origins*. Silver Spring: Linstok.

Whalen, R. E. 1971. The concept of instinct. In J. L. McGaugh (ed.) *Psychobiology*. New York: Academic Press.

Wilson, A. C. 1985. The molecular basis of evolution. *Scientific American* 253.4: 164–73.

Wilson, A. C. & Sarach, V. M. 1969. A molecular time scale for human evolution. *Proceedings of the National Academy of Sciences* 63: 1088–93.

Wilson, E. O. 1978. *On human nature*. Cambridge, MA: Harvard University Press.

Wind, J. 1983. Primate evolution and the emergence of speech. In Grolier 1983.

Wollberg, Z. & Newman, J. D. 1972. Auditory cortex of squirrel monkey: response patterns of single cells to species-specific vocalizations. *Science* 175: 212–14.

Wright, R. 1978. Imitative learning of a flaked stone technology – the case of an orangutan. In S. Washburn & E. McCown (eds.) *Human evolution: biosocial aspects*. Menlo Park: Benjamin/Cummings.

Yeni-Komshian, G. & Benson, D. 1975. Anatomical study of cerebral asymmetry in humans, chimpanzees and rhesus monkeys. *Science* 192: 287–9.

Yunis, J., Sawyer, J. & Durham, K. 1980. A striking resemblance of high-resolution G-banded chromosomes of man and chimpanzees. *Science* 208: 1145–8.

12 Linguistics and animal communication*

Richard A. Demers

12.0. Introduction

The linguist has reason to be interested in the communication system of other animals. Perhaps the most important reason is that since human language is the product of evolution, it is highly likely that some of the properties of human language have structural similarities (or even precursors) in the communication systems of other animals. By studying animal communication systems, we will therefore learn more about ourselves. Moreover, in studying these systems we may become aware of features that have not been fully appreciated in our own system of communication. Since we are 'inside' our own language, it is difficult to maintain a proper perspective on what may be the most salient properties of this system. The study of animal communication, then, in which we can be trained as outside observers, allows us to gain this perspective on our own system.

Once we have decided to look at animal communication, we must then decide on how to go about making comparisons among the various animal systems in order to facilitate their comparison with human language and communication. The problem is compounded by the fact that both human and animal communication systems are still the focus of ongoing research, and many features of the communication systems are still controversial. Nevertheless, the inquiry into human communication and animal communication has proceeded far enough so that fruitful comparisons are possible. I will begin with a brief, critical overview of some earlier systems which have been used for comparing human and nonhuman communication (section 12.1). In the next section (12.2) I provide a very brief summary of some of the central features of human language and communication. Next a brief description of some of the salient features of animal communication systems is given. The concluding section (12.3) summarizes the relationship

* I would like to thank Mark Lewis who made me aware of the vast amount of animal communication research that is being done at present. I would also like to thank Haywood Spangler for assistance in researching bee and other insect communication. I alone am responsible for errors in fact or analysis which appear in this chapter.

(similarities and differences) between human and other animal communication systems as they are currently understood.

It should be mentioned that this chapter will not deal with attempts to teach primates artificial communication systems. There is no uncontroversial evidence that these animals have acquired even a rudimentary syntax, although there is evidence that the experiments have advanced our understanding of the animals' cognitive abilities. The reader can refer to Premack & Premack (1983), de Luce & Wilder (1983), Terrace (1979), and Chapter 11 above for additional discussion and debate on these issues.

12.1. Earlier systems of comparison

There have been several systems proposed in the literature which have been influential in the comparison between human language and animal communication. Such systems have generally focussed on some set of features which are applicable to both human and animal systems. One type of comparative system which stresses the physical aspect of communication is the design feature framework of Hockett and Altmann (1968). Another important and widely adopted system of comparison is that of McNeil (1970). A third approach views communication from the perspective of the message model. These three comparative frameworks will be discussed in turn.

2.1.1. The design feature framework of Hockett and Altmann

Hockett and Altman propose the features listed below, all of which are found in (spoken) human language. Hockett and Altmann's strategy is to investigate the presence of these features in the communication systems of other animals in order to discover what is unique and what is common among all systems.

1. *Vocal–auditory channel.* The sender of the signal employs a vocal tract to produce a message, and the receiver employs an auditory system to process the signal.
2. *Broadcast transmission and directional reception.* A signal travels out in all directions from the sender because of the physical properties of the medium. The receiver, however, is usually able to locate the direction from which the signal has been sent.
3. *Rapid fading (transitoriness).* Because of the physical properties of the transmitting medium, the signal quickly disappears.
4. *Interchangeability.* Individuals can be both senders and receivers of messages.

5. *Total feedback*. Senders are able to monitor their own signals.
6. *Specialization*. The communication system is specialized to the extent that it does not serve any additional physiological function.
7. *Semanticity*. Linguistic signals function to correlate and organize the life of a community because there are associative ties between signal elements and features in the world; in short, some linguistic forms have denotations.
8. *Arbitrariness*. There is no necessary physical connection between the sign and its referent.
9. *Discreteness*. The signaling system can be sub-divided into repeatable units; for example, the sounds, words, and sentences of human language.
10. *Displacement*. The referent of the signal does not have to be immediately present in time or space.
11. *Openness* (productivity). The system allows novel messages to be sent.
12. *Traditional transmission*. The communication system is learned from those who have learned it earlier.
13. *Duality of patterning*. Every language has a patterning in terms of arbitrary but stable, meaningless signal elements, and also a patterning in terms of minimum meaningful arrangements of those elements.
14. *Prevarication*. Speakers can make utterances that are false or meaningless.
15. *Reflexiveness*. In a language, speakers can communicate about the very system in which they communicate (i.e. people can talk about language).
16. *Learnability*. A speaker of a language can learn any of a wide variety of human languages.

The result of comparing human language with other animal communication systems using the first thirteen design features, is shown in Table 1.

A critical weakness of the design feature system is that it does not separate out the central structural and abstract features of human language. Moreover, the design features are not defined carefully enough for someone to make meaningful comparisons. Two examples will make these criticisms clear. In Table 1, both the bee dance and human language are shown to have the feature of openness (or productivity). Bee dancing is productive in the sense that a scout bee is able to communicate the location of a potentially infinite number of food sources located in the vicinity of the hive. The openness of the bee dance is, however, a consequence of the properties of the continuum which allows lines and spaces to be divided *ad infinitum*. Human

Table 1. *Design feature characterization of some animal communication systems. Table 6 from* The acquisition of language: the study of developmental pragmatics *by David McNeill. Copyright © by David McNeill. Reprinted by permission of Harper & Row, Publishers, Inc.*

	A Bee dancing	B Western meadowlark song	C Gibbon calls	D Paralinguistic phenomena	E Language
1. Vocal–auditory channel	No	Yes	Yes	Yes	Yes
2. Broadcast transmission and directional reception	Yes	Yes	Yes	Yes	Yes
3. Rapid fading (transitoriness)	?	Yes	Yes repeated	Yes	Yes
4. Interchange-ability	Limited	?	Yes	Largely yes	Yes
5. Total feedback	?	Yes	Yes	Yes	Yes
6. Specialization	?	Yes	Yes	Yes?	Yes
7. Semanticity	Yes	In part	Yes	Yes?	Yes
8. Arbitrariness	No	If semantic yes	Yes	In part	Yes
9. Discreteness	No	?	Yes	Largely no	Yes
10. Displacement	Yes, always	?	No	In part	Yes, often
11. Productivity	Yes	?	No	Yes	Yes
12. Traditional transmission	Probably not	?	?	Yes	Yes
13. Duality of patterning	No	?	No	No	Yes

language, in contrast, is unlimited in the degree of openness that it allows in at least two ways. These two senses make human language different in quality from the openness property of the bee dance. First, the grammatical rules of human language permit a potentially infinite number of well-formed utterances. Second, given the ability of humans to create new words and to extend the meaning of words in new ways (lexical openness), human language achieves the property of *effability*, the characteristic of being *unbounded in scope*. Even if humans were limited in the number of sentence structures they could use, they would still have a system whose scope is potentially unlimited because of this second type of openness (lexical). The use of the term 'openness,' then, to describe the fact that both bee language and human language have an 'unlimited' number of messages, does not express the important different types of openness that the two systems possess.

The second criticism of the design features is that the term 'semantic' applying to both bee communication and human communication remains an unenlightening characteristic for comparison until a 'bee semantics' is developed. Not only have researchers of bee communication not been able to determine the meaningful properties of the bee communication system; they still are not even certain how the actual message is transmitted from the dancing bee to the potential recruits (Gould, Dyer & Towne 1985). Additional criticisms of the design feature framework are found in Akmajian, Demers and Harnish 1979.

12.1.2. McNeill's framework

McNeill's comparative system is based on two cross-classifying features: structural and functional. The two major structural features are called *grading* and *combining*. Grading systems are ones in which new messages are created by changing the signal along some uniform, physical dimension. The variation in the gravity-oriented tail-wagging dance of the European honeybee is a grading system. Gradual changes in the orientation of the straightline portion of this dance correspond to gradual changes in the direction that the recruited honeybee must fly with respect to the position of the sun to locate the 'intended' food source (von Frisch 1967). Combining systems are ones in which new messages are created by arranging elements from a set (or sets) in new ways. Human language is, of course, primarily a combining language.

McNeil identifies three meaning-related functional features, which are identified with the labels nominal, expressive, and predicative. Nominal systems function to pick out some object, event, or situation external to the sender: expressive systems reflect the internal state of the sender; predicative systems function to comment on either or both external events and internal states. A typical classification of communication systems using his system is given in Table 2. The weakness of this classification system is that its features are not 'fine' enough to differentiate the significant properties of the various animal communication systems, especially human language. McNeill himself notes, 'All communication systems include messages of both expressive and nominal types, and some systems are both grading and combining' (McNeill 1970: 38). McNeill's observation is correct, as it is impossible to find in animal

Table 2. *McNeill's classification of animal communication systems (McNeill 1970)*

	Grading	Combining
Nominal	bees	finches
	ants	cicadas
Expressive	wolves	
	gulls	
	monkeys	
	human paralanguage	
Predicative		grammatical speech

systems a vocalization that refers to an external object that does not also reflect an internal state. McNeill's distinction between grading and combining is, however, an important one, and I will have occasion to return to this feature below. In sum, McNeill's features do not represent the major distinguishing characteristics among the communication systems that he thinks they do.

12.1.3. The message model of communication

The message model characterizes a communication event, typically described in the following manner:

> A speaker has some message in mind that he or she wants to communicate to the hearer. The speaker then produces some expression E from the language that encodes the message as its meaning. Upon hearing the beginning of E, the hearer begins a decoding process that sequentially identifies the incoming sounds, syntactic categories, and meanings, and then composes these meanings in the form of the successfully decoded message. (Akmajian, Demers & Harnish 1984: 393)

This model does, in fact, appear to describe some of the communication acts which we find among animals. A description of each of the exchanges is given in Table 3. The examples in Table 3 are typical of the message model interpretations that one could make of animal communication events, and it would appear that analogous features would occur in human language. It is commonly assumed, in fact, that the message model does reflect the communication process in humans. I present here several inadequacies of the message model and introduce features of communication which will be used later in this chapter for comparing human communication with systems of animal communication.

Table 3. *The message model applied to different animal communication systems (Akmajian, Demers & Harnish 1984)*

Animal (sender)	Signal	Decoding	'Message' (in paraphrased English)	Subsequent behaviour of receiver
Vervet	Snake chutter	→	Warning: snake nearby	Surround snake ('mobbing')
	Aerial predator call	→	Warning: eagle overhead	Seek cover on ground
	Terrestrial predator call	→	Warning: leopard nearby	Climb trees, go to ends of branches
Bird	Aerial predator call ('seet')	→	Warning: predator overhead	Take cover in bushes and remain motionless
	Mobbing call ('chink')	→	Warning: stationary predator nearby	Surround predator ('mobbing')
	Terrestrial *song*	→	Warning: other males keep away	Other males keep out of territory of message sender
			Invitation: females come here	Uncommitted females are attracted to sender
Bee	Round dance	→	Instruction: seek food source within 10 meters of hive	Search randomly within designated area
	Sickle dance (Found in Italian honey bees)	→	Instruction: seek food source between 25 and 100 meters of hive	Fly in the direction of the bisector of the pattern of the dance (cf. Fig. 2.7)
	Tail-wagging dance	→	Instruction: seek food source of distance x, flying at y degrees with respect to the sun	Search for food at location indicated by the dance
Bottle-nosed dolphin	Distress whistle	→	Help!	Dolphins in the area come to distressed animal and raise it to the surface
Hump-backed whale	Song	→	?	?

As evidenced in the above quote, the message model carries with it certain assumptions, the most important among them being that the *message* of the utterance can be equated with the *meaning* of the utterance. I use the term *meaning* to refer to the narrowest semantic meaning of the utterance. The term *message* refers to additional communicative features of the utterance, some of which will be immediately explicated below. The point of discussing these additional communicative feature (pragmatic strategies) is to offer yet another perspective for the comparison between human language and animal communication.

The assumption of the identity between 'meaning' and 'message' breaks down in human language in several ways, as the following examples illustrate (Bach & Harnish 1979).

A. An utterance may have ambiguous meanings. When the hearer confronts the sentence *Norwegians eat more fish than Americans*, knowledge of the world guides the hearer to the correct interpretation. That is, the above sentence can be related to the longer sentence *Norwegians eat more fish than Americans do*, or even to another sentence *Norwegians eat more fish than they eat Americans*. Two (at least) very different meanings are available for interpreting the ambiguous sentence. The association of the correct (or most likely) meaning for any given sentence is context driven and this use of context occurs in parallel with the processing of all properties of the sentence. An adequate model of communication for human language, then, must include a component which can use context (knowledge of the world, previous sentences, and so forth) to arrive at the correct message.

B. Reference is not uniquely determined by the utterance. Hearers must constantly attend to problems of reference in processing utterances. Americans may associate the subject of the sentence *The great communicator will arrive soon* with the President of the United States. The expression, however, could also apply to many other people, such as a well-known news commentator (Walter Cronkite), so that additional context is needed to provide the listener with the basis for choosing which of the many possible referents is being referred to.

C. The communicative intent of the utterance must be recognized. The hearer must identify the intent of the speaker in order to assign the correct message to the utterance. The sentence 'I'll be there tonight' can be a threat, a promise, or a mere statement of fact. Unless the hearer correctly identifies the intent of the speaker, the intended message will not be communicated.

D. The utterance may be nonliteral. Nonliterality is a pervasive feature of human communication, and proper interpretation of the message requires more than knowing the literal meaning of an utterance. If one says, 'That meal was dynamite,' the listener must (under normal circumstances) know that the word *dynamite* has a slang use, with a meaning something like 'outstanding.' If, however, it is obvious that the meal fell short of one's expectations, one has just sarcastically conveyed an insult to the chef. The true message of an utterance may be the *opposite* of the literal meaning of the utterance.

E. The message may be indirect. The sentence *Is your mother home?* is frequently answered 'yes' by a cooperative child answering the telephone until the child learns that the message behind the question is an indirect request for the child to summon his or her mother to the phone.

F. The utterance may be devoid of a message *per se*. Certain ritualistic uses of language may serve to satisfy institutional requirements and do not have the primary function of conveying a message. When a baby is baptized, for example, the baby does not have to understand the utterances being used during the baptism. The survival of Latin in church liturgy for so many centuries testifies to certain noncommunicative uses of human language.

The point in discussing all of the above examples is to demonstrate that the 'meaning' of the utterance is not necessarily the same as the 'message' that is being conveyed. In human language, the core grammatical meaning of an utterance is only one component of the information that comes into play in the hearer's arriving at the message behind an utterance. Thus, any adequate theory of human communication must take into account all of the above inferential (pragmatic) strategies.

When we turn to animal communication, any comparison with human communication which strives for adequacy must seek correlates with the above-mentioned contextually determined variations in human communication systems. One particular difficulty resides in the fact that we arrive at these features of communication through introspection, a technique which is, of course, not available in the case of animal communication. In spite of the abstract nature of the six examples above, there is reason to believe that context is an important feature of animal communication and the message model, therefore, does not even characterize nonhuman animal communication.

12.2. Properties of human language and similarities found in animal communication

I present here some of the salient properties of human language and communication, and, using the most recent research results on animal communication, I show the extent to which these features are found in animal communication. I will consider structural, biological, and pragmatic (interpretative) properties of human communication, since this organization permits one to make comparisons with the properties of animal systems.

Structural properties

Human language is made up of several levels of discrete units, at each level of which units are combined according to abstract rules or organization. These structural units are *distinctive features*, which combine to make up *phonemes*; the *phonemes* in turn combine to make up *morphemes*; the *morphemes*, consisting of *words, affixes*, and *clitics*, combine to make up *words*; and words combine to make up phrases, including sentences. I discuss the existence of similar structural properties in animal communication below. A diagram of the levels of human language is displayed in Figure 1.

Biological properties

There are several aspects of the biological side of language that have correlates in the animal world. These are: (a) a developmental sequence during which the communication system is revised and refined; (b) a critical period for acquisition of the communication system; (c) an innate ability to discriminate among various types of acoustic stimuli; (d) cerebral dominance in the control of speech (lateralization). There are many other biological correlates between humans and nonhumans with respect to speech, language, and communication (for example, multimodal signaling), but these four areas suffice to show the value of biological comparisons.

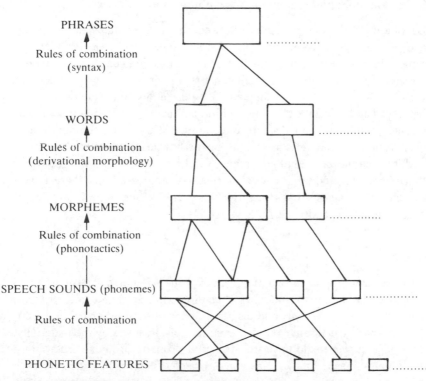

Figure 1. Simplified schematic of the structure of a human language, emphasizing the hierarchically organized levels of structure. At the level of the word or phrase, there is no limit to the number of well-formed expressions that can be constructed nor is there any limit on the meaning that a word may have. Human language is thus unbounded in scope, though built out of discrete units.

Pragmatic properties

In addition to being able to produce a potentially infinite number of utterances, humans also make use of a complex set of pragmatic strategies, such as those discussed above. Whether these strategies are part of 'grammar' or are part of some other system will only be decidable when the various components of language and communication are better understood. We will see below that there is reason to compare this aspect of human language with the communication system of animals.

The above-listed three properties (structural, biological, and pragmatic) do not exhaust the properties of human language by any means, but they do represent a few of the more prominent and well-studied features of human language. They are also features that lend themselves to comparisons between human and other animal communication systems.

12.2.1. Structural properties of nonhuman communication systems

Despite the evolutionary distance between the birds, whales and dolphins, and primates, their communication systems appear to be qualitatively the same. This is surprising given the fact that mammals are generally believed to possess a higher degree of intelligence than birds. Characteristic of all vertebrates is that they each possess a set of discrete sounds that are employed under specific eliciting conditions. These vocalization systems can be characterized as being discrete and bounded. That is, the number of these vocalizations is relatively limited (at most a few dozen), and the conditions under which they are employed appears to be restricted. We will see below that our understanding of these systems has progressed and there is now evidence that suggests that some primate systems possess a significant degree of structural complexity.

12.2.1.1. Birds

Bird vocalizations are of two major kinds: calls and songs. Calls may function to signal alarm, to announce a landing while in flight, and so forth. Structurally calls are short and discrete. Songs, on the other hand, are for the most part structurally complex and are typically given by the male only. Birdsongs, however, do have the structural property of linear order, since these songs can be analyzed as consisting of ordered subparts, and each subpart may in turn be made up of individual notes. One way of abstractly representing the song is in the form ABC, where each alphabetic letter represents a substring. There is no evidence, however, that birds create new messages by rearranging the parts of the song to BAC, or by substituting a new element, say ABD, to create new messages. Within a song, however, minor variations of the subparts are possible: for example, in a song where the B part consists of four trills, variations may exist in which the number of trills is more or less than the more common four. This type of variation does not constitute a new message, and, moreover, experiments have been done in which some parts of the song have been reordered (say BAC), and birds react to this song in the same way as they do to a normal song. Finally, some species of birds have elaborate duets between male and female, but there is no evidence at present that these songs have any structure beyond an alternating pattern between male and female. The exact function of the song (other than pair-bonding) is uncertain (Thorpe 1974).

2.2.1.2. Dolphins and whales

There still has not been a 'breakthrough' in arriving at an understanding of dolphin or whale communication. The following quote about killer whales is representative:

> Our ignorance about most facets of acoustic communication and interception in these animals is due not only to the problem of defining the behaviour which may be associated with sound production, but perhaps more fundamentally, with determining the actual source among a group of individuals. Present knowledge rests largely upon anecdotes gathered generally from animals held in oceanaria, from individuals during capture, or during strandings. (Hawkins & Myrberg 1983: 392–3)

The most studied cetacean (the group that includes both whales and dolphins) is the bottle-nosed dolphin; over half of all material published on cetaceans is on this species alone. The major types of dolphin vocalizations are pure tones and pulsed sounds, with the former being further divided into two types: clicks and another class of sounds consisting of barks, yelps, and moans. The function of dolphin vocalizations is still not completely under-stood. The pulsed sounds, i.e. the clicks, appear to function mainly for echolocation, although a communicative role is also suspected. The second class of pulsed sounds appear to express internal emotional states. The whistles and squeaks have still not been decoded, although some researchers (Caldwell & Caldwell 1977) have proposed that each dolphin has its own signature whistle that uniquely identifies it among other dolphins. There is at present no evidence that dolphins employ a sequence of subunits that conveys a particular message. Thus, it appears that dolphin communication does not entail the structural property of linear order.

The song of the hump-backed whale, in contrast to that of the dolphin, does have the structural property of linear order – the song consists of ordered subparts (Payne, Tyack & Payne 1983). Whale songs, moreover, possess a (newly) discovered degree of flexibility, which I will discuss below in the section on biological correlates of communication. The function of the whale song, in spite of the advances in understanding its structure, is still unknown.

12.2.1.3. Monkeys

Monkey vocalizations are being investigated with increasingly sophisticated techniques, and until recently, it was thought that their call systems were analogous to the vocalizations of cetaceans and even birds. There have been three areas of study, however, that show that monkey calls have a greater degree of complexity than had been thought to be the case. The species in which these advances have been noted are: (1) the vervet, (2) the cotton-top tamarin, and (3) the Japanese macaque.

Vervet

The principal insight gained in the study of the vervet is that it is a species which has evolved a class of distinct alarm calls to refer to distinct classes of predators (Seyfarth, Cheney & Marler 1980). One call is the snake chutter, a type of mobbing call given by females and juveniles. It is uttered when a dangerous snake enters the vervet band's territory. The vervets make the call while surrounding the snake and escort it while it passes through their territory.

A different call is given for terrestrial predators, and yet another call is given when a large avian predator is sighted. Experiments were conducted by Seyfarth *et al.* (1980) in the wild in which previously tape-recorded calls were reintroduced into the environment by means of loudspeakers. When the ground predator call was played, the vervets scampered to the trees and ran to the end of a branch. When the avian predator call was played, the vervets dropped from trees and took cover in the bushes. This evidence suggests that vervets clearly associated the form of the call with a certain evasive behavior. The fact that the vervets would scan the environment before acting appropriately, glancing upward if the avian predator call was played, for example, further suggests that the form of the call is associated with a certain type of external referent, similar to the way that particular words in human language can be associated with particular external referents.

Cotton-top tamarin

The cotton-top tamarin is a New World marmoset monkey whose vocalizations may exhibit not only systematic discreteness, but also primitive rules of combination (Cleveland & Snowdon 1985). Cleveland and Snowdon characterize these rules as follows:

1.   Vocal elements (chirps and whistles) can be repeated *ad libitum*.
2.   Where chirps and whistles are combined, all chirps precede all whistles.
3.   When chirps and whistles are combined, each successive unit has a lower overall frequency than the preceding units.

The following passage is from Cleveland and Snowdon's discussion of the 'meaning' of the combined structures:

> There were two sequences within the cotton-top repetoire that appears to be examples of lexical syntax. The inverted U + whistle (class 5) consisted of a Type E chirp plus a modified squeak syllable. The Type E chirp alone was used as a general alarm call in response to all intense disturbing stimuli. The squeak was used as a general alerting or monitoring call in a wide variety of situations other than alarm. Combination of these two elements occurred only after initial alarm calls had been given, at a time when the animals were stationary and scanned the environment. The piloerection [mane raising: RAD] that appeared with the Type E chirp was not present during the combined vocalizations. Thus, the addition of the squeak elements indicated vigilant animals with reduced fear or alarm. (Cleveland & Snowdon 1985: 259)

The term 'lexical syntax' is used above to refer to syntax-like constructions in which the meaning appears to be semantically compositional; that is, the meaning of the whole is a consequence of the meaning of the parts. The calls described above do appear to represent a combination of two calls, although there is a structural adaptation that occurs. In this sequence, linear order is clearly playing a role. The structure of the tamarin utterances clearly have a rudimentary combinatorial property which is similar to a combinatorial property found in human language. It should be noted that the alarm message used in the first part of the combination is shortened somewhat when the call appears in this combination. Moreover, the piloerection that appears with the isolated E chirp is not present during this combined vocalization. Thus, the 'meaning' of the whole is not entirely based on the meaning of the parts. In addition, the cotton-top tamarin call system also assigns discrete messages to points along a graded continuum. This property is also present in the Japanese macaque, the subject of the next section. The communication system of the cotton-top tamarin can be represented as in Figure 2, and this figure should be contrasted with Figure 1, a representation of the structural features of human language.

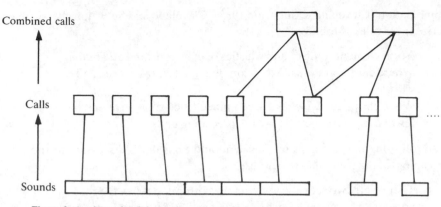

Figure 2. A schematic of the structural levels of the vocalization system of cotton-top tamarin. The lowest level consists of sounds, some of whose graded portions map into distinct vocalizations on the second level. This mapping is represented by the relationship between the continuous line on the bottom and the separate calls on the second line. Some of the tamarin's calls also appear in combined structures, shown in the top line, the 'meaning' of which is related to the meaning of the constituent parts. These combinations of two calls are limited in number.

Japanese macaque

Research on the Japanese macaque (Marler 1975) has revealed their ability to use a continuously variable vocal signal and divide it into distinct messages. The division of an acoustic signal into categorially distinct values is, of course, an important feature of human language. Gradual (continuous) variations in the formant frequencies produced by gradual changes in the shape of the vocal tract map into perceptually distinct entities. For example, by raising the blade of a forward-positioned tongue body from the floor to the roof of the mouth, the speaker of English produces perceptually distinct vowels from æ to *i*. Thus, the ability of monkeys to discriminate different signals along a continuously variable acoustic signal is a structural (and perceptual) correlate to the human ability to do so. In Figure 3, the contexts in which the graded variations in the 'coo' sound are used are displayed.

In sum, in some species of monkey structural analogs of important features of human language are found. The monkeys' systems have discrete elements that can be combined to form sequences, the 'meaning' of which is not inconsistent with semantic compositionality. Two-part combinations are a long way, of course, from the unlimited combinations found in human speakers, and the difference is one of quality, not just quantity. Monkeys also have the ability to assign discrete interpretations to regions along an acoustic continuum. This ability has been found in species other than the cotton-top tamarin and the Japanese macaque (Lillihei & Snowdon 1978; Eisenberg 1976).

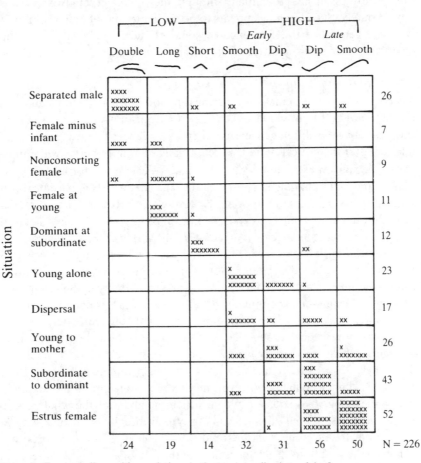

Figure 3. Conceptually sensitive variations in the 'coo' vocalizations of the Japanese macaque (Marler 1975)

12.2.2. Biological properties of nonhuman communication systems

Gradual acquisition

The human child gradually acquires language, and intermediate stages can be identified. Various developmental stages can also be identified in other species. Young vervets, for example, though born with the ability to produce the different alarm calls, must go through a stage of learning similar to that of human children. This is evident in cases where young vervets will emit the snake chutter when encountering sticks on the ground, nonpoisonous or

329

poisonous snakes; or they will emit the avian predator call when they see a bird, regardless of size. Eventually, though, the young vervet gives the calls appropriately. Such learning appears to be similar to that of human children who overgeneralize the reference of some of their vocabulary, e.g. the characteristic of small children to refer to any adult male as 'daddy.'

Critical period of acquisition

There is evidence in humans for a critical period, during which language is acquired most efficiently. Once the period of acquisition appears, usually at one year of age, children can learn numerous languages fluently. Languages learned after the critical period, which usually ends at puberty, will almost always be spoken with an accent. A similar critical period for learning has been found in the chaffinch (Thorpe 1961). The chaffinch is apparently born with an innate template of its song. Nevertheless, between ten and fifteen days after it is born it must be exposed to the male song of its species, if it is to acquire the song of its species as an adult. In the spring of the following year, the male chaffinch begins to sing its partially learned song, and perfects it in the weeks before breeding begins. Not all birds acquire songs in the same way as the chaffinch – there is, in fact, a great deal of variability in the acquisition of songs. Mocking-birds continually acquire new songs throughout their life, while other birds, such as the cuckoo, have a song that is completely innate.

It has now been learned that the hump-backed whale (unlike most songbirds) changes its song on an annual basis (Payne, Tyack & Payne 1983). The songs are structurally similar to those of songbirds in that they consist of repeated subunits. Whales, however, modify their song during the season in which they sing. It is still not known which members of the whale group initiate a new song, but all whales in a group eventually alter their song to conform to the new one. 'Major trends of song change in one year do not repeat in the next, thus the changes may be thought of as cultural rather than linked to natural rhythms or periodic phenomena' (Payne Tyack & Payne, 1983: 9).

Studies in the acquisition of communication systems in all species, including humans, are not very far advanced. Although the chaffinch appears to be the most thoroughly studied nonhuman, analogous studies on other species will likely yield important information for future comparisons.

Innate feature discriminators

There is good evidence that humans are born with the ability to discriminate among various types of speech sounds (Eimas 1975). Human babies are apparently born with the ability to discriminate among various onset times that correspond to the differences between voiced and voiceless sounds in human language. This ability is not, however, unique to humans – other mammals also have it. Chinchillas (Kuhl & Miller 1975), for example, have the voice-onset time discrimination ability, and monkeys appear also to be able to discriminate among acoustic signals that correspond to sound differences produced by the human vocal tract (Morse & Snowdon 1975). Nevertheless, it appears that only humans have incorporated this ability into their communication system. The inter-specific possession of this innate discrimination feature is analogous to the ability of many insect species to orient themselves with the direction of a light source or the force of gravity. Still, only the honeybee has incorporated this commonly available ability into its communication system (von Frisch 1967).

Lateralization

The clearest cases of lateralization of the control of vocalization other than in humans has been found in birds (Nottebohm 1971). But while the morphological effect is common, the function of the lateralization is not clear. The existence of speech centers as an explanation of lateralization does not seem to be required, since when speech-control centers in the left hemisphere in humans are damaged at an early age, the right hemisphere can take over the control of speech. 'The phenomenon [of hemispheric dominance in birds: RAD] is analogous to handedness and hemispheric dominance in man' (Nottebohm 1977). 'However, it is a more homogeneous phenomenon, because of 91 birds from 5 species tested, only 2 (a white throated sparrow and a Java sparrow) had right nerve dominance' (Seller 1983).

The above discussion has briefly touched on some of the biological correlates found in human speakers. These correlates range from similar developmental stages in acquisition to the hemispheric control of speech by the brain. But there is an important anatomical difference between the human and all other species with respect to the control of vocalization. It is only in the human that cortical portions of the brain have major control over vocalizations.

> The highest level of organization is structurally represented by cortical areas such as the precallosal limbic cortex with the dorsally adjacent supplementary motor area and the neocortical representation of the larynx. Within mammalian species, the first seems to play a role in phonation only in non-human primates, the latter exclusively in man. Thus, from an evolutionary point of view, cortical control over phonation seems to be a relatively recent acquisition. (Müller-Preuss & Ploog 1983: 145)

Human language, then, shares significant biological features with other species, but the more complex human linguistic system is, not surprisingly, associated with a more complex neuroanatomical organization.

12.2.3. Pragmatic properties of nonhuman communication systems

I noted earlier that the human communication system requires pragmatic interpretive mechanisms on the part of the hearer in order to arrive at the speaker's message, due to ambiguity in the meaning of an utterance, vagueness of reference, and so forth. Although we are not yet able to determine what the nature of these pragmatic interpretive mechanisms may be in animal communication systems, there is reason to believe that such mechanisms exist in animals. Their existence can be inferred from the heavy role that context plays in establishing the message behind the communication event. Three examples, from three different animal groups (bees, birds, and monkeys and primates) will serve to demonstrate the role that context plays in determining the message in animal communication.

Honeybees

The tail-wagging dance of the European honeybee is normally used to communicate the location of a food source outside of the hive. However, the dance can also be used to communicate the location of a new site for the hive. When, for some reason, the bee colony must move, scout bees begin to search the surrounding area for a suitable cavity for the hive. Frequently, different scouts will come back and indicate competing locations through their dances. The intensity with which a bee dances corresponds directly to the suitability of the future site. Sometimes a scout bee that earlier danced the location of a site will be recruited by another dancing bee. This newly recruited bee will then fly out to the location of the new site. Ultimately, the hive reaches a 'consensus' and the bees swarm out to the new location. The bees are thus able to distinguish between dances which are used to indicate the location of an available food source, and dances indicating the potential location of a new hive. Honeybees make use of contextual clues to distinguish food source dances from new-hive location dances.

Birds

Birdsongs appear to encode different messages, depending on which bird is listening to the song. The female of the species, for example, will be attracted to the song of a male. To other males of the same species, in contrast, the song will serve to repel. Furthermore, the repeling function is interpreted in one way by males who are settled, and in another way by males who are seeking new territory.

Monkeys and primates

Primate vocalizations are notoriously context dependent, communication between complete strangers being rare with communication generally restricted to members of a relatively stable social group. 'The context then, of any communicative act includes a network of social relations that have a considerable history behind them, all of which is relevant to the message and how it is received and responded to' (Lancaster 1975: 56–7). For example, 'a juvenile would ignore, or even respond with teasing to a threat from a female of lower rank than his mother, but would flee screaming from the same gesture from a female of higher rank' (Rowell 1972: 96).

The use of context (visual, tactile, olfactory, and so forth) in determining the message is a pervasive feature of animal communication. We see, then, that the traditional message model is too weak a model to handle even animal communication.

12.3 Conclusion

In a recent survey of primate studies and their relation to the evolution of human language, Linda Wiener writes: 'It is probable that many features of their [apes'] communication systems became building blocks for certain features that later evolved in human language' (Wiener 1984: 266). Recent research has certainly shown that the primates have communication systems which are more elaborate than was assumed earlier. What all nonhuman communication systems lack, however, is the unboundedness in scope that is the central feature of human language. The structural properties of the cotton-top tamarin's, depicted in Figure 2, appear to be similar to the lower levels of the structural properties of human language (see Figure 1). At the level of both word and phrase, however, human language achieves an openness and productivity totally beyond the capability of any nonhuman communication system. Finally, whether any structural correlates, or communication features in general, can be viewed as precursors to similar features in human language must await further research.

One feature common to all natural communication systems, and a feature which is underappreciated by many linguists, is the use of context in determining the message of a communication event. In the introduction I noted that research on animal communication may reveal the importance of a property of communication that is not adequately appreciated by researchers on human language. The importance of pragmatic strategies, the system of inference that functions to permit the receiver to arrive at the intended 'message,' may be such a feature. Interpretative systems which occur in addition to the physical signaling system itself are pervasive in natural communication systems.

Recent research on animal communication has demonstrated that animal communication systems are more complex than earlier researchers had assumed. As our knowledge of animal communication progresses, we are finding more and more correlates of the structural, biological, and pragmatic properties found in human language and communication. On the other hand, linguists have just begun to investigate many properties of human language, and have only recently come to appreciate the complexity and abstractness of the principles governing it. It is therefore too early to determine whether the gulf that appears between human language and communication and other animal systems will widen or narrow as our knowledge progresses.

REFERENCES

Akmajian, A., Demers, R. & Harnish, R. 1979. *Linguistics: an introduction to language and communication*. Cambridge, MA: MIT Press.

Akmajian, A., Demers, R. & Harnish, R. 1984. *Linguistics: an introduction to language and communication*, 2nd edn. Cambridge, MA: MIT Press.

Bach, K. & Harnish, R. 1979. *Linguistic communication and speech acts*. Cambridge, MA: MIT Press.

Caldwell, D. & Caldwell, M. 1977. Cetaceans. In T. Sebeok (ed.) *How animals communicate*. Bloomington and London: Indiana University Press.

Cleveland, J. & Snowdon, C. 1982. The complex vocal repertoire of the adult cotton-top tamarin (*Saguinus oedipus oedipus*). *Zeitschrift für Tierpsychologie* 58: 231–70.

de Luce, J. & Wilder, H. 1983. *Language in primates: perspectives and implications*. New York: Springer-Verlag.

Eimas, P. 1975. Linguistic processing of speech by young infants. In R. L. Schiefelbusch & L. Lloyd (eds.) *Language perspectives – acquisition, retardation, and intervention*. Baltimore: University Park Press.

Eisenberg, J. 1976. *Communication mechanisms and social integration in the black spider monkey, Ateles fusciceps robustus and related species*. Smithsonian Contributions to Zoology 213.

Frisch, K. von 1967. *The dance language and orientation of bees*, translated by C. E. Chadwick. Cambridge, MA: Harvard University Press.

Gould, J., Dyer, F. & Towne, W. 1985. Recent progress in the study of dance language. *Fortschritte der Zoologie*, Vol. 31. Hölldobler/Lindauer (hrsg.): *Experimental behavioral ecology*. Stuttgart: Fischer-Verlag.

Green, S. & Marler, P. 1979. The analysis of animal communication. In P. Marler & J. Vandenbergh (eds.) *Handbook of behavioral neurobiology*, New York: Plenum.

Hawkins, A. & Myrberg, A. 1983. Hearing and sound communication under water. In Lewis 1983.

Hockett, C. & Altmann, S. 1968. A note on design features. In T. Sebeok (ed.) *Animal communication: techniques of study and results of research*. Bloomington: Indiana University Press.

Kuhl, P. & Miller, J. 1975. Speech perception by the chinchilla: voiced–voiceless distinction in alveolar plosive consonants. *Science* 190: 70–2.

Lancaster, J. 1975. *Primate behavior and the emergence of human culture*. New York: Macmillan.

Lewis, B. (ed.) 1983. *Bioacoustics: a comparative approach*. New York: Academic Press.

Lillehei, R. & Snowdon, C. 1978. Individual and situational differences in the vocalizations of young stumptail macaques (*Macaca arctoides*). *Behavior* 65: 270–81.

McNeill, D. 1970. *The acquisition of language*. New York: Harper & Row.

Marler, P. 1975. On the origin of speech from animal sounds. In J. Kavanagh & J. Cutting (eds.) *The role of speech in language*. Cambridge, MA: MIT Press.

Morse, P. & Snowdon, C. 1975. An investigation of categorical speech discrimination by rhesus monkeys. *Perception and Psychopathology* 17: 9–16.

Müller-Preuss, P. & Ploog, D. 1983. Central control of sound production in animals. In Lewis 1983.

Nottebohm, F. 1971. Neural lateralisation of vocal control in a passerine bird: I. Song. *Journal of Experimental Zoology* 177: 229–62.

Nottebohm, F. 1977. Asymmetrics in neural control of vocalisation in the canary. In S. Harnard, R. Doty, L. Goldstein, J. Jaynes & G. Kranthamer (eds.) *Lateralization in the nervous system*. New York: Academic Press.

Payne, K. Tyack, P. & Payne, R. 1983. Progressive changes in the songs of the humpback whales (*Megaptera novaeangliae*): a detailed analysis of two seasons in Hawaii. In R. Payne (ed.) *Communication and behavior of whales*, AAAS Selected Symposium 76. Boulder: Westview Press.

Premack, D. & Premack, J. 1983. *The mind of an ape*. New York: W. W. Norton.

Rowell, T. 1972. *Social behavior of monkeys*. Baltimore: Penguin.

Seller, T. 1983. Control of sound production in birds. In Lewis 1983.

Seyfarth, R., Cheney, D. & Marler, P. 1980. Monkey responses to three different alarm calls: evidence of predator classification and semantic communication. *Science* 210: 801–3.

Terrace, H. 1979. *Nim*. New York: Knopf.

Thorpe, W. 1961. *Bird-song*. Cambridge: Cambridge University Press.

Thorpe, W. 1974. *Animal nature and human nature*. New York: Doubleday.

Wiener, L. 1984. The evolution of language: a primate perspective. *Word* 35.3: 255–69.

Index of names

Abbs, J. 296
Abelson, R. 13
Acredolo, L. 170
Ades, A. 16
Adjémian, C. 198
Aitcheson, J. 73, 86
Akmajian, A. 318, 319–20
Alajouanine, T. 216
Albert, M. 267
Allport, D. 124
Altenberg, E. 204
Altmann, S. 315–18
American Psychiatric Association, 259
Anderson, J. 6, 12, 41n
Anglin, J. 22
Aram, D. 268
Ard, J. 199
Armstrong, E. 301
Armstrong, S. 176n
Atchley, W. 299
Aten, J. 267

Baars, B. 28n, 88, 92
Bach, K. 70, 321
Badecker, W. 213
Baer, D. 266
Bailey, N. 196
Baillargeon, R. 170
Baker, C. 24, 167, 201, 226, 227, 229, 248, 249
Baker. E. 159, 179, 211, 218, 219, 221
Baker, L. 127, 131
Ball, W. 170
Ballard, D. 19
Barbeau, A. 304
Barton, M. 221
Baru, A. 297
Basso, A. 219, 220, 248
Bastian, J. 293
Bates, E. 2, 22, 119, 180
Batterman, N. 23
Baum, S. 228, 230
Baynes, K. 250

Beatty, G. 73
Beauvois, M. 128
Bellugi, U. 23, 156, 157, 225, 265
Benedict, H. 154n, 156
Benson, D. 242, 302–3
Benson, F. 127
Benton, A. 259
Berberich, J. 266
Berkovic, S. 239
Berndt, R. 227
Berwick, R. 8n, 16, 24, 201
Bever, T. 5, 8–9, 11n, 15, 16, 21, 26, 47n, 108, 110, 112, 164, 179, 277
Bias, R. 128
Bienkowski, M. 53
Bierwisch, M. 74, 75, 221
Birdsong, D. 80
Black, J. 13
Bladin, P. 239
Blasdell, R. 160
Block, N. 70
Bloom, L. 20, 164, 172, 179, 180, 266
Bloom, P. 51
Bloomfield, L. 38n, 131, 150, 165
Blott, J. 266
Blumenthal, A. 8
Blumstein, S. ix, 118, 210–36, 248
Bock, J. 29, 73, 74, 79–80, 87, 89
Boller, F. 220
Bond, Z. 100, 115
Boomer, D. 26, 75, 79
Booth, J. 216
Borer, H. 167
Botez, M. 304
Bouman, L. 215
Bourne, G. 284
Bowen, J. 196
Bower, G. 6, 12, 13
Bowerman, M. 21, 22, 24, 25, 179, 180–1, 186, 266
Boysen, S. 289
Bradley, D. 27n, 105, 227
Braine, M. 21, 24, 81, 164, 179, 180

336

Luce, J. de, *see* de Luce, J.
Luce, P. 163
Lucy, P. 11
Ludlow, C. 260
Lukatela, G. 228
Luria, A. 211, 215, 225, 237, 244–5, 246–7, 250
Lust, B. 163

Maassan, B. 29, 73, 79, 89–90
McCarthy, D. 262
McCarthy, J. 167
McCauley, R. 264
McClelland, J. 19, 25, 102, 228
McCusker, L. 128
McDonald, E. 265
McDonald, J. D. 266
Macdonald, J. 46
McGurk, H. 46
MacKay, D. 26, 28, 75, 88, 91
McKay, E. 261
McKoon, G. 13
Maclay, H. 26
MacNamara, J. 24, 159, 168, 179
McNeill, D. 20, 21, 71, 127, 315, 318–19
Macphail, E. 303
McReynolds, L. 265
MacWhinney, B. 2, 119, 180
Madden, C. 196
Madden, E. 168
Mairs, J. 197
Manelis, L. 105
Manzini, R. 176, 202
Maratsos, M. 16, 21, 160, 165, 178
Marcus, M. 16, 112
Marie, P. 242
Marin, O. 124, 125, 211, 226, 227
Markman, E. 174, 178
Marler, P. 326, 328–9
Marr, D. 14–15, 44–5
Marshall, C. 29
Marshall, J. C. 12, 125, 128, 132–3, 247, 249, 269
Marshall, J. M. 18
Marslen-Wilson, W. 10, 20, 46, 49–52, 53n, 102–4, 109, 119, 125–6, 137, 142–3
Martin, A. 215
Martin, J. 196
Martinet, A. 58
Masdeu, J. 238, 239
Massaro, D. 101
Masterton, B. 296
Mattingly, I. 47
Mayr, E. 286
Mazurkewich, I. 204, 206
Medin, D. 22
Mehler, J. 8, 101, 152, 159, 164, 269
Meier, R. 153n, 160, 161

Menn, L. 229, 259
Merringer, R. 26, 75
Mervis, C. 172
Metter, E. 238
Meyer, D. 143, 222
Meyer, K. 26
Meyers, D. 72
Miceli, G. 218, 220, 227
Milberg, W. 118, 211, 212, 222, 223, 230
Miles, H. 288, 289
Miller, G. 4, 6, 7, 8, 11, 18
Miller, J. 155n, 297, 331
Miller, J. 262, 263, 266
Milner, B. 250
Mohanan, K. 137
Mohr, J. 238
Montaigne, M. 281
Moody, D. 297
Moog, J. 261
Morehead, D. 265
Morgan, J. 153n, 160, 161, 166
Morse, P. 297–8, 306, 331
Morton, J. 12, 56n, 102, 104, 115, 124, 129–30, 137, 138, 142, 143, 269
Moskowitz, N. 298
Motley, M. 28n, 88, 91
Mowrer, O. 4, 5
Müller-Preuss, P. 331
Murphy, R. 276
Murrell, G. 104
Muysken, P. 198
Myers, R. 286, 306
Myerson, R. 226, 227
Myrberg, A. 325

Naeser, M. 238
Naigles, L. 185
Nakatani, L. 100, 156
Neiser, J. 105
Nelson, K. 22, 154n, 156, 172
Nemser, W. 197n
Nespoulous, J.-L. 215, 265
Neville, M. 238
Newcombe, F. 125, 132–3, 146, 218, 269
Newell, A. 4, 13
Newman, J. 297
Newmeyer, F. vii–ix
Newport, E. 22, 23, 153n, 154n, 156, 160, 161, 181
Niemi, J. 215
Ninio, A. 168n
Noback, C. 298
Nooteboom, S. 75, 98
Norman, D. 12
Norris, D. 12, 57n, 101
Nottebohm, F. 280n, 286, 297, 331
Nuutila, A. 218, 220

343

Index of subjects

Accretion hypothesis 279
Acquisition *see* First language acquisition, Second language acquisition
Activation model of perception 102
Addressed morphology model 139, 141
Agrammatism *see* Aphasia
Agraphia 242
Alexia 242
American Academy of Speech Correction 257
American Indian signs 291
American Sign Language (ASL) 23, 261, 287, 291
American Speech and Hearing Association 257
American Speech–Language Hearing Association (ASHA) 257
Amer-Ind system 267
Anaphora: and language acquisition 163; and language processing 12–13, 50–2
Anarthria 241
Animal communication: compared to human language 322–33; linguistics and 314–34
Anomia *see* Aphasia
Aphasia: 72, 83, 135, 160, 210–31, 237–44, 250, 258–9, 266–7, 291; adult 210–31, 258–9; agrammatic 211–17, 225–30, 243, 259, 263; anomic 72, 127, 220–1, 243; Broca's 211, 213–17, 222–7, 229–30, 241–3, 259; conduction 72, 242–3; developmental 259–60; lexicon in 220–4; linguistic investigations of 210–12; phonology of 214–17; speech perception in 217–20; syntax of 225–30; transcortical motor 242; transcortical sensory 242–3; Wernicke's 211–12, 214–17, 221–4, 229–30, 241–3, 259
Apraxia 243, 260
Artificial intelligence (AI) 3, 13–15, 18, 30, 99; influence of on psycholinguistics 13–15
Audiology 256

Auditory canal 296
Augmented transition network (ATN) 15–16, 112
Autonomy (of grammar) hypothesis 2–3, 17–20, 30–1; *see also* Modularity hypothesis
Autonomy-interaction debate 113–18; *see also* Modularity hypothesis

Bee communication 316–18
Behavioral homology 277–81
Behavioral homoplasies 280
Behavioral systems 281–91
Behaviorism 4–5, 20, 268
Biological basis for language 237–57
Biological clock 277
Bird communication 324–5
Bootstrapping, semantic and syntactic 180–6
Bracketed input hypothesis 166–7
Branching direction 198
Broca's area 240–2, 302–3; *see also* Aphasia

Caretaker speech *see* Motherese
Category induction programme 152
Caudate nucleus 238
Central (cognitive) systems 43–7, 57–66
Chomsky, Noam: effects of work on psychology 1–6, 38–41
Clausal hypothesis 108–10
Cloze effects 49–50, 53
Cognition, language and 4, 38–66
Cognitive impenetrability 48–57
Cognitive psychology 3, 5, 13, 98
Cohort model 20, 102–3, 125–8, 135–7, 139, 143
Communicative disorders *see* Speech–language pathology
Competence: communicative 22; linguistic 1–6, 39, 47
Comprehension *see* Language comprehension
Computational linguistics 30

345

Contents of Volumes I, II, and IV

Volume IV   Language: the socio-cultural context